Writer's Guide to 2013

Writer's Institute
Publications

www.WritersInstitutePublications.com

Editor in Chief: Susan M. Tierney

Contributing Writers:

Judy Bradbury
Michael Cooper
Chris Eboch
Sue Bradford Edwards
S. M. Ford
Mary E. Furlong
Carmen Goldthwaite
Christina Hamlett
Mark Haverstock

Casie Hermansson
Veda Boyd Jones
Suzanne Lieurance
Joanne Mattern
Mary Northrup
Patricia Curtis Pfitsch
Susan Sundwall
Katherine Swarts
Leslie J. Wyatt

Production Editor: Joanna Horvath

Contributing Editor: Pam Kelly

Publisher: Prescott V. Kelly

Cover image supplied by Big Stock Photo®.

International Standard Book Number: 978-1-889715-68-1

1-800-443-6078. www.writersbookstore.com
email: services@writersbookstore.com

Table of Contents

Markets

Style

Business & Career

Markets

Style

Business

Research

Ideas

Contests

Indexes

Are We There Yet?

The State of Book Publishing

By Patricia Curtis Pfitsch

Technological advances since the 1980s have been labeled the Digital Revolution, one that has changed the world in ways as profound as the nineteenth-century Industrial Revolution. For a long time to come, scholarly treatises will be written about the digitalization of the world across multiple disciplines—and the impact on the publishing industry, and thus on writers, is second to none.

Legal issues, new forms of publication, sales formulas, rights disputes, book promotion, and the traditional roles of publishers, authors, and even readers, are all in flux. As in many a revolution, new perspectives and new techniques come to the fore for good, creating opportunities that have never existed before for writers and publishers. But not without some casualties and ongoing debates.

Taking Aim at Amazon

Most visibly, the rift between Amazon and the rest of the industry widens, even as many of the company's policies and products drive publishing in new directions.

As Amazon strengthens its position as a publisher as well as a retailer, bricks-and-mortar bookstores are acting threatened. Last year, Barnes & Noble became the largest bookseller to boycott its rival, refusing to carry its print titles in bookstores because Amazon does not allow its ebooks to be sold on other websites. Barnes & Noble Chief Merchandising Officer Jaime Carey issued a widely reported statement declaring that Amazon's "actions have undermined the industry as a whole and have prevented millions of customers from having access to content. It's clear to us that Amazon has proven they would not be a good publishing partner to Barnes & Noble as they continue to pull content off the market for their own self-interest."

Traditional publishers have expressed similar views. Amazon is in a unique position to make sure its own books receive the most attention on its website, and a year ago, it upped the fees charged to promote other publishers' books by as much as 30 percent. For publishers, this came as fuel to the fire of Amazon's original ebook pricing when it launched the Kindle ereader in 2007. Most ebooks —including best sellers and new releases—were priced at $9.99. Selling ebooks at a loss was a move that eventually captured 90 percent of the ebook market for Amazon and made other publisher's print books look grossly overpriced. Publishers finally convinced Amazon to accept the *agency model* for ebook pricing, letting the publisher, rather than the bookstore, set the retail price.

Then in April 2012, the U.S. Department of Justice (DOJ) filed a lawsuit against Apple and five publishers (Hachette, HarperCollins, Macmillan, Penguin, and Simon & Schuster), alleging that the agency model represents collusion and it shuts off retail competition, that there was a conspiracy among the defendants, and that the practice will result in higher consumer prices. Simon & Schuster, Hachette, and HarperCollins settled with the DOJ without admitting wrongdoing. Apple, Penguin and Macmillan did not settle.

People in and out of the industry were disturbed by the suit. Many had expected an antitrust action—but aimed at Amazon. Senator Charles Schumer (D.-New York) expressed the opinion of many: "For the Antitrust Division to step in as the big protector of Amazon doesn't seem to make any sense from an antitrust point of view. Rarely have I seen a suit that so ill serves the interests of the consumer."

The *Wall Street Journal* interviewed antitrust experts who agreed there was evidence of price-fixing, however. ("U.S. Alleges E-Book Scheme, Lawsuit Says Apple, Publishers Colluded to Raise Prices; Three Will Settle." Thomas Catan et al, *Wall Street Journal*, April 11, 2012.) The *Atlantic* quoted University of Iowa law professor Herbert Hovenkamp: "Price fixing is kind of the first-degree murder of antitrust violations." He agreed that the government had to act on "what appears to be a strong set of facts that if true, are one of the most central of antitrust violations." ("Confused by the Ebook Lawsuit? So Is Everyone Else." Peter Osnos. *Atlantic*. May 1, 2012.)

During the 60-day period set aside for comments, the DOJ received a record 868 comments, most in support of the publishers and Apple. The American Booksellers Association (ABA) and Barnes & Noble filed *amicus curiae* (friend of the court) briefs objecting to the action. But some authors supported the settlement. David Gaughran, spokesman for 186 self-published authors, thanked Amazon for "creating, for the first time, real competition in publishing by charting a viable path for self-published books."

The DOJ responded by saying that the critical comments of the ABA and others had been submitted "by those who have an interest in seeing consumers pay more for ebooks, and hobbling retailers that might want to sell ebooks at lower prices," and that those in publishing were having difficulty accepting the "evolving nature of the publishing industry." The dispute, and its ramifications, are likely to continue for years.

The Copyright Battle

The other major corporate player that comes under fire from various sides of the publishing industry is Google. The Authors Guild, along with the Association of American Publishers (AAP), filed a lawsuit against Google seven years ago for scanning of millions of already published books without permission. In October 2012, the AAP dropped out of the suit, but the Authors Guild continues on.

From the authors' standpoint, the Guild has become their watchdog over digital books, making sure authors are fairly compensated.

New Ventures

The earthquakes rumbling through the publishing industry this year have not discouraged start-ups. Among the new ventures this year are quite a few small publishers.

~ Two years after Kate and Osman Kaynak launched the YA science fiction and fantasy press **Spencer Hill** (www.spencerhillpress.com) out of their home in Hopkinton, New Hampshire, they have added two new imprints, one for adults (Spence City) and a second for contemporary YA novels (Spencer Hill Contemporary).

~ **Opus** (www.opusbookpublishers.com) is a new book line by Glenn Young that will focus on the performing arts, and fiction. Young is the former publisher of Applause Books.

~ **Seven Stories Press** is starting its first children's imprint, called **Triangle Square** (www.sevenstories.com). The company has published children's books before, including picture books, but the audience for its first dedicated juvenile list is middle-graders and up. Among its first titles are *Trevor, a Novella,* by James Lecesne, and *Do You Dream in Color? Insights From a Girl Without Sight,* by Andri Magnason.

~ **Move Books** is a start-up dedicated to middle-grade books for boys. It published its first title in fall 2012. The Editor and Publisher is Eileen Robinson, whose last position was Executive Editor at Scholastic's Children's Press.

Larger publishers have started imprints in several genres.

~ **Redhook** is a new fiction imprint from Hachette (www.hachettebookgroup.com) that will publish science fiction, fantasy, manga, and graphic fiction. The first title, with an April 2013 release date, is Robert Lyndon's *Hawk Quest.*

~ **Bourbon Street Books** is HarperCollins's (www.harpercollins.com) newest paperback imprint, specializing in original and reprinted mysteries.

~ Educational publisher Capstone Books added a new trade line called **Capstone Young Readers** (www.capstonepress.com). The list will include original titles as well as modified editions of some of its existing titles.

~ Penguin has relaunched its **Dutton Guilt Edged Mysteries**—which published such writers as Mickey Spillane from 1947 to 1956—as a digital imprint. It will publish original crime and detective short stories and novellas.

New Ventures

The digital publishing revolution is continuing to encourage other new start-ups to serve the digital needs of the reading public and publishing community.

~ A Minneapolis firm, **Brain Hive**, provides a new lending service for K-12 schools, offering an alternative to borrowing ebooks from libraries. Membership in the service is free, and schools are charged $1 for each ebook borrowed. Titles are available immediately.

~ **HarperCollins** announced a new interactive platform to connect teen readers with authors and their books. Epic Reads (www.epicreads.com) is the landing page that features all HarperTeen books. Pitch Dark (www.pitch-dark.com/) highlights dystopian and paranormal stories, and Story Crush (www.storycrush.com) focuses on contemporary realistic fiction and romance.

~ The German company **BookRix** has launched an ebook distribution system to serve self-published authors. Writers can upload their work for sale to BookRix members for free or pay for a distribution package that will include more markets—Amazon, Barnes & Noble, Apple, and other platforms.

~ The digital company **Graphicly** has developed an automatic digital distribution system for both self-publishers and traditional publishing companies. While its main focus is on image-based content, the software can be used for any kind of digital content and will also provide data analysis.

~ The three-year-old online community of women writers She Writes has launched **She Writes Press** (shewritespress.com). It will offer editorial, production, and publishing options for writers, including a $3,900 publishing package. Other "tracks" are available, depending on how experienced a writer is and how close your book is to being publication-ready. Books will be released in both print and ebook formats. A POD-only option is available.

Google appealed a decision to make the case a *class action*, which is still to be heard by the Second Circuit Court of Appeals. The Guild had brought a similar suit against the HathiTrust, a consortium of libraries that allowed Google to scan their holdings. It argued that the libraries should compensate authors for the use of the books Google scanned. The libraries argued they should not have to pay under the principle of *fair use*. Also in October, a ruling came down agreeing with the libraries, and the case was thrown out.

Yet another copyright suit was resolved last year, again with possible repercussions. In 2008, four publishers sued Georgia State University for their use of *e-reserves*, a practice by which professors put digital copies of copyrighted material online for students to download and print, instead of making students check out print books and articles directly from the library. The university argued that these actions constituted fair use; the publishers argued they were copyright violations. The judge's final order came down in August, and was, reported *Publishers Weekly*, "a sharp rebuke to publishers." The decision sided with the university, even to the extent of ordering the publishers to pay its attorneys' costs. ("Final Order in GSU E-Reserves Case Is a Rebuke to Publishers." Andrew Albanese. *Publishers Weekly.* Aug 13, 2012.)

In the future, courts may similarly lean toward letting the public use digital versions of published works—within fair use—without compensating authors.

Print on Demand: Weapon or Wonder Drug?

Print on demand, or POD, technology was supposed to abolish remainders and books having to go out of print because of inventory costs. With the ability to print a book whenever a patron wants to buy it, publishers would avoid expensive storage costs for inventory. Books could stay in print forever. There is little difference between a book printed the traditional way and one printed in 15 minutes with an Espresso Book Machine.

Amazon has pressured larger publishers to use POD for backlist titles, but most have resisted out of a concern that the online retailer will "use its print-on-demand service to further tilt the economics of book publishing in its favor," according to anonymous sources who spoke to reporter Brad Stone for *Bloomberg Businessweek*. An infinite inventory would give Amazon yet another advantage over traditional bookstores. ("Amazon vs. Publishers: The Book Battle Continues." Brad Stone. *Bloomberg Businessweek*. April 26, 2012.)

Large publishers have long invested in the infrastructure of inventory and distribution, and may remain somewhat resistant to change. If most books become POD, publishers would have to split the wholesale book price differently—giving the author more and keeping less for themselves. Smaller publishers with less money tied up in warehouse space and distribution channels have been more willing to move to POD.

And companies like Ingram Content Group, a "publishing-service provider," are making POD more attractive. It has reduced the price for color POD projects by two-thirds. Previously, a single 120-page trade paperback would cost between $12 and $13.50. With new technology and cheaper pricing, the same project now costs $5, closer to the price of a traditional paperback. This development is particularly exciting for small publishers and self-published authors.

What Is a Publisher To Do?

Despite, or maybe because of, uncertain outcomes in legal and business battles, publishers are even more determined to succeed in a digital world. They are coming up with more innovative ways to produce and market books. As more writers opt for ebook and POD self-publishing, and as publishers rely even more on the authors themselves for promotion, new marketing techniques arise all the time. Some are destined to last, and some are not.

One promotional method is to use inexpensive ebooks to create interest in a print edition. Before Bloomsbury published Sarah J. Maas's first novel, *Throne of Glass,* in August 2012, it wanted to engage her many fans in the online community Fictionpress, which

Boosting the Bottom Line

~ In the biggest book publishing news of the year, and likely several years, **Random House** and **Penguin** agreed in late October to merge. The merger will take place in late 2013, if the deal passes government regulations.

~ Adult sales were up, according to Association of American Publisher (AAP) figures: Trade hardcovers were up 18.2 percent, paperbacks up 49.7 percent, and ebooks up 47.4 percent. Some of the credit is going to the *Fifty Shades of Grey* phenomenon. Children's/YA books fell 9.5 percent for the month, but ebooks rose 89.9 percent.

A *Publishers Weekly* report indicated that the reading public is excited about ebooks; sales accounted for about 20 percent of worldwide revenue at most of the largest publishers. ("A Mixed First Half for Worldwide Publishing; E-book sales continued to grow, but different factors weakened earnings. Jim Milliot. *Publishers Weekly.* September 7, 2012). But the slow economic recovery as well as the costs of litigation have cut profits.

~ Sales fell 4 percent and adjusted operating profit went down 48 percent at **Penguin Group** in first six months last year, attributable largely to the Penguin (USA) division. The company blamed a variety of causes: "a lighter schedule," the growing pressures of print publishing and retail, and the shift to ebooks. Penguin's children's and YA division did well, with international sales up 12 percent. The numbers for the second half of the year may show improvement, with new titles released by Neil Young, Ken Follett, Patricia Cornwell, Dolly Parton, and Zadie Smith.

~ **Random House** reported that sales for the first half of 2012 rose 20 percent, due mainly to huge sales of the Fifty Shades of Grey trilogy. This was the strongest growth of any of the biggest publishing companies. Other strong sellers were John Grisham's *Calico Joe*; Gillian Flynn's *Gone Girl*; and *The Lorax*, by Dr. Seuss.

~ **HarperCollins** announced a strong fourth quarter but gave no specific information about sales. Its parent company, Rupert Murdoch's News Corps, is still planning to split in two. HarperCollins will be part of the publishing and education side, with the second half television and film.

~ **Simon & Schuster** announced that sales rose 3 percent in its second quarter. Print sales slowed, but ebook sales rose 44 percent, amounting to 21 percent of total revenue. Revenue was offset by a $10 million decrease in operating

Boosting the Bottom Line

income because of the ebook price-fixing lawsuit brought against the publisher by the Department of Justice. The company's big sellers were Glenn Beck's *Cowards*; Stephen King's *The Wind Through the Keyhole*; and Mary Higgins Clark's *The Lost Years*.

~ **Lagardere**, the French-based, multinational parent company of Hachette, reported flat total revenue in the first half of the year. **Hachette** sales were up, but a weak list pushed U.S sales down 4 percent. Ebook sales were not strong enough to offset drops in print sales. Hachette is also named in the Department of Justice ebook price-fixing lawsuit. Profits are expected to rise in the second half of the year because of the release of J. K. Rowling's first adult novel, *The Casual Vacancy*, by **Little, Brown & Company**, part of the Hachette Publishing Group.

~ **Scholastic** reported that sales and earnings both fell in its most recent quarter, but that it anticipated meeting its fiscal year projections. The prior year had included the powerhouse book sales associated with the release of the last Harry Potter movie, and of *The Hunger Games* movie.

~ Despite increases in ebook sales reported by many publishers, the numbers are not completely clear. There is no doubt the trend is toward ebooks. But according to the most recent edition of the **Book Industry Study Group**'s *Consumer Attitudes Toward E-Book Reading*, the percentage of consumers who report buying ebooks "primarily or exclusively" fell 70 percent over a six-month period. The percentage who have no preference for either print or ebooks increased from 25 to 34 percent. The takeaway may mean the print-ebook battle is changing direction and consumers are willing to be diverse in their reading habits, and book purachases.

publishes original stories. In the year before the publication, Bloomsbury released four prequel novellas to *Throne of Glass* as 99¢ ebooks on Kindle, Nook, and other platforms, and announced their release on Maas's Facebook page. By August she had 6,000 Facebook fans, all waiting anxiously to buy her book.

Simon & Schuster used Twitter to reveal the cover for *Clockwork Princess*, the final book in Cassandra Claire's Infernal Devices series. The cover was posted on the series' website at 3 PM (EDT) on July 10, but the image was hidden behind a gauzy film. Each time a reader tweeted with the hashtag #ClockworkPrincess, a small puzzle piece of the gauzy film was removed. Within a few hours, 30,000 tweets had revealed the full cover. By that evening, 100,000 people had tweeted about the book. The first printing of *Clockwork Princess* was a million copies.

A similar venture is Togather.com, started by science writer Andrew Kessler. Its goal is to help authors with promotional book events through *fansourcing*, letting them find out about the level of interest in their event in advance. Possible event dates and times are posted on Facebook and Twitter and fans can go to the Togather.com site and commit to attending. Authors can learn how many fans plan to attend their event, thus avoiding the often embarrassing experience of arriving at a book talk to find an almost empty room. Fans can also propose events, which the author can then set up. The site is also set up to sell books.

Today, publishers expect writers to have blogs and a Facebook page and they are using Twitter chats to publicize books and authors. At a pre-announced time an author is available to answer questions from Tweeters about his or her latest books, writing process, and anything else interesting to fans. Tor Teen recently held a group chat with three YA writers to kick off a book tour. Random House held a series of Twitter author chats between August and November to create interest in their fall children's list.

Publishers are also aiming to increase their profits by releasing public domain classics like *Jane Eyre* with new covers that are designed to attract the young adults who made the Twilight books best sellers. The cover of a new Penguin edition of *Romeo and Juliet* has a t-shirted Romeo in need of a shave. The HarperCollins edition of *Wuthering Heights* has the words "Bella and Edward's Favorite Book" on the front; it has sold 125,000 copies since its 2009 publication, making the best-seller list.

Authors have also discovered the *crowdfunding* phenomenon. Sites like Kickstarter and Pubslush ("a publishing platform with a cause") provide a place for writers to publicize book projects, see what the market might be like—and solicit funding for publication. In return authors offer rewards that may be digital previews or free first editions or invitations to the launch party. Kickstarter accepts all kinds of creative projects, while Pubslush focuses on books, and as part of its services (it calls itself a "publishing imprint powered by readers") also helps some authors self-publish.

One example of *crowdfunding* comes from Book Riot, a book blogging site that began its campaign on Kickstarter in July 2012. The founders explained that the money contributed would be used for editorial and promotional costs, rewards, shipping, and fees. By the end of August, Book Riot had reached its goal of $25,000.

Finally, an Internet search on *book trailers* brings up thousands of hits for enterprises that create trailers for authors, and sites with instructions for creating your own. Will these approaches last? Will YouTube and social self-promotion endure or expand in publishing? What will they look like in one year, or in five?

The Dark Side

Not all author-marketing efforts are as up-front. In the publishing world, word of mouth is seen as very effective publicity for a book and the impact has mushroomed on social media sites and Internet bookstores. People are more likely to read a book with plenty of good reviews and a huge *buzz* on Twitter and Facebook.

The trouble is sometimes the fan base is artificial. Dubbed "social media scammers," they create false identities and load positive

People 2013

~ **Kelly Barrales-Saylor** is now Editorial Director at Albert Whitman & Co. She was formerly at Sourcebooks.

~ Houghton Mifflin Harcourt Children's Books Group named **Daniel Nayeri** to a newly created position: Digital Editorial Director. He oversees the ebook publishing program, acquires original e-content, and develops multimedia projects. He was previously an editor at Clarion Books.

~ **Susan Canavan** was promoted to Senior Executive Editor at Houghton Mifflin Harcourt.

~ Irish novelist **Anne Enright** won the first ALA Andrew Carnegie Medal for Excellence for her book *The Forgotten Waltz* (W.W. Norton). Robert K. Massie's book *Catherine the Great: Portrait of a Woman* (Random House) won for nonfiction. The medal, sponsored by a grant from the Carnegie Corporation, is the organizations' first national award for adult trade books.

~ **Frances Gilbert**, formerly at Sterling Children's Books, is now Editorial Director at Random House Children's Books.

~ Knopf Publisher **Pat Johnson** took early retirement at the end of the year "to pursue some long-held dreams." She was at Knopf for 16 years.

~ **Cindy Loh**, formerly Editorial Director at Sterling Children's Books, is now Publishing Director of Bloomsbury Children's Publishing.

~ **Josalyn Moran** stepped down as Vice President of Publishing at Albert Whitman, but remains in an advisory role.

~ **Brian Napack**, President of Macmillan, stepped down at the end of the year to pursue new business opportunities.

~ Perseus Books Group has made multiple changes. Publisher **John Sherer** left the company for a position in academic publishing at North Carolina Press and was succeeded by **Lara Heimert**, formerly Publisher of the Basic Books imprint. **Clive Priddle**, formerly Editorial Director at the Public-Affairs imprint, is now Publisher of Basic. **Susan Weinberg** is Group Publisher of Basic Books, Nation Books, and PublicAffairs.

At Perseus's Running Press, **Jennifer Kasius** became Editorial Director. She will focus the list more on lifestyle, cooking, and humor books.

Even thought the imprint boasts 17 *New York Times* bestsellers, Perseus is phasing out Vanguard Press.

People 2013

~ **Chip Gibson** left Random House after a 30-year career at the company. The last ten years he was in charge of the Children's Books division. **Barbara Marcus**, formerly at Scholastic, is taking his place. After leaving Scholastic, she was a consultant to Penguin and Open Road Integrated Media. She told *Publishers Weekly* she plans to "create new classics and reinvigorate the backlist."

~ **Ira Silverberg**, formerly an agent at Stirling Lord, left to become Literature Director for the National Endowment for the Arts.

~ **Kenneth Wright**, formerly an agent at Writer's House, became Vice President and Publisher of Viking Children's Books. He succeeded **Regina Hayes**, who remains as Editor at Large and continues to work with some of her authors, including Laurie Halse Anderson, Rosemary Wells, Joan Bauer, and Elizabeth George. Hayes had been at Penguin for 30 years.

~ **Lloyd G. "Buzz" Waterhouse** became President and CEO of McGraw-Hill Education. He was formerly CEO of Harcourt Education and also spent 26 years at IBM.

~ **Gretchen Young**, formerly of Hyperion, became Vice President and Executive Editor of Grand Central Press, an imprint at Hachette. She has edited books by George Carlin, Whoppi Goldberg, and Caroline Kennedy, among others.

comments on Amazon and Barnes & Noble, and in various online communities where books are discussed. Senior Writer Laura Miller has written articles about ebooks and spam for *Salon*, including a recent piece in which she quotes British writer Steven Leather about his promotional process: "As soon as my book is out I'm on Facebook and Twitter several times a day talking about it. I'll go on to several forums, and post there under my name and under various other names and various other characters. You build up this whole network of characters who talk about your books and sometimes have conversations with yourself." ("Social Media Scammers." Laura Miller. *Salon*. August 9, 2012)

This kind of fake reviewing is not very new. In 2004, Amazon's Canadian site accidently revealed the identities of anonymous reviewers. Visitors to the site could see that the authors themselves and their publishers wrote positive reviews for their books. Miller reports that the difference now is that, in addition to posing as anonymous readers or asking friends and co-workers to write positive reviews, authors can pay companies to post fake reviews, fill a Twitter feed, and post on Facebook—creating the impression that lots of people are reading and loving your book. The hope is that eventually real people will begin to buy it and post real messages and reviews. That may happen, but legitimate consumers are beginning to lose faith in customer reviews and social media recommendations.

Has the publishing world found a clear path through the maze of digital technology? Are we there yet? Given the hostility and continuing lawsuits among different areas of the industry, for this year at least, the answer is a definitive no. In fact, more earthquakes are likely, and the topology will change yet again.

But while some people see insurmountable obstacles, others see new paths and opportunities. When the digital publishing map is drawn a decade from now, it will not look much like the today's, but it is sure to take authors to exciting places never before imagined.

Obituaries

~ **Milburn Calhoun**, Publisher of Pelican Publishing, died on January 7. He had been a rare book expert and a practicing physician in New Orleans when he bought Pelican in 1961.

~ **Jerry Harrison**, former President of the Children's Book Division of Random House, died on January 19 at 83.

~ **Sam Vaughan**, former President, Publisher, and Editor in Chief of Doubleday, and later Editor and Senior Vice President at Random House, died January 30.

~ **Barney Rosset**, Publisher and editor of writers who included Samuel Beckett, William S. Burroughs, and Malcolm X died February 21. He fought for freedom of artistic expression, supporting the publication of books like *Lady Chatterley's Lover* and *Tropic of Cancer.*

~ **Atha Tehon**, award-winning children's book designer and art director, died on February 15, at 86. As Art Director at Dial Books for Young Readers and a freelance designer for Farrar, Straus and Giroux, she worked with many of the top authors and artists in the business, including Maurice Sendak, William Steig, Jerry Pinkney, and Stephen Kellogg.

~ **Jan Berenstain**, co-creator of the Berenstain Bears series, died on February 24 at 88. Her husband, and co-writer Stan Berenstain died in 2005.

~ **Maurice Sendak**, legendary author and illustrator of books such as *Where the Wild Things Are* and *In the Night Kitchen* died on May 8 at 83.

~ Well-known children's author **Jean Craighead George** died on May 15 at 92. Her best-known book, *Julie of the Wolves*, won the Newbery in 1972, and her *My Side of the Mountain* earned a Newbery Honor in 1960.

~ **Leo Dillon**, illustrator of more 40 children's picture books over his 50-year career, died at 79 on May 26. His work included *The People Could Fly: American Black Folktales,* by Virginia Hamilton, and he won the Caldecott Medal for *Why Mosquitos Buzz in People's Ears,* by Verna Aardema.

~ Legendary science fiction writer **Ray Bradbury** died on June 5 at 91. He was the author of 30 books, including *Fahrenheit 451* and *The Martian Chronicles*.

~ **Deborah Brodie**, long-time children's book editor, died on June 27 at 67.

~ **Stephen R. Covey**, author of *The 7 Habits of Highly Effective People*, died on July 16 at the age of 79.

Obituaries

- **Donald J. Sobol**, creator of the popular Encyclopedia Brown mystery series and numerous titles for young adults, died on July 11 at 87.
- Writer **Maeve Binchy**, called "Ireland's National Treasure," died on July 30 at 72. Her novels' strong characterizations and plots often focused on women's friendships, and evoked Irish village life. Her best-known books are *Light a Penny Candle, Circle of Friends,* and *Tara Road.*
- **Gore Vidal**, author, essayist, and playwright, died on July 31 at 86. His best-known novels are *Myra Breckinridge, Julian, Burr,* and *Lincoln.* He also wrote for the *Nation, Esquire,* the *New Yorker,* and the *New York Review of Books.*
- **Helen Gurley Brown**, Editor in Chief of *Cosmopolitan* and author, died on August 13 at 90. Her first bestseller, *Sex and the Single Girl,* was published in 1962.
- Five-time National Book Award finalist, historian, and author of 110+ books for children, **Milton Meltzer** died on September 19 at 94. His first book, *A Pictorial History of the Negro American* (1956), was co-written with poet Langston Hughes.
- Author of the early reader Little Bear books, **Else Holmelund Minaruk** died at 91 on July 12.
- Shoe String Press Publisher and founder **Frances Tompson Rutter** died on September 13 at 92.
- Publisher **Larry Sloan**, one of the founders in 1953 of Price Stern Sloan, died on October 15 at 89. The company was especially known in its early years for the Mad Libs books.
- The founder of Prometheus Books and an author of 50+ books, **Paul Kurtz** died at 86 on October 20. He was an ardent secular humanist.
- **Wendy E. Weil**, a literary agent for more than 40 years, died on September 22 at 72.

The Big Picture

The Year in Magazines

By Mark Haverstock

Play a game of *fun with statistics* and an article like this that reviews the year in magazines can take a negative angle, or a positive one. The negative: Circulation numbers and ad pages continue to decline, and magazines and newspapers are still being pushed toward digital to the demise of print. The positive: New magazine launches outpaced magazine closures by a substantial margin in the first half of the year. Startups continue to arrive. And digital magazines are vibrant and improving.

Newspapers and magazines have been in state of flux over the last few years as a result of the sluggish economy and an abundance of new media choices. But beware of reading numbers in a closed way. Declining circulations, and closing print versions of magazines such as *Newsweek*, can make the numbers seem dire—but how the numbers are to be read is changing as magazine media shift ground.

Accentuate the Positive

The Audit Bureau of Circulations reported that newsstand circulation was down almost 10 percent. The Publishers Information Bureau (administered by the Association of Magazine Media (MPA), formerly called the Magazine Publishers of America), announced that total consumer magazine ad pages declined 8.5 percent from the second quarter of 2011 to the second quarter of 2012. Total advertising revenues, based on official rate cards, slipped 3.2 percent to $5.5 billion.

But the MPA also reported numbers in October 2012 that, it says, "provide a more complete picture about the strength of magazines across platforms. The findings reveal a 57 percent spike in the number of brands advertising on magazine media platforms (tablet, online, and print) since 2010, and strong consumer engagement. Additionally, the data show year-over-year growth in the combined print and online magazine audience." (www.magazine.org/industry-news/press-releases/mpa-press-releases/mpa/ footprint)

MediaFinder, an online database of North American publications, reported in October that 181 new magazines launched in the first nine months of the year, with the largest number of new titles in the regional interest and food categories, continuing a trend. Magazine closures were down at 61, compared to 128 in the same period of 2011. In releasing the numbers to the media, Trish Hagood, President of MediaFinder's parent Oxbridge Communications, was bullish on the market, declaring, "The magazine industry has stabilized."

According to the 2012-2013 *Fact Book* of the Association of Magazine Media (MPA), 92 percent of American adults still read magazines, and the top 25 magazines reach more adults and teens than television. Facebook, Twitter, Pinterest, and other social media sites are playing a part in keeping the interest alive. A study released in August indicated how powerfully. "The results of MPA's new study clearly demonstrate that social media enriches the magazine reading experience, and that magazine media readers—on all platforms—are creating communities around and engaging with the magazines and editors they know and love," Chris Kevorkian, MPA's chief marketing and digital officer, said in a news release. (www.magazine.org/ industry-news/press-releases/mpa-press-releases/mpa/new-study-reveals-powerful-link-between)

Contrary to popular belief, younger readers are not necessarily abandoning magazines for other media, either. Data from consumer market research firm Gfk MRI shows that readers 18 to 24 actually read more print magazines now than they did 10 or 20 years ago. Fashion, beauty, and celebrity publications appeal to this group, as well as food and drink, travel, and luxury lifestyles. Twentysomething men gravitate toward lifestyle and fitness magazines, such as *GQ* and *Maxim.*

Among young adults, interest in general interest magazines like *Reader's Digest* and *TV Guide,* as well as women's titles like *Good Housekeeping* and *Redbook* is growing. Newsweeklies have lost ground with this demographic, which have become relics in a world of round-the-clock news reporting on the Web and television. Shelter publications, which saw a surge of readership a decade ago, have lost younger readers due to the slump in the housing market.

GfK MRI also reported in October the increase in interactivity with ads when magazines are read on a table or e-reader. A little over half of digital readers "noted" a digital advertisement on their tablet or e-reader, and among those who did 52 percent interacted with it.

The Face of Digital Magaines

People are used to purchasing apps and content for their electronic devices. According to a Nielsen survey, a majority of tablet owners have already paid for downloaded music (62 percent), books (58 percent), movies (51 percent), and magazines (41 percent). Low on the list is news, which only 19 percent have ever paid to read on tablets or readers. Some publishers are still stuck in print mode, hiring a coder to make an iPad version of the print magazine, instead of utilizing the features of this new medium.

One example of how *not* to go digital is the *Food Network Magazine* iPad edition. The layout is in spreads like a print magazine with some single pages not making sense until you see the following page. You have to keep your iPad in landscape mode through the whole process, but it is difficult to read the text without zooming in, and you need to zoom out for the next spread.

Interactivity is limited to tapping on recipes to add the ingredients to a shopping list. And the cooking videos are conspicuously missing. If there were ever a digital magazine that would have a stockpile of already completed videos, availability of star chefs, sets and camera crews, this would be it.

Successful publishers in the new media take advantage of the unique features it offers. *Wired*, published by Conde Nast Digital, manages to pull this off with style. The main attraction of the magazine is its interactivity. Besides filling the iPad's screen with high- resolution photographs, some stories and ads allow you to interact. An example is a Mars invasion story, where the main photograph could be spun around 360 degrees while pop-ups appear providing a short synopsis of each Mars landing. Other stories, including the cover story, are accompanied by embedded videos. There is so much interaction with the magazine that you may just neglect to read the stories themselves.

The ads are interesting too. Not only are they clean, crisp, and attractive, but some of them also have embedded video that opens up in full screen and a video starts playing right away.

Standardization is another challenge facing the growth of digital magazines. According to a GfK MRI survey, 72 percent of tablet owners who read a magazine on their device in the previous 30 days say they would prefer all digital magazines to be formatted in the same way. Almost the same percentage, 70 percent, said they would like to be able to buy items by clicking on the ads in a digital magazine, an additional incentive for advertisers.

The GfK MRI study also reported that 67 percent of tablet magazine readers said that, if available, they would rather read an electronic version of a magazine than a paper version. But 65 percent of tablet magazine readers said it is more *satisfying* to read a magazine the traditional way, on paper. Is there something wrong with the math?

"Although magazine publishers are experimenting with different formats in order to differentiate their digital brands, this is not necessarily resonating with digital readers adopting the new tablet technology," said Risa Becker, Senior Vice President of Research at GfK MRI. "Another really interesting finding is the seeming contradiction between the fact that most tablet magazine readers prefer to read electronically, and most also say it is more satisfying to read on paper. This may speak to the fact that although the convenience of electronic magazines, including the portability and immediate access, are highly valued by tablet readers, paper magazines still have a special tactile appeal." (www.gfkmri.com/assets/PR/GfKMRI_020312PR_DigitalUpdate.htm)

Ebooks, Ezines and Apps for Kids

Both established publishers and start-ups are experimenting with new ways of reaching young readers. With tablets and reading devices becoming less expensive and more accessible, children's publications also continue to migrate from print editions to more interactive digital ones.

For 40 years, the National Wildlife Organization's kids magazines entertained and educated children with their colorful print magazines. Now *Ranger Rick, Big Backyard,* and *Wild Animal Baby* are available in digital form for the Barnes & Noble Nook. Mary Dahlheim, Editorial Director of Children's Publications, told the press, "We're offering the same high-quality content with amazing wildlife photos and exciting stories, but we now have an additional delivery system to meet kids where they are." Plans for future issues include interactive games, songs, animation, and wildlife video.

Zinio (www.zinio.com), which bills itself as world's largest newsstand, is offering a variety of digital versions of popular print magazines and comics for children and teens. These include *American Girl, Chickadee, Girls' Life, Owl, Seventeen,* and *Transformers.*

Both tablet and smart phone apps are making their way to the market. *Timbuktu* is a tablet-based news magazine developed for kids that offers news with text, videos, and graphics developed by a global group of contributors. Editor in Chief Elena Favilli says the magazine's goal is to "combine education and technology to display everyday news. Children are usually completely cut off from [news]."

Cricket Magazine Group, part of Carus Publishing, which is now owned by the education media company ePals Corporation, is extending its brands by developing educational, reading-focused apps for *Ladybug* and *Cricket*. The *Ladybug*'s Bookshelf iPhone app offers stories with animation and sound so that kids can either read on their own or have the story read to them.

Constant, Continuing Change

As Isaac Asimov observed in *Asimov on Science Fiction*, "The only constant is change, continuing change, inevitable change that is the dominant factor in society today. No sensible decision can be made any longer without taking into account not only the world as it is, but the world as it will be . . . ."

This is completely true of the magazine market. *Integration, restructuring, consolidating,* and *streamlining* are among the publisher buzzwords for 2013.

~ Meredith Corporation, publisher of *Ladies Home Journal* and *Better Homes and Gardens*, continued cutbacks, eliminating 80 jobs that affected all the company's magazines. *Maxim* also downsized, laying off six staffers.

~ Hearst Magazines announced it would combine the editorial departments for its design group, which includes shelter titles *House Beautiful, Veranda,* and *Elle Décor*. Hearst president David Carey began the integration in October. An estimated dozen jobs in the group were scheduled to disappear by the end of 2012.

~ *Sports Illustrated*, a Time Inc. magazine, cut editorial staff through voluntary buyouts before resorting to layoffs with the goal of becoming more efficient. Bloomberg.com reported in June that Time Inc. has tried to reduce the impact of lower revenue from its print publications by increasing online advertising.

~ In an increasingly common reversal of the traditional paradigm, *Technology Review* is putting digital before print, posting articles online and only later publishing them on paper. It instituted the process between June and October 2012. Other digital-first publications are radio hobby magazines *CQ* , *Popular Communications, Monitoring Times,* and *QST*.

~ *Newsweek*'s last print edition was dated December 31, 2012. It is now being published digitally only. Other publications following this path are *Campus Technology* and *T.H.E. Journal*, which cover educational technology, and *Smart Money. Computerworld* and *CIO Canada* publisher IT World Canada is converting all its business-to-business publications to digital.

~ *Louisiana Cookin'* was acquired by Hoffman Media, which planned to increase circulation tenfold to 75,000.

~ *Star* and *OK!* reported layoffs in an effort to restructure.

~ *Reality Weekly,* which launched at the beginning of 2012, quickly moved to a tablet-only format because its print sales topped at 100,000, instead of the predicted 200,000.

~ *Forbes* is publishing a redesigned *ForbesLife*, to be sold on newsstands in New York, Los Angeles, and Las Vegas, and on iPad and e-readers.

~ The Internet's *Huffington Post* of Internet fame has entered the world of digital magazines with *Huffington*. The iPad weekly version has three sections: the week's top stories and events; in-depth features; and lighter "back-of-the-book" fare such as book, music, and film reviews.

~ *FamilyFun* introduced changes to its look and content in its October 2012 issue, months after the brand was acquired from Disney by the Meredith Corporation. The magazine is now structured around three categories—Create, Play and Explore. It has expanded coverage of learning, health, and travel departments.

~ The Association of Magazine Media (MPA) is reorganizing, and reducing staff. Its long-time President and CEO Nina Link has stepped down after 13 years. She had the distinction of serving

New Work Arrangements?

Out laid off its entire editorial staff, giving them a meager one month of severance pay, only to have Editor in Chief Aaron Hicklin announce he will hire back most of the 12 staffers as contract freelancers. Of course, there are no-full time paychecks or benefits in this arrangement.

Hicklin formed a company, Grand Editorial, to act as an editorial consultant for this company, and others in the future. He assumed the magazine's operations as a contractor for Here Media, and Regent Entertainment, which bought *Out* in 2008.

The positive side, Hicklin says, is that staffers will have more flexible hours and the opportunity to work on other projects for his company. Despite appearances, Hicklin insists this is not a cost-cutting measure. The magazine's content and frequency will remain the same.

longer at this post than anyone else, and was instrumental in guiding the organization through challenging economic times and the emergence of digital platforms.

Goodbyes & Welcome Backs

Good things eventually come to an end, and magazines are no different.

~ American Media's *Soap Opera Weekly* folded. It blamed the closure on the decline of the soap opera genre.

~ *St. Louis Commerce* closed its doors after 94 years in print.

~ *LA Times Magazine* ceased publication after a four-year run.

~ *Artnet*, an online magazine, folded after 16 years. Sources said the magazine was never able to pay its own way. At present, plans call for Artnet to remain available in an archive.

~ *Scrapbooks Etc.* ended its run with the August issue. Owner Meredith Corporation announced that the move was "due to the longer-term business forecast for the franchise and the industry."

~ Digital mags *Real Eats* and *Body Smart* both folded.

~ NFL ventures rarely fail, but *NFL Magazine* ceased publication after only four issues because the company that published the magazine, Dauphin Media Group, closed its doors.

~ Digital magazine publisher Nomad Editions closed down its three remaining titles: *Uncorked,* a wine magazine; *Snooth Wine Buyers' Guide*; and *Hemmings Classic Wheels.*

~ This year's comeback kids include some classics from bygone days. Inspired by the *New Yorker,* the original *Chicagoan* debuted in the 1920s and crashed with the Great Depression. A new biannual incarnation features long-form journalism about the arts, culture, and history of Chicago and the Midwest. Inside, readers will find profiles, interviews, fiction, reviews, and more. Daily coverage will be offered on their smartphone apps.

~ *Collier's* relaunched after a 55-year hiatus. Like the original publication, this new version covers current events and literary topics. Included will be features on the arts, cinema, politics, business, health, finances, and other aspects of American life.

~ The publishing rights to *Geek Monthly* magazine changed hands a couple of times since the original publisher, Fusion Publishing, ceased operations in 2010. Source Interlink Media now holds the rights, and is publishing a restyled and renamed *Geek Magazine* in print and tablet formats.

~ *Hot Rod* was relaunched in September 2012.

~ Golf publication *Fairways + Greens* rebranded itself as a print bimonthly print, with a monthly digital edition. The first relaunched issue appeared in November 2012, with a new focus on golf travel.

~ Condé Nast's Fairchild division resurrected *M*, which last appeared in 1992, and is now a quarterly. Its target audience is men with household income above $200,000. Each issue will be theme-based, with the debut fall 2012 issue about ambition. The plan is to go bimonthly in 2014.

~ Rodale is relaunching *Best Life*, which shut down in 2009. The first new issues are dated in fall 2012 and spring 2013. Target readers

Keeping in Touch

What about keeping in contact with magazine staff once they moved on? Email addresses change, rendering your contact list obsolete. But one thing increasingly remains the same: Twitter handles. They become part of individuals' identities, so much so that Twitter has policies to deal with impersonators. So if that favorite editor of yours moves on, and on again, try Twitter—or any of the major social media sites—to reconnect.

are men who "live the good life," with a median age of 45 and income of $150,000.

The comebacks of *M* and *Best Life* may represent a trend for publishers taking advantage of a resurgence in luxury advertising by returning to publications that had a strong reader following.

A Sampling of New Magazine Listings

~ *Cosmopolitan for Latinas* (www.cosmopolitan.com/cosmo-latina) is a spin off from *Cosmopolitan* for English-speaking Latinas. The bimonthly lifestyle glossy offers tips and features on style, beauty, entertainment, relationships, career, finances, food, entertaining and culture, tailored to bilingual, bicultural Hispanic women.

~ *Berkshire Magazine* (www.berkshiremag.com) is a new regional glossy that launched with a June/July issue. Covering culture, the arts, fashion and style in the Berkshires, the magazine will depend on editorial content from writers and photographers based in the area. It joins five other regional sister publications from the Morris Media Group. Eight issues per year.

~ *Edible Cleveland* (www.ediblecleveland.com) covers the local food community and is a resource for finding products seasonally. This is one of more than 50 editions published around the country by Edible Communities. Quarterly.

~ *Story* (storythemagazine.com) is a quarterly that targets Kentucky readers, with features on the arts, business, philanthropy, and Kentucky living. Quarterly.

~ *Huffington.* (www.huffingtonmagazine.com) is a weekly distillation of the best original content from the online *Huffington Post,* and includes original content as well. It covers politics, entertainment, business, culture, in the U.S. and around the world.

~ *The Growler* (growlermag.com), a lifestyle and craft beer bimonthly, hit the newsstands in the Minneapolis-St. Paul region in mid-2012. Besides focusing on craft beer, it includes articles on topics on team sports, hiking, biking, music, cooking, and the arts.

~ *EcoParent* (www.ecoparent.ca) is a Canadian quarterly catering to ecologially minded families. It gives parents the knowledge and inspiration to make healthy, green living choices. Content includes food, fashion, travel, health, books, and tips.

~ *Cycling News HD* (www.cyclingnews.com/cyclingnews-hd) is a weekly digest magazine for iPad. It covers the week's leading races, with expert analysis, and has in-depth stories. Its rider profiles and race routes are interactive.

~ *Moms & Dads Today* (momsanddadstoday.com) is a Minnesota bimonthly that is creating an interactive community where readers can learn and grow from sharing their parenting experiences. It offers tips and articles on health, hobbies, activities, and vacation ideas, as well as parenting.

~ *Wax, A Magazine for Urban Surfers* (readwax.com) is a biannual "exploring the intersection of art, culture and surfing in and around New York City." The print issue shares the stories of area surfers who are also artists, designers, authors, and is organized around a unique theme.

~ *Real: Authentic Austin Living* (www.statesman.com/life/real) is a monthly lifestyle magazine that highlights neighborhoods, home design, fashion, health, family issues, pets, events, and other topics of regional interest.

~ *Click* (www.clickonline.com) is a Canadian digital lifestyle

Gender Gap in Magazines

Two years ago, VIDA: Women In Literary Arts (www.vidaweb.org) started counting the rates of publication between women and men in many of the world's most respected literary outlets. The disparity is clear. Among the most recent numbers:

- *Harper's* ratio was more than three to one: 141 by men, 42 by women.
- The *Nation,* led by a female editor, published 440 articles by men, 166 by women.
- *New Republic:* 198 by men, 50 by women.
- *New York Review of Books:* 293 by men, 71 by women.
- *New York Times:* 968 by men, 641 by women.
- *New Yorker* published 613 articles by men, 242 by women.
- *Paris Review:* 46 by men, 2 by women.

monthly covering games, technology, and movies. It includes interviews, news articles, and reviews.

- *Destinations Uncovered* (www.destinationsuncovered.net) is a digital monthly underwritten by Educators Overseas, which finds teaching positions abroad. The publication provides destination information about history, culture, regions, cuisine and more.

- *Tailgating Digest* (www.tailgatingdigest.com) appears electronically and in print bimonthly and specializes in tailgating at sports events. Issues are seasonally based and cover events, food, product reviews, and other other topics related to tailgating. Each issue will focus on season-appropriate pro and college sports.

- *Los Angeles Fashion Magazine* (www.thelosangelesfashion.com) is the quarterly magazine of the greater Los Angeles fashion scene, as well as the Southern California lifestyle. Local designers, fashion news, and celebrity interviews are featured.

- *New York Home Design* (nymag.com/homedesign) is a twice-yearly, glossy spin-off of *New York* that targets professionals and others interested in interior design with a New York feel.

~ *Cigar & Spirits* (www.cigarandspirits.com) is a lifestyle bimonthly with a readership of people who appreciate quality cigars, spirits, fine dining, and fashion.

~ *Du Jour* (www.dujour.com) is a quarterly luxury magazine for the "one percent"—the wealthiest—especially in cities like Chicago, Los Angeles, and New York. Fashion, travel, fine dining, beauty, entertainment, culture, real estate, health, technology, finance, sports, philanthropy, and politics are featured subjects.

~ *What Makes You Happy* (www.happyhappyhappy.ca) is a Canadian quarterly with a focus on the positive and explorations of happiness. Editors hope the magazine "will amuse, stimulate and challenge" its audience.

~ *Miabella* (www.miabellamag.com) targets young women bimonthly, encouraging them in positive self-image, health, and fresh perspectives. It covers entertainment, fashion, social issues, the environment, fitness and nutrition.

~ *everydog* (www.everydogmagazine.com) is published quarterly by Continental Kennel Club to give dog owners news about the dog world, as well as improve life with dogs.

~ *The Box* (www.theboxmag.com) aims to serve the CrossFit fitness community with bimonthly advice on training and nutrition. It also includes news, research, and profiles of competitors.

~ *CommonCall* (www.baptiststandard.com) comes from Baptist Standard Publishing. The monthly offers human-interest stories about evangelism, family life, changing lives, church ministries, and Christians who put their faith into practice. Issues are theme-based, with real-life examples.

~ *South Carolina Hoofbeats* (www.schoofbeats.com) caters to South Carolina horse owners. All riding disciplines and breeds are covered. The quarterly features events, health, training, riding trails, horse-related business, and legal advice.

~ *Highlights Hello* (www.highlights.com/highlights-hello-magazine-for-kids) is a new children's monthly made for the children from birth to age two, and their parents. It features short, real-aloud stories and poems, picture puzzles, and fun activities, as well as articles for parents containing expert advice from pediatricians, psychologists, and educators.

~ *BYOU* (shop.beyourownyou.com/BYOU-Be-Your-Own-You-Magazine-p/mag.htm) is a bimonthly magazine made to empower young girls through interviews with positive role models, stories about girls making a difference in the world, self-esteem tips, activiies, games, contests, and fiction.

~ *Paleo* (www.paleomagonline.com) is the only magazine dedicated to the Paleo lifestyle—"modern-day primal living." Every other month it provides readers with information on a modern diet based on the foods that our ancestors ate to remain healthy and active. It includes research, interviews, interviews, inspirational stories, recipes, tips on nutrition and exercise, and reviews.

~ *Modern Cat* (www.moderncat.com) is a lifestyle magazines that features ideas for improving life with cats, and covers health and wellness, breed profiles, behavioral advice, and interviews with celebrities who love cats.

~ *Cloud Computing Magazine* (cloud-computing.tmcnet.com) is a quarterly about using the cloud, covering individual, community, and business use, security issues, innovations, and techniques for use.

Survival of the Fittest

History has proven that some magazine niches will do better than others. Publications serving intensely interested audiences should continue to thrive, despite the ups and downs of the market. Among them today, is *Game Informer,* published by Game Stop. Like the industry it covers, *Game Informer* has grown by leaps and bounds and in 2012 it had the third largest circulation among U.S. magazines, behind only long-established heavyweights *Ladies' Home Journal* and *Better Homes and Gardens*.

The shifting to digital technology overall has reached a tipping point, thanks to the growing popularity of tablets and e-readers. In the U.S., it is predicted that tablet users will number 133.5 million by 2015, representing 41 percent of the total population, an increase from 22 percent of the population in 2012. Publishers' biggest challenge remains monetizing tablet audiences to make up for the erosion of print revenue.

Although print is still far from dead, many print magazines will continue their transformation into digital publications that will be delivered in two forms: a downloaded version that can be read offline, and a networked cloud version that readers can access in real time.

The magazine industry will continue to evolve in 2013, and the bywords will continue to be adapation and survival of the fittest. At the 2012 Publishing Business Conference & Expo in New York City, Editor of *Bloomberg Businessweek* Josh Tyrangiel welcomed an audience tellling them, "Each day you have to fight for your right to exist. It is not a given anymore. Every new platform is an opportunity to define yourself to a new audience, to an audience that doesn't yet know you or hasn't even heard of you. It's also an opportunity to redefine yourself to an audience that does."

Big Fish, Little Pond

The Saga of the Midlist Writer

By Christina Hamlett

L et's be honest. A midlist author is the literary equivalent of a *tween*: old enough to pedal around a familiar neighborhood by herself and yet too young to trust behind the wheel of the family car. The midlist writer's dilemma became familiar to me with my first agent, a woman who only knew how to sell romance and tried to discourage me from pedaling beyond that particular genre. Transitioning to another form of fiction, she said, was as difficult a task as sitcom actors or comedians attempting to remake themselves and perform edgy drama.

That agent's viewpoint was wrong then because of its narrow perspective on writing and creativity, but it is even more wrong today. As the industry changes, midlisters have more and more choices, both within traditional publishing and outside of it.

The Numbers Game

Years after my agent's comments, I was researching an article about *RMS Titanic*, and another analogy came to represent the economic realities of the *midlist* label for me. The ships of the White Star Line were dependent on two classes of passengers: the multitudes who paid £5 a ticket to travel in steerage and the elite whose £870 fare bought them the privilege of dining with the captain. As long as the lower decks were consistently filled with passengers who require minimal attention, a crossing only needed a handful of the upper crust for the staff to fawn over to make for a financially successful voyage. Problematic, however, were second-class passengers—the midlisters who paid six times the cost of a steerage ticket but were not a large enough constituency and did not wield any significant social clout.

As traditional publishing venues downsize or reform today, a century after *Titanic*, it seems to be the midlist authors being abandoned by the ship and left to fend for ourselves. As a result, midlisters either pursue self-publishing routes or seek out the harbor of smaller houses that welcome their talents.

New writers tend to believe that once they get on board with a publisher, their futures are secure. Not so. Stellar reviews and awards, with modest sales, are no longer enough for the Big Six publishers (Hachette, HarperCollins, Macmillan, Penguin, Random House, Simon & Schuster) to keep midlisters on their payrolls, reported *Publishers Weekly* Senior News Editor Rachel Deahl in an article on small presses. It has grown harder for underperforming titles to get in-house support, and it is also more challenging for those with previously published books to lock down a new contract.

Deahl wrote, "A number of agents and publishers interviewed said editors at the big houses, who always consider the sales performance of an author's last book before signing the author's new book, need to see bigger figures to close deals." ("Smaller Presses, Bigger Authors." Rachel Deahl. *Publishers Weekly*. November 8, 2010.) Even if circumstances of poor performance are beyond a writer's control, publishing houses have become increasingly wary of taking fiscal risks. The result has been a downsizing of advances for debut novels and literary fiction, which attracts midlist authors.

On the other side of the equation, contract negotiations for presses of all sizes are becoming more complex with the rise of digital publishing. And authors are taking more of a stand. Mary DuBois is President of Trellis Publishing, a small press that publishes adult and children's titles. She says, "Authors are getting advice from every source about how to protect their rights and to make the most economic advantage that they can from their writing. And who can blame them, since most publishers are requiring authors to do significant book promotion?" Often the advice involves authors' retaining electronic rights.

This is a problem for DuBois, Trellis, and other small presses. "If you as an author retain exclusive ebook rights, then I as a publisher need to take the risk of the book manufacturing, which includes jacket cover design, final editing, print run and inventory storage costs (not to mention those pesky shipping costs), and initial promotion and marketing," she explains. "If I can't sell the ebook version, then I have taken most of the risk of the entire project and lost a profitable, growing sector. I just lost a contract because of this issue, and from that experience I no longer will enter the long, complicated negotiation process if an author wants to retain ebook exclusivity. It's just too stressful for everyone when the whole deal is likely to fall apart."

Fostering Collaborative Partnerships

With increased expectations placed on authors, Deahl says that even formerly best-selling authors are gravitating to independent presses. "Although small presses give less money up front, their model is more viable for a lot of fiction. The same book that disappoints by selling only 10,000 copies at one of the Big Six is a big hit at a small press—and that, many small press publishers note, often leads to a happier author."

The emergence of *hybrid* publishers has empowered midlist authors and encouraged them to create platforms that attract more readers. Influence Publishing in Vancouver, British Columbia, was launched two years ago by Julie Salisbury when she realized she could help authors by providing creative leadership that avoids some of the demands and problems of the fast-moving book market. "Most authors don't understand that a trade publisher needs to be guaranteed that a book fits into its existing, winning-formula genre, and will sell at bookstores— with little extra promotion—within two weeks of the launch date," says Salisbury. "If it's something *new*, it's too risky, especially since bookstores can return the book within 90 days if it doesn't move. What happens to those then? Do you really think the book is given a second chance?"

"Hybrid publishing," Salisbury continues, "utilizes print-on-demand (POD) technology so we don't have to risk a large print-run that might get returned. We turn our marketing to specific market sectors (usually not found in bookstores), identifying where readers are, and selling directly via online bookstores at associations or social media groups looking for specific knowledge. It's an entrepreneurial business relationship with the author that lasts a few years, not a few months, and certainly not the few weeks when most trade publishing houses expect a fast-moving book to succeed. It's a new wave of publishing that uses the book as a platform to promote the author's other activities, such as speaking, workshops, and teaching. Bookstores become another outlet [where] the reader can find the book, rather than being the only outlet to sell and market. With new POD technology and online marketing opportunities, the face of publishing is completely changing, [to be more] in line with independent movies and music."

Patty O'Sullivan, Associate Publisher at Prospect Park Media, has nothing but praise and enthusiasm for midlisters. "We consider the midlist to be our strategic sweet spot and are actively going after authors who have had underwhelming experiences with large publishing houses. In our experience, midlist authors are hardworking professionals who have a deep and realistic understanding of the publishing world. They realize that working with a smaller press will provide them with a team that has laser focus on helping their books achieve maximum sales potential. They also realize it's to our mutual benefit they participate in and even co-fund that marketing through social media efforts, blog and book tours, conference participation, and personal appearances."

O'Sullivan adds, "We typically don't replicate our marketing efforts from book to book. Instead, we'll work directly with the author and the material to identify the best way to cut through the wall of book marketing noise. And, unlike the big houses, we're nimble enough to change course if we discover that some-

> "We work directly with the author and the material to identify the best way to cut through the wall of book marketing noise."

thing isn't working. The last thing we want to do is waste our authors' time. As with any partnership, it all gets back to the basics. We communicate. It's an extraordinarily rare occasion when our authors haven't heard back from us within a few hours of reaching out. Usually it means we're on an airplane or on a sequestered jury!"

Becoming Buzz-Worthy

The best book in the world is not going anywhere if no one knows it exists. Indie presses such as BlackWyrm Publishing are taking an entrepreneurial page from the marketing and social media strategies of self-published writers, a lesson that midlist authors can learn from as well.

"As a small press, we study the self-publishing market closely," says BlackWyrm's president, Dave Mattingly. "Many of the techniques self-published authors use will also work for us, but on a different scale. While we can't devote one to two hours each day for each author—the way many self-publishers do—we can promote our author in general each day, and our individual authors can then build on that buzz to put in just a little time to keep themselves top-of-mind."

"The ideal author for us," Mattingly says, "is one that already has a platform established. If an author approaches us with a couple of thousand followers on Twitter, Facebook, LinkedIn, or Reddit, or has a podcast or YouTube channel with hundreds of fans, that author would probably get more attention from us than an author with no established base. Some of our authors use social media to reach audiences by giving away chapters as they're written, engaging fans as early as possible. Others tweet as their main characters, reacting to life's daily events as if they were real people. Some authors interact with other authors by interviewing them and promoting their respective books. There are also many writing and regional groups our authors belong to; when the audience is appropriate, tying in promotions with each of those is a great way to extend their influence."

"Even if a major publisher prints your book," says Publisher Alfred Poor of Desktop Wings, "you'll still be left on your own for marketing it. There are many useful strategies you can pursue but the most cost-effective choice in terms of time and money is online video. Put at least one video clip on your book's website. Some make a video *book trailer* like Hollywood does for movies, but most writers will be better served by simply posting an honest video message to prospective readers to start the conversation with them. This helps because Google loves video. One study showed that a video will make your site 53 times more likely to show up on the first page of a Google search. You can see the benefit in just 30 minutes. YouTube lets you store your video for free; you can even record and edit your video using YouTube and a webcam. Video helps you get your message across more effectively because people will spend an average of 344 percent more time on your website. More hits, more time on message, and, most important, all for free!"

Establishing a Smart Fit

If you are a midlist author seeking a new playing field—including the option of becoming your own publisher—it is critical you learn as much as possible about your target demographic.

Editor David Crumm, of Read the Spirit Books, says, "Large publishers today have far more data on readers than ever before and aim their books at big, well-defined groups of fans, racking up bestsellers with everything from celebrity cookbooks to murder mysteries for pet lovers. The authors they're turning away generally are writing books for audiences that are more difficult to identify and effectively serve. That's where I believe midlist authors and publishers can develop a significant advantage. At Read the Spirit, for example, we're ill-equipped to market mysteries but we're leading experts in marketing books that provide spiritual solutions for daily living. By understanding the key roles of the men and women who lead millions of small discussion groups in congregations nationwide, we know how to speak their language. We know spiritual subjects that are popular in these groups, and subjects that are fading. My advice to midlist authors is to spend time researching smaller publishers that are developing special expertise in niche markets that interest you. Walking in the door for a meeting with an acquisitions editor will be more promising if you already understand how your book proposal is a perfect fit with that publisher's core audience."

Publishers are also more receptive to midlist writers that have incorporated adjunct activities and marketing strategies into their business plans. Psychologist Eileen Kennedy-Moore, author of *Smart Parenting for Smart Kids* (Jossey-Bass) and *What About Me? 12 Ways to Get Your Parents' Attention Without Hitting Your Sister* (Parenting Press) has made book promotion a natural fit with her speaking engagements at schools and conferences. "I generally end up selling books to one-third to one-half of the audience, probably because people can see firsthand that I genuinely care about the concerns of parents and children and that I know lots of practical ways to help. Some of my speaking gigs come through event organizers finding my website (I have a page dedicated to speaking information that lays out everything they need), but many come about because I've submitted a proposal to a conference or I've sent an email directly to a principal, head-master, guidance counselor, or PTO president explaining what I could offer."

"My advice to midlist authors is to spend time researching smaller publishers that are developing special expertise in markets that interest you."

Kennedy-Moore also enthusiastically recommends Reporter Connection (www.reporterconnection.com), ProfNet (www.prnewswire.com/profnet), and HARO (Help a Reporter Out, www.helpareporter.com) as great resources to find and respond to journalists seeking experts. "Journalists are often on tight deadlines and being able to offer useful, quotable, on-topic comments makes the reporter's job easier and makes you a memorable source for future stories," says Kennedy-Moore.

In addition to getting reviews and doing radio shows, Kennedy-Moore's research-based blog on the *Psychology Today* website does not just garner thousands of views, it also reinforces her credentials as an expert readers can trust. "For nonfiction authors, the key question to ask yourself is, 'What information, perspective, or strategies can I offer that people will find useful?'

By focusing on sharing valuable information, we create genuine connections with potential readers and avoid that icky *Me! Me! Me! Buy! Buy! Buy!* tone that's so off-putting."

The Label Syndrome

"Who is your publisher?" is a common question writers are asked when they announce they have sold a new book. Yet readers today rarely base their purchase decisions on whether a publishing label is a prestigious one. They are just looking to find a book that will entertain, inform, or enlighten them regardless of who put it into circulation.

"Breaking into publishing is like joining an exclusive club," says Lucy Leitner, author of *Working Stiffs* (Necro Publications). "Most major publishers will not look at a manuscript that does not have the representation of an agent, and agents will only represent already published authors. The catch-22 inherent in the process of getting the novel published is further complicated by the confusion brought about by the ubiquity of self-publishing. When I was looking to publish my debut zombie comedy novel, I found my options limited due to the fact I wasn't an established author. Luckily, however, my book fit into the horror niche which has an extensive selection of specialty publishers willing to gamble on first-time authors. Unfortunately, these houses are also small and lack the marketing budget of Random House. When Necro Publications released the book in June 2012, I was left to do much of the promotion myself."

Leitner soon found that booksellers and reviewers often mistake midlist works from small publishers for self-published books. "The proliferation of vanity presses has made debut books like mine appear to be self-published. Accordingly, when I visit a bookstore to request they carry my novel on their shelves, I have to explain that the book was professionally edited, already passed through a screening process and that I didn't pay for its publication."

While naysayers continue to decry the escalating popularity of nontraditional publishing routes, industry statistics reveal that earlier perceptions of *midlist* as *second class* are rapidly falling by the wayside. And the new concept of *wagging the long tail*— keeping many old titles in print and available, a concept that was essential to Amazon's growth—bodes well for the midlist author. The ability to generate small, steady sales through the Internet and micro-markets can translate to large profits over the long run. For the creative midlister feeling stuck on a ship bound for nowhere, publishing now offers the opportunity to take the helm and strike out in a bold new direction.

The World Wants Your Opinion

By Susan Sundwall

"Your assignment is to write a 400-word essay on the strongest and the weakest elements of democracy."

A collective groan goes up, pencils snap, and glares are directed at the poor social studies teacher who is only trying to give an assignment that will enlighten students. Condensing any developed thought into 400 words sets the bar too high for some, but whatever the word count, the assignment can seem burdensome if you are the hapless, challenged student who finds democracy a complete mystery.

But that dreaded high school assignment represents a form of writing that is found across magazine, newspaper, and online markets. It runs the gamut from engaging personal essays to scathing political commentary. Each variation of the form has its charms and challenges, but each adheres to the prescribed structure for crafting a solid essay. If you learned to write those essays well in school, you are a step ahead.

Three Essay Types

Aldous Huxley, perhaps best known as the author of the novel *Brave New World*, was also an essayist and wrote about the form. He divided essays into what he called three *poles,* or forms: the personal, the factual, and the abstract. Essays are brief, and often speak from a personal viewpoint, even if analyzing factual

Two Editors Weigh In

Leslie Moore of *Sasee Magazine* and Charity Bishop of *Prairie Times* are two editors who seek well written essays for their publications.

Why do you think the essay form works so well for your readers?

Bishop: It lends itself to nostalgic narratives, which is what our readers most like. They want to read stories about real life, people, and events, not fiction. Many of them are former city people who have long dreamed of being part of the country, and living a simple life. Today, we don't milk cows by hand, or hook up the buckboard to go to town, or sew dresses out of flour sacks. The real-life experiences of our writers let [readers] step back into another time, or cause memories of their own to resurface.

Moore: *Sasee* is a women's lifestyle magazine and women love reading about what other women are experiencing in their lives. It helps us to understand that the experience of being female is universal. Plus, it's just fun to read essays!

How can writers best prepare for writing an essay?

Bishop: The best possible way to prepare to write is to simply do it. Write it, put it in a drawer, and walk away from it. Go back to it in a couple of weeks. You may find you have more to add, or a new angle comes to mind, or

information. They may reveal autobiographical information anecdotally (the personal essay), objectively analyze an issue or critique something like a book or exhibit (factual/objective), or discuss ideas (abstract/ universal). Among the most well-known American essayists are Ralph Waldo Emerson, Henry David Thoreau, H. L. Mencken, E. B. White, and James Thurber. Writers today known for their essays include John D'Agata, Marilynne Robinson, David Shields, Sarah Vowell, and the late Christopher Hitchens and David Foster Wallace.

I have written and sold personal essays about such diverse subjects as the family recipe box, pennies, doll patterns, huckle-

Two Editors Weigh In

it doesn't flow as well as you thought. Writers can make the mistake of being in a rush. They cram their heads with research, pound out something good, and send it off. Your best writing isn't your first draft. It may not even be your second draft. It takes time. If you work on it too hard all at once, you'll get sick of it. Slow down, let it breathe, and then polish it.

Moore: Writers, I believe, are always looking for a good story. Life is a good story! Journaling would be a good way to practice writing personal essays—everyone's life is full of good material.

What are some of the more popular topics with your readers?

Moore: "We have an editorial calendar that lists topics for each month and some do go over better than others. "Memories" was a big one this year. I received nearly 150 essays that month. "Generations" was another big hit, but it's very similar. Writing about a special memory or important person from your past can be very powerful."

Bishop:"Our readers most love animal stories. Whether they are cranky bulls, blind cows, cats that chase dogs, or man's best friend. I think the love of pets is so universal that it is easy to identify with the author in his or her predicament."

berries, childhood holiday memories, and the antics of various animals I have owned. These are autobiographical and anecdotal.

Anyone who listened to the late Andy Rooney heard a personal essay verbalized every Sunday night at the close of that week's *60 Minutes*. Rooney took the most common occurrence, household item, or social situation and gave it back to us with his own humorous twist. Millions of viewers tuned in every Sunday evening to find out Andy's spin on his chosen subject.

I have also tackled tougher issues like abortion and atheism, in essays that veer toward either the factual or the abstract. My oldest son writes political commentary essays with titles like "The

Bloody Nose Statists" (www.ericsundwall.com), where objective/ factual and abstract/universal come into play and his political views blaze through. We each have our readers. We each follow the same generally accepted principles of good essay writing.

The Schematic

There is hardly a topic or area of life that could not be covered by one or more of Huxley's essay forms. But whichever the form, from personal to universal, the schematic of essay writing is straightforward. According to Jim Cullen, Editor of *The Progressive Populist* in Storm Lake, Iowa, "Essays should have a beginning, a middle, and an end. You'd be surprised how many submissions are missing one or more of those ingredients."

Essay writers must also leave the reader with a takeaway. You have read essays that have stuck in your mind, sometimes for years, because the writer's thoughts and conclusion left a crater-sized impression. The takeaway may have been intensely, passionately conveyed, or composed with irrefutable reasoning, or adroitly used humor may have made the essay memorable. Humor falls into the abstract/universal category and is a favorite of editors.

Leslie Moore is the Editor of *Sasee*, where essays, humor, satire, personal experience, and features on topics relating to women are the primary editorial focus. "I look for essays that are evocative or humorous. I believe humor is harder," she says. "The personal essay should resonate with readers; it should include them in the experience being related. Of course, good writing is hard to define. Once the basics are down, I think you either *have it* or you don't. And, I believe writers have to believe in what they're writing. We all make creative embellishments when putting together a story, but if the writer feels strongly about their subject, it shows in the finished product."

Prairie Times, a bimonthly news magazine in Byers, Colorado, uses essays extensively. Editor Charity Bishop also appreciates the humorous aspects in the submissions she receives. "The best pieces of writing connect on a level that is more than superficial, and provoke memories. Humor is also very popular. Life is serious . . . but why should it be?" she says.

Personal essays are written with no attempt to hide the fact that the writing is yours. Your words, thoughts, observances, and opinions expressed all come from your own quiver. The true you emerges, and you do not care who knows it. The autobiographical essay is not academic, but rather a personal narrative of experience meant to entertain or evoke emotion or empathy. The author's own perspective and insight are key.

A Point Well Made

Core to the essay form is that it offers your thoughts, your attempts at conveying perceptions. When writing an essay, your brain will also be flooded with thoughts and images readers probably will not care much about. You might think it important to examine exactly why you named your dog Monster in your autobiographical essay, but if that has nothing to do with the point of the piece, leave it out. Be sure that you have a core idea, understand yourself what you wish to say and convey, and how to say it effectively.

"If you cannot articulate your point," says Bishop, "your heart isn't behind what you are writing. You must believe it to write it. Usually, hitting writer's block is an indication that you are not happy with where your story is going. If you cannot write through it, go back to the last place the words were flowing naturally and head off in a new direction."

Beating your point to death will also work against you. Making a point with just the right amount of emphasis is a struggle, but worth the time. Moore says, "I believe beginning writers sometimes write what they think the reader wants to hear. While that has some validity, it's important to always write for yourself first." At the same time, she cautions, "Be sure you're not using

Commentary Writing

Steven Greenhut, Vice President of Journalism at the Franklin Center for Government and Public Integrity, gives an inside look at his commentary writing.

"I operate from a set of ideas, from a fairly well-thought-out sense of how the political system should operate. My readers know that I am a libertarian, but my views are infused with myriad other influences. I'm forthright with my readers about what I believe, which allows them to discount my biases. I start there, but it's crucial nonetheless to be somewhat unpredictable and driven by sound reporting. Writers who are too doctrinaire are boring. Too many opinion writers don't do enough original reporting.

"I have at times surprised myself at the topics I embrace. In my newspaper career, I have spent much of my time writing about police abuse issues, eminent domain abuses, and other takings, and since my 2009 book *Plunder*, I've been writing so much about public employee unions. The common thread is the issue of justice. I am motivated by exposing injustices—by people losing their property so that cities can hand over their land to developers; by the authorities abusing their power; by the undue influence unions exert in politics and how they have twisted the meaning of public service. I have also come to focus on California's particular situation. This is a magnificent state and I want to write about ways that we can fix its ongoing dysfunction. I find that people across the country have a newfound interest in California. Perhaps it's *schadenfreude*. But I am keeping busy writing about this state for national audiences."

Greenhut also shared this about some of his favorite commentary writers.

"I always admired George Will, who is one of the most elegant writers out there, and an adult voice in a conservative movement that often has become shrill and vulgar. I like Glenn Greenwald of *Salon* and his anti-war commentary. I've always been a big fan of Pat Buchanan's writing. He's a clear thinker and powerful writer. I like writers who try to convince readers rather than impress them or win praise from those who already agree with them. I still like to read Mencken. My mark of a good commentary writer: someone I love to read even when I disagree with their conclusions."

your writing to work through some strong emotion, such as anger or grief. It's certainly okay to write about those feelings, but not for publication when they're still so raw it hurts to read. Wait until you have some perspective and can be of service to your reader."

Sometimes the point you want to make does not fully emerge until you are halfway or more through a piece. Keep writing, but watch the verbosity and tangents, and check for them in your revisions. "Maybe you set out to make *this* point, but another one is bleeding through instead. Don't limit yourself so severely

> Mark Twain said, "The time to begin writing an article is when you have finished it to your satisfaction. By that time you begin to clearly and logically perceive what it is that you really want to say."

that you cannot go with instinct and inspiration," Jerry Bishop advises. Maneuver that point to the core, the nugget of your essay.

"I often hear from people who want advice on how to write. I ask them what they are trying to say. They will often provide a concise explanation of it. I tell them, 'Write that,'" says Steven Greenhut, Vice President of Journalism at the Franklin Center for Government and Public Integrity in Alexandria, Virginia. "Writing is thinking. People need to think through what they want to say and then start writing. I had an editor early in my career who would tell me, 'Don't make your problem the reader's problem.' As writers, we need to figure things out first then write, not take readers on a convoluted journey. Mark Twain offered a lot of great writing advice. This is one of my favorites from him: 'The time to begin writing an article is when you have finished it to your satisfaction. By that time you begin to clearly and logically perceive what it is that you really want to say.'"

Tone is an essential element that can make or break your piece. Read and reread the publications you are targeting for your work. Determine if the tone in them is consistently the same, or if there is room for variety. *Prairie Times,* for instance, is flexible. "Some subjects are more serious than others, but I like stories best that are lighthearted or thought-provoking," says Charity Bishop.

As much as you want to convey your thoughts, perceptions, or opinions in an essay, your goal is also to appeal to readers, especially in an autobiographical essay. "Reading is a form of escapism. You can learn from it, but mostly it is our chance to step outside of ourselves for a time. If as a writer you set out to entertain your readers, they will love you for it, far more than if you set out to lecture them. Make the most of your story. What is better, to capture your grandma in one biographical work that may be meaningless to anyone outside your family, or to make others appreciate what a truly wonderful woman she was through a series of individual anecdotes?"

Commentary

Commentary essays differ from personal ones in that a journalistic tone predominates. The bulk of your narrative will be objective and factual, Huxleys's second essay form, although you may express an opinion in the end. Topics are taken from the world at large—local to global—and may include trending social issues, current political struggles, the impact of pending legislation, various ethical dilemmas, and much more.

Jerry Bishop writes commentary for each issue of *Prairie Times*. "I write about whatever I feel is the most pressing need at the moment—a topic that needs to be addressed right away, some revelation I just got or that came to my mind, or a topic that I feel a burden about."

Stay focused when writing commentary pieces. That is good advice for all writers and for all kinds of writing, but it is especially germane to the essay, where brevity is king.

"To maintain focus, imagine that you are explaining the subject to someone with little or no knowledge of the subject," Cullen advises. This is where your command of the facts comes into play and evidence of your objectivity is revealed. "You should have the facts before you have the opinions. Facts should lead to opinions."

Still, you must be creative in your presentation so your reader's eyes do not glaze over at paragraph two. It helps to have a plan. "Make an outline of the points you feel are most important," Jerry Bishop suggests. "Then go back and flesh out each point."

Editors have style and topic preferences too. The *Progressive Populist* is "not much interested in *sound-off* articles about state or national politics, although we accept letters to the editor," says Cullen. "We prefer to see more journalistic pieces, in which the writer does enough footwork to advance a story beyond the easy realm of opinion."

That easy realm of opinion is to be avoided if you want to be convincing. Feedback from readers can put into perspective how well you succeeded with a commentary piece.

"You can't put people in a box," says Jerry Bishop. "Everyone is complex, with many different views on subjects, sometimes which are contradictory, but reinforced through their own life experiences. Everyone thinks everyone else is like they are, with the same likes, dislikes, and opinions. For every response you get, at least a hundred other people wanted to ask the same question, make the same point, or voice the same objection, but didn't. Most of the feedback has been positive" for Bishop's own commentary pieces.

He continues, "I like commentators who come up with unique perspectives on a topic that challenges me to think differently about an issue. If the same 20 commentators are saying the exact same thing, I want to hear the one person who is approaching it from a different perspective."

"Readers have over the years been a great source of advice and help," states Greenhut. "Of course, they provide useful tips and critiques. When I worked at the newspaper, I had an informal group of readers who I would call and run ideas by. I only would consult truth-tellers. Writers need good feedback. I've learned to ignore the nasty folks, who seem to have grown nastier in recent years. I love the new, open media world, but one of its downsides has been a coarsening of the discourse as everyone yells and shouts at each other via email and comments. I think the act of sitting down and writing a letter to the editor filtered out the angry folks. On the good side, I love how quickly articles get vetted thanks to comments. I often read comments to help bulletproof my arguments."

Flow Freely

Keeping Huxley's rule of three in mind, the final form is the abstract/universal. These essays have nothing to do with the personal or autobiographical, and they do not objectively rely on facts. They consider universal principles or abstract thoughts, perhaps philosophies. The writings of Michel de Montaigne (who coined the word *essay*, from the French *essayer*, to try), Francis Bacon, Ralph Waldo Emerson, Henry David Thoreau, and Huxley himself provide examples here, although all wrote essays in all the categories.

You may have knowledge and skills that direct you toward the analytical and therefore favor the commentary essay. Or you may be a writer who has a warehouse of personal anecdotes or memories to share. Or, less common today, you may desire to wax abstract on universal concerns. Whichever form allows thoughts and ideas to pour from your cup, let them flow. Editors are waiting.

A Wide World of Faith

The Judaeo-Christian Book Market

By Katherine Swarts

However high-tech the world has become, whatever topics modern readers may favor, attachment to religion remains alive and well, and book publishers know and address it.

In today's diverse and technological world, many people have more knowledge of life in other cultures they see on television or in news stories than they do about their own ancestors' cultural traditions. The days when it was assumed that every American child was raised on the Bible (Jewish, Catholic, or Protestant) are past. Today there is a large market for books that fill in the gaps in basic religious and cultural education, but even more for books that offer insight into living out faith in a changing world.

It's a Whole New World

Sally E. Stuart, author of the Christian Writers' Marketplace blog and former compiler of the annual *Christian Writers' Market Guide* says readers, including youngsters, are "interested in books on how to live a Christian life within today's cultural pressures."

Across the Judaeo-Christian spectrum, publishers are trying to meet the broadened interests of their potential readerships, while remaining true to their tenets and valued perspectives.

From the Editorial Department of the Catholic publisher Pauline Books and Media comes this: "What we're seeing now, and project we will continue to see, are books that speak to living as a Catholic in the world, along with books that present the positives of a Catholic approach to life. Scriptural spirituality, lives of the saints, Marian themes, adult faith formation, the theology of the body, family life, and prayer are strong sellers. Also, as the Church garners more media attention amid growing discussion of cultural and policy shifts, there will be more books that explain Church teaching in a way that appeals to broader audiences—not just those already committed to Church teaching, but [also] those curious and struggling, embracing their new faith or getting fresh understanding of their faith. Titles presenting the faith and its aspects in daily lives, and titles aiding people in nurturing their spiritual and prayer lives, are increasing."

"A growing Jewish library for children," Kar-Ben Publishing is "a liberal publisher within the world of Jewish-content books," says Publisher Joni Sussman. But she also describes its list as wide. "Kar-Ben offers content that appeals to the broad-based Jewish community, from relatively observant Jews to those unaffiliated or even quite secular—any family on the spectrum of Jewish observance that wishes to express itself Jewishly in some way. Gone, at least for us, are didactic stories of 'this is how one celebrates a Jewish holiday.' Readers appear to be interested in a great variety of Jewish-themed stories, both fiction and nonfiction."

Today's technology can impact religious publishers in unique ways, as Devorah L. Rosenfeld, Editor in Chief of Hachai Publishing, reveals: "We publish children's picture books with a traditional Jewish viewpoint. Ebooks are very handy for busy parents. However, hard copies remain necessary if books are to be read and enjoyed on Shabbat, during which [many conservative Jews] do not use computers, Kindles, or other electronic devices." Traditionally, kindling a fire was considered work on the sabbath day of rest; activating a current by turning on an electronic device starts a fire of sorts.

"Trends may come and go," observes Rosenfeld, "but a good story, told in a charming, age-appropriate way, will never go out of style. And, rather than preachy explanations, it's the personal and emotional core of religious life that will surely dominate in the future of religious publishing. A Torah lifestyle is full of joyous, meaningful, and sensory observances that children love, and our most popular authors are able to capture that lively spirit in their work."

The Individual & Faith

As emphasis on the individual has increased, so has the need to respect every individual's choices—which has led to an expanded variety of popular religious or spiritual book topics.

At the "fairly conservative" Seventh-Day Adventist publisher Pacific Press, Book Acquisitions Editor Scott Cady reveals that Biblical novels remain popular. Traditional scriptures still continue to drive fiction and nonfiction at some publishers.

But the emphasis on the individual, balanced with established beliefs, challenges other publishers to offer titles for a variety of perspectives within a single tradition, and to take on new subjects.

Sussman notes that "one of [Kar-Ben's] new books for spring 2013 is *The Purim Superhero* [by Elisabeth Kushner], about a boy with gay dads, a subject we may not have tackled a few years ago" and which most conservative publishers still won't touch in anything resembling a sympathetic manner.

Another sign of individual-mindedness is the increased popularity of self-publishing, and of small presses where writers can receive more personalized attention from editors. Some publishers are also experimenting with new business models that can work to the advantage of religious writers.

Small-press owner Tracy Ruckman says, "In 2011, I started two publishing companies. Pix-N-Pens Publishing is our evangelical line; all the books we publish through PNP have a strong Gospel message. Write Integrity Press is more general; we publish books that are clean, wholesome, inspiring, entertaining—and may or may not have a strong Christian message. [Both companies] stand out in

Religious Book Markets

Article Sources

~ **Hachai Publishing:** 527 Empire Blvd., Brooklyn NY 11225. www.hachai.com

~ **Kar-Ben Publishing:** Lerner Publishing Group, 241 First Ave. N., Minneapolis, MN 55401. www.karben.com

~ **Pacific Press Publishing Association:** 1350 North Kings Road, Nampa, ID 83687. www.pacificpress.com

~ **Pauline Books and Media:** 50 St. Paul's Ave., Boston, MA 02130. www.pauline.org

~ **Pix-N-Pens Publishing/Write Integrity Press:** 110 Prominence Point Pkwy. , #114-330, Canton, GA 30114. www.pixnpens.com, www.writeintegrity.com

More Religious & Spirituality Markets

~ **Abingdon Press:** www.abingdonpress.com

~ **ACTA Publications:** www.actapublications.com

~ **Ambassador International:** www.emeraldhouse.com

~ **AMG Publishers:** www.amgpublishers.com

~ **Ave Maria Press:** www.avemariapress.com

~ **Baker Publishing Group:** www.bakerpublishinggroup.com

~ **Barbour Publishing:** www.barbourbooks.com

~ **Beacon Hill Press:** www.beaconhillbooks.com

~ **Behrman House:** www.behrmanhouse.com

~ **Bethany House:** www.bethanyhouse.com

~ **B & H Kids:** www.bhpublishinggroup.com

~ **Bondfire Books:** www.bondfirebooks.com

~ **R. H. Boyd Publishing:** www.rhboydpublishing.com

~ **Bridge-Logos Foundation:** www.bridgelogosfoundation.com

~ **Cedar Fort:** www.cedarfort.com

~ **Christian Ed. Publishing:** www.christianedwarehouse.com

~ **Christian Focus Publications:** www.christianfocus.com

~ **Conari Press:** www.conari.com

~ **Conciliar Press:** www.conciliarpress.com

~ **Concordia Publishing:** www.cph.org

~ **Covenant Communications:** www.covenant-lds.com

~ **Crossway Books:** www.crossway.org

Religious Book Markets

- CSS Publishing: www.csspub.com
- Deseret Book Company: www.deseretbook.com
- Wm. B. Eerdmans Publishing: www.eerdmans.com
- Focus on the Family Book Publishing: www.focusonthefamily.com
- Forward Movement: www.forwardmovement.org
- Franciscan Media: www.franciscanmedia.org
- Friends United Press: www.fum.org
- Gefen Publishing: www.gefenpublishing.com
- Group Publishing: www.group.com
- Guideposts Books & Media: www.guideposts.org
- Harcourt Religion Publishers: www.harcourt.com/bu_info/harcourt_religion.html
- Horizon Publishers: www.ldshorizonpublishers.com
- Ideals Books: www.idealsbooks.com
- InterVarsity Press: www.ivpress.com
- Jewish Lights: www.jewishlights.com
- The Jewish Publication Society: www.jewishpub.org
- Jonathan David Publishers: www.jdbooks.com
- JourneyForth: www.journeyforth.com
- The Judaica Press: www.judaicapress.com
- Judson Press: www.judsonpress.com
- Kregel Publications: www.kregel.com
- Leadership Publishers: www.leadershippublishers.com
- Legacy Press: www.legacypresskids.com
- Lighthouse Publishing: www.lighthousechristianpublishing.com
- Liguori Publications: www.liguori.org
- Lillenas Publishing: www.lillenas.com
- Master Books: www.masterbooks.net
- Thomas Nelson: www.thomasnelson.com
- New Hope Publishers: www.newhopepublishers.com
- New Leaf Press: www.nlpg.com
- O Books: www.o-books.com
- Paulist Press: www.paulistpress.com
- The Pilgrim Press: www.ucc.org/the-pilgrim-press

Religious Book Markets

~ **Prometheus Books:** www.prometheusbooks.com

~ **P & R Publishing:** www.prpbooks.com

~ **Quest Books:** www.questbooks.net

~ **Rainbow Publishers:** www.rainbowpublishers.com

~ **Randall House:** www.randallhouse.com

~ **Resource Publications:** www.rpinet.com

~ **Revell:** www.revellbooks.com

~ **Rose Publishing:** www.rose-publishing.com

~ **Saint Mary's Press:** www.smp.org

~ **Scarecrow Press:** www.scarecrowpress.com

~ **Servant Books:** www.servantbooks.org

~ **Standard Publishing:** www.standardpub.com

~ **Tyndale House:** www.tyndale.com

~ **Unity House:** www.unityonline.org

~ **URJ Press:** www.urjbooksandmusic.com

~ **WaterBrook Multnomah:** www.randomhouse.com/waterbrook

~ **Weiser Books:** www.weiserbooks.com

the marketplace because, although we're traditional publishers, we're a little different. We don't pay advances, but we do pay higher-than-average royalties, and authors begin earning money from the first sale. We offer authors a little more control than traditional publishers—more input on cover design and editorial processes—but we don't charge authors [money] like self-publishing companies do. We're the best of both worlds."

And it is true that "the number of small publishing companies is growing," continues Ruckman. "There has never been a better time for authors, and small publishers provide a great way for authors to be involved in every aspect of the business. Years ago, I heard a writer say that her publisher was her champion—he believed in her book enough to publish and promote it. I want to be that champion for my own authors. I'm privileged to work closely with every author on every book, so not only are my time and money invested, but my heart as well."

It's a Digital, Visual World

Of course, the continuing improvement in ereaders and tablets and the corresponding skyrocketing popularity of ebooks has not been missed by religious publishers. Neither has the still-growing popularity of graphic novels in fiction and graphic narrative in nonfiction. "Young people today are used to functioning in a visual world," says Stuart. "Kids today also live in an electronic world; ebooks are taking over the stage and will soon be the go-to form for nearly all of [their] reading—including textbooks." Because the world now values expediency, multitasking, and mass storage, the digital and graphic trend is permeating adult publishing as well. Pacific Press's Cady says "portability" and "ease of use" are the major advantages of ebooks, and he points to "book subscriptions" as a rising trend.

"As parents know," says Kar-Ben's Sussman, "it's always a good idea to bring a variety of books on outings with young children, and ebooks are infinitely more portable. Fortunately, most [current] technology portrays art beautifully, assuming the device is big enough for kids to appreciate the art, which is so critical to picture books."

"Ebooks are a growing market for Catholic publishing," say the Pauline Books and Media editors. "The greatest advantage is the quick and easy way to reach more readers, especially those who don't have access to bookstores that carry many religious books. Also, sometimes the more traditional bookstores don't have as great an appeal to the tech generation, so ebook versions are a great way to speak to this population."

"Even many traditional publishers have opened or will soon open ebook divisions. They have no choice," says Stuart. "We are likely to see more stores or some sort of [public] access that makes ebooks more accessible to everyone. The publisher's biggest battle will be trying to keep up with the changes in technology. All those changes are also likely to affect how publishers deal with authors. All this makes the negotiating of contracts more difficult and intense, requiring the help of an agent or knowledgeable advisor."

Sussman notes: "There have been a number of significant changes that affect both religious and secular publishers, particularly the advent of ebooks and the development of social networking as a marketing tool. In both these cases religion publishers are trying to leverage these changes for the positive and give the reading public what it wants. As niche publishers, we also now have some unique opportunities in terms of ways to market and deliver our content. Most important, though, is what hasn't changed. A good book with excellent content is still a prized commodity, regardless of the delivery mechanism or marketing device."

It's Still a Human World

Others recognize possible risks in being too eager to chase the "latest thing," whether technology or topic. "I'm not much of a trend-watching person," says Ruckman. "As soon as one trend settles, another pushes it away. So we base our decisions on what's best for all involved—reader, writer, publisher—rather than what's trending next. Readers appreciate good stories, writers like to write them. If we've got a good story, we'll buck the trends to get it published." Rosenfeld concurs: "Trends may come and go, but a good story, told in a charming, age-appropriate way and accompanied by beautiful illustrations . . . that's the heart of a great picture book, and that will never go out of style. A Torah lifestyle is full of joyous, meaningful, and sensory observances that children love, and our most popular authors are able to capture that lively spirit in their work."

"Religious [nonfiction] editors are looking for the same qualities found in general nonfiction books," adds Pauline Books and Media: "engaging voice, superb writing, and clear and accurate information."

Besides overall good communication skills, respect for others—readers and editors alike—is a vital and timeless characteristic of the successful writer. "Our most popular authors," says Sussman, "are those who can really speak in kid-friendly language and make readers feel comfortable in their skins." Ruckman adds: "Writers of Christian books have a tremendous responsibility. They, individually and as an entire entity, represent Jesus to readers." Religious writers who come across like the stereotypical holier-than-thou preacher rarely get a following.

Or a publisher. A frequent complaint among religious editors is writers who not only open with "I know you don't normally publish fiction but mine is worth making an exception for," but add "because God Himself gave me this message to share with the world." Good writing or no, wholesome message or not, it's the height of arrogance—and a sure mark of an amateur—to expect a publisher to adapt its mission to suit the book. Professional writers seek out publishers with compatible missions. "Review online catalogues to get a sense of the market a particular religious publisher serves," says Sussman. "Be sure your manuscript is a good fit."

"Both writer and editor will want the manuscript to be the right fit so the project helps people on their spiritual paths," says Pauline Books and Media. "It's crucial to read writers' guidelines to see if your work fits that house's particular mission statement and tone. Additionally, approach the process of getting published in this genre like you would discerning your vocation. Think of your manuscript as a form of ministering to the reader, evangelizing, or offering pastoral care—in other words, it's not about you."

The world still craves good religious writing. The secret is to be religious about being a good writer.

Keep Moving with Action Fiction

By Chris Eboch

Action fiction, while not a clearly defined genre in itself, encompasses fast-paced, plot-heavy genres: crime novels, spy novels, adventure tales, sports stories, and Westerns. It has a broad, entertaining appeal, but can also be written at a high quality level. And it sells.

"I love the emotional impact of action fiction," says Karen L. Syed, President of Echelon Press. "It's about a well-written scene that puts you on the edge of your seat and [leaves you] dying to turn the page before you are truly finished reading it, just to see what happens next. Action in fiction is about putting the readers in the jump seat and making them hold on for dear life."

Action appeals to writers who crave intensity, at least in their writing. Suzanne Morgan Williams is the author of the young adult novel *Bull Rider* (Margaret K. McElderry), about a teen who decides to ride the meanest bull around in an effort to help his injured Marine brother. She says, "I love reading books where things happen. I like writing about risk and challenge and prefer settings that play into that. I get to write about things I might never do."

Jason Hunt is the author of *A Midsummer Night's Gunfight* (Wild Oaks Press/Oak Tree Press), about a man who hunts down the people who killed his family. "I write Westerns because they are the sole genre that is wholly American," says Hunt. "Sure,

Edgar Allan Poe (an American) is the father of both horror and detective fiction, but those genres now deal with every time, location, and theme you can imagine. The Old West or the Wild West, will always be about the Americans in America. It will always be about rugged individualism and justice."

The quest for justice also shows up in spy and crime novels. P. A. Brown is the author of *L.A. Boneyard* (Bristlecone Pine Press), a crime novel about human traffickers. "The hard science and search for answers to solve intricate crimes fascinates me," Brown says. "Each novel I've written requires research into a new field,

> "The joy of writing suspense boils down to this: It rights an unjust universe, parceling out equal amounts of satisfaction for every danger faced and obstacle overcome."

and I learned something new each time. While researching human trafficking for *L.A. Boneyard*, I became aware of the disturbing fact that there are more slaves in captivity today than at the height of the African slave trade."

Despite the strong entertaining factor of action fiction, it can also address important issues, and allow authors to reveal and comment on the world. Jenny Milchman is the author of *Cover of Snow* (Ballantine), in which a woman wakes to find her police detective husband missing. "For me the joy of writing suspense boils down to this: It rights an unjust universe, parceling out equal amounts of satisfaction for every danger faced and obstacle overcome," Milchman says.

While action fiction has its share of stereotypes—the laconic cowboy, the suave spy—modern authors are demolishing those clichés to share their own world views. Neil Plakcy is author of the Have Body, Will Guard series (Loose Id), about two men who are partners in life and as bodyguards in Tunisia. "I love writing about strong, intelligent, gay men who defy stereotypes and become action heroes," Plakcy says.

Action fiction can blend genres, and attract readers with multiple interests. Rob Kresge is author of *Death's Icy Hand* (ABQ Press), which is set in 1872 Wyoming. "I love combining mystery, history, and romance," Kresge says. "When I started writing this series, there were few historical mysteries set in the Old West. Before I got published, though, my friends Ann Parker [author of the Silver Rush mystery series] and Steve Hockensmith [author of Holmes on the Range series and *Pride and Prejudice and Zombies*] became successful with their sleuths."

Keeping Action Real

By definition, action fiction needs plenty of change, obstacles, movement, conflict—action. But that does not excuse writers from developing character depth and believability. Plot is core, but it never stands alone in any kind of action fiction. "Getting the plot *right* (Read: *believable*) is always the hardest part for me," Milchman says, "especially those niggling small details. When I write, my justification for each scene often tends to be 'because it is so freaking cool.' I have to pull back and remind myself, 'Yeah, but it has to do double duty for the story and work for the character, too. Interesting action isn't enough.'"

Action needs to be real. Action and fantasy fiction definitively intersect, but be sure even in fantasy and science fiction, the action is true to life—even life in another world must seem believable to the reader.

"I tend to immerse myself in my subject and never stop researching," Brown says. "I own a growing variety of books, some actually textbooks used at a police academy. A lot of research material can be found online through Google and Google Scholar. I've also toured police stations, taken citizens' academies [training], and attended a three-day workshop at a police academy taught by the school instructors. The biggest challenge is being as accurate as possible in the police procedures and forensics I use, but never let the action slow down or become tedious."

A historical setting can add complications for the writer. *Three Seconds to Thunder* (Oak Tree Press), is an action-packed mystery set in the late 1890s, by C. K. Crigger. The author says that matching her "female wannabe detective" China Bohannon's "persona with the strictures of the times" has to be just right.

For Kresge, "The major challenges are getting the real history right without being pedantic, giving readers a rewarding mystery to unravel, and keeping readers engrossed in the evolving relationship between my two protagonists." To do the research, he uses "everything from the Internet to actual site visits, including forts and towns in Wyoming, historical societies, and museums and libraries."

Fortunately for us all, despite the necessary cautions about accuracy, the Internet makes research easier for us all. "For my most recent book, *Olives for the Stranger* (Loose ID), I watched YouTube videos of the protests in Tunisia, read news articles, and constructed a timeline for the political events. [I did] lots of online research, including viewing images and travel diaries, to get the details of my locations correct," Plakcy says.

The Internet cannot always take the place of hands-on experience, however. John Brantingham, author of the thriller *Mann of War* (Oak Tree Press), says, "Sometimes I use the Internet, but I like to be out in the field the most. I want to see and smell a place or a thing before I write it."

Jody E. Lebel, author of *Playing Dead* (The Wild Rose Press), is a court reporter who works criminal cases. For her research, she says, "I show up to work every day." But even that direct experience

Back in Print

Ebooks and print on demand (POD) are giving old works new life. Philip Athans is Curator of Science Fiction and Fantasy at Prologue Books, an ebook publisher for out-of-print titles. He explains, "Every day I become more and more convinced that not just the future, but the present of the book is predominantly in the digital space. What we're still lacking, though, is the full spectrum of available content. While the ebook has allowed a boom in self-publishing, and given birth to a new wave of small, niche publishers, it's also provided an opportunity to rediscover forgotten classics."

Prologue Books focuses on previously published books in the genres of crime, romance, Westerns, science fiction, fantasy, and young adult fiction. "Since becoming part of this project I've become quite skilled in the role of literary detective," Athans says. "For the most part I target an author, investigate that author's bibliography, search for what's already been published in ebook form, and if there are still books out there to be published, hunt for the rights holder (many of the authors we're publishing are deceased), and work with the fine people at Adams/F+W to contract for the rights."

needs to be adapted for novels. One issue is "balancing the black humor used in courtrooms and by cops at crime scenes—used to help us handle the horrific things we have to deal with—with the reality of crime. I don't want the humor to come across as callous or cold."

Keeping characters real is essential. "The challenge is to find a balance between the action and writing a true story about believable characters with hopes and dreams the reader can care about," Hunt says.

"I write action-adventure stories with a romantic heart," Plakcy says, "and it's challenging to find new ways to explore the romance between my protagonists in the midst of an action-oriented plot."

That heart is important for the action scenes to ring true.

Action Fiction Markets

- **Bristlecone Pine Press:** www.bcpinepress.com. Ebooks only, in many genres including mystery, suspense/thriller, historical fiction, and GLBT. Send email query following guidelines on website.
- **Echelon Press:** 2721 Village Pine Terrace, Orlando, FL 32833. echelon-press.com, quakeme.com. Follow submission guidelines very carefully. Any deviation gets one deleted without explanation or consideration.
- **Istoria Books:** 1125 Old Eagle Road, Lancaster, PA 17601. www.istoria-books.com. Publishes fiction in a variety of genres, in digital format. Email query with a one-paragraph summary of the book, its genre and word count, plus writing credentials. No advance; splits royalties.
- **Kensington Publishing:** 119 West 40th St., New York, New York 10018. www.kensingtonbooks.com. Publishes many genres, including mystery, suspense, true crime, thrillers, romantic suspense, and historical. Send cover letter, first three chapters, and synopsis by mail, with SASE, or query by email.
- **Loose Id:** www.loose-id.com/submissions. Publishes erotic romance in subgenres including mystery, suspense, Western, multicultural, and historical. Email query, synopsis, and three chapters to submissions @loose-id.com.
- **Musa Publishing:** musapublishing.blogspot.com/p/submissions.html. Ebooks only, in genres including mystery/suspense, horror, and historical. Email to submissions@musapublishing.com following guidelines.
- **Oak Tree Press:** 140 E. Palmer St., Taylorville, IL 62568. www.oaktree-books.com. Mail or email queries to query@oaktreebooks.com. Publishes novels in many genres but with a special emphasis on mysteries and crime fiction.
- **Prologue Books/Adams Media:** 57 Littlefield St., Avon, MA 02322. www.pro-loguebooks.com. Only accepting submissions of previously published books in the genres of science fiction, fantasy, Western, and mystery.
- **The Wild Rose Press:** www.thewildrosepress.com. The primary genre must be romance. Email queries to queryus@thewildrosepress.com following the writers' guidelines.

Action Fiction Markets

More Markets

- **Academy Chicago:** www.academychicago.com. Mystery, war, military fiction.
- **Amulet Books:** www.amuletbooks.com. Adventure for young readers.
- **Anaphora Literary Press:** anaphoraliterary.com. Mysteries.
- **Avon Books:** www.harpercollins.com. Historical romance, mystery, science fiction, fantasy, YA.
- **Ballantine Books:** www.randomhouse.com/BB. Many genres, including mystery, war, military.
- **Berkley Publishing:** us.penguingroup.com. Many genres, including adventure, mystery, suspense, Western.
- **Black Rose:** www.blackrosewriting.com. Genre fiction, including action, horror, suspense, fantasy, romance.
- **Canterbury House:** www.canterburyhousepublishing.com. Romantic suspense and mystery, emphasis on Southern U.S. settings.
- **Graphia:** www.graphiabooks.com. Books for teens, including adventure and graphic novels.
- **Gryphon Books:** www.gryphonbooks.com. Small press that specializes in crime fiction and science fiction.
- **Hard Case Crime:** www.hardcasecrime.com. Small press specializing in crime fiction.
- **Minotaur Books:** us.macmillan.com/Minotaur.aspx. A mystery, suspense, thriller imprint of Macmillan, a division of St. Martin's Press.
- **Mulholland:** www.mulhollandbooks.com. The suspense imprint of Little, Brown.
- **Pegasus Crime:** pegasusbooks.us. Crime imprint from Pegasus Books launched in 2011.
- **Poisoned Pen Press:** www.poisonedpenpress.com. Specializes in mysteries, for adults and young adults.
- **Tyrus Books:** www.tyrusbooks.com. Small press that features crime and mystery fiction.

"Anytime you write about something you haven't actually experienced, like bull riding, the challenge is to find the emotion and physical responses to the action and report it accurately," says Williams. "That requires talking to people who do do it, and translating their experiences to something you and your readers understand. It's challenging but amazingly cool."

That accuracy requires more research. "I interviewed professional bull riders, ranchers, and people who work with wounded veterans," Williams says. "I watched some kids take their first bull ride. Then I had a couple of my contacts vet the manuscript for corrections."

Today and Tomorrow

Some action genres are written in a traditional style that readers have come to expect. "For me, the most difficult part was learning to write in the style at the sentence level," Brantingham says. "There is a spareness to the writing and that's often difficult to attain" in thrillers.

That is not to say the styles of action fiction have not changed over time. Action novels have been influenced by the increase in explicit violence on TV and in movies. "I'm not sure if this is a good thing or a bad thing, but action fiction has taken a turn toward the violent," Syed notes. "I remember the days when action might involve being chased down a mountain by a boulder, or being caught in a storm on the sea. Now, it almost always means exploding bombs and lots of automatic weapon fire."

The pendulum may be swinging back to more traditional styles of suspense, however. "I think the readers are bored with serial killers," Lebel says. "I think we are returning to richer stories in the vein of Alfred Hitchcock. More tension, less blood and guts."

Trying to mimic media violence can actually weaken storytelling. "In fiction, you don't have visual aids," Syed points out. "You must rely on your word choices to make an impact and so few authors these days know how to do that." That means writers who do know how to balance dramatic action with emotional authenticity have the best chance of impressing editors and readers.

Authors need every advantage they can get in a changing publishing climate. "It's tougher than ever to crack into print with agents and large publishing houses," Kresge says. "However, it's easier than ever to be published by small POD presses or independently on various ebook platforms."

But some authors are optimistic about the market. "I'm lucky in that the market for M/M [male/male] romantic suspense is booming," Plakcy says. "Right now I work with four different publishers, for different kinds of books. By networking on writers' sites and groups, I hear about who's looking for what."

Brantingham also values personal connections when it comes to the publishing business. "Most of the time a publisher has picked up a book from me, I have talked to that person beforehand. The writer-editor relationship can be a close one. No one wants to work with someone he or she doesn't like."

Milchman notes that with independent publishing growing because of technology, more authors can make a living off their writing. "The e-volution has allowed for books that would've been sadly missed by a [publishing] model that depends on larger sales, and happily resurrected the career of the so-called mid-list. It's given authors freedom to publish in multiple ways. But because it is so fast and easy to publish nowadays, the writer's apprenticeship, of writing draft after draft of novel after novel before seeing publication, is getting harder to stomach. There's a temptation to publish before the work might be ready—and I think that temptation must be resisted if quality is to remain high."

For her own path to publication, Milchman says, "I queried agents and wrote novels and sent out submissions over a period of 11 years. Three agents, 8 novels, 15 almost-offers. Finally, I found the editor I feel I was always meant to be with. How would I generalize this approach for other writers? Decide which publishing path is right for you and go after it with every cell in your body, every ounce of heart, every single thing you've got."

Despite the advantages of technology at all stages from research to publication, it's the human touch that makes for strong writing and sales. "The current market is good as long as the writer is willing to work," Brantingham says. "If the writer can figure out how to connect with people on a personal level, he or she will have readers."

Action scenes keep the pages turning, but ultimately, you have to have heart.

Diversity in Writing & Publishing for Young Readers

By S. M. Ford

"In 2010, more than 90 percent of books for children and young adults in the United States were written by white authors about white protagonists. What does this mean for the almost 40 percent of U.S. children who come from different backgrounds?" author Suzanne Morgan Williams asks.

In 2011, the Cooperative Children's Book Center (CCBC) received 3,400 books ranging from picture books through young adult. The number of books with significant multicultural content, themes, topics or characters was broken down this way: African or African American, 123; Asian/Pacific or Asian/Pacific American, 91; Latino, 58; American Indian, 28. That amounts to 300 books, or less than 9 percent of the total.

Alvina Ling, Editor at Little, Brown, told Williams for an aricle on diversity in the *SCBWI Bulletin*, that as a young reader, "I was always searching for Asian American characters whose lives reflected mine in some way. . . . A lot of the books I've acquired and edited are books I wish I could have read as a child." ("Diversity: Everybody in the Pool!" *SCBWI Bulletin* May/June 2012)

Editor Namrata Tripathi of Atheneum Books talked with the CCBC about her experience reading *The View From Saturday,* by E. L. Konigsburg: "I think initially I was simply happy to see a half-Sikh character in a story where I didn't expect to, but then I read a few simple, powerful lines in the novel that seemed to make everything fall into place [and as] I read the lines a jolt went through me, and a path was created between my brain and my heart. I had always been intellectually dedicated to the concept that we need books in which kids can see themselves. But I finally understood this on an emotional level. It seems crazy that it happened a decade into my career as a children's book editor. But for the first time, I felt understood." ("An Unexpected Mirror," July 6, 2012, www.cbcdiversity.com/2012/07/unexpected-mirror.html)

Note how neither of these experiences centers on books about race issues, but on books that feature multicultural characters.

The Children's Book Council Diversity Committee was created to discuss issues of diversity in children's books. Committee Chair, and Executive Editor at Macmillan's Roaring Brook Press, Nancy Mercado says that the committee has discussed authors who "avoid the portrayal of diverse characters for fear that they may perhaps not 'get it right,'" as well as editors who "worry that reviewers will heavily scrutinize books that feature diverse characters." ("It's Complicated," May 21, 2012, www.cbcdiversity.com/2012/05/its-complicated.html)

The Society of Children's Book Writers and Illustrators (SCBWI) is also concerned, and in 2012 created a new grant called the On-the-Verge Emerging Voices Award. Executive Director Lin Oliver says, "Each year, it will be given to two people who are from a racial, ethnic or religious minority who have a ready-to-submit completed work for children."

The Market

"The market for multicultural books is growing," says Leap Books Publisher Laurie J. Edwards. "All readers deserve to have books written about them, to see their faces on book covers. Publishers have realized the importance of this, so most are eager to receive submissions that portray diversity. Leap Books would love to publish more multicultural books. We hope to reach a diverse audience, so we are always looking for well-written tween fiction that portrays life in various cultures."

"Multicultural books at all levels are absolutely essential to Carolrhoda and Darby Creek," says Andrew Karre, Editorial Director of Carolrhoda, an imprint of the Lerner Publishing Group. "Our Coretta Scott King Award-winning books have pride of place on display in the reception area of our building. I cannot imagine a year going by without publishing something in this area."

Karre adds, "I think there is a strong library market. People in that community are passionate about this topic. I don't have a strong sense of consumer demand, however. It may be there, but it's less clear to me."

"I think the market for diverse middle-grade books is a lot higher than it is [for teen books] because publishers aren't using sales to measure success in that category," says Claudia Gabel, Senior Editor at the HarperCollins imprint Katherine Tegen Books. "When you look at all the recent award winners, most of them feature a multicultural story. Case in point: Thanhha Lai's *Inside Out and Back Again*, which is set in Vietnam, won the National Book Award."

"I think our company has a made promoting diversity in the publishing industry a big priority," continues Gabel. "As for my own personal interest, I love reading about cultures that are not familiar to me. In fact, I published a middle-grade novel a few years ago, *1001 Cranes,* by Naomi Hirahara, about a California-born Japanese girl who spends a summer folding paper cranes in her grandparents' flower shop. I just love slice-of-life novels that drive home a deeper message about identity and family."

"Schools and libraries are often essential in getting multicultural books in the hands of kids in low-income communities," says Arial Richardson, Chronicle Books Editorial Assistant. "Marketing a book written cross-culturally to the community it is about can be difficult, most especially if the artist is an outsider or the story feels inauthentic. In addition, an artist creating art cross-culturally may not have as many contacts within the community they're writing about, making book promotion more challenging."

Richardson says she is thrilled by the creation of the CBC Diversity Committee, and would encourage anyone interested in writing multicultural children's literature to read their blog, attend their events, and submit to the editors on their committee."

"There is a definite hunger for diverse, multicultural books for any age group. How can there not be? Census data alone cannot be overlooked."

At Chronicle Books, says Richardson, "Our Publishing Director, Ginee Seo, is interested in multicultural publishing, as am I. I studied sociology as an undergraduate at UC Berkeley; I am interested in the sociology of children's literature and am always looking for books with themes of social justice."

"There is a definite hunger for diverse, multicultural books for any age group," says Marietta Zacker, an agent with Nancy Gallt Literary. "How can there not be? Census data alone cannot be overlooked, not to mention the many other factors that help us see the need for amazing literature that reaches *all* young readers. An accurate and authentic look at the world we live in is essential if we are to truly foster a global community in which we can recognize, acknowledge, and celebrate our differences—all with the hope that we gain a greater understanding of ourselves and our world. I would say it is the same for both fiction and nonfiction."

Diversity Blogs & Websites

~ **American Indians in Children's Literature** (AICL): americanindiansinchildrensliterature.blogspot.com. Offers "critical perspectives and analysis of indigenous peoples in children's and young adult books."

~ **The Brown Bookshelf, United in Story:** thebrownbookshelf.com. Increases awareness of African American writers for children.

~ **CBC Diversity:** www.cbcdiversity.com. A Children's Book Council committee dedicated to "diversity of voices and experience" in juvenile literature.

~ **Exploring Diversity: Themes & Communities:** www.cynthialeitichsmith.com/lit_resources/diversity/multicultural/communities.html. Found on author Cynthia Leitich Smith's website, a list of titles—ethnic, regional (Appalachia), for girls, for children with disabilities, and more.

~ **InCultureParent:** www.incultureparent.com. A website "for parents raising little global citizens."

~ **Masala Reader:** masalareader.wordpress.com. The blog of a community college librarian that highlights multicultural children's and YA literature.

~ **Mitali's Fire Escape:** www.mitaliblog.com. Author Mitali Perkins's blog. She calls it "a safe place beween cultures to chat about books."

~ *Multicultural Familia*: www.multiculturalfamilia.com. An online magazine for multicultural families.

~ **Multicultural Literature Resources, Cooperative Children's Book Center:** www.education.wisc.edu/ccbc/links/links.asp?idLinksCategory=4. Resources, links, and recommended reading.

~ **Paper Tigers, Books + Water:** papertigers.org. A website, blog, and outreach program on multicultural books for children, especially those related to the Pacific Rim and South Asia.

~ **World Full of Color Library:** www.librarything.com/catalog/shelftalker. A list of multicultural titles for children from the Library Thing community.

~ **Writing with a Broken Tusk:** umakrishnaswami.blogspot.co. A blog by Uma Krishnaswami, an instructor at the MFA/Writing for Children and YA program at the Vermont College of Fine Arts. Its focus is "overlapping geographies" and writing for children.

Multicultural Markets

~ **Atheneum Books for Young Readers:** Simon and Schuster, 1230 Ave. of the Americas, New York, NY 10020. imprints.simonandschuster.biz/ atheneum. Agented manuscripts only. Namrata Tripathi, Executive Editor.

~ **Carolrhoda Books, Darby Creek:** Lerner Publishing Group, 241 First Ave. North, Minneapolis, MN 55401. www.lernerbooks.com. Puts out occasional calls for submissions, and looks at agented manuscripts. Andrew Karre, Editorial Director.

~ **Chronicle Books:** Children's Division, 680 Second St., San Francisco, CA 94107. www.chroniclebooks.com. Open to queries and mansucripts. See the writers' guidelines. Ariel Richardson, Editorial Assistant.

~ **Nancy Gallt Literary Agency:** 273 Charlton Ave., South Orange, NJ 07079. nancygallt.com. Marietta Zacker, agent.

~ **Leap Books:** P.O Box 112, Reidsville, NC 27323. www.leapbks.com, leapbks.blogspot.com. Agented submissions only. Laurie J. Edwards, Publisher.

~ **Little, Brown and Company:** Hachette Book Group, 237 Park Ave., New York, NY 10017. www.lb-kids.com Agented submissions only. Alvina Ling, Senior Editor.

~ **Roaring Brook Press:** MacMillan, 175 Fifth Ave., New York, NY 10010. us.macmillan.com/roaringBrook.aspx. Agented submissions only. "When hearing an editor speak at a conference, there's usually a window of opportunity to submit directly," says Nancy Mercado, Executive Editor.

~ **Katherine Tegen Books:** HarperCollins Children's Books, 1350 Ave. of the Americas, New York, NY 10019. www.harpercollinschildrens.com. Agented submissions only. Claudia Gabel, Executive Editor.

Multicultural Markets

More Markets

- Abbeville Family: abbeville.com
- ABDO Publishing: www.abdopublishing.com
- Abrams Books for Young Readers: www.abramsbooks.com
- Bess Press: www.besspress.com
- Boyds Mills Press: www.boydsmillspress.com
- Children's Book Press: www.leeandlow.com
- Cinco Puntos Press: www.cincopuntos.com
- Egmont USA: www.egmontusa.com
- Hartlyn Kids: www.hartlynkids.com
- Interlink Publishing Group: www.interlinkbooks.com
- Just Us Books: http://justusbooks.com
- Kensington Publishing: www.kensingtonbooks.com
- Lee & Low Books: www.leeandlow.com
- Mage Publishers: www.mage.com
- NorthSouth Books: www.northsouth.com
- Pinata Books: www.latinoteca.com
- Raven Tree Press: www.raventreepress.com
- Rubicon Publishing: www.rubiconpublishing.com
- Salina Bookshelf: www.salinabookshelf.com
- Seal Press: www.sealpress.com
- Second Story Press: www.secondstorypress.ca
- Shen's Books: www.shens.com
- Star Bright Books: www.starbrightbooks.com
- Third World Press: www.twpbooks.com
- Tilbury House, Publishers: www.tilburyhouse.com
- Toy Box Productions: www.crttoybox.com
- Tradewind Books: www.tradewindbooks.com

The Writers

Mainstream writers can write about children under-represented in books and stories, but publishers often look for writers who come from the culture they are writing about.

"Writers develop a deep empathy and awareness that allow them to imagine living another person's life," Edwards says. "They write from the viewpoints of characters quite different from themselves—various ages, genders, personalities, and time periods. So using that intuitive sense, they should be able to envision life in another culture. That said, though, authors need to have others from the ethnic group or culture provide feedback to be sure their stories are accurately and sensitively portrayed."

Karre does not believe a writer's ethnicity needs to match the characters of a book or the nonfiction topic. "To believe this would be to deny the very core of all creative writing. It's much less about the topic than you might think, and much more about how well you tell the story. 'It's multicultural' is not a lead selling point. 'It's a great story with a diverse cast of characters' is."

"I do think that sharing the experience of the protagonist can help a writer to create an authentic narrative, but no, I don't think it's necessary," says Gabel. She cautions that "a writer who is crossing culture lines needs to expect that some people are going to challenge and question their right to tell the story of a race, religion, etc., to which he or she does not belong."

"Although often preferable, ultimately I think it is too rigid to say that an artist's ethnicity must match that of their protagonist.," says Richardson. "Writers should be able to write outside of their experience, whether about a fantastical world of magical adventure or another culture. However, it must be done thoughtfully, preferably [as] the result of extensive research and vetted by someone with insider knowledge of the culture."

Zacker agrees. "I don't believe someone's background should dictate who or what they can write about. However, in my opinion, a writer or illustrator needs to be able to step into someone's shoes or feel well-steeped in that world in order to accurately and authentically write or illustrate the experience." She adds that writers must reach "deep to find the innermost part of a character or situation" and recommends that authors "write or illustrate from the inside looking out, rather than the other way around."

There are other caveats, especially in writing multicultural fiction. Mitali Perkins is the author of *Bamboo People* (Charlesbridge), about two teens caught in Myanmar's ethnic conflicts. She commented in a *Publishers Weekly* blog, "When to cross a border of race, culture, or power in creating fiction? If a particular community is processing a shared experience of suffering through the healing power of story, maybe it's time for our *outsider* version to wait. When we have more power in society than our protagonist, it's always good to ask whether to speak on his or her behalf. If we still feel compelled by the story, we must lean heavily on research, imagination, and empathy. Always, love deeply within that community and listen well." ("Great News on the Diversity Front—Plus Twibbons" by Elizabeth Bluemle, *Publishers Weekly ShelfTalker,* February 9, 2012, blogs.publishersweekly.com/blogs/ shelftalker)

"Although I spent most of my childhood in Ethiopia," says author Jane Kurtz, "I never assume that I can blithely leap in to write a book set in Ethiopia or [understand or convey] the brain of an Ethiopian child. I love using what craft tools I have to show glimpses of what I've seen and experienced. But I add in lots and lots of research." Kurtz's books include *Jakarta Missing* (Greenwillow), which takes place in North Dakota but is about a family from Kenya, Ethiopia, and Egypt.

Being Culturally Sensitive

"One of the major problems of writing cross-culturally is not knowing cultural taboos," says Edwards. "Another is not being aware of the inside life of a culture. Often groups act and speak differently when outsiders are around, so writers see only the surface and miss the cultural richness that an insider can bring to a story."

Eugie Foster, author of *Returning My Sister's Face and Other Far Eastern Tales of Whimsy and Malice* (Norilana Books), has written, "We are conditioned from birth to acquire social competence in a single culture—our own. While beneficial sociologically, it can leave us with preconceived notions that even the most conscientious and well-meaning may not be aware of. In order to avoid imbuing our writing with unwitting prejudice, writers of children's multicultural fiction need to methodically scrutinize these boundaries for possible cultural bias." ("Writing Multicultural Fiction for Children" (part 2), www.absolutewrite.com/novels/writing_multicultural2.htm)

For example, Seattle suburban teens who prepared to visit the Yakima Indian nation in Washington state were told by a Yakima not to wear deodorant or to bring two-piece bathing suits as both would be offensive. That is a detail that would belong in a book about the two cultures meeting.

More important to get right are the deeper issues of culture. Debbie Reese, Assistant Professor of American Indian Studies at the University of Illinois, has written, "Most people don't know anything at all about tribal sovereignty and what it means. Without that knowledge, it can be difficult for outsiders to write stories that ring true to our experiences as American Indians. In fact, it can be difficult for someone of a sovereign tribal nation at one end of the country to write about a nation at the other end, but someone who knows their nation, its history, its ways of being, and the ways it has been misrepresented has a leg up on anyone else." (It is Even More Complicated than Most People Know . . . ," *CBC Diversity*, May 25, 2012)

Artists "are always exploring what calls to them and stirs their curiosity and passions," says Kurtz. "So I'm one of those writers who thinks that of course we need to be humble and careful and thoughtful but assume that we and other writers will never exactly match the characters we create and write about. That's fiction (and creative nonfiction) for you."

The State of YA

By Casie Hermansson

If the December 2011 release of the film *Young Adult*, featuring Charlize Theron as a writer for teens, is anything to go by, YA literature is very much in the public eye. Massive franchises derived from best-selling teen books like Suzanne Collins's Hunger Games trilogy (Scholastic) have proven not only that YA is thriving, but that it continues to grow as a crossover market for an adult audience.

Ben Rosenthal, Associate Editor at Enslow Press says, "In general, YA literature is in a great position, mostly because of the upward trend in YA fiction. With the wild success of Harry Potter, *Twilight*, and *The Hunger Games*, YA fiction has seen a massive growth in readership. Successful YA fiction books have rabid fans and followers, helped along by strong social media and marketing campaigns. . . . In addition, YA fiction has a lot of crossover appeal as more and more adults are reading the genre. Many titles are not only becoming popular, but are also achieving critical success. Looking in the library and bookstores, YA fiction shelves always seem to be growing."

Another New YA Imprint

The fiction shelves will have to grow some more: "Enslow Publishers, in fact, is launching its own YA fiction imprint, Scarlet Voyage, in spring 2014. I have already begun acquiring

A New YA Tool

Fortunately for YA writers, a new digital resource for writers interested in staying current in their YA reading has arrived. In June 2012, the American Library Association announced a new YALSA (Young Adult Library Services Association) app, the Teen Book Finder, for the iPhone, iPod, or iPad. An Android version is expected soon.

The free app helps readers learn about books from the recommended and awards lists both current and dating back three years. Titles can be located in local libraries, through a WorldCat search, or they can be added to a favorites lists, and shared. The home page features three titles each day.

titles for our imprint, and we're very excited about this new trade market for us," says Rosenthal. Comparing YA fiction and nonfiction trends, Rosenthal points out that YA nonfiction has had "a more steady path" in recent years. Enslow has traditionally been a nonfiction publisher.

Narrative is important in nonfiction today, however, says Rosenthal. "Because of the easy accessibility for nonfiction content on the web, YA nonfiction has become less about presenting factual information and more about telling a great story. For example, we recently released a new series of Holocaust books called the Holocaust Through Primary Sources. Each book in the series focuses on a different aspect or event from the Holocaust, such as Auschwitz, the Kindertransport, the Warsaw Ghetto Uprising. Using accounts from diaries, letters, memoirs, as well as photographs and artifacts, each chapter looks at the book topic through the perspective of a person who experienced it. The book *Auschwitz: Voices From the Death Camp* provides a tremendous wealth of information, but in the process, tells a gripping story of a tragic place that keeps the reader intrigued. While, of course, it remains important that a book be factually accurate and historically relevant, it needs to tell a story that keeps young adult readers engaged and interested. When it comes to YA non-fiction, a book either needs to fill a void (provide content that's not out there yet or has not been presented in that format), or entertain. If it can do both, all the better."

Universal & Timeless

Jessica Anderson, Associate Editor at Peachtree Press, also insists on the fundamental importance of good storytelling in teen writing. "I'm always excited when I find a book with a distinctive and relatable voice. For me, that's at the top of the list where YA is concerned: Do I want to spend time with this narrator? Good storytellers are harder to find than good stories."

Anderson hedges her bets about the future of YA because the changes are lightning fast: "In publishing you might think you know what's coming, but then a novel might be an unexpected hit and suddenly the whole landscape shifts before your eyes as everyone scrambles to replicate that success."

Instead of chasing trends, Peachtree is looking for consistently good-quality fiction, says Anderson. "Peachtree has always been pretty solidly focused on literary fiction for the YA market, and I don't see that changing anytime soon. Genre fiction is a minefield —it's so hard to execute with a sense of originality and emotional honesty. Lots of people do it, but few do it well."

The best YA authors are "getting it right" today, says Anderson. "Personally, I feel the experience of becoming an adult is timeless and universal, and books that get it right will keep their place in the market for a long time to come. I'm talking about books that speak candidly and fearlessly to the young adult experience."

Claire Caterer writes fantasy to address timeless and universal themes. *The Key and the Flame* is Caterer's first novel and the first in a contracted series being published by Margaret K. McElderry Books. She says, "So many things we read or hear about are fleeting—they come and go so quickly—and we read about them two years later and don't know what they're about anymore." In contrast, "a certain core" of ideas or topics "is accessible to everybody" in the form of "universals, like mythology [that offer] basic conflicts, themes [such as] authoritarian regimes, standing alone against others." Caterer sees fantasy as an exciting means by which teen readers can feel empowered. "The reader can escape to this place where people are dealing with issues (feeling alienated, trying to find independence and their own identities) and can work them out in this different setting. [As a young reader,] you can have powers that you don't have ordinarily, but you still have to find those things in yourself to solve your problems. You can't solve them with a magic wand."

Stretch Yourself

Kimberly Pauley, author of the Sucks to be Me series (Mirrorstone), and *Cat Girl's Day Off* (Tu Books), notes that the particulars of YA are why she loves writing it: "You can take more chances and really stretch yourself in ways that I don't feel you can do in the adult market. There aren't the same expectations and limitations, at least to my mind. The audience is also so receptive and honest. Emotions and everything are just rawer and newer in those teen years."

But, like other YA writers, editors and publicists, Pauley warns that it is crucial to hit the right note for teen readers: "They know when an author doesn't *get it*. I like that. It is a challenge to be truthful and even though I mostly write light funny fantasy books, I still try to keep everything real and authentic."

The way to find that authenticity, says Pauley, is to stay connected: "I not only write YA, I read it too and have been doing so since way before it was cool to do so. I listen to teens and talk to them. I follow them on Twitter (but not in a stalkery way) and Facebook. I have my nieces and nephews read things for me. I also tend to read the dialogue out loud to make sure it sounds right."

In a recent blog post, British YA author Marcus Sedgwick notes that he writes with only one teen in mind—his former self

("Writing Teen Novels," writingteennovels.com, April 18, 2012). "I write for me, and if there's something youthful about my writing, it's because, I believe, that those of us who write for children or teens are still deeply in touch with that part of their lives, in some part of their brain at least, and are seeking to understand it. At the most, then, I concede I might be writing for a part of me, one that is still thinking as I thought aged 16 or so."

"You can take more chances and really stretch yourself in ways with YA that I don't feel you can do in the adult market."

Pauley concurs. "I remember myself as a teen—not so much the specific things that happened to me or that I did, but how I felt and where I was emotionally. One of the things I think most of the YA authors I've met have in common is that we all can remember our own teen years more clearly (and without rose-colored glasses) than the average person."

Among the recent notable books that have attracted attention because of taking chances is Julie Anne Peters's LGBTQ fiction for teens, including *It's Our Prom (So Deal With It)* (Little, Brown). In an online interview with Cynthia Leitich Smith (Cynsations, cynthialeitichsmith.blogspot.com, June 14, 2012), Peters commented on the challenges of this subject matter: "All these fears burbled up inside me about writing a *gay* book. At the time I'd been working for ten years to establish myself as a children's writer. I thought, 'If I do a book like this, I'll be blacklisted by every teacher and librarian on the planet. My books will be banned. I'll be labeled as a gay writer and expected to write more gay lit.'

YA Publishers

- **Abrams Comicarts:** abramsbooks.com. Graphic novels.
- **Action Publishing:** www.actionpublishing.com. All ages.
- **Algonquin Books:** www.algonquinbooksblog.com. Publishing middle-grade and YA for the first time in 2013.
- **Amulet Books:** www.amuletbooks.com. Agented submissions only.
- **Atheneum Books:** www.simonandschuster.com. Agented submissions.
- **Baen Books:** www.baen.com. Science fiction and fantasy.
- **Balzer & Bray:** www.harpercollinschildrens.com. Agented submissions.
- **Behler Publications:** www.behlerpublications.com. Nonfiction, books of social relevance for teens.
- **B & H Publishing:** www.bhpublishinggroup.com. Christian. Launching a new juvenile imprint.
- **Bloomsbury USA:** www.bloomsburykids.com. Agented submissions.
- **Blue Sky Press:** www.scholastic.com. Agented submissions.
- **Candlewick Press:** www.candlewick.com. Agented submissions.
- **Carolrhoda Lab:** www.lernerbooks.com. Dedicated YA line. Periodic calls for submissions. Check the website and blog.
- **Chronicle Books:** www.chroniclebooks.com. Wide-ranging list.
- **Clarion Books:** www.hmhbooks.com. Diverse list. Open to unsolicited manuscripts.
- **The Collaborative:** alloyentertainment.com. Division of multimedia Alloy Entertainment looking for middle-grade and YA fiction for development.
- **Cool Well Press:** www.coolwellpress.com. Small publisher changing its focus to YA, especially fiction.
- **Dial Books for Young Readers:** us.penguingroup.com. Open to submissions. Check guidelines for novels.
- **Egmont USA:** www.egmontusa.com. Agented submissions.
- **Enslow Publishers:** www.enslow.com. New YA fiction imprint is called Scarlet Voyage.
- **Entangled Publishing:** www.entangledpublishing.com. Fantasy, romance, science fiction. See the Entangled Teens imprint.
- **Farrar, Straus & Giroux:** us.macmillan.com/FSGYoungReaders.aspx. Agented submissions.
- **Feiwel & Friends:** www.feiwelandfriends.com. Agented submissions.

YA Publishers

~ **Margaret Ferguson Books:** us.macmillan.com/fsgyoungreaders.aspx. Agented submissions.

~ **Fire:** sourcebooks.com. Dedicated YA line.

~ **Flux:** www.fluxnow.com. Dedicated YA line.

~ **Frances Foster Books:** us.macmillan.com/FSGYoungReaders.aspx. Agented submissions.

~ **Graphia:** www.graphiabooks.com. Dedicated YA line.

~ **Greenwillow Books:** greenwillowblog.com. Agented submissions.

~ **Harlequin Teen:** www.eharlequin.com. Agented submissions.

~ **HarperTeen:** www.harperteen.com. Agented submissions.

~ **Henry Holt Books:** us.macmillan.com/holtyoungreaders.aspx. Agented submissions.

~ **Houghton Mifflin Books for Children:** www.hmhbooks.com. Diverse list.

~ **Kensington Teen:** www.kensingtonbooks.com. Relatively new YA fiction line from Kensington Publishing that focuses on self-discovery for teens.

~ **Alfred A. Knopf Books for Young Readers:** www.randomhouse.com/kids. Open to queries. Review guidelines online.

~ **Wendy Lamb Books:** www.randomhouse.com/kids. Open to queries. Review guidelines online.

~ **Leap Books:** www.leapbks.com. Focuses on teens, tweens, and reluctant readers.

~ **Arthur A. Levine Books:** www.arthuralevinebooks.com. Scholastic imprint open to submissions for all ages.

~ **Little, Brown and Company Books for Young Readers:** www.lb-kids.com. Agented submissions.

~ **Margaret K. McElderry Books:** imprints.simonandschusterbiz/margaret-k-mcelderry-booksAgented submissions.

~ **Musa Publishing:** www.musapublishing.com. Small ebook publisher specializing in genre fiction. Has a YA imprint.

~ **MuseItUp Publishing:** museituppublishing.com. Ebooks for middle-grade and YA fiction, and adults.

~ **Philomel Books:** us.penguingroup.com. Diverse list. Open to submissions.

~ **PUSH:** www.thisispush.com. Dedicated YA line from Scholastic. Agented submissions.

YA Publishers

- **G. P. Putnam's Sons:** us.penguingroup.com. Diverse list. Open to submissions.
- **Pyr Books:** www.pyrsf.com. A science fiction publisher that has recently launched a new YA line because of the strength of the teen market.
- **Quirk Books:** quirkbooks.com. Open to submissions. Publisher of the best-selling *Pride and Prejudice and Zombies.*
- **Razorbill:** us.penguingroup.com. Dedicated middle-grade and YA line. Open to submissions.
- **Roaring Brook Press:** us.macmillan.com/roaringbrook.aspx. Agented submissions only.
- **Schwartz & Wade:** www.randomhouse.com/kids. Open to queries. Review guidelines online.
- **Seven Stories Press:** www.sevenstories.com. In 2012, opened its first juvenile imprint, Triangle Square Editions, including YA titles.
- **Simon Pulse:** kids.simonandschuster.com. Dedicated YA line. Agented submissions only.
- **Tanglewood Press:** www.tanglewoodbooks.com. Small press for children of all ages; has recently been more interested in middle-grade and YA.
- **Tor Teen:** www.tor-forge.com. Dedicated YA science fiction and fantasy line. Open to submissions.
- **Viking Children's Books:** us.penguingroup.com. Diverse list. Agented authors preferred.
- **Albert Whitman Teen:** www.albertwhitman.com. Dedicated teen fiction line. Open submissions policy.
- **White Mane Kids:** www. Specializes in middle-grade and YA historical fiction.
- **Paula Wiseman Books:** http://kids.simonandschuster.com. Agented submissions; accepts some submissions through writers' conferences.

There's such a small niche market for LGBTQ books, I thought, how would I ever make a living with my writing? But my worst fear was that I'd get hate mail. It took me a year to work through all my fears. They weren't unfounded, but the response from readers who told me this book saved their lives made me wonder if writing for my community wasn't what I was meant to do."

Once again YA asserts its uniqueness. "The teen market is its own animal," says Susan Raab, marketing expert and founder of Raab Associates, a New York agency that has specialized in marketing and publicizing children's books and products for more than 25 years. Raab is also a marketing advisor for the Society of Children's Book Writers and Illlustrators (SCBWI), and author of *An Author's Guide to Children's Book Promotion* (now in its eleventh edition). She explains what distinguishes the teen market: "They're considered a very vibrant and dynamic audience. If they like or don't like something, they have no problems voicing their opinion. They also influence each other, and that's one of the reasons why what is important in that market is the dynamic between the author and their fanbase. Really what you're trying to do is find potential to fold more teens in the fanbase."

Teens comprise an audience of direct and capable consumers, Raab says. They want to feel consulted, to feel invested in what they consume, and they have a more "personal relationship" with authors who have respectfully listened to them. Raab advises writers that it is essential to research this market, to know what other authors in the genre are doing, what interests teens have in pop culture, and what is happening in social media.

Marietta Zacker, a literary agent with Nancy Gallt Agency also speaks to the wide interests of teens, and why YA matters to her: "The ability of young adults from all backgrounds, with varied interests, to read a book that gives them a different perspective or allows them to find a piece of themselves within the pages is important to me." Zacker praises Nora Raleigh Baskin's novel *Surfacing* (Candlewick Press), saying it will "undoubtedly speak to many young adults." But she cheerfully notes that writers across the board are rising to the YA challenge, saying, "It has been a pleasure to receive a richer variety of YA manuscripts that encompass a wider range of genres—from contemporary to horror to mysteries to fantastical."

The state of YA is thriving. The consensus is, write as well as you can irrespective of the market, but also do your due diligence in learning about the literature and the teens themselves. After all, as Raab expresses it, "This is an audience you don't want to make assumptions about."

Style

Markets

Business

Research

Ideas

Contests

Indexes

Foreshadowing

A Hint of What Is to Come

By Veda Boyd Jones

"Add details, add details," I tell myself when I'm writing. "Let the reader see the scene in his mind." But there are details, and there are details. A writer must be selective, and the details must have purpose.

"If you show the shotgun hanging on the wall, it must go off," I've heard said since I started writing here in the Ozarks, where years ago a shotgun rested horizontally on two wall supports at my uncle's house. That shotgun is a detail that foretells something is going to happen. In literary terms, the principle is called 'Chekhov's Gun' because the Russian playwright wrote, "One must not put a loaded rifle on the stage if no one is thinking of firing it."

Author and playwright Sandy Asher has heard the adage another way: "If a character coughs in Act I, he'd better die of consumption by Act III."

Writers use many details in creating a scene. While you can get away with almost anything in the name of character development in a novel, you cannot get away with showing something unimportant in minute detail. The detail will stick in the reader's mind, and the reader will feel cheated if it does not come back in play.

The reader wants to feel smart. If a writer sprinkles in details—to develop character or to give a glimpse into the plot—then the details must not be inconsequential. Even red herrings in mysteries must be meaningful, so the reader feels they are justified.

Well-chosen words that hint at what will occur later, create suspense, or convey information. Those are the meaningful details that foreshadow.

Backward and Forward

Author and freelance editor Suzann Ledbetter Ellingsworth has a strong aversion to author-intrusive foreshadowing. Ellingsworth says, "Phrases like *little did she know* or *before the day ended* typify author intrusion. This is futuristic stuff. Who's supplying the information? The writer. If it's a future event, circumstance—or whatever—a character isn't aware of, it's blatant the hint derives from outside the character's realm. The sole party responsible is the writer butting in like a narrator."

That type of foreshadowing is unfortunately done all the time, often as cliffhangers meant to get the reader to start another chapter. A point-of-view switch from a character to the narrator or writer is likely to be remembered for the wrong reason: It jars the reader. Careful writers avoid such intrusion and plant little details along the way to help a character at a moment of crisis. Clever readers appreciate the subtlety.

Foreshadowing is easy to see in films. Visualize a scene fully set in a living room. The viewer can see all kinds of details, from the couch and lamp tables to the pictures on the walls. If the camera zooms in on a deck of cards carelessly left on the table beside the recliner, that is a signal to the viewer that the cards will be important. Comparably in a written account, many specifics about the room may be described, but one feature may receive a few extra words, or a character could comment on it to bring it into focus. In that way, the reader will not find it coincidental when the item becomes important to the story.

It is not always an object that merits focus. In my personal tribute to the late Kathryn Joosten, the actress who played Mrs. Landingham on *The West Wing,* I recently watched the second season finale. In the episode "Two Cathedrals," writer Aaron Sorkin cleverly foreshadows using the gestures of a central character. Flashbacks reveal President Jeb Bartlett's boyhood habit of putting his hands in his pockets, glancing to the side and then straight ahead with a slight smile. The gestures indicate that the boy has decided to take on a challenge, and in the flashbacks, a young Mrs. Landingham comments on them. Back in the present, a reporter asks Bartlett if he will run for a second term, amid rumors and an earlier decision that he would not. The adult Bartlett puts his hands in his pockets, and glances to the side and then straight ahead with a slight smile. The scene is so much more effective than Bartlett simply saying, "Yes."

This flashback is a foreshadowing device that helps the reader know more about the character. A story might depict a character's skills or knowledge that will aid him later on, or it might describe a character tic like Bartlett's, which reveals how he thought and acted then, and thinks and acts now.

Plausibility

Sometimes we write ourselves into a corner when a plot goes in a direction we did not see coming. We cannot always anticipate necessary details, but foreshadowing can be inserted at any stage. Go back and add the necessary elements to make the plot work.

In Joan Banks's thriller *Edge Of Darkness* (Diamond Books), the story hinges on a foreshadowed detail. On a trip through the Ozarks, Lesley and her husband Robert stop at a dilapidated diner for lunch. After eating, Robert heads to the men's room and does not return. He simply vanishes. Lesley appeals to the sheriff but gets no real help, and goes home to await news.

"I needed a way to get Lesley back into the scene unbeknownst to the sheriff so she could investigate her husband's disappearance on her own," Banks says. "I went back to the beginning of the manuscript and placed a 'Help Wanted, Waitress' sign in the window of the diner. Robert sees it and jokes that Lesley could get a job there. After his disappearance, she changes her appearance, returns to the town, and applies for the job. Now she is embedded in the community, ready to investigate. Had she not seen the sign before the disappearance, her method of returning to the town would have seemed too contrived, too coincidental. Foreshadowing makes things feel plausible."

Timing is crucial. You cannot wait until your hero needs a way out of a cave to reveal that he always carries a penlight and matches, which he will use to see how the air moves slightly so he can make a tight, crawl-on-your-belly exit.

The cavalry cannot suddenly show up to save the hero. *Suddenly* is a word, and idea, to avoid. Sometimes things do happen suddenly, but a story always works better if the reader has a hint

Suddenly is a word, and idea, to avoid.

that something may occur. If the cavalry comes riding up, the reader will find it more believable if he knew earlier that soldiers were in the vicinity.

Sneed B. Collard III presents a clue early in his middle-grade mystery *Hangman's Gold* (Bucking Horse Books). After seeing a weird man they suspect of stealing some paintings, Slate Stephens and his pal Daphne take their geologist dads and law enforcement officials to an old mine shaft to look for clues, but no one finds anything. Here is how it reads:

> I am just about to return when my eye catches something small and brightly colored tangled up in some sagebrush branches.
>
> Litter.
>
> Anger rises up inside of me. I swear I just don't get people who throw their trash everywhere. Most Montanans would never dream of throwing their garbage out in a beautiful place like this. Unfortunately, there are still a few litterbugs who treat the outdoors as their personal garbage dump. They don't think twice about tossing cigarette butts out car windows

or dropping soda bottles and candy wrappers anywhere.

"Idiot," I mutter. I lean down and pull the plastic—a wrapper from a watermelon-flavored Jolly Rancher candy—out of the sage bush and shove it into my pocket. Then, I make my way back to join the others.

This passage not only develops Slate's mature character through his passionate rant, but it lays the groundwork for his discovery later that the real thief is sucking on that same type of candy.

Obstacles & Warnings

Besides presaging solutions to story problems, foreshadowing can be used to create obstacles. In Dandi Daley Mackall's 2012 Edgar Award-winning *The Silence of Murder* (Knopf), the heroine notices something odd after her love interest, Chase, leaves her house.

Finally, I turn to go back inside. And that's when I see it. An old white pickup truck, headlights out, creeps from the shadows and inches up the street. I step back as it passes my house and keeps going. At the corner, it turns right, just like Chase did. The truck lights come on, and the truck speeds off, disappearing into the darkness . . . just like Chase.

Two pages later, Mackall inserts the truck again and it is not even visible. She writes, "Outside, there's a faint rattle of an engine creeping by, but not passing, the house. It could be a white pickup. I know it's stupid to think like this, but I can't help it." Nearly 70 pages later, the white pickup reappears in a great chase scene when the heroine is pursued by the driver.

Foreshadowing gives readers a warning of events to come. In her middle-grade novel, *Just for You to Know* (HarperCollins), Cheryl Harness has pregnant Mama tell her 12-year-old daughter Carmen that she lost a baby early in her marriage: "'It was a medical thing,' she went on. 'Things—pregnancies, I mean—sometimes go wrong.'" Later on, things go terribly wrong again.

Foreshadowing Tools

~ Use phrases that hint at what is to come.

~ Make imagery and metaphor work to suggest.

~ Use your setting—weather, location, environment—to foreshadow.

~ Build on small events to prefigure your climax.

~ Let a character unknowingly comment in a way that predicts a future event.

~ Show secondary characters' reacting or acting in a way that suggests what might be to come.

~ Rely on a backstory to echo or foreshadow the main plot line.

Seeing Ahead

"I know foreshadowing is key in works for older audiences. But it occurred to me during work on a picture book that this element can also add more than a modicum of richness to a picture book story as well," says author Lynda Graham-Barber.

In Graham-Barber's current picture book project, "a small dog has been abandoned on gritty urban streets. She eventually ends up being fed scraps near a dumpster behind a Chinese restaurant called the Fortune Cookie. She's captured by animal control shortly after she begs for a cookie. At the shelter she's given the name Cookie because of where she was found. And in the end when a small child hoping to adopt a dog repeats her name, the little dog sits up and begs. This time her begging gets her a home."

In a picture book, the illustrations may also provide story hints. "To foreshadow story events I've suggested the artist illustrate on the very first spread (in advance of actually seeing the restaurant) a flyer advertising the Fortune Cookie, posted on a graffiti-splattered wall," says Graham-Barber. "There's also a poster for a lost cat, and a lost dog, which lend muscle to the plight of urban animals in stray or abandoned situations. Further, I've indicated that a white

Metropolitan Animal Control truck be pictured in the distance a few spreads ahead of the actual capture. I think these visual clues add a layer of interest especially during subsequent rereadings of the picture book story."

True Foreshadowing

Although we think of foreshadowing in fiction, nonfiction can also use variations by playing with time. Here is how Judith and Dennis Fradin begin their book *Stolen into Slavery* (National Geographic Children's Books):

> When Solomon Northup awoke in the middle of an April night in 1841, his body was trembling, his head was throbbing, and he couldn't remember where he was or how he got there. Sitting in total darkness, he gradually figured out that he was on a bench in some kind of damp, foul-smelling dungeon. He could hardly move, for he was wearing handcuffs and his feet were chained to the floor.

After this emotional description of Northup, the reader learns that he has been kidnapped, and that he is a free black man. Beginning with the flashback and playing with chronology signals to the reader what will happen before it actually does, and foreshadows all the events along the way.

Jan Greenberg and Sandra Jordan have written many biographies of famous painters from birth to death to afterwards. In *Andy Warhol: Prince of Pop* (Laurel Leaf), the first paragraph describes the artist's boyhood fascination with celebrities, which finds its way into his paintings later in his life.

In his history *Wicked Joplin* (The History Press), about Joplin, Missouri, author Larry Wood introduces some gamblers in his chapter on saloons, although the gamblers were not heavy drinkers. He wants the reader to be aware of them and their influence before the reader gets to the chapter on gambling, where Wood simply reintroduces the gamblers and shows that the seedy sides of town were very interconnected.

However you use foreshadowing, whether to create suspense or convey information, those details must be skillfully added to give the reader hints of what is to come. Plant details carefully to keep your reader guessing, yet not be led down the wrong path nor figure out the ending. By book's end, the reader will have had a most satisfying read.

Cinematic Scene-Building

By Chris Eboch

Script writers understand the value of a good scene. Screenwriter Karen Stillman says, "A good scene can accomplish several things at the same time. It can move the story forward, reveal something interesting about the characters, and thoroughly entertain the audience. This sounds simple to say, but it can often be surprisingly difficult to accomplish in just two or three pages."

A scene "moves the story forward while revealing character. Or, more precisely, characters reveal themselves by moving the story forward," says Paul Guay, who conceived and co-wrote *Liar, Liar* and co-wrote *The Little Rascals* and *Heartbreakers*.

In movies, the scenes are obvious. Each one starts when the camera switches to a new location or jumps ahead in time. The camera angle may change in the scene, perhaps by focusing on the different characters, but the scene endures for as long as a single action or dialogue sequence continues.

In books, scenes may not always feel so delineated. If you can imagine a sequence of action or dialogue from your novel playing out on film in one continuous episode, you have a scene. Beware, however: If you have sections of writing where nothing visual is happening—nothing that could be filmed—you may have slipped out of your scene into an information dump in an attempt to provide background information. Even interior monologues should be filmable. Ask yourself what your character is doing while he thinks.

Every novel has some backstory that is necessary for readers' understanding. Weaving backstory into your scenes through action and dialogue can pick up a novel's pace, make the writing flow, and create a cinematic story—if done well. But simply adding scenes with background is not enough to make a novel dramatic.

Ron Osborn, a TV and features writer whose credits include *Moonlighting, The West Wing, Duckman,* and the feature *Meet Joe Black,* has tackled novel writing with his comedic religious thriller

"In screenwriting, the writer's job is to visually manifest character through action. . . . In prose narrative, it is all about the details, about exploring the scores of thoughts behind the action, that color and define the world."

The Lost Ark of the Sacred Movement (CreateSpace). He compares screenwriting and prose. "In screenwriting, the writer's job in a scene is to visually manifest character through action," Osborn says. "We suggest/imply/show what the character is thinking through that action, and we let the audience fill in the blanks as to the specifics of that thinking. Furthermore, set designers, costumers, prop masters, hair stylists, all work to fill in those blanks."

When Osborn switched to writing a novel, the job changed somewhat. "In approaching prose narrative . . . it was now all about the specifics, the details, about exploring the scores of thoughts and prejudices and outlook that were behind the action, that color and define the world, as much or more than the action that was being manifested. I couldn't let descriptive action—or other working professionals—do most of the work for me."

Screenwriters work with action, dialogue, and brief setting notes. Novelists have more more tools and more options, but also more responsibility. Osborn says that, for him, "In screenwriting the text of the scene, what was going on visually on the surface took descriptive precedent, but in the prose, the subtext, what was going on beneath the surface, came to the fore and became key."

Novelists can and should take advantage of all the tools in their toolbox. The disadvantage of such a surfeit of techniques is that it can be tempting to dawdle on loving description, to explain decades of history, or to let a character ponder the world through long interior monologues. All these options, used unwisely or too often, can slow a story and bore the reader. By focusing primarily on the action and dialogue in a scene—by writing in a cinematic way and using other writing tools sparingly —a writer can create fiction with good pace and intriguingly active characters.

Came Late, Left Early

A strong scene typically includes action *and* dialogue, which may include a character's thoughts. The action and dialogue should support each other, although not necessarily mimic each other. Stillman offers an example: "I loved the show *House* because it used dialogue in such a clever way. The characters would often be having just one conversation but bouncing back and forth between two topics—the medical case and a personal issue. And they'd often be having this conversation while treating a patient, so there was action as well."

"In a screenplay, it's necessary to think visually and economically," says Guay, "i.e., to write each scene no longer than it needs to be, to balance interiors and exteriors, to keep the focus on the protagonist and the antagonist rather than on peripheral characters, etc. There's a lot to balance."

A script consultant as well as a screenwriter, Guay knows first-hand that in screenwriting, "It's dangerous to write pages covered with paragraphs of text, because readers—producers, studio executives, directors—might not read them. So, screenwriters try to have a lot of white space on each page. Among its other virtues, dialogue helps to create that white space and to break up blocks of action. Part of our job as screenwriters is to make the read as simple and as compelling as possible. Hence our concern with the aesthetics of the page." While novelists do not often have the same white space concern, finding the right mix of dialogue and action remains an important principle.

Part of making a screenplay simple and compelling involves starting and ending a scene in the right place. "Most screenwriting books say to start late and end early, and I totally agree," says Stillman, whose credits include the TV movies *Smoke Screen; They Shoot Divas, Don't They?;* and *Hit and Run.* "Have faith that if you start late, your audience will be able to figure out what's been said until that point. And, whenever possible, leave them wanting."

Osborn found this principle true for his novel writing as well. "The screenwriting tool that helped me the most in making the transition [from screenplays to novels] is true of all good scene writing: Get into the scene as late as possible, get out as soon as possible, get the job done and move on. Think how films jump-cut in both time and space without preamble, leaping continents and centuries; audiences for quite some time have been visually sophisticated enough to make the leap with the filmmaker. The same is true for prose. The growing vocabulary of film has come to influence the style of writing over the twentieth century. You can find examples of this in certain writers who have worked in both mediums. Graham Greene, Ray Bradbury, and Elmore Leonard are three who come to mind, whereas the storytelling of, say, Edith Wharton, who wrote at the dawn of visual storytelling, would never make such leaps without very deliberate transitions."

Keep It Moving, Keep Them Reading

For Osborn, "Another screenwriting approach that transfers well to prose is that every scene has a beginning, middle, and end; the end to a scene doesn't have to be a resolution, but it does have to have a calculated end point that advances us to the next scene. By the same token, in screenwriting, every scene (like your protagonist) has a goal, and the dramatic or comedic tension to that scene comes from whatever obstacle stands in the way of that goal. All of that helped keep me on point in switching to prose."

> "Get into the scene as late as possible, get out as soon as possible."

Focusing on story goals is also helpful when considering which scenes to keep or cut. "If in doubt, throw it out," Stillman says. "Executives receive so many submissions; the one thing I never want to do is bore them. Sometimes when I'm writing, I'll give a draft of my project to a few colleagues and say, 'Mark the pages where you stopped to make a phone call, to go to the fridge, to check your email.' If two or more people stop at the same spot, I know I have a problem there." The advice holds true as much for book publishing as for filmmaking.

"I outline the entire screenplay before I begin writing," Guay says, "so I know my beginning, middle, and end. I know my act breaks, and I pretty much know at least the kind of scenes I'll need to tell my story. I choose those scenes that most effectively show characters revealing themselves by moving the story forward."

"If I can find a clever or interesting way to transition out of one scene and into the next, I will," Stillman says. "But sometimes a hard cut is the only thing that makes sense."

Experienced scriptwriters naturally think cinematically, even when reading novels. Guay says, "I tend to notice when things aren't cinematic—for example, when there's interior monologue, or constant switches in point of view, or an emphasis on language (in the prose rather than in the dialogue), or side trips away from the narrative and thematic spine of the piece. I have no problem with the first three—they are among the virtues of prose as opposed to screenplays—but I have to admit that after years of writing screenplays, I tend to judge side trips away from the spine more severely than I once did."

Osborn remarks, "Melville might be able to get away with 30 pages of blubber rendering, and Tolstoy might veer off into an extended chapter about Levin working among the serfs harvesting his crops, but [such diversions] wouldn't have flown in any modern era screenplay. In today's prose, a writer will have a tough time getting such literary side trips past an editor. Get the job done, get out, move on."

Novelists who can learn to think cinematically can write more dramatic books, and also have a greater chance of catching a movie studio's attention. "I'm reading a novel now called *Bond Girl*," by Erin Duffy (William Morrow), Stillman says, "and I just finished a scene where a woman in very high heels rushes around Manhattan in a cab, trying to transport a huge wheel of cheese. The minute I read it, I thought, I bet this book has been optioned. And it had. Granted, the theme of the novel is fresh and interesting, and there are several scenes that have memorable visuals. But that wheel of cheese was just so, well, cinematic."

Osborn says, "I can't help but visualize a novel as I read it, even if it's two people talking in a drawing room over tea and crumpets. I don't know if this is unique to screenwriters, but it brings to mind a favorite quote of mine from Edith Wharton: '[F]or reading should be a creative act as well as writing.' In screenwriting, it's a one-way street. The writer and director are doing most of the work for the viewer, visualizing every aspect of

Resources

Books

~ *Advanced Plotting*. Chris Eboch (Pig River Press, 2011).

~ *Elements of Fiction Writing—Scene & Structure*. Jack M. Bickham (Writers Digest Books, 1999).

~ *Make a Scene: Crafting a Powerful Story One Scene at a Time*. Jordan Rosenfeld (Writers Digest Books, 2007).

~ *Plot & Structure*. James Scott Bell (Writers Digest Books, 2004).

~ *The Plot Whisperer: Secrets of Story Structure Any Writer Can Master*. Martha Alderson (Adams Media, 2011).

Other Resources

~ Let's Schmooze: letsschmooze.blogspot.com. Screenwriter Douglas Eboch's blog with articles on story structure and script writing techniques, many of which can be adapted for novels. Also on Let's Schmooze, Paul Guay (www.letsschmooze.com/PaulGuay.html) leads pitching and screenwriting workshops and offers script consultations.

~ Scriptnotes Podcast: Available on iTunes, these podcasts from John August and Craig Mazin cover screenwriting and industry topics.

~ Wordplay: www.wordplayer.com. A website about writing scripts, with essays and a discussion forum.

~ Screenwriter Karen Stillman suggests reading scripts as a resource for writers. "I'm currently writing a pilot for Lifetime [television network] in which I need to introduce—and distinguish—six characters relatively quickly. So I've been reading pilots and movies that do so effectively. I think it helps to study writing in the same way one would study math or science. On what page does the writer reveal character traits? Relationships? Various plot points? What's said? What's not said?"

the characters and their world; it is a very passive experience. Wharton's point is that the novel is far more of a collaboration between the writer and the audience, the former providing enough facts and clues to engage the latter enough to want to bring his or her own point of view to the experience, and making it all the richer for both. The better the writer, the more collaborative the experience with the reader."

Novelists can embrace the special opportunities of the printed page. But if they can also sometimes think like screenwriters, they can make their stories more cinematic, which translates into more drama and excitement for modern readers raised on film.

Characters in Conflict

By Chris Eboch

A t its simplest level, a story is about a character with a problem. The story follows a character (preferably an interesting one) as he or she struggles to reach a goal or overcome a challenge (preferably a difficult one). Story is character in conflict.

Exceptions exist, of course. A bedtime picture book designed to lull a child to sleep may not have conflict. Other stories may succeed primarily because of humor, beautiful language, or a powerful message. But the vast majority of stories need interesting characters in conflict.

Narrative Structures

You probably learned the following basic types of conflict or narrative structures in high school English class.

Character versus character: The enemy is another person. This enemy could be a villain trying to take over the world, or something more prosaic, like a bully at school or a family member with different goals. Variations include character versus an anthropomorphic creature, or a machine such as a robot, or a supernatural entity—although some people designate another, distinct category for *character versus deity,* or *character versus destiny,* as described on page 118.

Character versus nature: The enemy is a wild animal or a natural force like a snowstorm or hurricane.

Character versus self: The main character must wrestle with his or her own internal flaw, overcoming a weakness in order to succeed. The flaw could be a personality trait like a short temper, emotional feelings such as guilt or anger, or physical characteristics like poor health, which may make it difficult for a character to achieve a goal.

Character versus society: The protagonist's enemy is not a single entity but rather a legal or moral system, or attitudes like racism or sexism.

Character versus destiny: In ancient Greek literature, from which this system of conflicts ultimately derives, a protagonist might have struggled with a deity, such as one of the Fates—destiny. *Star Wars*'s Luke Skywalker is a hero who battles his destiny as a Jedi warrior. Medieval stories like some of the Arthurian legends, including *Parsival* and *Gawain and the Green Knight*, and other quest stories, fall into this category.

Quest legends can contain more than one of these conflicts, and often do. The hero may be the suspect in a crime, and have to avoid the law (society) while chasing after the bad guys (character) during a dangerous storm (nature). In the epic Harry Potter series, Harry faces not only the main villain, Voldemort, but also an assortment of mean kids, tough teachers, cruel relatives, and supernatural nasties, while struggling to understand his destiny and handle the personal angst of teenage hormones.

Which Came First, the Character or the Conflict?

Many short story or novel writers begin with either an interesting character or a plot idea and build from there. "I definitely start with character," says author Judy Alter. "For my Kelly O'Connell Mysteries (Turquoise Morning Press), I decided on a realtor who restored Craftsman houses in a historic inner-city neighborhood. Only then did I think about what sort of conflicts or situations this woman might get into. I made her a single parent of two young girls because whatever happened to her in the outside world in the way of mystery, danger, etc. would provide conflict immediately. She had to protect her daughters above all else. That was her strongest challenge."

Author Stacy Juba puts a plot idea first: "I always start with a plot, or concept. Then I start thinking about what kind of protagonist would best fit into that concept. I'll fill out a character chart, answering a list of questions on everything from childhood memories to physical characteristics to employment history and relationship history. This exercise helps me to identify the character's strengths, flaws, and internal conflicts. Knowing all of this helps me to come up with the most fitting challenges."

Allison Brennan is author of the Lucy Kincaid series (Minotaur Books/Macmillan), about an FBI recruit with a tragic past. "Because I have a series character," she says, "I always start with a situation. My character approaches the situation colored by her experience and world view and past. I come at every plot point from my character's perspective: How does this impact her, if at all? How might this change her?"

Plot and character intertwine for Marilyn Fisher, author of horse racing thrillers that include *He Trots the Air* (American Book Publishing). "When inventing the people who will inhabit the major plot or subplots, I ask myself who is needed to flesh out the story. A plot twist called for one of the villains to need certain information on the workings of a prestigious horse farm, but security barred him from getting onto the property. It seemed realistic that he wouldn't hesitate to seduce a woman who works there, who so wants another husband and normality that she deludes herself that the man loves her. One of the best things about writing a novel is the invention of the characters, whether large, small, or even incidental."

As you are developing a story, work back and forth between plot and character. Think about how your character and plot intersect, and design your character for your plot, your plot for your character. Could you drastically change your main character and have the same plot? The answer should be *no*.

Inside and Out

Every story benefits from an internal conflict that ties into the external. An internal struggle adds emotional depth and dramatic challenges to an external problem, as the character overcomes weaknesses or flaws.

"I do a detailed outline that tracks not only plot points and external conflict, but the character's internal conflict," says Juba. "The character arc goes hand in hand with the plot arc, as character drives plot. There needs to be a clear reason why the character makes certain choices. For example, in my young adult thriller *Dark Before Dawn* (Thunder Horse Press), the external conflict is that the protagonist, Dawn, has been taking secret psychic classes from a fortune-teller and she discovers that her new friends may be tied to some mysterious deaths in town." Her internal conflict is that she has always felt like a misfit and has finally found people who accept her and share her psychic abilities. As part of her journey, Dawn learns that acceptance comes from within.

Linda Joy Singleton, author of the Seer series and its spinoff *Buried: A Goth Girl Mystery* (Flux), explains, "Characters and plot are a marriage. Each plot turn should be motivated by what your characters want. I always give characters inner and outer goals. For instance, an outer goal could be for a budding girl detective to solve a mystery, but the inner goal could be for a girl to gain her father's respect. So, a plot turn could involve both inner and outer goals, perhaps [in the form of] finding a clue that she uses to solve the mystery, which impresses the father."

That sounds simple enough, but Singleton warns against resolving conflicts too easily. "Build conflict by using plot turns to stir up trouble. A better plot twist in this situation would be for the girl to find a clue, but the clue has to remain a secret that builds conflict between the girl and her father, so that instead of gaining respect, the father turns away from his daughter in anger. Blending the character's outer goals with her inner desires deepens plotting."

Putting a character in situations that oppose his or her needs and desires, or force the character to face fears, escalates conflict. Basic, strong human desires that give rise to story obstacles and that influence the way a character behaves include:

- ~ *Security:* feeling safe, knowing the future.
- ~ *Change:* a desire for variety or excitement.
- ~ *Independence:* having a sense of personal identity and freedom.
- ~ *Connection:* feeling part of a group.
- ~ *Growth:* working toward a personal goal.
- ~ *Contribution:* feeling needed or worthwhile.

To come up with an internal conflict for your story, consider which desires would be strongest for your protagonist. Then decide what situations or experiences would oppose the character's desire, and create the external conflict. If the protagonist prefers security, force him into a dangerous and unpredictable situation. If she craves connection, isolate her.

To get fully inside your character's head, ask, "How would this character define him or herself?" If her view of herself is accurate, a situation that challenges that perception will create conflict. If she is fooling herself, a situation that exposes that self-deception will create conflict. For example, a character who claims, "I never lie," will struggle through a situation that gives her a very good reason to do so.

Complex Characters

The challenges characters face should be difficult enough to be dramatic—we must believe the hero could fail—yet not so great that no real person could resolve them. Your hero should have the qualities needed to overcome the obstacles, realistically.

The people you love have flaws and irritating quirks, and so should your characters. Give them a mix of good and bad traits. These traits may sometimes work against each other. A character who is bright may also be undisciplined. One who has strong leadership skills may not take feedback. Some traits may have positive and negative aspects: A character may be so generous that others are encouraged to take advantage.

In any story readers look to a protagonist who changes, who makes errors and learns something. "It's essential in a standalone book that the main character grows by the end of the novel," Juba says. "In a series, the growth might be more subtle from book to book, but it should still be evident."

"Sometimes, characters' conflicts may be external and easily resolved," Fisher says. "But other characters, both in the major plot and the subplots, have had their lives so disrupted by what

Challenges should be difficult enough to be dramatic—we must believe the hero could fail—yet not so great that no real person could resolve them.

happens to them that they suffer internally and act on frustration and anguish. What is happening to them internally accounts for their behavior. A writer, I believe, must develop some characters beyond just the external conflicts, [and] delve into the deeper internal problems that are to blame for what ultimately happens."

With every character, Singleton says, "Even if you don't show scenes with their inner and outer goals, you as the author should know their goals to motivate their behavior and enhance plotting."

"It's vital that how the character acts and reacts is believable for what the reader knows about the character, and that there is always movement in the story—plot and character growth (and

Important & Difficult,
Complex & Challenging

If you typically start with a plot concept, ask yourself what kind of person would have the most trouble in that situation while still being able–just barely–to succeed.

If you typically start with character, focus on the characters' primary needs and how they would define themselves. Then figure out which situations would most challenge them.

Once you have your basic character and plot goal, two questions can help you discover and build conflict.

> ~ Why is this problem important?
> ~ Why is this problem difficult?

A simple problem gains impact when it is important and difficult for that particular character. Say a businessman has to give a presentation at a meeting. The situation alone is not interesting, but you can add drama by making it important: This presentation will determine whether the business-man gets a promotion or gets fired. Setting high stakes adds tension, and if your readers care about the character, they will care about the outcome.

But even that is not enough. You have to show why the challenge is difficult. Maybe the businessman suffers from a public speaking phobia, or his opponent has stolen his notes, or he was up all night helping a family member who ended up in the emergency room.

Suddenly your simple conflict is complex and challenging.

You can use these two questions to generate ideas or to analyze your current work, by connecting characters to their conflict.

sometimes backtracking after a setback)," says Brennan.

That does not mean every character has a complete and successful character arc, Fisher points out. "Some of the actors and actresses in the drama of the novel will fail to grow at all, indeed sink lower and lower until their arc comes to an end and they perish in some way. Some will remain stable with little or no growth. And some will win some measure of growth."

"The essence of plotting is having a character who wants something, then building conflict as they strive to achieve their goals," Singleton says. "Sometimes a book will end with the happy ending of goal achieved. Other times the ending is bittersweet; a journey traveled and lessons learned along with way. Ultimately, it's not important whether your characters get what they want, as long as your readers get the well-crafted story they deserve." That comes from the connection between character and conflict.

Not All Grandmothers Have White Hair

Making Minor Characters Fresh

By Chris Eboch

When creating a new story, you probably spend the most time developing your main character. The protagonist is, after all, the star of your show, more important than any other actor. But do not neglect the rest of the cast. Major secondary characters should also be realistic, complex, and vivid.

Joanna Campbell Slan shares her approach to secondary characters: "I chart out the arc for each of them before I begin a new book in my Kiki Lowenstein Mystery Series (Midnight Ink). Since each person has his or her own problems or drama in life, this adds more tension to the overall book. Furthermore, by seeing each character as a discrete entity, I get maximum mileage out of their varied personalities. I try to visualize myself as an orchestra conductor, with each character being an instrument. My protagonist is the soloist who gets the most attention, but the other artists matter, too. It is that interplay of personalities that keeps the story moving along."

Sandra Levy Ceren draws on real life for some secondary characters. "In the Dr. Cory Cohen psychological mystery series (Loving Healing Press), the protagonist discusses her psychological diagnoses and treatment plans with her best friend and colleague, Betty—a secondary character based on my best friend, a wonderful woman who died of cancer much too early, long ago. I keep her alive in my novels, often asking myself, 'What would Amy say about this?' The fictional character Betty has many of Amy's characteristics, i.e., she falls in love too easily, is exhilarated but winds up disappointed, yet springs back and gets on with her life, having enjoyed the ride while it lasted. Her fine understanding of human nature, her empathy, and intelligence make for a fully dimensional character."

Your major secondary characters should feel just as real as your main character—or the people you know. Kathleen Shoop, author of the historical drama *The Last Letter* (CreateSpace), says, "To help secondary characters stand out from main character, they need their own habits, gestures, voice."

In short stories and some children's books, you do not have much time for developing complex secondary characters. Even in novels, chances are you will have some minor characters who do not have an important role. It is easy to grab a recognizable *type*: the geeky scientist, type-A businessman, difficult mother-in-law, bratty little brother. Because these types are so familiar, the reader recognizes the character with a few quick clues, saving time. Beware negative stereotypes—the ones based on race, gender, religion, size, and so forth, which are hurtful or reinforce prejudice.

You might also twist a character type to make your story world more interesting. Maybe you want your young heroine to turn to a grandmother for comfort. Easy, you say. Gran is a sweet, white-haired lady who bakes cookies. We recognize the type, she fulfills her role, and such people do exist.

But she is hardly memorable. Think of the grandmothers you know. Some may be in their 40s, while others are much older. They might be retired or hold a variety of jobs. Their hobbies and interests could range from crafts to social activism to extreme sports. They may live with a spouse or partner, other family members, a friend, a professional caregiver, or alone. The real world is full of variety. Try making your minor characters as fresh and surprising as the people you know.

Maybe Granny dyes her hair black and gets donuts from the corner gas station. Maybe Nona is an archaeology professor whose house is full of strange artifacts. Maybe MeMa is a bowling fanatic who consoles her granddaughter while sitting over bowling alley burgers. Maybe Babi is an immigrant who only speaks her native language. As you develop her, some quirky characteristics may spark new story ideas. Regardless, Gran is now more memorable than that old cliché.

Causing Trouble

Your cast of secondary characters may include family members, friends, teachers, bosses, aliens, mythical creatures, or even pets. Some will be nice. Some will be annoying. Ideally, one or more should be trouble.

> "Enrich secondary characters with specific skills to drive the plot forward or cast light on other characters."

Mary Reed, co-author of the John the Lord Chamberlain historical mystery series (Poisoned Pen Press), says, "Enrich secondary characters by giving them specific interests or skills. But don't stop there. Use these skills or interests to drive the plot forward or to cast light on other characters."

"All the great sitcoms on television succeeded because the cast of secondary characters played off the strengths and weaknesses of the central protagonist," Slan comments. "Think of *Gilligan's Island*. While Gilligan is the hero, it's his daily interactions with the Professor, MaryAnn, Ginger, Mr. and Mrs. Howell, and the Captain that made each episode enjoyable."

Even well-meaning secondary characters can make your main character's life more complicated. In stories for children or teenagers, loving parents may want what they see as best for their child—but if that is not what the child wants, it causes trouble. These challenges could add complications interfering with the child's goals.

Parents can cause trouble in adult novels, too. Mom may pressure the heroine to marry the wrong man because she wants grandchildren. Bosses can add challenges, whether it is pushing the main character to do something illegal for the company or simply demanding long work hours that interfere with other goals.

Do not forget friends. A friend could turn out to be using the hero, or secretly trying to interfere with his plans. Even good friends can give bad advice or provide distractions with their own emotional problems.

Jaden Terrell, author of *Racing the Devil* and *A Cup Full of Midnight* (The Permanent Press), explains how secondary characters can both challenge and reveal your main character. "When I started writing my private detective series, I knew I wanted to explore the life of a man who seems, on the outside, to be a stereotypical tough guy, but who also has a complex emotional landscape and a deeply compassionate side. I decided to reveal these traits through a cast of secondary characters, among them an ex-wife he still loves, a son with Down syndrome, and a best friend battling AIDS. I don't need to tell readers that Jared is a loyal man with a strong need to protect others. They'll see it when he defends his housemate against a bigot, when he cradles his son in his arms, and when they learn that he once accepted disgrace and the loss of his job in order to protect a woman who had betrayed him."

To see if you are making the most of your secondary characters, go through your work in progress and list every major one. What is their basic personality and role in the story? What do they want? Then ask:

- Could I make this character more interesting?
- How could these characters be causing problems, even if they do not mean to?
- If the character is already causing trouble, could those problems escalate?

Balancing Minors

Secondary characters will not appear as often as your main character, but important ones should have a strong and consistent role. You can check how much "screen time" each character gets using an outline or your draft. Highlight each secondary character in a different color to create a visual map of how often someone appears.

I did this exercise while outlining a middle-grade novel. The main character was a 12-year-old boy. His little sister was important to both plot and theme, but she showed up in my outline mainly at the beginning and end. That made me realize I needed to include her in some middle scenes.

You can do this exercise with a complete draft as well, to find holes where you ignored a subplot or major secondary character for too long. You do not have to track characters who only appear once, in passing—just those who have an important role.

If you have lots of minor characters who drop in and out, or several secondary characters who fill the same supporting role, consider combining or eliminating some of them. "This is especially important when it comes to writing about groups of friends," says author Kathleen Shoop. "Each needs to complicate the plot or go."

If you do not have many secondary characters, consider adding some, space permitting, to add complications and drama. However, make sure any newcomers fit smoothly into the plot and do not feel like they are just shoved in to cause trouble.

"When I began writing my new series, The Jane Eyre Chronicles (Berkley), I encountered a new challenge," says Slan. "Since the first book, *Death of a Schoolgirl*, begins where Charlotte Brontë's classic *Jane Eyre* left off, there were no strong secondary characters. So I created a secondary character, Lucy Brayton, who is the exact opposite of Jane Eyre Rochester. Where Jane is reserved, Lucy is brash. Where Jane is asocial, Lucy is a member of society. Each character serves as a whetstone, to sharpen the defining edge of her corollary."

Classic Secondary Characters

~ Bertha Mason Rochester, *Jane Eyre,* by Charlotte Brontë, and protagonist in *Wide Sargasso Sea,* by Jean Rhys.

~ Wicked Witch of the West, *Wizard of Oz,* by Frank Baum, and protagonist in *Wicked,* by Geoffrey Maguire.

~ Milton's Satan in *Paradise Lost,* whom many critics say is the epic poem's most successful character.

~ Rosencrantz and Guildenstern, *Hamlet,* by William Shakespeare, and the protagonists of Tom Stoppard's play *Rosencrantz and Guildenstern Are Dead.*

~ Doctor Watson in E. Conan Doyle's short stories is often the narrator, and may not be the most well-developed secondary character in literature, but he has made a great impact on the cultural mindset. Witness the variations on the character in the recent BBC's *Sherlock* and CBS's *Elementary.*

~ The emperor of great secondary characters is, not surprisingly, Shakespeare, but other classic fiction has given us unforgettable support players. Among them are: Shylock (*Merchant of Venice*), the Fool in *King Lear,* Iago; Miguel de Cervante's Sancho Panza in *Don Quixote*; Charles Dickens's Mr. Micawber and Uriah Heep (*David Copperfield*), Bill Sikes and Fagan (*Oliver Twist*); Mark Twain's Pap Finn (*Huckleberry Finn*); Victor Hugo's Inspector Javert (*Les Miserables*); Margaret Mitchell's Melanie (*Gone with the Wind*); Harper Lee's Boo Radley (*To Kill a Mockingbird*); and J. K. Rowling's exercises in opposition, the Dursleys and the Weasleys (the Harry Potter books).

"When developing secondary characters, consider the movies," Shoop says. "Many actors will take a small role if the character is a scene-stealer. Your secondary characters should inspire the desire to play their part—they should be that good."

Use Your Villain
Your villain's role is to make your hero's life difficult, right? Yet

sometimes a villain sets trouble in motion and then disappears, twiddling his thumbs offstage while you focus on the hero's actions.

If your story action is sagging or you cannot figure out what happens next, check in with your villain. Get him actively trying to thwart your hero, plotting new complications and distractions. By keeping your villain active, you will keep your story moving.

Of course, not every book has an actual villain in the "evil genius trying to take over the world" sense. But even if you don't have a major villain, an antagonist can cause trouble, either in the main plot or as a subplot.

In my Haunted series (Aladdin), each book's main plot involves kids trying to help ghosts. In *The Ghost on the Stairs,* I introduced a fake psychic, Madam Natasha. In *The Riverboat Phantom*, Madam Natasha figures out that Tania can see ghosts. Madam Natasha uses the secret as a threat, demanding Tania share information about the ghosts. In *The Knight in the Shadows,* the kids go to war with Madam Natasha, determined to expose her as a fraud. This is secondary to trying to help the ghost, but it adds complications and emotional drama.

Your villain or antagonist might be a bully, a competitor, a nasty boss, a difficult sibling, a manipulative friend. Whatever the villain is, his job is to make your hero's life miserable.

Here is another place to avoid lazy stereotypes. A villain should be complex and well-rounded, just like the hero. Whether or not you reveal it in the story, you should know why the villain is nasty. Is she actually evil, or just ignorant, or does she have reasonable goals that conflict with your hero's? A villain with good qualities and understandable motives creates a more subtle and complex story.

Consider your work in progress. Do you have a major villain? If so, is the villain as active as possible, aggressively trying to stop, hurt, or kill your hero? Do you have secondary characters with villainous tendencies? Can you enhance these, so they cause even more trouble?

Your main character may be the star, but major secondary characters also need to come alive. Think about their motives, their strengths, and their flaws. Add some surprising and contradictory qualities. Then let your whole cast of characters put on a fabulous show.

Point of View in Nonfiction

By Carmen Goldthwaite

Scribes of true stories write for the curious—for readers who want to know more—and for the perplexed, who want to make sense of life's happenings. Whether the form is memoir, biography, essay, or journalism, or the subject is travel, social issues, community life, science, history, or sports, authors of nonfiction can turn to age-old storytelling tactics to engage the readers.

Nonfiction can use many of the same techniques as fiction, to the point that the only major distinction is factuality. One tactic is for the narrative nonfiction writer to commandeer a point-of-view character, as in fiction, whose life is the portal through which the reader enters the true story. Facts, and the point-of-view character's perception of them, drive the nonfiction story.

Single Viewpoint

To convey viewpoint, a writer may select real people to express their views or describe their experiences. Sometimes, one individual stands out as the just right person to show a reader about a particular world.

Ken Wells found such a real life point-of-view character for *The Good Pirates of the Forgotten Bayous: Fighting to Save a Way of Life in the Wake of Hurricane Katrina* (Yale University Press), which was nominated for a Pulitzer Prize and won the Harry Chapin Media Award. Wells used the singular perspective of Ricky Robin: "He had an incredible story to tell and he is the great embodiment of an American," says the author.

Wells's book about the Robin family's experience when Hurricane Katrina slammed into New Orleans focuses on a parish south of the Crescent City, one overlooked by most news coverage. Who better to tell this story than the son and grandson of shrimp boat builders, a man who built his own boat in high school, and years later rode out Katrina aboard her the same boat? Afterwards, Robin focused on helping hundreds of stranded and flooded neighbors.

Through Wells's point-of-view character the reader experiences the power and devastation of the storm and desperation encountered by survivors. Wells asked Robin to take him aboard his boat, asking questions about exactly where he was on the boat, and what he saw, so that the author could to recreate the day of the storm. Who better to tell the story than a man who knows the people of the particular area by first name, knows what they needed and how to reach them, who told the then-*Wall Street Journal* reporter Wells, "If you're looking for a story, I've got a story for you"?

Robin provided not just the narrative drama of the story, but also the texture and complexity that arise from deep knowledge and history of the place, and the seafaring way of life along the bayous of southern Louisiana. Robin embodied the particularities of place, of a way of life, and of an attitude about hurricanes. "Ricky stood for a whole lot of things interesting about Louisiana, and attitudes toward hurricanes and the wetlands," Wells says.

Through Ricky Robin's eyes, personality, and attitude—conveyed by Wells' attention to history and details of the scene—readers enter the point-of-view character's world. Readers can hear and feel the storm winds, see and ride the tidal surge, imagine the taste of slurping good gumbo with beer, bog down in the depth of the mud, weep at the desperation of those who are doomed. Yet Wells could let the drama and tragedy of the story unfold with a touch of humor because of his main character. "Ricky is funny, [with] some unintentional humor. He's interesting, agreeable, and an intelligent sort of guy." Out of the tragedy that struck the Robin family and so many more, the reader gets to witness the resiliency of the bayou country spirit, of those rising out of the muck to begin again.

"His was a sea adventure—riding out the storm in a safe harbor, the storm surge, and surrounded by a subdivision where he and other shrimp boat captains helped save hundreds of people, 10 days before the government forces arrived with food and water," says Wells. Robin led the author, and ultimately readers, through the drowned district. Wells recounts the story with Robin's unabashedly subjective viewpoint, displaying the Louisiana native's own skills as a storyteller. Wells explains that the entire "Robin clan are great storytellers, with good family stories of hurricanes that his great grandparents had survived."

Double Vision

Shoe-leather reporting led Wells to a hero that propelled his story, but not all stories work best with a single viewpoint. Dubbed 'father of the New Journalism' by Tom Wolfe, Gay Talese gave this advice on point of view in nonfiction at the Mayborn Literary Nonfiction Conference in 2006: "Tell a story from many points of view . . . [It is] your choice of whom you talk to." Talese advocated using minor figures to bring important information and viewpoint to bear, and recalled a piece he wrote about Frank Sinatra as seen by a cigarette girl in a night club.

Author Susan Casey chose two points of view for *The Wave* (Doubleday): a scientist and a surfer. Fascinated by ever-increasing waves and the surfers who challenge them, Casey chose Laird Hamilton as the surfer, a man readers could identify with in values and goals. Laird follows the Pacific shore with his passion to skim the surface of waves towering 60, 70, even 100 feet. Casey also turned to North Sea scientist Dr. Penny Holliday, a researcher of extreme waves, to lead the reader through the troughs and curls that swallow large marine vessels, and to help explore why these waves seem to be gaining in intensity. The author then braided the two stories together, using a first-person, subjective viewpoint but incorporating details of personal experience and science. Casey, also the Editor in Chief of *O Magazine*, told the 2011 Mayborn Literary Nonfiction Conference that she is "big about writing about smells and noises and other people's reactions."

Comedy or Tragedy

Setting the stage for a story, award-winning historian Jim Crutchfield tries to find a character to "get him into the first paragraph." Long an advocate of writing to entertain as well as inform, Crutchfield has written, collaborated on, or edited 50-plus books about regions across the nation. The books have garnered fans and awards, many for local and regional history. The Tennessee author was a major contributor to and editor of *The Settlement of America: Encyclopedia of Westward Expansion from Jamestown to the Closing of the Frontier* (M. E. Sharpe). In 2011, Western Writers of America (WWA) honored Crutchfield with their acclaimed Owen Wister Award for his lifetime achievements as a writer.

Crutchfield's challenge has been to write history "to make it engaging, to give the reader the same thrill that you get out of reading a cowboy shoot 'em up." To do that he "borrows a lot of ideas of a fiction writer." He identifies his subjects as those that "need to be covered, a story I wanted to tell because there was nothing out there about it, to tell a story that needed telling." Then he searches for the character to open the story, "to give the reader that episode of history through the ideas of a strong central character."

Crutchfield often puts the point-of-view character in action immediately, as he did in *It Happened in Texas* (TwoDot/Globe Pequot), where he wrote, "On a hot summer day in 1534 in what is now southern Texas, Álvar Núñez Cabeza de Vaca crouched over a young man with a serious chest wound." Through this character's experiences the reader learns about the terrain, the hardships, the vastness of the lands, and the early peoples of Texas.

Fascinating, sometimes edgy, personalities intrigue this historian, whether they are good guys or not. In *It Happened in Montana* (TwoDot/Globe Pequot)), Crutchfield introduced an episode like this: "Mike Fink was a rowdy, no doubt about it. By 1823, his reputation had spread up and down the Missouri River. . . . He was known as a bully and a brutal, deadly fighter." Readers of this book know what they are in for from the first paragraph. The facts are true, although the author recreated the scene with details, to bring an unforgettable character to life.

I Did It My Way

Not all narrative nonfiction stories feature the good guys or have positive endings. But Jack Hart, retired Managing Editor and writing coach of the *Oregonian* thinks, "The more satisfying stories end successfully. They tell you how to cope with challenges thrown your way, the comedies rather than the tragedies."

Nonfiction writers approach a story wanting to understand why something happened, how it happened, or how the person at the story's center got into a predicament and then coped. Readers of narrative nonfiction are looking for the same. Sometimes that information is conveyed directly from the point of view of the writer.

Johnny D. Boggs is a journalist, feature writer, author of teen fiction, and of Western fiction and nonfiction, including *Jesse James and the Movies* (McFarland). He talks about how nonfiction perspectives vary from genre to genre: "In travel writing, it's your own impressions a lot of times. It needs to be fun. I'm looking for a point of view that's maybe kind of folksy but covering the facts and slipping the fun and folksiness in there a little bit." Currently, Boggs writes "a lot about art," and the award-winning novelist contributes regularly to *Persimmon Hill, New Mexico, Western Art and Architecture, Wild West,* and *True West.*

While Boggs says that the point of view of his stories and 42 books may change from subject to subject, "it's likely my point of view driving the story." There are exceptions, particularly for the subjects of art, history, and films. In these stories, Boggs is more likely to "hook onto one character that's going to drive that story." He is "intrigued" by historical characters like Frank James (brother of Jesse), and by people like Samuel Fuller, who directed the movie *I Shot Jesse James*.

Although one real individual may be the way into revealing a story, Boggs says, "I'm not writing about good guys and bad guys but values, to find a real hero in history. It makes writing about real people interesting—finding their flaws, making wrong choices that can sometimes leave you cringing [over] why this person made this decision."

In narrative nonfiction, writers explore the edges of the real people who become point-of-view characters. They work because of what distinguishes them from most people, but also because of universal traits that bring readers to empathize with them or want to understand them.

In his book *Storycraft* (University of Chicago Press), Hart shares what he taught reporters at the *Oregonian*: "Look for someone who has something to solve—something thorny—[and] someone you can like, so you can see yourself struggling with the same kinds of complications." Once a subject is selected, the reader can then benefit from the writer's hewing to the narrative arc of fiction, telling the story so that the character experiences a transformation, preferably one of his or her own doing, as in any good storytelling.

You Have to Be Convincing

Argumentation as a Writing Form

By Katherine Swarts

Dale Carnegie, that self-improvement salesman and guru of another century, said that the only way to get the best of an argument is to avoid it. That holds true as long as you define *argument* as a verbal battle and *getting the best of it* as convincing someone you are right. Argumentation as the art of a logical and reasonable persuasion of others to accept a debatable position, however, is another matter. Argumentation is an art all writers should understand on some level, whether they write expository nonfiction, true narrative, or pure fiction.

Persuasion

Long before Carnegie came Plato and his Socratic dialogues, and *dialectic* as the foundation of argumentation in Western literature. "Dialectic, which is everywhere in human experience, shapes the thematic elements of any work of fiction or nonfiction," says Steven Womack, Senior Partner at Whiskey Creek Press. "Dialectic is the intellectual part of our humanity, complemented by and usually in conflict with our emotional–physical state."

"The purpose of argumentation is to win agreement for an issue that may be controversial and is morally significant," says author Nancy Carol Willis, owner of Birdsong Books. "The writer must anticipate arguments against her position and must present facts, rigorous reasoning, and compelling persuasion designed to evoke the desired response from the reader."

"I believe every novel is an argument," says Melanie Ann Billings, Submissions Editor at Whiskey Creek. "As with any good debate, a novel lays the groundwork in persuading the reader to suspend disbelief, to follow the story—the argument—to the end. Throughout, the author will use conversation, whether between the narrator and the characters, between the characters themselves, or directly aimed at the reader, to bring the story to a logical or emotional conclusion. The entire story, any story, is a work of persuasion—full of argumentation strategies."

Argumentation under Any Other Name

Most people who hear the word *argumentation* think of essays or social commentary—a specific effort to convince directly. Starting there can actually be a great help to writers of all stripes. "I teach freshman writing at the university level," says author and writing instructor Heather Gemmen Wilson, "and one of the staples for the course is persuasive essays. Students have to know how to formulate thoughts to convince others; nearly all writing is persuasive by its very nature. Whether writing Facebook posts or editorials or full-length novels, authors are presenting a point of view that they hope will be received positively."

"I've been using argumentation in essays and commercial free-lance pieces without knowing the formal term," says C. Hope Clark, Editor of *Funds for Writers*. "I state my point, explain why I'm qualified to state the point, provide examples and proof, confirm my credentials and the credentials of my quoted experts, cover perceived rebuttal with qualifiers, and reclaim the point, now endorsed with very clear qualifiers and support. It's simple logic, a subtle, three-point message of claim, points, and conclusion proved."

You will be most convincing if your writing radiates concern and empathy, as opposed to condescension and criticism. Think in terms of opening new perspectives, of gently encouraging readers to challenge the norm. "Many of my teen and YA nonfiction books concern a controversial discussion," says Dale Carlson, President of Bick Publishing House. They may include "experimental dialogue," and promote young people's self-awareness and understanding in ways that are "unlike what they are told at school or at home." Bick's books on the human condition might be considered argumentation in the sense of promoting "psychological freedom from psychological prisons, and are based on the need for psychological freedom to decide, to keep what you want and rewrite what you don't, without harming anyone else."

Argumentation can work with readers even younger than teenagers, says Louise May, Vice President and Editorial Director of Lee & Low Books, "as long as the opinions on both sides are expressed at a level the targeted audience can understand, and the resolution is age-appropriate. Emotional appeal [at any age] comes from the successful, logical, positive resolution of opposing positions."

Audience Ages and Argumentation

"The age of our audience should affect how we attempt to convince them," notes Wilson. "We may use an authoritative voice for children that wouldn't work for a peer audience; or young people may demand more evidence because they are at a stage when everything is changing and nothing can be taken for granted."

"The younger your audience," says Megan Friel, Founder and Editor of Sparrow Tree Square, "the simpler your argument should be. For the picture book audience, this may mean limiting yourself to issues that are immediate to a child's world, as Charlotte Zolotow does in *William's Doll*; or it may mean simplifying complex issues to their bare bones, as Dr. Seuss does with discrimination in *The Sneetches*. Middle-graders can understand wider-ranging issues addressed from a child's perspective, as Jane Langton does with hunting in *The Fledgling*. Young adults have the intellectual and emotional maturity to handle complex, nuanced arguments, such as Elizabeth George Speare's discussion of religious persecution in *The Witch of Blackbird Pond*."

Vivian Owens, author and Publisher of Eschar Publications, echoes the principle: "In [Russell Hoban's] *Bread and Jam for Frances,* a book for very young readers, Frances argues for decision-making power with one strong point; she repeatedly says, 'I do not like . . . .' The story is written lyrically. In *Lord of the Flies,* a book generally read by ninth or tenth graders, William Golding uses multiple examples [to show] the savagery in a mankind stripped of mandates. Throughout, the main characters confront this question with a presentation of place and circumstance, voice rendered through the eyes of the beholder."

Regardless of audience age, consider what tone of voice best speaks to the reader's mindset, and balance your focus to suit. "Tone of voice is harder to control in writing," notes Wilson, "so crafting arguments has to be done carefully. Avoid belittling your audience; instead, think of them as people who could be on your side."

"Language is usually the tipping point between argumentation and argumentativeness," says Friel. "Writers should address both sides, but they should be careful to use a neutral tone and avoid derogatory language. Using positive language when presenting your own view is more effective than trying to denigrate the opposition, especially when writing for a young audience."

With such a delicate tipping point, awareness of all the techniques and effects of argumentation is key. "Keep in mind the strategies for arguing," says Billings. "Logos is the appeal to reason. Ethos is the appeal based on ethics. Pathos is the appeal to the emotions. Keep in mind all three."

Argumentation Without Arguing

If you fail to find balance, you risk becoming the crusader-writer who considers it his life mission to let everyone know how brainless and evil his opponents are, and who succeeds only in encouraging those opponents to dig in their defensive heels, while he either bores or embarrasses almost everyone else.

Katie Barry, Editor at Next Step Publishing, says, "Whenever a writer approaches a topic with any sense of negativity, bias shines through. The best writers are able to persuade without ever seeming anxious, angry, or malicious. Stating your case in a positive manner, while addressing the opposition in a respectful and factual way, will only help your cause. [I like] political debates because they are entertaining, but [they are not known for being] particularly well-constructed or persuasive."

Clark notes the perils of "pointing fingers when making points. Great debate is when points are made without belittling the opposition. The reader throws up blinders once a writer starts taking sides instead of proving a theory. The writer must sound open-minded, having reached a conclusion based on pure logic,

"The best writers are able to persuade without ever seeming anxious, angry, or malicious."

lacking any emotional or pre-established opinions. [My favorite blogger,] Justine Musk (justinemusk.com), writes as if she's discovering as she goes. It attracts the reader, keeping him hanging on to the end."

"To argue just creates antagonism. Non-authoritative questioning and dialogue work better," says Carlson.

The second you let your emotions run away with your writing, the moment your tone hints that your my mind is made up and you see red even thinking about any other point of view, you have already lost your argument. This is as true when argumentation techniques are used in fiction as in nonfiction. "A writer's passion toward a particular viewpoint can blind her," notes Owens. "As the plot grows in a direction that favors one type of characterization, it is easy for the writer to lose sight of balance.

The story then becomes warped and loses vitality. As you plan scenes, describe in your outline how you will achieve pace in your story. Ask yourself, 'Is there balance in their discourse?'"

"Express the logic first," says Clark, "not overplaying the emotion. When an essay or feature piece turns into an op-ed, I know that the writer entered the forum to hammer a point. Sure, a writer usually has a point to prove, but when he sounds like Everyman trying to learn like everyone else, he maintains a larger readership. Someone who is strong *right* or strong *left*—or strong anything that I don't agree with—will not likely reach me. But if [the writer is] known for being open-minded enough to listen, regardless of his leanings, I just might [listen to him in return]. It's called *intelligent discourse* instead of falling prey to knee-jerk emotion. The emotional appeal in a piece has to be shown and not told, like any other type of writing. We love to be convinced. We hate to be told."

"Avoid generalizations," says Willis, "and present an argument using facts that can be observed and tested. Two common writing traps involve assuming that what the writer is trying to prove ("It's common knowledge that caffeine is bad for one's health") and inferring one idea from another ("Because caffeine is bad for one's health, it should be regulated as a controlled substance"). The conclusion may logically follow the premise and still be factually untrue. Is caffeine in any amount bad for everybody? I hope not!"

"Logic should not be confused with fact," explains Barry. "Logic, while often fact-based, is about convincing your audience that your argument is not only truthful and accurate, but one they agree with. There is an element of persuasion that accompanies logic, and that is often emotional. However, a purely emotional approach is not often logical. A delicate balance of both makes for the best arguments."

Beware also of ironic humor, which easily gets out of control. "Check the sarcasm unless you target a select market or are priming the audience for debate," says Clark. "Ease into your points, showing via examples, not opinion, connecting the dots ever so subtly so the reader travels with you to the end and isn't dared to take issue. He rides on your journey, feeling he is absorbing as you, the writer, are. Assume the audience is wanting an education, and prefers not to be an adversary. With that mindset, you can lead a reader to the water and have him drinking before he knows it."

Billings concurs: "Use material and characters in a way that subtly manipulates the reader to keep reading, that persuades the reader to support, emotionally or logically, the characters or situations you want the reader to identify with. If an author feels unintentional antagonistic tendencies coming forward through a situation or character, if there is any doubt as to whether an author has pushed the argumentative boulder too far over the cliff, stop and reevaluate."

A Legacy of Argumentation

Finally, read other writers whose persuasive writings have stood the test of time, as well as influential modern authors. Learn from Plato and Kant, but also learn from *Twilight* author Stephenie Meyer. Study techniques and approaches: What gives these writers' arguments staying power? Why are many of them read long after the original purposes for the arguments passed into history? What gives force to an argument in modern fiction?

And think of yourself as a writer first and a persuader second. Those who love argument for its own sake are already on the wrong track. "Before you employ [outright] argumentation," says Friel, "ask yourself if it's really the best approach. Simple exposure is often just as effective, and may be more palatable."

It's not about you, it's about your readers. That's one rule that no one experienced in publishing will argue with.

Sources

~ **Bick Publishing House:** Dale Carlson, 116 Marion Road, Branford, CT 06405. www.bickpubhouse.com

~ **Birdsong Books:** Nancy Carol Willis, 322 Bayview Road, Middletown, DE 19709. www.birdsongbooks.com

~ **Eschar Publications:** Vivian Owens. P. O. Box 1194 , Mount Dora, FL 32756. www.escharpublications.com

~ **Funds for Writers:** C. Hope Clark, 140-A Amicks Ferry Road, #4 , Chapin, SC 29036. www.fundsforwriters.com, www.chopeclark.com

~ **Lee & Low Books:** Louise May, 95 Madison Ave., # 1205, New York, NY 10016. www.leeandlow.com

~ **Next Step Publishing:** Katie Barry, 2 West Main St., Suite 200, Victor, NY 14564. www.nextstepu.com

~ *Sparrow Tree Square:* Megan Friel. www.sparrowtreesquare.com

~ **Whiskey Creek Press:** Melanie Ann Billings, Steven Womack, P. O. Box 51052, Casper, WY 82605. www.whiskeycreekpress.com

~ Heather Gemmen Wilson: www.thisheather.com

Snappy, Solid, Sold!

The Well-Crafted Synopsis

By Judy Bradbury

You have written a fascinating article, a riveting novel, or a groundbreaking nonfiction book, and you finally feel ready to offer it to the world. You are happy with the tweaks and polish, your critique group has given it a thumbs up, and you (or you and your agent) have identified the publishers who may be interested in considering your project for publication. There is just one more hurdle to leap: Writing a synopsis. It must grab the attention and entice a prospective editor, and have the promise of writing that will appeal to your target audience down the line. The synopsis is a crucial step in getting your project read, considered, and sold.

Features of the Synopsis

"I think of a synopsis as a combination summary, writing sample, and sales pitch. I want the synopsis to show an editor why my magazine article or book idea is worthy and also assure this editor that I can write well," says Melissa Abramovitz, author of *A Treasure Trove of Opportunity: How to Write and Sell Articles for Children's Magazines* (E + E Publishing). "In the case of a magazine article, which must have a very narrow focus, I want the synopsis to clearly reveal its angle. And any good synopsis, whether it is for a book or magazine article, conveys the tone, along with the essence and direction the article or each chapter of the book will take." Abramovitz incorporated part of the synopsis for her book into the introductory chapter, and the publisher chose to use it on the book's back cover and in promotional material. "The synopsis lets the reader know what the book covers and what makes it unique. Plus, it reveals that the tone is conversational and directly addresses and engages the reader," notes Abramovitz. (See the sidebar on page 150 for an excerpt of the synopsis that helped Abramovitz cinch the contract.)

Peggy Thomas, author of numerous nonfiction books for both children and adults, including *For the Birds: The Story of Roger Tory Peterson* (Boyds Mills Press), and *Anatomy of Nonfiction: Writing True Stories for Children* (Writer's Institute Publications), co-authored with Margery Facklam, lays out how the synopsis fits into the project's presentation to an editor. "For a nonfiction writer, a synopsis is part of the proposal package, along with a cover letter, bibliography, résumé, and a sample chapter or two. I prefer to write a chapter-by-chapter breakdown to show how the book will be organized. I also think it is easier to scan than a big block of text. In just a paragraph or two I give the key focus of the chapter and what issues I'll discuss. I highlight the new and exciting material I've uncovered—what makes my take on the subject different. I may name the people I will interview for that particular chapter, or mention some other aspect of the research, such as the archives where I've spent countless hours. I might also give an example of a sidebar or other feature I expect to include. Oftentimes, I incorporate the first sentence or two from the chapter just to give the editor or agent a flavor of the text and a sense of my style. It is a lot to pack into a little space, but not if you focus on the points that make your story different, timely, and irresistible."

The Editor's Perspective

A well-conceived synopsis is vital for a fiction project. David Dilkes, Editorial Director of Enslow Publishers, offers insight into what grabs his interest when reviewing the piles of queries that

A Winning Fiction Synopsis

~ *Hook* the reader with a smart and snappy opening paragraph that reveals the premise of the story. If *setting* is important to the story, be sure to offer salient details.

~ Introduce the main *characters* and their relationship to one another: offer insight into their dreams, their goals, their strengths and weaknesses, and their problems. Avoid getting bogged down with minor details, however. Be word choosy!

~ Craft brief paragraphs outlining the highlights of the progression of your *plot* and the developing *conflict*: actions, tensions, and results. Use vivid verbs and sensory language.

~ Offer a solid paragraph or two detailing the *resolution* of the main *conflict* in your story. Be sure to offer particulars that reveal the logic, connection, and ultimate satisfaction of a well-conceived resolution to a meaningful conflict.

arrive at his office: "When we receive a fiction submission, I look for the first paragraph of the synopsis to catch my attention immediately with a recap of an exciting scene or dilemma taking place in the manuscript. Preferably, the scene in this first paragraph will pertain to the main plot. Then the main plot of the story should be revealed in the following paragraph.

"My next expectation is that the author will introduce all of the main characters, themes, and subplots in the story. It's best if some snippets of dialogue are included so that I can get a feel for the author's voice. Finally, it's best for me if the synopsis runs about one page, or less, for every 30 pages of manuscript. Anything beyond that," Dilkes warns, "runs the risk of getting pushed to the side."

An Author's Calling Card

"In addition to conveying vital information about your manuscript, a synopsis indirectly serves as your calling card and shows

Sample Synopses

~ The following paragraph-length synopsis was crafted for *A Treasure Trove of Opportunity: How to Write and Sell Articles for Children's Magazines,* by Melissa Abramovitz.

The need for children's magazine nonfiction is one of the best kept secrets in the trade. At the risk of divulging well-kept secrets and tips for succeeding in this market, I've written this book to provide a comprehensive guide to planning, researching, writing, and marketing magazines nonfiction for children and teens. There are books out there on writing nonfiction in general and on magazine nonfiction in general, but they offer limited insight into the specifics of writing and selling articles for children and teens. This book will give you the specifics you need to get started in a richly fulfilling and financially rewarding full or part-time career.

~ Abramovitz also offers a comparison between a weak lead and a strong one for a synopsis about an article on dog heroes.

First, the weak opening: "The article begins with a child getting near a rattlesnake in his backyard, and the family's little dog interfering."

To improve the synopsis lead, she chooses vivid words and shows, rather than tells: "Two-year-old Jack toddles toward a coiled rattlesnake in the Jenkins family backyard. Binky, the Jenkins' beloved ten-pound poodle, races across the yard and plants himself between Jack and the snake." Abramovitz suggests the next sentence might read, "Binky's brave stance nearly cost him his life, but, like other dog heroes, his overriding concern was for his family."

Which version would make you want to read the article?

~ For unlimited examples of winning synopses, peruse recently published books at your public library or local bookstore. Read and analyze the flap copy. Consider what the author or marketing copy writers did to make you want to flip to the first chapter and dive into the book. If you do not want to read more, why not?

~ See also these websites for an array of sample synopses:
- www.charlottedillon.com/SynopsisSamples.html
- www.eharlequin.com/images/pdf/SampleSynopsis.pdf
- pred-ed.com/pesynop.htm

an editor what type of writer you are. While the synopsis does not list your qualifications as a résumé or query letter does, its quality speaks volumes about you," says Abramovitz.

"Although the synopsis is not nearly as detailed as the manuscript itself, you can still employ writing techniques that will make it a winner, just as these techniques contribute to a winning manuscript," she continues. "If your synopsis is well-written and error-free, this speaks well for your professionalism and writing ability. If it contains typos, misspellings, poor grammar, questionable facts, and unclear thoughts, this reveals that you are a sloppy, unreliable writer who takes no pride in her work. Even if your article or book idea is good, you will not get the assignment or a request to see your book."

> "Although the synopsis is not as detailed as the manuscript, employ the same writing techniques to make it a winner."

Perusing the flap copy on successfully published books often reveals the merit of a well-conceived and well-crafted synopsis. Abramovitz offers concrete advice: "Use vivid, specific words rather than vague, general words to create a clear picture. Show, don't tell. Don't use two words when one suffices. Hook your reader with a strong beginning, sustain interest with a dynamic middle, and create a memorable ending for your synopsis just as you would in your manuscript." She emphasizes that these strategies apply to nonfiction as well as fiction. "Many people wrongly believe that nonfiction consists of a boring list of facts. On the contrary, salable nonfiction manuscripts (and synopses) employ many of the same techniques as salable fiction does; the difference is that everything in the nonfiction is true."

A winning synopsis is concise and focused—absolutely to the point in every aspect. It should contain no minor details, no tangents, and no vague or wasted words. To summarize an entire article or book briefly and yet engagingly, Abramovitz advises, "Choose the most interesting of the important elements of each section of your article or each chapter of your book and highlight them with short, vivid descriptions. Ideally, tie the featured elements to your main theme or focus." For an example, see the dog hero article lead and follow-up sentence featured in the sidebar on page 150.

> "The single most important part of a synopsis—and one that is easy to overlook—is *panache*, otherwise known as *voice*."

The Heart of Your Package

"The single most important part of a synopsis—and one that is easy to overlook—is *panache*, otherwise known as *voice*," claims Elizabeth Partridge, author of numerous award-winning nonfiction titles, including *Marching for Freedom: Walk Together Children and Don't You Get Weary* (Viking). "You can get everything else right, and without a compelling voice in your synopsis you won't get an editor to jump out of her seat, saying, "I have to publish this book!"

In sending a proposal package, Partridge notes, "Voice doesn't show up so much in your list of competing volumes. It's in your cover letter, your chapter titles, and most significantly, carried through your sample chapters. Look over what you've written. Is there some nuance or mystery or thrill in what you've written? Can you make your verbs more vibrant? Are your sentences tight? Paragraphs in the right order? Flabby prose ruthlessly thrown out? Does what you've written in your sample chapters make an editor go back and read over your chapter titles, hungry for more?"

"It seems paradoxical, but you need to know the heart of your book before you can submit a really great synopsis," says Partridge. "Whenever I put a book together, I am always searching for that heart. It doesn't usually come to me in words at first," she reveals, "it's more of a tingling sensation, a feeling of excitement, that I'm getting close to what I want to say. It's fine if it's not in words at first, because you don't want to be flatfooted about the heart of your book. Words will form in their own time."

Partridge offers a personal example. "When I was putting together *This Land Was Made for You and Me: The Life and Songs of Woody Guthrie* (Viking), I struggled to understand what made Guthrie tick. Gradually—and then with a sudden rush of *aha!*—I realized his childhood had been destroyed by his mother's Huntington's disease, and he both knew and denied fairly early in his adult life that he too was getting this inherited, fatal disease. I scribbled 'Haunted by Huntington's' on a Post-It, stuck it to bottom of my computer screen, and started writing." The rest is history. *This Land* went on to win a truckload of awards and applause-filled reviews.

A well-conceived, heartfelt, focused, and snappy synopsis is a critical part of your book proposal package or article query. Get it right and you, too, may be shouting *"Sold!"*

Sentences & Syntax

The Threads of Revision

By Carmen Goldthwaite

Most writers I know are in the "get it down quick and then revise" school of thought, which is my own method of working. Yet we also all know people who labor over every word and sentence as they write, not advancing their story or article until they have penned each small piece as well as they can. They prefer everything to be done in the *right* order to carry the mood and tone forward. Ultimately, it does not matter which approach a writer takes. In the end both the whole of the story and the individual components of words, sentences, and syntax should be merged and perfected.

What matters is that we rewrite and revise. As Kurt Eichenwald, Contributing Editor at *Vanity Fair*, former *New York Times* reporter, and author of best-selling books has said, "Anybody can write. It takes a writer to rewrite."

Rewriting means making a story, article, or book "sound right," whether it is written all in one fast draft, or in slow, one-by-one words and phrases.

Rhythm & Structure

Fantasy and mystery author J. Suzanne Frank says that she reads her work out loud because "writing is closer to music than any other art form. You can *hear* it that way." A writer who prefers to write the first draft as soon as possible, she is the author of seven novels—four time-travel books in a series from Grand Central Publishing/Hachette (*Reflections in the Nile, Shadows on the Aegean, Sunrise on the Mediterranean,* and *Twilight in Babylon*) and three mysteries from Kensington Publishing (*Going Out in Style, Designed to Die,* and *Fashion Victim*) that trade on her experience in the fashion industry. Her newest book is *Laws of Migration* (Tyrus Books).

Reading her drafts aloud, Frank hears and can correct "unintentional rhyming and pronoun confusion," which are among the discordant notes that can annoy or misdirect the reader. "Rewriting is the bulk of the work for me," she says.

Other writers find the rhythm of writing comes naturally. "Because of my experience in acting and improvisation through college, and teaching theater to kids, I developed vocalized storytelling, and developed an ear," says Rosemary Clement-Moore. The young adult author has published several books with Random House's Delacorte Press. *Prom Date from Hell, Hell Week,* and *Highway to Hell* she characterizes as "more fantasy overt," while her later books, *The Splendor Falls, Texas Gothic,* and the new *Spirit and Death* are "more ghost and gothic" stories.

Clement-Moore says her cadence as a writer also "comes from being a voracious reader. I learned early on that different authors will have rhythms. Prose has a rhythm to find." From her stage training, she recognizes "a conversational flow where one extra word can make a difference." For instance, for her first book, *Prom Date from Hell,* Clement-Moore was excited and nervous about being published and confronted the copy editor about a single word. The copy editor had "changed *leapt* to *leaped.* For the rhythm of this particular sentence, it had a whole different sound; for the rhythm of the sentence, I wanted to change it back." The editor agreed.

Johnny D. Boggs, YA and Western author, acknowledges that readers have told him "they like the rhythm of how [a] story flows." But he adds, "I don't know that I want to be too aware of that. The voice is always varying. I want to kind of mix it up. I never want to be predictable in fiction." He would prefer that people "pick up a Johnny D. Boggs book and not know what they will get." Boggs won the 2012 Western Writers of America Spur Award for best short novel with *Legacy of the Lawman Five* (Five Star), along with awards for several other adult books, and for the young adult *Western Hannah and the Horseman* (Avalon), the story with which he moved him from journalist to novelist.

Boggs is keen on performing revision, of reviewing structure and syntax. "I rewrite a lot," he said. He looks for "clarity and

> ## The first draft is "the ugly version— just get it on paper." Then attack at "first with a scalpel and then with a meat cleaver."

brevity" and "does [the writing] make sense. I look for sentence structure, how am I beginning each paragraph and the length of each paragraph. I have to get it as perfect as possible." He does his revisions on the computer until he prints the book out for his wife to read, and "I'll read it again on hard copy. . . . Then, at some point the deadline takes over."

Pared & Punchy

Ken Wells calls the first draft "the ugly version—just get it on paper." His first draft is usually long and he attacks it "first with a scalpel and then with a meat cleaver." He cites his *Crawfish Mountain* (Random House), a fictionalized account of Hurricane Katrina. Wells says he overwrote the novel dramatically. "I cut 40,000 words and it still came out as an 80,000-word book." Currently Senior Writer at *Bloomberg News* and *Business Week,* Wells's novels also include a trilogy of mysteries for Random House, and a YA novel, *Rascal, a Dog and His Boy*, from Knopf/ Random House.

Wells credits his style in part to a college professor who told him "you're better than this," and pointed to the young writer's florid, fluid style. Wells said "the light clicked on" as a reporter on an offshore oil fire assignment. He experienced the power of his story as "the recognition to pare down my style, write punchier sentences; not to be afraid of adjectives [but] not to overuse them. After that it's been a great deal easier. There are still days . . . " he says, when he succumbs stylistically, "but over-all it's easier. When there's a sentence you write that you hate, throw it away. I've become a ruthless self-editor—very uncharitable to myself on the ugly version."

Wells describes his self-editing: "I do an autopsy on the sentence. Why did the sentence rankle me so? And [then] I do the opposite. You have to be smart enough to recognize when you've written a dud."

Wells agrees with Boggs, however, saying "Writing's always a collision between the longing to write the perfect sentence and meeting deadlines."

Strong, Crisp, & Metaphoric

"The fine points are in rewrite," agrees Jack Hart, retired Managing Editor of the *Oregonian*. At the time of the interview for this article, Hart is in the middle of a rewrite of his novel *Skookum Summer* (University of Washington Press). He is in the process of "streamlining sentences with more active, stronger verbs, figurative language." He finds that "most similes and metaphors come in rewrite, not banging out the first draft." His goal is to craft "crisper, plainer language, language that's more appropriate to the character."

But if effective imagery comes as a piece of writing unfolds, there is a divide over adjectives. Adjectives were a tool of choice for the purple prose of some writers long ago—and were then condemned by Mark Twain's mantra to "kill all adjectives."

Adjectives do have their place, but are worthy of special

attention in rewriting. Pictorial words and phrases contribute to a rhythmic syntax when used well. Consider this sentence with with its run of descriptive phrases:

> A horse-drawn cart, a dusty lane, a well-thumbed Bible, and a handkerchief in his pocket, John Dickinson departed on his self-prescribed mission.

"Most similes and metaphors come in rewrite, not banging out the first draft."

The parallel phrasing creates a rhythm, a specific way to begin and carry the sentence. The four adjectives or adjectival phrases —horse-drawn, dusty, well-thumbed, self-prescribed—create a picture that works pointedly.

Frank in fact favors adjectives, shunning Twain's advice. She follows more in the spirit of the syntax and style of Pulitzer Prize winner Eudora Welty. Recognizing that adjective use can go overboard, Welty said: "I try to write a lush book because I like reading lush books. But then my characters tend to be pretty straightforward so it keeps it from becoming overblown, I hope." Welty found a balance in her novels and short stories.

In her own fiction, Frank says, "I probably use a lot of adjectives simply because I try to write about places or situations that are so extreme (like the Nile River) or so fast (the fashion industry), that we need that kind of underlining to understand them. I like to write on a really, really big screen in terms of color and sensory input."

Ways to Vary Syntax

~ Vary sentence length.

~ Vary sentence type: simple, compound, complex.

~ Vary paragraph structure.

~ Use adjective phrases and participial phrases well.

~ Change the "internal order" of sentences. Sometimes hold off your main point to the end, sometimes place it up front, sometimes let it stand simply on its own.

~ Watch your punctuation. Do not use em dashes repeatedly or fall into a love of colons or semicolons everywhere.

~ Check your own verbal tics. Do not rely on rhetorical questions too often. Look for phrases that you rely on too regularly in your writing.

~ Pay attention to voice. In a given piece of writing decide if simplicity and clarity serve the subject best, or if the language would be better if full and suggestive.

~ Consider your word choice, as in what novelist Gustave Flaubert called *le most juste*—the perfect word perfectly used.

Good & Long

Adjectives also have strong supporters in nonfiction. James A. Crutchfield, author of more than 50 books and countless magazine articles, believes nonfiction writers have good reason to write with even more complexity than writers of fiction. In his four decades of writing, Crutchfield has published many books on the states, including Georgia, Montana, Tennessee, Texas, and Montana, and on American expansion. "In history, you're trying to keep facts together and thought processes together. I use some pretty lengthy sentences in books and articles to get everything I [am] trying to get across in a sentence, a long sentence," he says.

"I'll just sit down at the computer and change a sentence (or a paragraph) a dozen times before [the story] gets released, until it's gotten the point across." As much as he believes in "rewrite, rewrite, rewrite," Crutchfield admits that he did not start out believing this. Now, he says, he "never picks up anything of mine that I don't think, 'I wish that sentence had gone this way [instead].'"

Unabashed about writing long sentences in a cultural world that often clamors for short and simple, Crutchfield crafts all the parts of a sentence: the left-branching introductory phrases or descriptive clauses; the core statement; the right-branching clauses that amplify the main part of the sentence. He works on the sentence until "it holds my thought processes together—describing a boat, the river, etc. I can say those same things in one sentence, one good-sounding sentence, where each part of the sentence has led [to] the next one."

Clement-Moore strikes a different note. "I try to straddle the line between literary versus simple. I like a balance of a contemporary, moving, well-paced story but enough language and literary illusions." For her young readers, she says, "I tend to overwrite and [then] cut. It's something I have to work at in the rewrite." With too complex language, the plot can slow and she can lose her audience, so she will "tune that up and get going again." Clement-Moore finds that being true to the character in her story "makes it a lot easier" to tame the language and syntax.

Her favorite sentences "come more naturally. I can always tell the sentences that I'm not going to have to rewrite; they're the most natural, and I don't have to move them around. They don't feel like work." Then she tackles the others. "The sentences that I have to work on the most are transitional, for efficiency, or for a real clear emotion I want to convey [in equally] clear words."

Clement-Moore refers to the sentences and syntax as the flutes of the writing orchestra. The best ones may sound easily and smoothly, but others may come only after the skills of a dozen rewrites are played and the "ugly version" becomes a composed work of art.

Web Writing

More Than Just Putting Your Work Online

By Sue Bradford Edwards

The most successful writers today have an online presence. For some, this means writing for ezines, websites, and blogs. Others work with print magazines that also need online material. Some writers have published books in print and are developing apps in conjunction with them. The gap between print and the web has shrunk to the point that it is virtually nonexistent.

"Print-only publications had to adapt to new media to fit their audience's needs, and that may include blogs, social networks, video, audio, apps, mobile, or other emerging technologies," says *WOW! Women on Writing* ezine Editor in Chief Angela Mackintosh. "At minimum, traditional media [have] adapted by pushing their content out on social networks and blogs to amplify their message. So, if you're writing for a print magazine, they may ask you to repackage the content for their website or write a shorter companion piece to go with a slideshow."

With the overlap between web content and print media, writers need to understand today's e-content to remain competitive, because although the differences are smaller than ever before, web content is much more than simply putting your work online. And web content today is different from web-content yesterday.

Then and Now

When the World Wide Web was new, writers were told to write short and tight. No one wanted to spend all their time reading at their desk.

"It's no longer necessary to write for the attention-deficit skimmer," says Mackintosh. "Most online content is available via apps for e-reading devices, and many premium blog themes come with mobile-responsive design, so the reader is not sequestered to a desktop. They can curl up on a couch with a cup of tea just like they would with a good book. That said, *WOW!* has always broken every rule about web writing. 500 words? That's 1,000 words too short for us. We publish in-depth articles similar to those you would find in a print magazine."

How do you know how long your web content should be? "Remain flexible and, above all, consider the audience you are writing for," says Mackintosh. "Study your market, read what they publish, and always follow their editorial guidelines."

Not only are people spending longer with their electronic readers, but the way they find content is also changing. At one point, search engine optimization (SEO) was the only way for readers to find your work. Author Chynna Laird explains, "SEO words are crucial and something online content editors are quite adamant about. What it means is that the writer needs to be more aware of using specific words in their piece that are searchable."

For writers who do not understand how keywords work, Mackintosh offers advice. "Choose one main and two secondary keywords that are search-specific to your article. Make sure you include your primary keywords in your title. Repeat your main keyword in the first sentence of your article. Include your keywords and phrases in the first 150 words of your article, as long as it's readable and not ridiculous! Spread your secondary keywords throughout the rest of your copy. If you are writing a long article, make sure that you include your main keyword or phrase in at least every other paragraph. Include your keyword or phrase in your conclusion paragraph. This is always changing, but it won't hurt to sprinkle your keywords throughout your article."

This is no longer the only way for readers to find your work. Editors now look for *clickable content* with the potential to go viral.

Banishing Myths

No matter how necessary it is for writers to get their work online, some still hesitate. "Some writers are worried about people stealing their work or ideas just because it's online when, in fact, it's [now] easier to figure out if someone is copying your words," says Angela Mackintosh, Editor in Chief of the ezine *WOW! Women on Writing*. "There are online plagiarism checkers where you can paste text in a box and run a check to see if there is anything similar online, or you can use Google Alerts to notify you via email whenever it finds the keyword/phrase/link that you specify."

Author Sue Ford has a warning for fellow writers: "At a reputable site, online markets have just as stringent requirements for quality work as a print magazine." Fail to meet their research standards or appear to plagiarize and you will find yourself persona non grata.

Writers also worry about pay for online markets. "Another myth is that online publications don't pay as much as print," says Mackintosh. "I could point out specific examples that say just the opposite, but print-only publications are having a hard time, while online publications have low overhead and are really just growing legs."

Ensure the opportunity for decent pay by submitting to web venues that have quality content. "On *WOW!*, we interview a lot of experts who give outstanding tips on many areas of writing. These are researched, edited articles," says Contributing Editor Margo Dill. "There are many websites like ours in many different subject areas."

"SEO is still there but content has taken a turn where it is more about share-ability. It is resonating with users. Are they engaging with the content? There's more of a human side with the writing that goes viral. It's more about optimizing for the web, but the over-arching principal isn't SEO. It's about writing a piece that's engaging and resonates and is shareable," says Education.com Editor Carlee Gomes. Publications that focus on the possibilities of content going viral make it easy by positioning buttons for Pinterest, Twitter, Facebook, emailing, or somehow sharing an article on each page.

Whether the focus is SEO or clickable content, readers will not connect with a piece that is hard to identify. "I would say I have to

Submitting Your Work

As with any type of submission, check to see what each individual publication prefers.

~ **Education.com** wants submissions in the form of attachments. "I find them easier to work with. I save those copies of my writer's work in case I need to see the original," says Editor Carlee Gomes, who admits that the formatting wizardry of Word attachments can quickly become a hardship. "With articles painstakingly formatted with number and bullets—all of that is corrupted the second I put it into our system." So keep submissions as clean as possible.

~ For similar reasons, *WOW! Women on Writing* has very specific formatting requirements. "Each publication is different, so it's important to follow individual guidelines. At *WOW!*, we don't allow attachments on submissions sent over the transom for safety reasons—we prefer that the article be pasted in the body of an e-mail. For submissions we have contracted, we ask writers to send their article as a Microsoft Word attachment in our specified font and formatting. We will always reformat a writer's submission per our specifications, but it gives us a clean starting point for graphic artwork and web formatting if they follow our directions," says Editor in Chief Angela Mackintosh. "We prefer web-friendly formatting—this means no indents, text flush left, and skip a line between paragraphs. We also prefer titles and subtitles so we can create heading tags (H1, H2, etc.) for web pages. Book titles should be italicized, rather than underlined. In fact, text should not be underlined unless it's a hyperlink. That's a tease!"

~ Author Sue Ford reminds fellow writers that some publications only take submissions via their own online submission forms.

revise around 75 percent of the titles I receive," says Mackintosh. "Take a look at your article, see what questions it answers, and think about what readers will be searching for. Does the article tell you how to do something? Is it breaking news? Are you interviewing someone? What is the focus of the article? Why did you write it? Abstract ideas do not fit here. And if you want to get more advanced, you might try using Google AdWord's Keyword Tool and type in the phrase to see how many queries it receives and its popularity." Readers cannot read what they do not find.

Talk to Me

To use keywords effectively or write clickable content, you need to know how today's readers use the web. "Web content tends to be easily digestible," says Gomes. "Around here we call it *grocery aisle content.* You're browsing and there is so much to look at and consume. You see something that catches your eye. Web content is that sort of grocery aisle."

Web consumers go online for specific reasons. "People go to the web when they are looking to solve a problem like 'my kid isn't sleeping,'" says Gomes. "We'll still talk to our mom [for advice], but people will chose web over print when they are going to solve an immediate problem."

This also affects how readers approach individual pieces of online writing. "Web content has to be engaging from the first word. Online, people want to know upfront: What is this article about, what am I going to learn, what can I expect?" says author and *WOW!* Contributing Editor Margo Dill.

Part of engaging the reader is delivering information in an acceptable voice. "You have to write in a voice that makes sense for the content. Our voice is an older sister voice—authoritative but friendly and approachable. When we get something that doesn't feel like that, it doesn't do as well. Readers are expecting to be talked to in a certain way and they pick up on it if its off," says Gomes. "The voice has to be endemic [to] the environment. Web readers are fickle." Give them something that feels off, and they will click away from your writing to someone else's.

Although connectivity means that readers can easily move away from your content, it also means that you can connect with readers more easily than ever before. There are many ways that web-savvy writers do this.

"Authors can link to references to support their research, and

Selected Online Markets

~ *About.com:* www.about.com
~ *AKA Mom:* www.akamommagazine.com
~ *Amazing Kids!:* www.amazing-kids.org
~ *American Athlete:* www.americanathletemag.com
~ *Anotherealm:* www.anotherealm.com
~ *BabagaNewz:* www.babaganewz.com
~ *Babble:* www.babble.com
~ *Bamboo Magazine, Whole Family Living:* www.bamboofamilymag.com
~ *bNetS@vvy:* www.bnetsavvy.org
~ *Christian Work at Home Ministries:* www.cwahm.com
~ *CKI Magazine:* www.circlek.org
~ *COLUMBIAKids:* columbia.washingtonhistory.org/kids
~ *Craftbits.com:* www.craftbits.com
~ *The Dabbling Mum:* www.thedabblingmum.com
~ *Denver Reign:* www.denverreign.com
~ *Dyslexia Online:* www.dyslexia-magazine.com
~ *Earlychildhood News:* www.earlychildhoodnews.com
~ *The Education Revolution:* www.educationrevolution.org
~ *Edutopia:* www.edutopia.org
~ *EFCA Today:* www.efcatoday.org
~ *Enchanted Conversation:* www.fairytalemagazine.com
~ *Encyclopedia of Youth Studies:* www.centerforyouth.org
~ *Entertainment Magazine:* www.emol.org
~ *FatherMag.com:* www.fathermag.com
~ *For Every Woman:* women.ag.org
~ *Fried Fiction:* www.friedfiction.com
~ *GeoParent:* www.geoparent.com
~ *Girlworks:* www.girlworks.ca
~ *Go! Magazine:* www.go-explore-trans.org
~ *Grandparents.com:* www.grandparents.com
~ *Guardian Angel Kids:* www.guardian-angel-kids.com
~ *Gumshoe:* www.gumshoereview.com
~ *Home Educator's Family Times:* www.homeeducator.com/familytimes
~ *A Hundred Gourds:* www.haikuhut.com/ahg
~ *The Illuminata:* www.tyrannosauruspress.com
~ *Imagination-Café:* www.imagination-cafe.com
~ *Inspired Mother:* www.inspiredmother.com
~ *Kaboose.com:* www.kaboose.com
~ *KidSpirit:* www.kidspiritonline.com
~ *The Kids' Storytelling Club*: www.storycraft.com/co
~ *Knowonder!:* www.knowonder.com

Selected Online Markets

~ *Kyria:* www.kyria.com

~ *Lightspeed:* www.lightspeedmagazine.com

~ *Literary Mama:* www.literarymama.com

~ *Little Bit:* www.littlebitmag.com

~ *MetroKids:* www.metrokids.com

~ *M.L.T.S.:* mltsmag.wordpress.com

~ *My Light:* www.mylightmagazine.com

~ *Natural Child:* www.naturalchildmagazine.com

~ *North Texas Kids:* www.northtexaskids.com

~ *Parenting Special Needs:* www.parentingspecialneeds.org

~ Parents' Choice: www.parents-choice.org

~ *The Pink Chameleon:* www.thepinkchameleon.com

~ *Rainbow Kids:* www.rainbowkids.com

~ *Rainbow Rumpus:* www.rainbowrumpus.org

~ *RUGBYMag.com:* www.rugbymag.com

~ *School Librarian's Workshop:* www.slworkshop.net

~ *See Jane Fly:* www.seejanefly.com

~ *Simply You:* www.simplyyoumagazine.com

~ *SingleMom.com:* www.singlemom.com

~ *Sisterhood Agenda:* www.sisterhoodagenda.com

~ *SLAP:* www.slapmagazine.com

~ *Spaceports & Spidersilk:* www.samsdotpublishing.com/spacesilk/main

~ *Still Moments Publishing:* www.stillmomentspublishing.com

~ *Stories for Children:* www.storiesforchildrenmagazine.org

~ *Strange Horizons:* www.strangehorizons.com

~ *Supportingstudents.com:* www.supportingstudents.com

~ *Survive Parenthood:* survivemag.com

~ *Sweet Designs:* www.sweetdesignsmagazine.com

~ *SweetMama:* www.sweetspot.ca/SweetMama

~ *Texas Child Care Quarterly:* www.childcarequarterly.com

~ *Third Flatiron:* www.thirdflatiron.com

~ *Tots to Teens:* www.totstoteensmagazine.com

~ *TQR:* www.tqrstories.com

~ *The Universe in the Classroom:* www.astrosociety.org

~ USA Synchro: www.usasynchro.org

~ *VegFamily:* www.vegfamily.com

~ *Women Today Magazine:* powertochange.com/women/

~ *Work Your Way:* www.workyourway.co.uk/

~ *WOW! Women on Writing:* www.wow-womenonwriting.com

~ *YARN:* www.yareview.net

~ *Young Bucks Outdoors:* www.buckmasters.com/resources/young-bucks-outdoors.com

readers can connect to the source to gain better understanding," says Mackintosh. "We can create hashtags on Twitter to chat about a topic or follow it. We can spread stories in social circles in Google+ that may garner the interest of news outlets and other forms of media. And we can mash up stories from all around the web—including video, blogs, tweets, photos, and more—to create a complete picture like they do with many citizen journalism news sites or sites like Storify that curate social media," says Mackintosh. "We can read an article and immediately share our feedback, ask a question, or link to another reference."

These are not the only ways to use connectivity. The best web writers network."They do things such as commenting on other writers' work, tweeting or otherwise sharing other writers' work, or even highlighting another writer's articles. Networking is one of the top three things that get a writer out there and with the online world being so competitive, writers should be making these connections as often as possible," Laird says.

What is the point of doing all of this when you could be researching or writing? The share-ability of an author's work is often impacted by their efforts to connect. "You have to be a champion for your own work. You have to talk about it. It's all about resonating with social communities on the web. That's become a metric for success. Is your piece resonating with these people in these communities? Are they commenting? Are they sharing it? You have to ignite that fire," says Gomes. Get your name out there, interact with your readers, and you'll connect with them and they will connect with your work.

Writers seeking to carve a place for themselves in the current publishing landscape cannot afford to ignore the web. With for-mer print publications appearing online and producing original web content, the two publishing worlds are no longer separate entities. The web has come into its own with many worthwhile publications putting out well-researched content. Find one with a voice that matches your own, and you will find yourself attract-ing new readers and new editors.

Business

Markets

Style

Research

Ideas

Contests

Indexes

Advertise Yourself

By Christina Hamlett

Probably the most depressing advice a writer on a shoestring budget wants to hear is the adage that "you have to spend money to make money." Paid advertising to hype your new book can be pricey and, unfortunately, carries no guarantee of creating a demand or a buzz. Free resources like social media, blogging, and do-it-yourself websites, however, make up an already overcrowded platform with too many voices shouting "Buy this!" So how do you solve the problem of making your voice rise above the din?

Psychologist Norman Maier used a connect-the-dots puzzle in 1939 to support his theory that problem-solving attempts often stem from human assumptions and restrictions. To unleash true creativity, he believed people must free themselves of conventional perceptions. Maier called it "thinking outside the box." Writers doing their own advertising might call it "thinking outside the bookshelf."

Life Imitating Art Imitating Life

Co-authors Beatrice Dee Pipes and Charles Wilbur Yates Jr., who write under the pseudonym Dee Wilbur, put creative talents of various kinds to clever use when they set out to promote a trio of their titles. "Ladies' organizations, church groups, and book clubs are always looking for *different* programs or outings. Our three books *A Jealous God, Justice Perverted,* and *A Foolish Plucking*

(Comfort Publishing), are all set in the small Texas town of Richmond. We offer two-hour tours of the book sites: the church where the couple married, the factory where the poisonous gas was made, the world-famous dip, etc. We finish with a Dutch-treat lunch at the characters' favorite restaurant. We only ask that participants have read one of the books!"

The intersection between real and imaginary took on a rock-star cast for author Michael T. Fournier. "My novel *Hidden Wheel* (Three Rooms Press), focuses on art and music scenes in a fictional town named Freedom Springs. The town's biggest musical export is a punk band named Dead Trend. As I was writing the book, I also wrote their songs which, like the band, are 25 years in the past and talk about Reagan, Chernobyl, Ollie North and the Berlin Wall." In concert with the book, Fournier and some musician pals formed an actual group. "The band helped me promote the book and generate a buzz. As a result of Dead Trend, the novel got great press in the *Boston Globe* and we played for 250+ people in the New York City opening for Mike Watt, bass player for the Stooges, fiREHOSE and Minutemen." Fournier also does readings at traditional venues like bookstores, and in basements and art galleries on both coasts.

Can an endorsement from beyond the grave give your book a boost? Tea Del Alma Silvestre is the author and self-publisher (through Amazon Digital Services) of *Attract and Feed a Hungry Crowd: How Thinking Like a Chef Can Help You Build a Solid Business*. Silvestre says, "One of the out-of-the-box things I did was create a YouTube video in which a [supposed] psychic dials in a conversation with the late Julia Child. It didn't end up going viral (at least not yet!) but I did get a few sales out of it, so I think in terms of the no-cost investment of producing it with a friend, the ROI [return on investment] was great."

Here is another idea for advertising yourself inexpensively. Consider what your novel's characters might say if they blogged. Had the Internet been available in Victor Hugo's time, Inspector

Javert might have hooked readers with the following: "I saw him last night in an alley off Boulevard Saint-Germain. I'm sure it was Valjean—a shadowy figure clutching a croissant in one hand and a bottle of fine Margaux in the other. His (stolen) evening meal perhaps? I shall return to the same alley this evening and hope that confidence renders him foolish."

You have already brought your characters to life. Why not get them a free blog site at Blogger.com, Wordpress.com, or Thoughts.com and invite them to share their insider version of what happened next? Remember that the *Fifty Shades of Grey* phenomenon started out as online *Twilight* fan fiction.

Armchair Producers

According to a recent Google study, YouTube is the second most popular social media website, with 790 million monthly visitors and 100 billion page views. Since there is no cost for uploading content nor extensive filmmaking expertise required to produce short promos, it is no surprise that authors are using YouTube to "go Hollywood" and post creative book trailers. Use either MovieMaker software on PCs or iMovie on Macintoshes. Import your own audio/video or avail yourself of free resources at from sites such as morgueFile.com (digital images), Stonewashed.net (sound effects), and Musicbakery (royalty-free tunes).

Not comfortable with such do-it-yourself technology? Consider advertising a contest to outsource your trailer's production. For YA books, pitch a contest through School Video News (www.school-video-news.com) to attract the talents of aspiring young filmmakers throughout the country. Encourage online judging of the finalists' entries and generate even more curiosity about your book.

Do not stop with YouTube once your video is finished. Blazing Trailers (www.blazingtrailers.com), BookTrailers (www. book-trailers.net), and the Red Room (redroom.com) are just a few free sites to upload your commercial.

Tie-ins, Networking, & Partnerships

Co-op ads that promote your book and a colleague's are an economical way to pool resources and maximize exposure. There are also creative options for pairing your title with organizations and upcoming media events.

"When I started my book, *Movies and the Battle of the Sexes*, I set up Google Alerts that bring me numerous hits per day," says ZetMec (a pen name). "Usually the hits reference hard-core gender battle info, entertainment news, or stories about the 2013 anniversary of the Battle of the Sexes tennis match between Bobby Riggs and Billie Jean King. I decided to hook up with a network before they started planning their fortieth anniversary specials to see where movie versions of the Battle of the Sexes fit into their gender-bender tennis story!"

Rick Lauber, author of *Caregiver's Guide for Canadians* (Amazon Digital Services), recommends approaching local businesses serving the same demographic as your target readers. "Suggest a consignment deal with a percentage for all copies sold. Introduce yourself and your book to all media. Tie your press releases in with current linked news and that will increase your chances of being interviewed." Establishing oneself as a subject-matter expert is an additional component of Lauber's advertising plan. "Write and submit free articles relating to your book's content to print and online publications. Regular submissions will help sustain name recognition."

When author Jennifer Bannan acquired several copies of her previously published short story collection *Inventing Victor* (originally published by Carnegie Mellon), she decided to advertise an event to sell them. "I put together a National Short Story Month reading featuring local writers, and charged admission. The event was fun and got my name out there as a promoter, and writer, of literary fiction. I'm planning a ten-year-in-print promotion; *tin* is the theme, so I'll give away a can of beer with every book sold. I'm not sure what the anniversary sales will do, but I definitely made back my investment on the reading event!"

To promote Parenting Press's release of Janan Cain's picture book *The Way I Feel,* Linda Carlson of the publisher's marketing division came up with a Fish Lips Face Photo Contest. "This encourages libraries and booksellers to photograph kids imitating the face on the book cover. We provide a book for the prize plus publicity for stores and libraries that do displays for the contest," Carlson says. "Some co-sponsors are creative. One photographed its mayor's fish lips face for the ad announcing the contest. Author Janan Cain attended some of these events and helped select winners. The advantage to this approach is that it's inexpensive, gets kids and parents into appropriate venues, and generates local media publicity for the book."

Award-winning author Charmaine Hammond (*On Toby's Terms*, and *Toby the Pet Therapy Dog*, published by Bettie Youngs Books) bonded with fellow animal lovers with the innovative marketing she used to build her platform. "Our Toby series is about our dog. We created an award after he passed away to recognize other animal assistance therapy dogs. It generated media, but most of all it keeps the legacy of our special friend. I also host three radio shows to talk about our books during conversations with incredible guests. We created a website, too, for sharing marketing tips with other authors, holding contests and, as a condition to enter, asking contestants to *like* the social media pages related to the book."

James W. Lewis combined the popularity of online contests with the *friending* aspects of social media. "For my second book, *A Hard Man Is Good to Find* (The Pantheon Collective/TPC Books), I started a Facebook contest; specifically, whoever used the book cover as their profile pic was eligible to win a $50 gift certificate and an autographed copy. Twenty people entered the contest. The book was constantly exposed to over 10,000 Facebook members who were in no way friended to me. Many of them were curious about the book cover, which led to interest in the book, and ultimately, secured sales prior to the contest ending."

Nontraditional Venues

Intriguing potential readers, and making them happy, can lead to unusual places and events.

"For Aristotle," says Dr. Bruce Weinstein, "the essential ethical question was, 'What is happiness?' In my experience, the happiest place on earth is a bakery, so I decided to launch my latest book, *Ethical Intelligence: Five Principles for Untangling Your Toughest Problems at Work and Beyond* (New World Library), at a famous New York cupcake shop. I pitched over 1,000 media contacts with the hook: 'First-ever book launch at Magnolia Bakery (for an ethics book).' Reporters, editors, and hosts of several major national media outlets came or asked for the book, which I continued promoting after the party. I wound up doing interviews on the *Today Show* and CNN, and an article I wrote based on the book appeared in American Airlines' in-flight magazine, *Nexos*, in Spanish!"

I have a story of my own related to unusual venues: My former hairdresser was the quintessential party planner and offered to host my first-ever book signing. His salon was on the second floor of a Victorian mansion, quite an upscale alternative to a mall bookstore! Not only were several guests impressed enough by the ambiance to become Jim's clients, but in the weeks leading up to the party he gave autographed copies of my book to anyone who booked extra services during their scheduled appointments. Depending on the category of your title—a cookbook, a mystery, a romance, a sports biography—consider businesses with which you already have a relationship that draw your target demographic, and are also receptive to attracting newcomers.

The Freebies

Unless you are the cranky baby in Jimmy Fallon's Capital One commercials, you want to save money. So do your readers. Anything you can give them for free, and any advertising you can get for free, is worth a look.

"Nothing works like *free* for an unknown author," says Mary E. Twomey, author of the Saga of the Spheres series (Amazon Digital Services). "I had a five-day period in which I gave away Book One as a free ebook download. It's part of a four-part series that was released simultaneously. The free book ends in a cliffhanger, which leads the reader to download Book Two, and hopefully, finish the series. Cross-promotion is easier than you think. I put the first chapter of another author's series at the end of my Book Four; she's going to do the same for me. This will lead her fans to me, and mine to her. We both write cliffhangers in the same genre, so our fans would like the other's work."

Dayna Steele, author of *101 Ways to Rock Your World: Everyday Activities for Success Every Day* (iUniverse/Amazon Digital Services), recommends, "Give a free signed book or ebook to everyone in your network along with a note asking them to blog, review, post, share, tweet, or host a book signing. Word of mouth is a very powerful force. Though it will cost you up front, the PR you'll get is invaluable in terms of people subsequently buying it as a gift or recommending it to others."

Take inspiration from Kermit's whisper campaign in *The Muppets Take Manhattan*. To get his play into the bright lights of Broadway, Kermit and his pals start some chatter under the tables at Sardi's to make patrons think he is a famous producer. Recruit your friends to talk effusively about your work in settings conducive to eavesdropping—elevators, cabs and airplanes.

Attending a writers' conference? Bring freebie giveaways such as magnets, mugs, t-shirts, bumper stickers, pens and keychains. With vendors like Vista Print (www.vistaprint.com), these are relatively low cost for long-term remembrance.

Always remember your best free asset: You! Every time you blog, send an email, participate in a chat room, post a Facebook update, or talk about your book with a total stranger in a checkout line, you are engaging in a media moment and it is not costing

Post It or Give It

~ Is the first sentence of your book a grabber? Post it at TwitrLit (www.twitrlit.com) to tease buyers' curiosity. The site posts "literary teasers" with a link to Amazon.

~ If you are an ebook author and are offering titles for free as a way to build a future readership, check out:
- authormarketingclub.com
- www.freeebooksdaily.com
- bargainebookhunter.com
- digitalbooktoday.com
- www.pixelofink.com
- thefrugalereader.wufoo.com/forms/frugal-freebie-submissions
- GalleyCat on Facebook at www.facebook.com/galleycat/ app_4949752878.

you a dime. The energy and enthusiasm you bring to the moment makes you the functional equivalent of a walking sandwich board whenever you connect with the outside world. Make the most of it.

Build a Magazine Career

By Chris Eboch

Beginning writers often focus on trying to publish books. Many career writers who make their living from writing, however, do at least some nonfiction work for magazines. Nancy I. Sanders, author of *Yes! You Can Learn How to Write Children's Books, Get Them Published, and Build a Successful Writing Career* (E + E Publishing), describes the advantages of magazine writing: "There's an unending opportunity to get published and build your writing credentials, especially in the smaller magazines. There are countless topics to write about for each different magazine's focus, so it's easy to find one that matches your personal passion. And finally, there are a significant number of magazines that pay—and pay well."

"Realize that magazine writing [requires] two sets of skills," author Loretta Hall says. "One is the craft side—researching, interviewing, organizing, and writing interesting articles. The other is the business side—getting assignments, building relationships with editors and sources, and establishing yourself as an experienced, respected writer for certain types of readers. Developing both types of skills is essential for a successful career. Do that by reading books and magazines and by attending classes, workshops, and conferences in both the writing profession and in the subject areas you want to write about."

Marcia E. Lusted is an Assistant Editor and Staff Writer for ePals Publishing, which acquired Cricket Magazine Group and Cobblestone Publishing about a year ago. "My advice would be to really pay attention to what magazines' needs are, particularly if they are themed," she says. "We get so many good queries that just don't fit any of our upcoming themes and we can tell that the writer hasn't bothered to notice that we are themed! I don't think most writers realize that the marketing aspect of writing— figuring out what a magazine needs and matching ideas—take a great deal of time and effort."

Author, instructor, and freelance editor Bobi Martin's focus is writing for children. "If I come across a topic that intrigues me" she says, "I study the Writer's Institute's *Magazine Markets for Children's Writers* to find magazines that my idea might be a good fit with. Next, I check to see if the age range and word limits of the magazines I've targeted fit with what I had in mind for the article. When I don't have a topic in mind, I study the listings to see what magazine editors are looking for. When I have two or three magazines in mind, I visit their websites for their most current information. This is a great way to generate new topics to write about." For writers for adult markets, use the market directory *Best of the Magazine Markets 2013* and follow the same process as Martin. (Both directories can be found at www.writersbookstore. com.)

One big advantage to writing magazine nonfiction is that you can usually pitch an idea instead of submitting a completed article. Even if a magazine only accepts finished articles, you can suggest additional ideas in your cover letter. "When you submit a manu-script or query a magazine with your idea, it also helps to add a list of three to five ideas that might fit well into their particular magazine if your main topic doesn't fit their current needs," Sanders says. "I've landed more magazine writing assignments over the years by including a short list of other ideas in my query or cover letter for the editor to consider. Giving them the chance to choose another topic if they find merit in your writing helps avoid the constant stream of ambiguous rejections from editors saying, 'Doesn't suit our current needs.'"

Start Small & Focused

While new writers often aim for the best-known magazines, it is easier to break in at smaller specialty or regional publications. *Highlights for Children* may be found in homes, libraries, and doctor's offices across the country, but because it is so well known, the editors receive about 800 manuscript submissions every month. Meanwhile, the lesser-known classroom magazine *Current Health Kids* only receives one or two.

Magazines with a narrow and unusual focus may have a hard time getting enough material, so when they find a good writer they want to build a relationship, as Martin discovered. "When my daughter became interested in Junior Showmanship, a special class for young people at dog shows, I saw an opportunity to write an article for *Dog World Magazine*. I did my research and sold the article, happy just to have made a sale." Then the editor asked Martin to cover two dog shows tht year for the magazine, which led to doing related feature articles and eventually to six years of writing a regular column for junior handlers.

You will find thousands of these specialty magazines listed in market guides. Where to start?

Consider your own interests, talents, and experiences. Melody Groves, author of *Hoist a Cold One! Historic Bars of the Southwest* (University of New Mexico Press), says, "I love everything to do with the West." Because of this passion, she works regularly with Western magazines, and has been published in *True West, NM Magazine, abqARTS, Desert Exposure, Albuquerque,* and *Humps 'n Horns.* "Once a strong relationship is built with an editor, doors open for other opportunities," Groves says. "Editors talk to other editors. It's a good way to get recommended."

Hall optimizes her own specialties as well. "Although I occasionally write for general interest periodicals, my primary activity is

Moving to Books

Many writers dream of publishing books. A magazine career does not harm that dream, and might even help. "Magazine writing and book writing can have a useful symbiotic relationship," author Loretta Hall says, using her book *Underground Buildings: More than Meets the Eye* (Linden Publishing), as an example. "I found that the magazine work had helped me develop my skills at researching, interviewing, and writing. It also established my credentials and facilitated access to resources in the engineering and architecture communities. After the book was published, my status as an author added credibility to my queries to editors of magazines in those subject areas. And the articles I wrote increased my visibility with the book's target audiences."

contributing articles to trade publications. These are generally in the fields of civil engineering, construction, and sustainable building. Some companies publish several trade magazines, and writing for one of them can lead to requests to write for others within the same company." This is a narrow niche that includes publications such as *Concrete Décor* and *Traditional Masonry*. "There is less competition" with trade magazines, Hall says. "In fact, many trade editors want to find more writers. Identify an area of interest or expertise and develop relationships with editors at a couple of relevant publications. Produce good articles, on time."

Specializing helps you meet new clients. "One of the best ways I have found to develop new markets is to attend trade shows in my areas of specialty, engineering, construction, and space exploration," Hall says. "Publishers of related trade magazines have booths in the exhibit halls, and I introduce myself to them and offer my services."

"When possible, I visit with the editor," Groves says. "I'm a firm believer in conferences and conventions where you meet editors. You learn a lot in a five-minute chat over a cup of coffee."

Even if you cannot meet face-to-face, editors who see a handful of queries a month are more open to starting a dialogue than those at popular magazines seeing hundreds or thousands of submissions. "Another technique I use is to email the editor, explaining my interest and experience in writing about their subject area," Hall says. "Sometimes I pitch an article idea, and sometimes I just let them know I am available for assignments." That technique works best with editors who are not overwhelmed by submissions.

> ### "Many trade editors want to find more writers. Identify an area of interest and develop relationships with editors."

Freelance work can even lead to a full-time job. Rob Spiegel is a freelance writer and Senior Editor of the trade magazine *Design News*. "For 12 of the last 15 years I was a full-time freelancer," he says. "I typically worked regularly for 5 to 7 magazines. These relationships usually lasted 5 to 10 years. I freelanced for *Design News* for 10 years before they brought me on full-time."

If you still dream of being featured in a well-known magazine, specialty magazines can be a step in that direction, even if writing for them does not feel ideal. "You may find that you are happy with that not-so-glamorous but rewarding type of writing career as it grows," Hall says. "However, if you still aspire to write for high-profile consumer magazines, you can use your proven record as a successful writer in the trades to establish a foothold in the popular press."

Get in and Stay in

As these writers' stories show, the best way to build a magazine career is to cultivate long-term relationships with a few publications. Most editors are delighted to find writers who will take on regular assignments. "As an editor, I believe it is important to work with the same writers on a constant basis," says Susan M. Espinoza, Editor of *enchantment*, the magazine of the New Mexico Rural Electric Cooperative Association. "You get to know the writing style of the writer, and know what type of stories to assign the writer. A regular writer knows what *enchantment* is about, who the readers are, so he or she know what types of stories to pitch. Regular writers also understand your deadlines. We build a relationship over time."

"Editors want to work with a regular crew of freelancers. It saves them time. If you make the editor's job easier, you're in for years."

As both an editor and a writer, Spiegel understands the benefits of long-term publishing relationships, and a *stable* of writers. "Editors want to work with a regular crew of freelancers. It saves them time to work with writers who know how the magazine ticks. If you make the editor's job easier, you're in for years."

Although editors like to work with the same writers, they also constantly need new ones. "I believe in giving new writers an opportunity to write for our publication," says Espinoza. "It spices up the writing, and a new writer may have a new story idea we have never come across before." Just be prepared to work harder on that first job. "Research the publication ahead of time," she suggests. "What is the magazine's target audience and focus? As a new writer, establish a relationship with the editor. Meet the editor's deadlines. Don't hesitate to ask the editor for feedback."

After you make that first sale, the door is open a little wider. At the Cobblestone magazines, Lusted says, "If someone has written for us just once or twice, they generally follow the same query process as everyone else, although the editor will definitely look at them more favorably because they've already written for us. [The editor] might also be more willing to give some feedback on a query, or tweak it a little." As the relationship develops, it typically gets even easier to make a sale. For regular writers, "queries might be slightly less detailed, and they won't need to send a writing sample."

That can turn into steady work. At Cobblestone, some writers query for nearly every issue, and the editors may even ask these regulars to fill empty slots. "They know these people write well and will deliver a quality product on time," Lusted says, "and there aren't any unexpected nasty surprises when someone's actual article doesn't live up to their query. I can think of five or six writers for each of our magazines who are published in almost every issue, and some have even ended up doing regular departments. However, to get to this point, a writer has to be willing to write on any topic that the editor gives them."

Follow Your Passion

Whether you are just starting to build your magazine career or already have steady jobs, it's important to keep finding new markets. "Shifting editors can threaten your work," Spiegel warns. "It's easier to let a freelancer go than to fire an employee, so your work is not as secure." Keep cultivating relationships and looking for new areas where you can build expertise.

"Recently, I developed an interest in the history of space exploration and wrote a book about it," says Hall, author of *Out of this World: New Mexico's Contributions to Space Travel* (Rio Grande Books, 2011). "I am now writing magazine articles in that area as well."

Successful magazine writers agree that the most important quality you need is a passion for your topics. "Fall in love with your subject, and read everything on your subject," Spiegel says.

"If you're interested, truly interested, then it comes through," Groves says. "Writers spend a lot of time on a subject, so it should be something they like and are interested in. Then find a different way of looking at it."

"Write about topics that matter to you," Martin advises. "You can always research for more information, but if you don't care about your topic, that will show in your writing."

To build a magazine career, the path is clear: find your passion, explore a niche, target specialty magazines, and develop long-term relationships with editors.

Balance Life & Career

By Joanne Mattern

You have a brilliant idea for a story. Or you have finally gotten that coveted assignment from a magazine or book publisher. You cannot wait to sit down for a few hours of uninterrupted writing time to transfer your creative vision from your head to the computer screen. But first you need to drop off your kids at school and do the grocery shopping. Or check on your elderly parents before you head to work at your *real* job. Before you know it, another day has gone by and you have not written a word. "Tomorrow will be different," you vow. But it is not. Once again, you spend the day taking care of life at large, instead of devoting the time you want and need to your writing.

All writers have been there. Even one who does not have the responsibilities of children or other family members has a life outside of writing that needs time and attention. So how do you keep the home fires burning and still make time to write? We asked several published writers to share their stories and tips for making writing a priority while still having a fulfilling personal life.

Distractions? Let Me Count the Ways

A seemingly endless number of distractions can unnerve a writer. For many, the number one distraction is their children. Vijaya Bodach, author of *India* (Compass Media), and *How Do Toys Work?* (Macmillan) shares, "I began writing when I was pregnant with my second child (the first one was only one at the time), so writing always had to fit in between the cracks. The hardest part was when they were very young and dependent on me and I started getting assignments and being on deadline. I would happily say yes to the assignment, then look at the children and panic."

Complications continue as children grow. Yes, they are at school most of the day, but you are still needed to help with homework, ferry them to activities, and just be the loving, involved parent you want to be. As middle-grade novelist Marcia Hoehne points out, "Here's what happens when the kids get older: They play ball. They take ballet. They need a class mom, a team mom, a band mom. They need you for college applications, college visits, packing up and getting to college. Then there's graduating, moving, wedding planning, and *boom*, grandkids. Are you going to wait till they get older too? Because by now, your parents are older, your dog is older, your house is older, and you are older, and stuff starts falling apart. You have less control than you used to."

Many writers care for elderly parents or other relatives. Writers may also face their own health crises. Or they may work long hours at a steadily paying job. After a long day of handling real-life responsibilities, most of us are too tired to think about writing that novel or researching that article. And so another day goes by.

Taking Control

Writers do not have to neglect their families and let responsibilities slide to become successful. What they do need to do is take control of their schedules and their lives. That means making writing time a priority, just as you do with your personal life.

"I encourage writers to avoid the mindset that they will write 'when life settles down,'" Hoehne says. "Wherever you are in life, *carpe diem*!" That means carving out writing time every day and making that time as set in stone as the time you allot to running errands.

Many writers find schedules essential and block out a certain amount of time each day as writing time. Kelly Milner Halls, who published several nonfiction books and edited a YA anthology in 2012 alone, is very strict about her writing time. "I require myself to write every day, with very few exceptions. When I take a day off, I'm usually sick." Halls travels often for research and school visits, but she sticks to her writing schedule even when she is on the road. To meet her deadlines during several days away from home on a recent school visit, Halls wrote whenever she was not sleeping or speaking to children. "I did revisions until 1:00 AM, slept five hours, then did my first school visit. When I got back to my room, I did the next round of revisions that were waiting for me." Among Halls's books last year were *Tiger in Trouble!* (National Geographic Kids), and *Hatchlings: Life-Size Baby Dinosaurs* (Running Press).

Deanne Durrett, author of *Searching for My Destiny: George Blue Spruce Jr.* (University of Nebraska Press), is lucky enough to be able to write full time, but she faces distractions too. Her advice is to "keep the priorities in order. When setting a deadline, allow more time than you expect to need. I keep a very strict schedule when I'm on deadline. When I write on spec, I have a deadline of my own so I'm always working toward a deadline."

Taking control also means finding the time when you are most creative. For Christine Kohler, author of the ebook *Words Alive! Christian Writers' Skills and Prompts,* and *Music Performance: Vocals and Band* (Rosen Publishing), "My brain is freshest in the morning. Before I lived with my grandchildren, I worked from 9 or 10 AM to 2:30 PM. I'm hoping to go back to that schedule this fall when the baby starts school."

Hoehne is a writing instructor, and she also finds that keeping a schedule makes her writing life more productive. "Right now, I write and teach on alternate days," she explains. "I've also used mornings/early afternoons for writing and afternoons/evenings for teaching. But I'm not afraid to change it up for variety, or if I feel something else will work better."

Family First Doesn't Mean Writing Last!

Another part of taking control is making your family and friends understand that writing is your job, and a non-negotiable part of your life. Halls, who has raised two daughters as a single parent, made sure her family knew where everything stood. "Putting the family first was essential. My kids knew they were my number-one priority. But they also knew my work kept us fed and housed. I always described the three of us as a team, and my assignments as *our* assignments—my money as *our* money. When they felt invested, they felt more inclined to help me, even if that meant giving me quiet to meet a deadline or finish an interview."

Bodach also believes her children play a vital part in her ability to be a productive writer. "I try to do as many chores as I can with the kids. Not only do they learn how to cook, clean, and do basic maintenance, but it frees up time for writing. While they work on their independent art projects or homework, I can write." Bodach also limits her children to one sport or activity per season.

Having a supportive spouse makes the writing life easier. Bodach considers herself lucky because her husband has a flexible work schedule that has allowed him to share many of the family responsibilities. "He works a very early shift so that he could be at home with the children when they come home from school. Having him home means that he can help with homework, cooking, or driving them to practice, especially when I have deadlines to meet."

You can find creative ways to combine family and writing time. Kohler enjoys taking business trips with her husband. "While he is working or at a convention, I stay in the hotel room and write up to 10 hours a day. Usually he is gone for an entire week and I can move mountains on a new draft or revision." Kohler and her husband then get some precious alone time together after they have both fulfilled their work commitments for the day.

Most of all, do not neglect your family to get your writing

done. It might sound counterproductive to say you can write more by spending less time doing it, but all the writers we spoke to agree that family has to come first. Prolific author and blogger Kristi Holl says, "The best advice I ever got on this topic was in a workshop run by Dandi Daley Mackall, an extremely prolific [writer and] wife and mother. She said not to take your writing time away from the family, or you'll hurt them and have to deal with a lot of guilt. She said writing is what you want to do, so it needs to come out of your extra time: your TV viewing time or your lunches out with friends, your shopping, fun, surfing the Internet, whatever. So when my kids were little, I gave up reading and snacking during their nap time and wrote instead. I gave up TV at night, and I read books in the area where I wanted to be published. My children always knew they came before the writing. I was not a slave to my kids, but I didn't want to let their child-hood slip by because I was too busy trying to make it as a writer."

Balance Is Key

Holl's advice may mistakenly sound like writers need to forego their own needs. It is very common for people to put themselves last. Even though writers may need to carve writing time out of their own time, it is essential that they give themselves time to recharge their batteries.

Many writers turn to reading as a way to get rid of stress and stay motivated. "I make sure my pleasure reading stays pleasure reading," says Hoehne. "The love of reading is what got me into writing, and I figure it will do neither me nor my writing work any good if I lose that."

Bodach has found the best way to refresh her creative spirit is to take a day of rest. "My faith is very important, so going to Sunday Mass is non-negotiable. We also make it a day of rest and spend it in Bible study, bike riding, music, playing games, etc. The funny thing is that when you keep this the center of your life, everything else pretty much falls into place. To take a break from work on Sundays is not only refreshing, but necessary."

It is also important to take a break from sitting at the computer screen. Halls reports, "I'd say it's crucial to allow yourself little escapes. So if you're frustrated or blocked, taking the dog on a walk or grabbing an ice cream cone with your kids is not only recreational, it's helpful. I allow myself to walk away briefly, knowing when I get back, my answers will present themselves. It's like magic, how honoring balance in my life makes me more productive."

Balancing life and career is never easy. No matter what your situation and responsibilities are, there will always be times when you feel your writing time slipping away into the abyss. The key to being a productive writer and having a happy personal life comes down to priorities and balance. If you make writing a priority and put it ahead of other distractions in your life, you really might be able to have it all.

Keep Them Real

Legal & Personal Consequences of Using Living Models for Characters

By Mary E. Furlong

As part of our local bicentennial celebration in 1976, I wrote a historical play about the Village of Lewiston, New York. Patterned after Edgar Lee Masters's *The Spoon River Anthology,* my play included monologues delivered by actors portraying regional historical figures, some of them based on real people, some the products of my imagination. At a party following the final performance, one of the younger cast members reported that she had looked up all the characters in the play to discover which ones had made it into the history books. "Daisy Campbell was real," she said, referring to the part she herself had played.

"Oh, no, hon," I told her. "Daisy wasn't real. I made her up."

She shook her head. "Daisy was real," she insisted. "Daddy and I found her grave."

She and her father had indeed found Daisy Campbell's grave. It was off by itself in a wooded area a mile or so beyond the boundary line between Lewiston and neighboring Niagara Falls. The gravestone gave her age, 11; the cause of her death, a fever; and the year, 1821.

The similarities to the fictional Daisy were striking, but a quick review of the script revealed differences as well. My Daisy also died of a fever at around the same age, but the year was 1811. Her grave did not have a stone or a marker of any kind.

But what if the differences did not exist? What if I had somehow re-invented a real person? What if living members of Daisy's family objected to what they might term an invasion of privacy? What if they refused to believe that I had never heard of the real Daisy Campbell? There can be serious repercussions when a writer bases story characters on real people, or appears to have done so. Some of those repercussions have to do with the law. Others relate to personal relationships.

> # Misstated facts are not enough to support a defamation claim by a *real* character. Authors must be shown to intend harm.

The Legalities

When it comes to the law, the real Daisy Campbell does not present a problem. It is possible to invade the privacy or defame the character of a living person, but not a dead one. The outrage of surviving relatives carries no weight in court, unless of course the executor of an estate or memorial foundation were to object to my enriching myself at the expense of legitimate heirs or beneficiaries. Daisy was unlikely to have had an estate, and my enrichment was not of a material kind.

A living Daisy who thought she saw herself in a story character might sue, claiming that the publication had injured her by invading her privacy, by using her name and reputation for financial gain (the personal enrichment issue), or by defaming her character.

To recover damages in the U.S., however, Daisy would have to prove that her likeness to the story character would be obvious to most observers. Further, misstatement of the facts by a writer is not enough to support a charge of defamation. Daisy would have to show that the author intended to cause harm. Preserving the principle of free speech would more than likely trump Daisy's rights.

Despite these protections, there are legal and personal hazards in using real people in fictional settings and situations. Anyone who feels injured or taken advantage of is free to sue for compensation whether or not an objective observer would support the claims. Authors are not free to ignore such lawsuits. Nor, in most cases, can they prevent their publishers from settling even the most frivolous suits out of court and charging the costs to the author. Thus, it is always a good idea to double check your contract as to your responsibilities in such cases. In addition, if you have borrowed a personality who plays a negative role in your story, it would be wise to ask your own attorney or one of your publisher's legal staff to assay possible repercussions.

Compelling Personal Consequences

The personal consequences of using real people in fiction stories are often a more compelling deterrent than any legal considerations. What is regarded as an entertaining foible in a story character might turn out to be a serious embarrassment for the person portrayed. Your neighbor who wears argyle socks with her flip flops might not see the humor of your story character with a similar fashion sense. Your child's teacher probably sees herself as serious and concerned, not as Old Sourpuss Sullivan, who serves as the ongoing antagonist in your chapter book. Your teenage daughter may be mortified when her friends read about your spirited *discussions* regarding allowances and curfews and spending Sundays with the family. As youngsters grow up, they might change their tunes about what is okay with them, forgetting their previous little-kid enthusiasm for seeing themselves in a book.

Such was the case with Christopher Robin Milne, the real boy whose childhood was chronicled in *Winnie, the Pooh, The House at Pooh Corner, When We Were Very Young,* and *Now We Are Six.* As a toddler, Christopher took delight in being the central figure in his father, A. A. Milne's, famous stories and poems for children. But later, at boarding school, he came to loathe their sentimentality and subtle irony. Speaking of his father's poem "Vespers," the younger Milne said that the piece filled him with "toe-curling, fist-clenching, lip-biting embarrassment" whenever his schoolmates recited it or created parodies of it. He never found a way to cope with their relentless teasing. Even into adulthood, he felt cheated by his father's invasion into his childhood privacy, convinced that there was no benefit to him in being famous in this way. The discrepancy between the warm, paternal tone of the poems and stories and his father's emotional distance in real life caused a resentment that remained with Christopher Robin until late in A. A. Milne's life.

On the other hand, the use of real people in fiction stories can create singularly positive experiences. Author Jan Czech's daughter Carly was happy to be the protagonist in Czech's picture book, *Garden Angel* (Centering Corporation), the story of a child's way of coming to terms with the death of her grandfather. Carly is not mentioned by name in the book, but artist Susan Aitken chose to use her as a model for the illustrations. A middle-schooler at the time, Carly had the task of selecting the photographs Aitken would use as references, a way of allowing her to choose exactly how she would be portrayed. Czech believes that *Garden Angel* gave Carly a sense of closure about the loss of her grandfather.

Annie, a Korean-born child adopted by an American family, is the protagonist in *The Coffee Can Kid* (Child Welfare League Press), another of Czech's picture books. The story traces Annie's history from her birth in a Korean village to her present life with her adoptive family, who keeps treasured mementos of their daughter's experience in an empty coffee can. Despite several distinct fictional details in the book, it is clear that Annie's story is based upon Carly's. The book is a favorite of Carly's, who was delighted when one of her English teachers chose to use it as a teaching tool.

It is fairly easy to account for Carly and Christopher Robin's sharply contrasting reactions to the experience of being an identifiable character in a work of fiction. While the Christopher Robin poems and stories were meant to be read aloud to small children, many of them are clearly *about* children rather than for them. The poem "Vespers" is a prime example. Christopher

The use of real people in fiction can create singularly positive experiences —although Christopher Robin Milne might not have agreed.

Robin's innocence is the subject of humor in these stories, and while we may read them today and see no intentional harm in them, no one likes to be laughed at no matter how gently it is done. That the humor turned into ridicule from Christopher Robin's contemporaries suggests that adult condescension by father A. A. Milne was the experience of Christopher's generation as well.

In Czech's stories, however, children's ideas are taken seriously. In *Garden Angel*, Carly receives support for her belief that she can somehow communicate with her deceased grandfather. In *The Coffee Can Kid*, Annie's curiosity about her past is seen by her father as an opportunity to make her feel loved by both her birth mother and her adoptive family. A third Czech picture book, *An American Face* (Child Welfare League of America), also focuses on international adoption and features a boy who looks forward to looking like his adoptive parents when he becomes an American citizen. His hopes and fears are treated with sympathy, not derision. All three books stress acceptance of children's deepest emotions.

Six Degrees of Separation

No matter what the hazards, authors use real people as models for the characters in their fiction stories, even unconsciously. There is no other way to come up with characters that readers can believe in. But to establish the right kind of reality, and at the same time to protect themselves legally and personally, authors need to find ways to separate their story characters from their real life counterparts. Here are six ways to do it.

> ~ *Disclaim.* This is a strictly legal maneuver. A disclaimer at the beginning of a book may not protect the author completely, but it will be a legal starting point if a defense becomes necessary. The word *novel* may be inserted beneath the title, followed by some working similar to the following disclaimer: "This is a work of fiction. Any resemblance to real persons or events is entirely coincidental."
>
> ~ *Double up.* Turn two or more characters into a composite. In my book, *Real Dog, Super Dog* (Zane-Bloser Publishing), the protagonist's blind neighbor, who plays a brief but pivotal role, demonstrates the coping strategies of two real life blind friends of mine—humorous acceptance of inconveniences and imagination in the way one seeks help from others
>
> ~ *Distance yourself.* Some stories are not ready to be told. In time, thoughts of the unfair teacher, the crabby neighbor, the careless handyman will become annoying rather than enraging. Wait until that happens before you include them even as minor characters.
>
> ~ *Dialogue and dignify.* These are twin approaches that

go hand in hand. Czech advises authors to "be up front with the person" before the writing even begins, an excellent idea when stories are as personal as her picture books. Few people will take offense at characterizations that show respect for their real life personalities.

~ *Disguise.* Change the name, using different initials. Turn a child into a childlike adult, a blonde into a redhead, a boy into a girl. Describe a fanciful new setting, or turn an exotic one into Anytown, U.S.A. Give an only child siblings. Turn brothers into sisters, cousins into the kids next door. Annie's name and other changes in details in *The Coffee Can Kid* gave Carly the option of detaching herself from the story if she wanted to. Give your real life prototypes similar choices.

~ *Decompose.* Take your real life characters apart, figuratively, of course. Then, reassemble the parts into brand new characters, composed of this one's way of saying everything twice, that one's curly red hair, a third one's freckled nose, a fourth one's habit of humming under his breath, a fifth one's toe-tapping restlessness. A journal full of notes on the small everyday gestures of ordinary people will give you all the ideas you need for making your characters real, regardless of whether they are based upon real people.

It should be noted that very little of this applies to historical figures. They are in the same legal position as Daisy Campbell, so there is no need to disguise them or to fear their wrath. But so much is known about them that there is not much room for further character development. Their actions in your story have to be supported by the established facts. All things considered, the less famous your inspiration people are in real life, the more real they will seem in your fiction.

Bouncing Back from Rejection

By Veda Boyd Jones

A t our monthly writer's meeting at the public library, we celebrate first rejections. Many of our members are beginners, and a rejection means they are now part of the club—brave enough to put writing out there for some young whippersnapper editor to drive a truck over. The newbies take it fairly well when they publicly confess they have earned a rejection, but in private they may not deal with it as well. Neither do seasoned writers.

The writers in this article who share their rejection stories have published enough collectively to fill a small bookstore with adult and children's books, fiction and nonfiction, and fill the entire magazine section besides. Their stories are inspiring and show that successful writers are determined, but may also harbor hidden hostilities.

It Ain't for Us

~ **Lisa Collier Cool**, author of *How to Write Irresistible Query Letters* (Writer's Digest Books): "When my father was young, he once submitted a poem he'd written that had a cowboy/country theme to a literary magazine and received the following four-word rejection: 'It ain't for us.' He took it as a snarky critique."

Cool shares her own story: "I found what I considered to be a very touching true story of a little girl who was able to kiss her mother for the first time, at age eight, after successful treatment for a facial birth defect that previously made this impossible. After five magazines rejected the story, I got discouraged and probably would have given up, except that a colleague urged me to try more magazines, including *Parents*. As a result, I not only made the first of many sales to *Parents*, but the article subsequently won an award. I titled it, 'Ashlynn's First Kiss.'"

~ **Julie Catalano:** "My book, *The Women's Pharmacy: An Essential Guide to What Women Should Know About Prescription Drugs* (Random House/Dell) was rejected by every publisher my agent sent it to, and maybe even a few she didn't. I don't know—all I remember was getting the latest list of houses that did not want my book. It was beyond crushing, having to see in writing

"The moral of the story—besides that publishing is a lot like dating—is that rejection isn't forever."

how many people didn't want me. Then suddenly I got a phone call from [my agent] telling me she got a nibble from Random House, and I said 'Take it, take it, take it!' She said no, she was going to use it to leverage some other offers. I almost had a heart attack. The next phone call was that the book was now in a bidding war between Random House and another publisher who decided they wanted it if somebody else was after it. I recognized it as a house that had already rejected it—why now? She said, 'Because you suddenly got a lot more interesting.'

"The moral of the story—besides that publishing is a lot like dating—is that rejection isn't forever."

Nice Payback

~ **Caitlin Kelly**, author of *Malled: My Unintentional Career in Retail* (Portfolio/Penguin): "My pitch to *Woman's Day* for an essay about my divorce was rejected soundly by them. I sold it to *Elm Street* (now defunct) a national Canadian women's magazine; it won me the Canadian National Magazine Award for humor. Seems like a nice payback! In all seriousness, I think the only way to survive rejection, emotionally and financially, is to remember that it's only one person's opinion, not the [voice] of God saying, 'You stink, now and forevermore.'"

~ **Beth Levine** has written for many magazines, including *AARP Bulletin, More,* and *Woman's Day:* "I can't remember which magazine this was for, but I sent a pitch on marriage tips that was rejected as totally not appropriate for their audience, blah blah. A few *years* later, a new editor comes in, sees the pitch somehow and calls me and assigns it because it is so perfect for their audience."

~ **Susan J. Gordon**, author of the memoir *Because of Eva: Uncovering Secrets in My Family's Past*: "Years ago, I had an experience similar to Beth's. I submitted a humor piece about ways in which language can make you feel hungry to *Weight Watchers Magazine*. The articles editor didn't think it was funny, and said no. I put the piece aside, having tailored it to fit a *Weight Watchers* reader. About a year later, I perused the masthead, noticed that the naysaying editor had left, and resubmitted the very same piece. The new articles editor thought my piece was very funny and bought it right away. *Weight Watchers*'s rates had gone up, so I sold the piece for more money than I would have before.

"If there's a moral to my story, it's keep going, and don't quit. If your work is good, sooner or later you'll sell it!"

~ **Patti McCracken**, freelance journalist who has written for the *Wall Street Journal* and *Christian Science Monitor*, and teaches journalism at Webster University Vienna: "In 2005, an idea for an article was rejected by all U.S. papers and magazines I pitched (way more than a dozen). It was rejected by several U.K. publications, but accepted by the *Guardian*. I'm now at work on a book for Simon & Schuster based on the original historical true crime article."

Revenge!

~ **Sandy Asher**, author of *Writing It Right: How Successful Children's Authors Revise and Sell Their Stories* (Writer's Institute Books): "My antidote has always been *revenge!* In the early days, I used to lie down on the sofa and bemoan my fate: 'I can't write. I give up. I'm hopeless. I'll never get anything published.' Or a variation: 'I'll never get anything *else* published.' My husband and kids would wander by now and then and ask deeply sympathetic questions, such as, 'How long is this going to last (this time)?' and 'What's for dinner?' Eventually, self-pity would give way to daydreams of revenge. 'I'll show them. I'll revise this and get it published and it'll be so successful, they'll eat their hearts out that they didn't accept it when they had the chance!' The resulting adrenalin rush would get me off the sofa, get dinner on the table, and get the revision done and in the mail. Hopefulness restored! Until the next time. I no longer stretch out on the sofa in despair, and my kids are grown and gone. The journey toward revenge has all been internalized over the years, but it still works for me."

~ **Brenda Seabrooke**, author of *Wolf Pie* (Clarion): Seabrooke visited with a great aunt and learned about one of the aunt's childhood Christmases. "I wrote 'Christmas Day 1914' and sent it to *Redbook*. It was rejected. Seven more magazines rejected it. Meanwhile I was sending other stories to magazines. When one of those was [also] rejected by *Redbook*, the new fiction editor sent a note asking if I had published the Christmas story and if not, would I send it to her? Of course it went by return mail and was published in the December *Redbook*.

"Rejections have always made me work harder. I look at the manuscript as if it were clay and try to see how I can improve it, reshape it, polish it, change the tense, change person—first, second, or third—rewrite part or all of it, write a new ending, add a new character, lengthen or shorten it, or turn it into something else. Sometimes it takes years. One story about walking with my grandfather, 'Country Ways,' made it to the final cut at a literary review but was rejected. I rewrote it as a picture book, and it was published at Cobblehill as *Looking for Diamonds*."

~ **Vicki Cox** has written for *American Profile, New Pioneer,* and more): "I once had an assignment from an editor with specific instructions on what to provide. When I did, he wasn't satisfied and asked for a rewrite. I rewrote. Still not satisfied, he wrote me, 'Vicki, you may not be ready for the big time.'

"I wrote that sentence on an index card and taped it to my desk. Several children's biographies and untold number of published feature credits later, I use that card for inspiration. If I start to get down on myself, I just look to my right and read that card. It's enough to bring fire to my eyes and send me back to the computer—typing."

~ **Joan Carris**, author of *Aunt Morbelia and the Screaming Skulls* (Aladdin): "On rejections I speak with authority. *Welcome to the Bed and Biscuit* was turned down pretty much everywhere, and I have a good agent. At the time it was being submitted I'd written about 17 books, so I wasn't exactly a novice. But publishing is very trendy, in my opinion, and at the time my manuscript was circulating, no one really wanted animal fantasy.

"Finally, after about nine years, disgusted and ready to spend a long weekend crying, I asked my agent to send the manuscript to Candlewick Press. That really was the most logical place, because Candlewick understands fantasy and animals, so I should have hollered sooner. To end this tale of woe, I summarize with joy. The first book has had two sequels: *Wild Times at the Bed and Biscuit,* and *Magic at the Bed and Biscuit.*

"Overall, I think my story illustrates the fact that writers must do their homework. What house is publishing the books that *you* like to write? Submit to those houses."

~ **Ben Mikaelsen**, author of *Touching Spirit Bear* and *Ghost of Spirit Bear* (HarperCollins): "My favorite story about rejections comes from the last rejection I received before my first publication. At the time I had been working full time at writing for five years, belonging to two writer's groups, attending every workshop, conference, reading every book, and consumed each day with writing. At the time, I had written three full-length novels and received 126 rejections on those novels from either agents or editors. The last rejection I received was on the manuscript for my novel *Rescue Josh McGuire*. It came from a large publishing house and the editor tore [the book] to shreds saying it was much too long for a middle-grade novel because everybody knows kids won't read long books (this was six months before the first Harry Potter book), that the characters were shallow and two-dimensional, that the story wasn't realistic, that I changed points of view, and I was writing about something the average reader would have no interest in reading. She suggested I quit wasting her time and my time and take up a different vocation.

"That was my last rejection before having that identical manuscript picked up by Disney's Hyperion Press. With almost no changes, it went on to win the International Reading Association's Award, Western Writer's Golden Spur Award, the Nautilus award, many state readers' awards, starred reviews, as well as a handful of other recognitions. Incidentally, the publishing house that rejected it so viciously was the same house that later paid handsomely for the U.K. rights to that same novel.

"Point being: Rejections, the same as rave reviews, should be taken with a grain of salt. Believe in yourself and keep pushing forward. By definition, you have never failed until you quit."

A Welder, Not a Writer?

~ **Fred Minnick**, author of *Camera Boy: An Army Journalist's War in Iraq* (Hellgate Press): "Filled with fragments, run-on sentences, misspelled words, and dreadful grammar, my high school essay showed imagination with little structure or proper training. My English teacher held my essay in her cold hands. 'Fred, you

> **"Believe in yourself and keep pushing forward. By definition, you have never failed until you quit."**

should become a welder, not a writer,' she said. 'This isn't for you.' I was not devastated or defeated. I was pissed."

Minnick went on to sell articles to national magazines. His memoir of his time as a photojournalist in Iraq received countless rejections over several years. He never gave up. "I used every rejection as motivation." The memoir eventually sold to a small press, had a small print run, and was filed as an ebook. Amazon chose it as Kindle book of the day, and the next week, it was number ten on *Wall Street Journal*'s list of best-selling ebooks.

"There's only so much we writers can control in this business. We can choose to let agents' and editors' comments bring us down, or we can let them spur us on. I chose the latter."

~ **Lois Ruby**, author of *The Secret of Laurel Oaks* (Tor/Starscape) and the upcoming *Rebel Spirits*: "This was my first book, and I was unagented and green. I had no idea how long it might take to get responses from editors. After about a year of various rejections, I sent it to Dial. Months passed with no word. This was years before we could gently prod an editor with a jocular email message reminding him or her that here, in the hinterlands, there was a desperate author who hadn't been breathing normally for the past three months. So, I sent a real letter. I got word that the book was being read by a second editor. Thinking an offer would be forthcoming, I was already planning a lucrative future. More months passed. It went to a third editor. More months passed. Other letters were exchanged, without results.

"Finally, after 18 months of this nonsense, I demanded that the editor return the manuscript to me immediately so I could send it elsewhere. I realized I was biting my own foot, but I couldn't endure the agony one day longer. She phoned and made an offer! It was a modest offer, of course, but I was on my way. So, I assumed every subsequent book would be a breeze. Not so. Three decades have passed, and it still takes months and months to get responses, whether they're rejections or acceptances, but I'm grateful when each book meanders aimlessly through the maze and gets the nugget at the end."

Armor & Attitude

~ **A. LaFaye**, author of *Walking Home to Rosie Lee* (Cinco Puntos Press): "Whether it's being picked last for the team or being told your plot is too confusing to follow, rejection is always an arrow to the heart. And with such injuries, you can respond by donning armor and attitude. First, feel free to say *ouch*! Who wouldn't with a proverbial arrow sticking out of your chest? Once you've acknowledged the sting, arm yourself with the fact that any rejection is part opinion, part market analysis, and part literary response. It's your job to figure out how much of each is at the base of it.

"If the comments reflect a reader-based response like, 'I'm not that fond of . . . ,' then you can surmise that that portion of the rejection is personal [to the editor]. Some editors aren't fond of certain genres or even certain things. I had an editor reject a book of mine because one of the characters was elderly and she wasn't that fond of old people! If the editor talks about having a tough time selling marketing on the idea or calls it a 'quiet' book or mentions its lack of broad appeal, then you know the issue is marketing.

"On the other hand, if the editor critiques the craft—the development of the characters, the plot, etc., then you know the issue was the level of development. In response, find an editor who loves what you're writing based on other books he or she has worked on; seek a publisher who markets the type of book you're writing (different publishers have different target audiences); and hone the craft of your manuscript. It also helps to get a variety of opinions. Do you see a pattern in the types of responses editors are giving you? Then follow the pattern where it leads you.

"Above all, remember that what you are is a writer, it's a part of you—what you write is a product and when an editor critiques your work—it's not you that's being critiqued, it's just one thing you've written and that story may or may not merge into something new over its lifetime. You certainly have plenty more to say in the many stories you'll write over your lifetime, so don't take it personally. Publishing is part of the profession of being an author, writing is our passion. Focus on the passion and leave the book selling to the professionals."

~ **Stephen Morrill**, author of 1000+ articles: Morrill creates an on-paper marketing plan before he submits a query. With different slants, he targets five types of magazines, and within each type, he selects the top five magazines for each type and submits to the top one in each type. One reason for his marketing plan: "The ability to swiftly, with no thought, almost mechanically, send out another query is *very* important. When you get a rejection letter, you are going to feel like someone kicked you in the gut. You are going to want to quit the business. You are going to want to kill the editor. If you have been bragging to all your friends, you are going to want to kill yourself. You get over this, eventually. But in the meantime, it helps to go on autopilot and just send off more queries. And lo and behold, you already have a list ready."

~ **Cheryl Harness**, author of *Just for You to Know* (Harper-Collins): "Gee, rejection has gotten to feel like such a common-place affair. One more dull thud. It's part of the game, like what football players face when they're having their progress impeded down the field, just no concussions. Wahoo! And after all, how can rejection *not* be part of the game? Many are called, but few are chosen. One keeps sending in box tops, hoping to win the contest. All you can do is do your best to know the game and to get in the game, stay in it, and not let the disappointments defeat you, silence you. Kill you. And maybe there's a message to be gotten: You haven't told *the* story that you're meant to tell. And/or you haven't found *the* vehicle/soapbox/publisher by which you can tell it. Like true love, you only need one."

Your Readers = Your Customers

By Joanne Mattern

For most authors, writing is a passion. For many of us, writing is also a career—a business. But when was the last time you thought about customer service? While it is easy to remember customer service if you work in a bank, store, or a sales-oriented business, the benefits of good customer service are not as obvious when you are sitting at home writing a book or articles.

Writing may be a solitary profession, but writers have customers too: readers! Authors can apply some common customer service tips to improve their reach and service to readers (including writing quality), and boost their careers.

Know Who's Boss

At the entrance to Connecticut's Stew Leonard's grocery stores—"The World's Largest Dairy Store" and named one of *Fortune*'s 100 best companies to work for—is a large rock etched with the company policy: "1. The customer is always right. 2. If the customer is ever wrong, reread #1."

As a writer you often work independently, but you are not exactly your own boss. Every successful business owner knows that the ultimate boss is the person who buys your product or service. If you are a business owner, the customer pays your salary. If you are a writer, the reader determines whether you will succeed or fail and makes your career possible.

Of course, it can be tricky to know how to please your readers when they are not in front of you as you create your books or stories. Michelle Bisson, former Publisher of Marshall Cavendish eBooks, stresses that understanding your readers is key. "Make sure the book is relevant to them." For Marshall Cavendish that means a book "should be on grade level, interesting, to the point, and, if applicable, should contain some humor. Learn what your readers are interested in and tailor your books to them."

Mary Rodgers, Vice President and Editor in Chief of Lerner Publishing Group, agrees that learning what your readers want is extremely important. "Do your homework to choose topics wisely,"

Many authors visualize their readers as they are writing. They ask, "What would I like to know if I were reading a book or article on this subject?"

she says. "Don't write in a condescending way. Craft a good story that makes full use of the beauty and diversity of our language. Pay strong attention to pacing your story for maximum impact. Give a sense of time, place, and sensory experience."

A frequent contributor to parenting magazines such as *Mothering, Scouting,* and Seattle's *ParentMap,* Loralee Leavitt always has her readers in mind as she scouts for article ideas. "I think about what I need and what other parents might need. When I visit a tourist attraction, I note the questions I have or the things I need, or think of what another parents might need to know. Is this area stroller-friendly? Can parents bring snacks? Will my writing help families navigate this attraction?"

Many authors visualize their readers as they are writing.

Barbara Alpert, who has written articles for *Cosmopolitan* and *Hemispheres*, and books published by Penguin, Berkley, and Kensington, always asks herself, "'What would I like to know if I were reading a book or an article on this subject?' I want to offer a satisfying menu of possibilities to explore a topic. I also talk to friends and colleagues about my chosen subject to get a sense of what they would like to know about it."

Ana Maria Rodriguez co-wrote *The Iron Butterfly: Memoir of a Martial Arts Master* (Pelican Publishing), a Korean woman who is the highest-ranking woman in the martial arts of Kuk Sool Won. "When I wrote *The Iron Butterfly,* I had women in mind. Although the story has also appealed to men, I decided before I began writing that I would write it almost as if I was having a conversation with a group of middle-aged women who would understand personal and professional challenges as they get married and have children and grow old. I just thought I was telling the story to a friend."

Although the reader is the boss, several writers point out that the writer's needs remain important too. Chris Eboch, who also writes suspense and romance novels set in the Southwest as Kris Bock, notes, "During early drafts, writers should write for themselves. During revisions, you might start considering what readers like, and if you are targeting traditional publishers, what editors are hoping to buy. But focus too much on the reader in the early stages and your work might seem stale and derivative. You need to walk that fine line between meeting expectations and following your heart."

Viji Chary, who has written for several anthologies, including *Chicken Soup for the Soul: Food and Love,* agrees. "I focus on the writing, not the reader," she says. "I focus on the plot, conflict, story line, etc., to produce quality writing. I think that readers want the story to flow with action, excitement, and unexpected resolutions. Anytime the reader can feel the emotions of the story, a bond is created. As a writer, I need to convey emotion."

Anticipate Needs

Part of pleasing customers is understanding what they want and need. Customers may buy a product, but what they really want is good feelings and solutions to problems. Customer service experts know that most purchases are emotional rather than logical, and that includes book and magazine purchases. The better you know your customers, the easier it is to anticipate what they need and give them what they want.

One excellent way for writers to anticipate needs is to spend time with your audience. If you are a children's writer, spend time in the world of children—your own, nieces and nephews, or volunteer at a local school, playgroup, or after-school program. What are these children interested in? What makes their eyes light up with excitement? What problems are they facing? What do they care about or worry about? These insights are the keys to learning what stories will touch them as readers.

If you write for adults in a particular category, learn about their interests—writing for women's magazines targeted at thirtysomethings or fiftysomethings means finding out about what is relevant to women today living through those decades of their lives. If you write thrillers geared toward young men 25 to 40, what appeals to them? Of course, you must write the best story you can and be true to your own writing vision, but you are writing to an audience and you want them to buy and read your work.

Sue Ford, who writes for both adults and children, always "thinks about what my readers want, whether it be information in nonfiction or meaningful entertainment in fiction. I know in neither case do they want to be bored! When writing fiction, I think about what I enjoy when reading—sensory details, learning something new, a character I can identify with and root for, a logical procession of the plot, a satisfying ending."

Social media can give insights into readers' lives, especially in today's diverse world. Rodgers advises "mining the social media opportunities that kids use. Monitoring social media where kids and adults talk about what's of importance to them can be very helpful."

Writers can also understand audience needs by studying the marketplace. Peruse the shelves of your local bookstore or library and talk to the staff about what is selling. What books grab your attention and why? What market trends can you spot? "Talk to librarians," insists Stephanie Fitzgerald, an author who is also the owner and Editorial Director of Spooky Cheetah Press, a book producer. "Librarians know what the kids need to learn about, perhaps write reports about, and whether sources exist. They also know what kids are looking for when they browse the shelves."

While following the crowd is never a good way to provide the best customer service, understanding what is popular and why can be the key to discovering what your audience needs and wants. Tamara L. Britton, Nonfiction Editorial Director at Abdo Publishing Company, agrees that knowing the market is very important. "Follow trends and keep hip on your reader's culture. Know what your audience is into and what they want to know more about," she advises. At Abdo, this is especially true for non-fiction writers, who must stay in touch with the needs of the school and library market. "If curriculum support is your genre, then read trade journals and follow curriculum changes."

The same is true when writing for adults. "I look at what's out there for readers now and try to anticipate what might be the next step in the subject matter or way of presenting," says author Nancy Sweetland, who writes for children and also writes adult mysteries and romance.

Understanding what your audience wants is especially important in genre fiction. Deanne Durrett, who writes Christian fiction, knows that her readers "are looking for an entertaining story with main characters who share their values. I think my readers want to identify with my characters, see them struggle as they would, and find acceptable solutions based on their faith. They don't want a sermon—they go to church for that!" Marcia

Hoehne, who writes regularly for the adult devotional magazine *Pathways to God,* agrees. "I don't teach readers as much as relate to them. I am asked not to explain the Bible passage to readers, but to give an example of how the principle in the passages works or is evidenced in everyday life."

Give More Than Expected

Customers love to get extras, whether it is a free product, an upgrade, or personal attention that goes above and beyond a standard business interaction. As writers, we must also be aware of ways to give our readers more than they expected.

Caring about your topic or story line is a vital part of being a good writer and creating a powerful product. While it might be tempting, even smart, to follow a trend, do not be a copycat. An original idea, approach, style, or voice is always the strongest and the best. "Write about what matters most to you," says Bisson. "If you deeply care about something, and invest the time to research and understand it thoroughly, your readers are most likely to care about it too."

"Write with care," says Rodgers. "Don't rush your work. Be part of a critique group whose honest feedback can help you improve your work." This attention to your craft will pay off in richer, better writing that will give readers more than just an average book or magazine article.

Britton believes that a successful book "must exceed its competition. It must have the best writing, the best illustrations, the best presentation, and its content must fit an unserved niche in the market."

Customers want to feel respected, and readers are no different. Britton urges authors to write "lively prose that is not condescending, but respectful of the reader's intelligence." Rodgers encourages authors to be genuine. Adults and "kids can smell a false voice a mile away."

"Make sure your writing is about them, not about you," says

Hoehne. "Most professional writing is about the writer being of service to the reader. If we can convey that it's about them, not about us, I think that more than meets their expectations. Rather than 'What do I want to say or teach?' ask yourself 'What do my readers want or need that I can provide or help them find?' I have found that newer writers, especially, can make a big leap forward in their writing if and when they understand that professional writing isn't primarily about getting their voice heard. It's about considering what will best serve the reader."

"Newer writers can make a big leap forward when they understand that writing isn't primarily about getting their voice heard. It's about what will best serve the reader."

Be Prepared

The old Boy Scout motto "be prepared" is great advice for anyone who is running a business—or writing. If someone started a business selling products without researching the market, odds for success would be low. Similarly, someone who markets an inferior product that does not work as promised or make customers happy is doomed to fail.

Writers deliver a quality product by knowing their subject and conveying it to readers with the highest quality in information or story, and style. For nonfiction subjects and writing quality, Britton says, "Writers should have education and experience or have researched extensively in the subject matter they wish to write about." Getting the details of a time period and setting are essential for fiction authors too.

Lori Shein is the Managing Editor at nonfiction publisher ReferencePoint Press. She believes research and careful writing are essential to success. "Write well," she says. "Create a strong narrative and use primary sources and anecdotes or examples wherever possible to illustrate and support main ideas. Provide context so that readers understand important events and ideas."

"Pay attention to your audience," says Bisson. For Marshall Cavendish books, "Don't make references to things kids don't understand, particularly historical references, or use language from another era when they are writing a book set in the present, for example."

Alpert found "be prepared" very good advice when cowriting cookbooks with JoAnna M. Lund. "Lund was a woman who believed wholeheartedly in delivering more than expected—more flavor than a healthy recipe typically had," for example. "So I keep that in mind when I write: How can I give more than an easy Google search? I interview knowledgeable experts when appropriate, visit museums and other sites if useful, and seek out whatever primary source information and experience I can. I believe that this extra effort makes a measurable different in the final product and in the reader's experience of my book or article."

Get Feedback—Good and Bad

Understanding what your readers want and need does not stop once you have written your manuscript. Your customers can also provide important feedback about your story. Bisson advises children's writers to "run your manuscripts by young readers you know before submitting them for publication."

Readers can be an important source of feedback even after your book is published. While you cannot be with your readers as they read the book, keeping in touch with them is an easy, eye-opening, and entertaining way to find out what they thought about your book and why. Set up a Facebook page and a Twitter account and encourage your readers to follow you and comment on your work. Create a reader feedback page on your website and ask readers to submit comments, thoughts, and criticism.

Online sites such as Amazon and Goodreads also allow reader comments and feedback. Just keep in mind that many authors find Amazon and Goodreads commenters to be overly negative, so you might want to take harsh remarks from these sources with a grain of salt.

The personal touch is still important, even in today's fast-paced digital age. Make appearances at bookstores, organizations or relevant to your writing (museums, historical sites, small businesses, associations), schools and libraries.

In the long run, we are in the market of selling a product. While a book might not be the same as a plastic widget or a can of soup, it is still a product that needs to meet the needs of its audience.

In the long run, we are all in the market of selling a product to customers. While a book might not be the same as a plastic widget or a can of soup, it is still a product that needs to meet the needs of its audience. As authors, we need to promote ourselves and our products, understand our customers, and work hard to keep those customers happy. In the long run, you will produce a better book or story, and your readers will be able to enter the world you have created. If we succeed at keeping our customers happy, everybody wins.

Maximize Your Writing Productivity

By Leslie J. Wyatt

Unlike many professions, freelance writing has no crisply defined boundaries. For most of us, our schedule is our own, with no office expecting us to appear and spend a clearly allotted amount of time. If we want to rise at 10 AM and type in our PJs while sipping a bottomless cup of coffee, or stay up until the wee hours churning out our next novel, we can do that. Our time is our own. We get to create in the anonymity of our own environment, far from the tyranny of time clocks and rush hour traffic.

Yet this very freedom—the privilege of ordering our own day—can be one of our greatest challenges. Indeed, time—that "illimitable, silent, never-resting thing . . . rolling, rushing on, swift, silent, like an all-embracing ocean-tide," as Thomas Carlyle wrote —can swallow us up. If we are not intentional in our writing, we find ourselves at the end of the day with disappointingly few words committed to paper. We must find and use techniques to enhance our output.

Ever Increasing

One of the primary ways writers can boost their productivity is by setting goals. At first glance, this may seem to rob the concept of *free* from the word *freedom*. Without a firm and realistic picture of what we plan to accomplish, however, we may circle around

Time-Saving Tips

~ Set goals, short and long-term:
- word counts per day or week
- projects or chapters completed per month
- queries or manuscripts sent out per week or month
- earnings per month, per year

~ Review how you divide and schedule your writing tasks:
- the writing itself, and the various porjects you are working on
- research and idea generation
- career considerations: finances, promotion, etc.

~ Determine your most productive work times, each day, and throughout the year. One highly successful author, Sneed B. Collard III, divides the year into writing seasons and marketing seasons.

~ Be willing to change your goals and schedule to adjust to changes in your life and work. Author Emily McIntyre calls this *recalibration*.

and around like a piece of driftwood caught in an eddy. Christina Katz, a.k.a. the Writer Mama (christinakatz.com), is a national speaker, instructor, and author. She advises, "Create a vision of what ongoing success would look like for you, and then go for that. Don't dwell on or pursue other people's glory."

Kansas City-based freelancer Emily McIntyre, whose work appears in such publications as *Missouri Life, Rails to Trails,* and *KC Parent,* agrees. "You don't have to please or imitate anyone else when it comes to any aspect of your writing career. You can decide where you want to go and the steps you must take to get there. . . . If you fall short, you disappoint no one but yourself, which means that you have the right and privilege of adjusting your expectations when you need to."

A per-day or per-week word-count goal works well for some writers. Sneed Collard III, author of more than 60 acclaimed books for young people, including *Lizards* (Charlesbridge), and the middle-grade novel *Double Eagle* (Peachtree), says, "I feel productive if I complete at least one good chapter in a novel. Sometimes, I can do more than that, but a chapter a day is satisfactory progress."

Others want or need to earn a minimum amount per month. When asked about the single most important productivity booster, Collard states, "Bills!" and Jody Feldman, journalist, speaker, and author of *The Seventh Level*, and *The Gollywhopper Games* (both from Greenwillow), says: "Quite simply, treating it like a job."

Rather than targeting word count or income, some writers aim for spending a certain amount of time on separate aspects of their freelance load—perhaps querying a new publication, making progress on a favorite fiction project, or putting X number of manuscripts in the mailbox each week. These are not absolute rules, but rather motivation for working on idea generation and productivity.

"I consider my writing to be three-phased: my novel, nonfiction, and short stories," says McIntyre. Endeavoring now to adjust her expectations while meeting the demands of being a stay-at-home mom with a newborn, she says, "If I am able to pay significant attention to two out of three of these [categories], I consider that a productive day."

What works for one person may not work for another. And we may each need to shake things up once in a while. What works for us today may not work next winter or even next week. We change, and what it takes to keep us writing at peak levels may very well change too. So tap into your own rhythm. Are you most creative in the morning, afternoon, or at midnight? Schedule your writing tasks to maximize your window of productive potential.

Deadlines can be a powerful motivation. Katz says, "Without deadlines I am essentially lost. By having deadlines and meeting them, I have learned the basic rhythms of successful writing for publication." She continues, "At some point I started putting deadlines into effect in every area of my career. Anywhere I am successful today, whether it's as a teacher, coach, speaker, author, or journalist, you can be sure it's because somewhere out there is a deadline with my name on it."

Productivity Pirates

Since freelance writing is by nature self-directed, it comes with its own unique set of challenges. Goals, deadlines, and a business-like approach can set us up for success, and we must be wary of time-eroding possibilities. Perhaps the biggest one is procrastination in its various guises. One of the worst is the Internet. "I wish I could be more original here, but the universal truth is the Internet is a veritable time vacuum," Feldman says. Collard agrees: "Do not get distracted by Facebook, the Internet, phone calls, etc. This is not productive time. To paraphrase Stephen King, you've got to sit your butt in the chair and turn off all outside distractions. Do not start the day by checking out Facebook. Reward yourself at the end of the day, after you have completed your hard work."

The key is self-regulation. Although Feldman once had a mantra of *none before noon*, referring to email, she says, "I don't fight it anymore. I will check my email when I first turn on my computer." She scans those messages that may be too interesting or important to wait, and holds the rest in reserve for the afternoon when productivity naturally wanes for her.

Internet activities, games on your smartphone, or *Downton Abbey* are not the only time pirates. Other people can undermine writing productivity. Yes, even those we love. They do not always understand that writing is serious business. Once people realize that we are at home (albeit working), we are often fair game for whatever they need at the moment. It is up to us to communicate that writing is our job. Feldman says she has had to help people understand that she is serious about her work. "I don't do lunch. I don't sit all day eating bonbons and watching soap operas. Yes, I am in my house. Yes, I set my own hours. But no, I am not bored and am not waiting for the phone to ring."

About that: Let your answering machine or voice mail screen phone calls. If people do not leave a message, they must not need you very badly, and if they do leave one, you can determine at your leisure whether, when, and how you want to respond. Katz says, "I get a steady stream of unrequested time inquiries. If I were not selective and discerning with unsolicited time requests, I would never be able to meet any of my paying deadlines. So I've learned how to say no and how to say it regularly."

Internet activities, games on your smartphone, or *Downton Abbey* are not the only time pirates. People, yes, even those we love, can undermine productivity.

Besides the Internet, people, and phone calls, countless other time-frittering occupations abound. Take household tasks. It can be mighty tempting to trade a particularly stubborn chapter or plot point for the instant success of folding a load of laundry, sweeping a floor, or waxing the car.

To counteract procrastination, McIntyre sets small writing goals and forces herself to complete them even if working feels futile. "Often I find upon reviewing my work that it wasn't that bad, and it gets me out of the funk I was feeling," she says. "A thousand words on my book, for example, or spending just 15 minutes plotting a short story, or locating one expert for an article" are ways to boost both confidence and productivity.

"It used to be when I hit rough spots," says Feldman, "I would often decide that I desperately needed to dust under my bed or rotate my hangers or run to every supermarket until I found something as essential as kumquats. Funny thing, the problem areas wouldn't disappear. So now I have an unwritten rule to face them head on, get something down in print that might work. Then, when I hit a natural stopping point or have accomplished some mini-goal, I can take that break."

Even writing-related activities such as research and marketing can be counterproductive if they take us away from keyboard or pen for extended periods of time. The most necessary of these must inevitably yield to the act of writing itself. Collard divides his year into *marketing seasons* (fall and spring), during which he is on the road speaking much of the time, and *writing seasons* (winter and summer), during which he tackles and finishes projects.

Customize

Solid goals, specific deadlines, and a big dose of self-discipline go far toward boosting writing productivity. But like some New Year's resolutions, goals that do not fit your individual personality and vision or that impose too many limits, may fade away—or even sabotage your levels of production.

"Taking time to re-evaluate every once in a while has greatly boosted my productivity as a writer. I call these times *recalibrations* and use them to assess my goals and the daily efforts I'm making toward them," McIntyre says. "Every once in a while I find that I'm lacking motivation and not really accomplishing anything in my work. These times usually coincide with changes in my personal life—moving, having a baby, starting a new job, beginning school." If not under a deadline, McIntyre gives herself a break, then as she feels motivation returning she will sit down and harness it, making new weekly goals and starting a new to-do list. This allows her to plunge back into writing renewed and rejuvenated.

Katz explains about her own ways of working, "I'm very right-brained and because of this it might be easy to be scattered.

What helps is viewing my job as providing services for people rather than seeing myself as a content-generating machine." This viewpoint enables her to focus on her readers rather than on efficiency, which she finds boring. "Committing to the ongoing, steady evolution of my ideas takes more time and effort, but has paid off in the long run, since I am a niche writer."

When asked regarding elements that have been important in boosting his writing productivity, Collard replies, "Having wide-ranging interests helps create an endless supply of projects I am eager to work on." He advises writers to give themselves plenty of raw materials to spark interest and keep themselves motivated.

It may appear counter-intuitive at first glance, but spending too much time at the keyboard can hinder production. Turning back to writing after an intense session of other activities can help recharge your energy. Try walking or biking. Read. Spend a bit of time in a flower bed or hanging out with friends or your favorite animal. Feldman shares that when she comes to a natural pause in her writing she will allow a short, specific time for checking social sites. "Like a corporate coffee break," she quips. "Five minutes, 10, depending on the workload. It's enough to satisfy my curiosity, and it works to let me refresh and hit my story with a little more energy."

For optimal productivity, strive for balance. Collard advises fellow writers to "take time to go out and explore new things, read a lot of nonfiction books, and take notes about everyday life. All of these give you the raw material to write, and when you get enough of it, well, you just can't help yourself. You've got to sit down and let it out by creating a new literary masterpiece!"

"Work hard, but not too hard," says Feldman. "Find things you love and live them. They'll not only give you a release, they'll enrich your life and inform your writing." As McIntyre puts it, "Look inward, not outward, for direction, and you will find your writing journey to be deeply satisfying."

Author Blogs

Why, What, When, & How to Use Them to Sell Your Writing

By Suzanne Lieurance

Authors today need to do more than write books, articles, or stories if they are to succeed in their chosen career. They also need to promote or market what they write. A website is one way to do this. An arguably more effective marketing tool is an author blog. A website tends to be static, often updated only every few months or so. A blog is updated regularly (sometimes daily), so it offers a more immediate and personal connection between author and readers.

Why Blog

Audrey Macks Mitnick, Senior Publicist for Sleeping Bear Press, says, "Blogs are a great PR tool for authors. Once an author engages an audience through their purchase of a book, maintaining contact through a blog is a cost-effective way to nurture and grow that audience. Friends (in both the traditional and virtual sense) share with their friends."

An author blog can also develop a ready-made market even before a writer has a published book or articles. For that reason it is never too early for a writer to create a blog. "Blogging is a great way to create buzz for an upcoming book," says Faye Levow, author and President of Launch Pad Publishing, which provides publishing services to readers. "Through an author blog you can share your thoughts and ideas as you write your book, share

Free Blog Resources

Blog Platforms

~ **Blogspot platform:** www.blogger.com. Google's blog platform includes customizable templates and layouts.

~ **Wordpress:** www.wordpress.com. Includes templates and themes to choose from, and wide plug-in choices. See http://wordpress.org/extend/plugins/social-media-widget to add links to all of your social media and sharing site profiles.

Other Resources

~ **My Live Signature:** www.mylivesignature.com. This site allows you to create electronic signatures and custom logos.

~ **PRLOG:** www.prlog.org. A free press release distribution service.

~ **StatCounter:** www.statcounter.com. Track the traffic to your blog to see how many visitors you are getting, where they are coming from, and what they are coming to see on your blog (the most popular posts, etc.).

~ **Stock.xchng:** www.sxc.hu. Free stock photos. The site is owned by Getty Images.

~ **SurveyMonkey:** www.surveymonkey.com. Create a free survey on your blog to find out what your visitors want.

chapters and get feedback, and generally let people know what you're up to. You'll be attracting the niche audience for your book even before your book is published."

Generally, feedback is obtained on a blog in the form of comments left in response to posts. But authors can create surveys and questionnaires on the blog for this purpose, too. Many best-selling authors do not allow comments on their blogs because they do not have the time to respond to them. Other authors welcome and encourage this interaction with their readers.

Blogging can also lead to opportunities for author visits and other speaking gigs that can bring in additional income as well as increased sales. Children's author Kelly Milner Halls speaks frequently at writers' conferences. Every year she also makes author visits to schools across the country. When she speaks at a conference or visits a school, she posts photos of these events on her blog, along with short articles that give her readers an inside look at her presentations. These posts position Halls as an in-demand expert in her field, making her attractive to conference organizers, school principals, and librarians who might visit her blog looking for a speaker.

Doreen Pendgracs is a Canadian author who writes nonfiction. She started her blog more than three years ago, "right after returning home from a writers' conference where the keynote speaker insisted that each of us absolutely had to have a blog in today's world. Creating my blog was one of the best things I've ever done," she says. Nowadays, Pendgracs uses that blog to position herself as an expert speaker as well as an author in much the same way Halls does. When Pendgracs attends or speaks at a writer's conference, she blogs about it and includes photos of the event, thereby showing how involved she is in the publishing industry. Her posts often receive 30 to 40 comments, which she responds to, making it a highly interactive site. "To me, reading and replying to readers' comments is as important as creating new content."

What to Blog About

Even with so many good reasons to blog, many authors are hesitant to get started because they do not know what to blog about or they are afraid they will not have enough ideas to keep blogging on a regular basis for very long. That does not have to be a problem.

"Authors can blog about anything they love," says Mitnick. "Hopefully, the list begins with their book(s), the writing process, interviews with other people involved in the book (the illustrator, editor, publisher, etc.), and experiences (both humorous and challenging) they had along their journey to publication."

"Write about your books, your characters, your subject matter," says Levow. "Even if you're a private person, you can throw in some facts about when you write, where you come up with your ideas, random interests, or other things that might be engaging to your particular audience."

One author who does this successfully is mystery and suspense writer Billie A. Williams. She is the author of several dozen mysteries, so it is easy for her to come up with topics to blog about. "I'm blogging about each of my books in alphabetical, not chronological, order right now," she says. "Having the alphabet as a prompt triggers my muse. I don't have to search for topics. I already know what the books are about and what might interest my blog readers, so it's fairly simple, quick, and straightforward."

"I blog about whatever I want to promote—my new book, a review, or an upcoming event," says children's author Margot Finke. "I might blog about something similar for writing friends, or something I find online and think readers will giggle over, enjoy, or find interesting."

Halls finds that photos are often how she gets ideas for her blog posts. "When I get photos that capture a moment," she says, "that's usually my inspiration for starting a blog post. And I take my camera with me everywhere I go. Images from my daily life spark my blogs, almost always."

How to Attract Readers

No matter how great an author blog might be, it will not be of much use unless plenty of people visit it. That means authors must constantly drive traffic to their blogs.

Dianne de Las Casas is a professional storyteller and author. She has a website and a blog and receives as many as 10 million visitors, combined, to her sites each year. She is also active on Facebook (with more than 3,000 friends, and 1,250 fans) and Twitter (more than 5,500 followers)."I cross-post to Twitter and Facebook when I have a new blog post," she says. "I also include links to blog posts in my monthly email newsletter, which goes out to over 10,000 subscribers." She adds, "There are lots of great tools available that make blogging easy. I blog straight from my iPhone using the WordPress app and even include photos I take with my phone."

Like de Las Casas, many authors use social media to drive traffic to their blogs, but that is just one way to increase the number of visitors. Personal email invitations may seem outdated, but they can still be effective. "Periodically, I personally invite all my editors and publishing contacts to stop by my blog for a special event," says children's author Nancy I. Sanders. "I always see an increase in visitors when I do this."

Media releases can also be created and submitted to free online distribution services whenever an author has something special on a blog, like an interview or excerpts from a new book. These releases also create new incoming links to the author's blog, thereby helping the site improve its ranking on Google and other search engines. Williams finds that "having a link to my blog in my email signature is probably the biggest traffic generator. I also use it as a signature in my Facebook and Twitter posts. Whenever I do anything, I include the link. When I send out invoices, bill payments, or even greeting cards (which I always snail mail so I can include bookmarks and/or business cards) I add the blog link to them."

Contests and giveaways can also be used to generate interest in an author's blog and thereby increase the traffic. Halls regularly gives away gift bags and other fun items related to her new books. "I gave away dinosaur egg replicas to celebrate the release of *Hatchlings* (Running Press). Giveaways are great fun!"

Sanders enjoys hosting giveaways too. "I always get a bunch of new people who stop by my blog when I have a contest or give-away, so this definitely builds networking and sometimes helps sales, too." But, she cautions, "I don't ever like to give away a free copy of my book because then I think people wait to see if they won the contest instead of buying it." Instead she offers freebies that are directly of interest to her target audience. "For example, I like to give away manuscript critiques when I'm targeting other writers. I like to give away autographed bookmarks or theme-related calendars when I'm targeting teachers or other educators."

Once visitors make it to an author's blog, the next challenge is to keep them there long enough so they read the posts and other content. "I *always* post pictures in my blog posts," says de Las Casas. "People are visual and pictures make the reading experience more visceral and immediate."

Mitnick recommends, "Artwork and photos are important additions to any blog. Photos and excerpts of works in progress are a great way to pre-premote. Related photos sent by readers (finding the book on the shelf in a bookstore, checking it out at the library, trying a recipe found in the book, reading at the beach) are a fun way to brighten the blog format and engage the audience. Photos of author family experiences, book tours, and interests outside of the publishing world are all of interest to readers."

Finke agrees. "The old adage, 'A picture is worth a thousand words,' still rocks! I always add book covers, art work, pictures, or even clip art that fits a particular theme and might get a giggle."

Pendgracs includes photos with most of her blog posts for two reasons. "First, I'm a visual person, and I think many people like posts with images. Second, I'm on Pinterest, and people can *pin* my posts if there is an image in the post."

Knowing what to blog about and how to drive traffic to an attractive blog is still only part of the blogging process. Authors also need to make a commitment to blogging at least somewhat regularly.

When to Blog

Many authors blog on a daily basis, much like keeping a diary. Other authors post a once-a-week update. It really does not matter

Author Blogs to Visit

- Dianne de Las Casas: www.storyconnection.net.blog
- Margot Finke: www.margotfinke.com
- Kelly Milner Halls: www.wondersofweird.blogspot.com
- Doreen Pendgracs: http://doreenpendgracs.com/
- Nancy I. Sanders: www.nancyisanders.wordpress.com
- Billie A. Williams: www.billieawilliams.com

how often an author blogs as long as posts are made somewhat regularly. The real trick for authors is make sure they do not get so involved with blogging that it becomes the only writing they do.

With more than 80 published books to her credit, obviously Sanders spends most of her writing time writing books, not blogging. She warns, "Many wannabe authors spend so much energy building a blog and keeping up with social networking that they never earn a solid income as writers. Then they quit trying and stop writing altogether. If they used all that energy first to focus on writing to earn money, get published, and meet their personal writing goals, then they could spend much less time blogging yet have bigger and better results."

More Success Tips

Overall, knowing what you have to give, and your audience's interests make up the necessary foundation for a blog. "Great content and consistency is key to a successful author blog," says de Las Casas. "Give readers value and give it on a regular basis. Your readers will become your lifelong fans."

Finke suggests "fun, freebies, and great content. Know your audience and cater to it."

"Having a wide range of subjects and truly engaging with your audience" are key, says Pendgracs. "Blogs are not meant to be one-way communication!"

"Be aware of your target audience's interests," advises Sanders. "For example, I have a board on Pinterest where I pin blogs that have huge numbers of visitors. I study these blogs and ask myself why so many people love coming to these blogs and commenting on them. Then I ask myself what I can do in the days and weeks ahead to meet my current target audience's interests better and provide them with something they really want. I experiment with things and offer different stuff to my readers (helpful links or theme-related interviews, for example). I observe the reactions and see which types of posts produce more comments or page views or get more first-time visitors than other posts. Then I try to put more of these posts on my blog to give my audience more of what they want."

"A great blog is more than what an author did or where he went," Mitnick explains. "A blog engages the audience. Whether by introducing readers to authors and books with whom they may not be familiar, or by providing additional details from research that didn't make it into a recent release, or by sharing a meaningful quote or a family moment, a blog should be a personal commentary that entertains and even possibly, educates the reading audience."

Software for Writers

By Mark Haverstock

G one are the days when authors could submit handwritten or typed manuscripts. Those of you who remember the television series *Murder She Wrote*, which ran from 1984 to 1996, recall that mystery writer Jessica Fletcher started on a vintage Royal typewriter, but eventually upgraded to an Intel 386-based PC word processor to keep up with the ever-changing publishing industry.

Today, most of us cannot imagine starting a writing project without the aid of a computer. Basic word-processing applications are the staple of writing these days, but there are dozens of other software packages that can make life easier for writers. Whatever you want to do, someone has developed a software package to accomplish. The software can help you plan and structure a novel, share documents online with other people, format your screenplay or script correctly, minimize writing distractions, improve your English, organize your research, and more.

If that is not enough, there are now hundreds of apps for your smartphone and tablet computers. These portable tools help with everything from organization to field research.

Modern Word Processing

The word processor was the first tool that writers embraced in the computer age. Who was first to produce a novel with this new technology? No one knows for sure, but Matthew Kirschen-baum, Associate Professor in the Department of English at the University of Maryland and expert on the early days of fiction writing on word processors, believes Jerry Pournelle, Stuart Woods, and Stephen King are among the contenders.

Word processing has come a long way from the early, cryptic key combinations to today's user-friendly graphic interfaces—and more features than most people will ever use.

~ *Microsoft Word* (Microsoft. PC/Mac. www.microsoft.com/office/preview/en/word-2013-preview)

Word has become the defacto program of choice in business, education, and publishing. The first thing most notice about Word 2013 is how clean the interface is. With the ribbon interface—the tabbed toolbars—hidden away, you can really focus on your writing. A simple click or tap on one of the ribbon headings instantly brings it into view. Microsoft's new generation of software pays close attention to touch, in reaction to the recent popularity of tablets and touch screen computers. You can tap charts or images to zoom in; you can tap to expand or collapse sections of a document; and you can hold your finger on a word or phrase to access context-sensitive options.

Word 2013, one of the applications in Microsoft Office, also takes you to the cloud, instead of you relying on local storage. *Cloud* is the buzzword of the moment and Microsoft, like Apple and Google, wants you to utilize this new way of keeping your files. Now documents, presentations, spreadsheets, photographs, and more can all be stored in the cloud, ready to be accessed from whatever device you happen to have to hand, whether a tablet, a computer, or your smartphone. The cloud Microsoft is promoting is their SkyDrive service. Office saves documents to SkyDrive by default, so your files will always available on all your devices.

The new Office on Demand means you can also subscribe to

the Office as a cloud-based subscription service. Microsoft is moving away from the software-in-a-box philosophy to a yearly subscription model. To sweeten the deal, pricing for the subscription service will be lower than the cost of the physical software. In addition to Word, Office 2013 (released December 2013) includes Excel (spreadsheets), PowerPoint (presentation manager), OneNote (note gathering), Outlook (email), and Access (database).

The cost of Office Home and Student 2013 (Word, Excel, Power-Point, OneNote) is $139; Home and Business (adds Outlook) is $219; Professional (adds Access and Publisher) is $399. The cloud subscription package, Office 365 Home Premium, is $99 a year, including 20GB in SkyDrive and a monthly hour of Skype. Office 365 Small Business Premium, with additional features, is $149 a year per user.

Word includes improved versions of the traditional template library. A large number of useful and popular templates are organized in the New tab as user-friendly tiles. In addition, the search bar allows you to browse, view, and select from hundreds of online templates in the Office Library. Office apps like the Merriam-Webster Dictionary and eFax app for Word 2013 can be added to increase functionality and productivity.

~ *Word Perfect X6* (Corel. Mac/PC. www.corel.com. $99.99.)

Writers and editors have used WordPerfect since the last millennium because in many ways, it is the best available instrument for writing and formatting text. Nothing matches its ability to put together multi-chapter documents from separate, editable files. Although it is not the most widely used program today, it has a very loyal group of followers.

The major attraction of WordPerfect is that it is the only modern word-processing program that gives you almost total control over the way your documents look, using a *reveal codes* feature that allows you to make adjustments quickly. Microsoft Word, in contrast, sometimes seems to have a mind of its own—formatting documents in ways never intended, or unpredictably retaining or discarding formatting in text imported from a Web browser.

Another perennial favorite of WordPerfect is the macro feature. Not only can you create quick, on-the-fly macros, you can also record complex macros, or record macros to be used in a certain template or to interact with another program.

This newest version also adds a unique electronic publishing module to create documents for the Kindle and other reader apps. It adds the ability to open documents in separate windows, finally making it easy to use the program on two monitors.

~ *Apache Open Office 3.4.1.* (Apache Software Foundation. Mac/PC/Linux. http://www.openoffice.org. Free.)

A rival to Microsoft Office, OpenOffice (OO) includes a word processor and other desktop applications, such as a spreadsheet program, a presentation manager, and a drawing program, with a user interface and features similar to those of Microsoft Office suites. Not only does OO let you edit basic documents such as letters and faxes, it also handles equations and complex multi-part documents with bibliographies, reference tables, and indexes.

The interface is similar to that of Microsoft Office 2003, and even advanced Office users will find almost everything they are used to: templates, collaborative features, macros, and even a programming language. OO lets you open and save documents in formats as diverse as Office formats, PDF, HTML, and XML. It can also import files from those formats, as well as WordPerfect and others, but it normally saves files in the open-standard Oasis OpenDocument XML format, for compatibility with other applications.

The latest versions of OpenOffice have a larger variety of extensions available for the program than previously. These include templates for professional writers, an export tool for bi-directional functionality with Google Docs (the ability to read languages that read right to left, such as Arabic and Hebrew),

Selecting Software

If you decide you want one of the many writers' programs available, how do you go about selecting the right one for you?

Decide what you need: First, consider if the kind of program you are interested in will actually help you be more productive or better organized. Some programs waste significant amounts of time by creating extra busy-work when you could be writing.

Identify which features are important to you: Clarifying your needs first can save you from being caught up by advertising hype. Maybe you do not need all the bells and whistles. Also consider if the program is compatible with your writing and research style.

Make a short list: Once you have worked out your needs, examine the available software and make a short list of ones that have features you want.

Test drive: If possible, test-drive each program on your short list. Many programs, such as Microsoft Office and Scrivener, offer trial versions you can download from the web. Set aside enough time to become familiar with each program and learn what it will and won't let you do. Set up a realistic trial, using the same material each time so that you are making a fair comparison.

Do not choose on price alone: A free or cheap program may meet your needs exactly, especially if all you want are the basics. Why pay for features you do not need and will not use? But some free or cheap programs may not have the important features you need to do your work, or good tech support when you need advice. Always consider your future needs as well.

blog publishing, and more.

~ *Google Docs* (Google. Online based. All operating systems with browsers. docs.google.com/demo. Free.)

The no-cost Google Docs is perfect for people who travel frequently or need collaboration capabilities. As long as you have access to the Internet, you can write and edit word processing documents. One of the best features of this program is the ability to store your documents online, so you can access them from any computer. You will find this handy if you take work home.

There is no need to worry about transferring documents to removable media or syncing your documents.

If you collaborate with others, help is built in. You can make a document public or show it to others by sending a link. If you want to allow others to work on the document, you can notify them that they can access the document, rather than email documents back and forth.

Docs has a nice selection of standard word processing features. It covers the essentials for most writing purposes. Google Docs's ability to export PDFs is a handy bonus, since not all word processing programs export to that format automatically. On the downside, it still lacks features found in conventional desktop word processing applications, such as grammar checks, templates, and the ability to handle larger documents.

~ *AbiWord* (Abisource. Mac/PC/Linux. www.abisource.com. Free.)

If your word processing chores are simple and straightforward, you may want this freebie. AbiWord features a simple interface; you will not need to spend hours trying to navigate your way through ribbons or multi-level menus. It was created to match the look and feel of Microsoft Word, and be compatible with Word's DOC files.

The features you need are presented right in front of you in simple icons and menus across the top of the page, without clutter. You will also be surprised by the number of features this free word processor offers. AbiWord handles images, mail merges, insertion of page numbers, date and time, and other auto-text. It also has tools for handling tables.

Abiword's tools and plug-ins are one of its best features, and are accessible from their website. These extensions provide Abiword with a host of integrated features, including spell check, thesaurus, image editing, online collaboration and more.

Writers' Tools

Just as your mechanic or plumber has a specialized set of tools, writers sometimes need their own tool kit to enhance their writing. Though writing software does not ensure you will be a top-selling author, playwright, or screenwriter, it does provide a series of tools to help you think about writing and story development, to organize your creative thoughts into recognizable and standard story formats. Here's a sampling of several popular programs.

~ *Scrivener* (Literature & Latte. Mac/PC. www.literatureandlatte. com/scrivener.php. $40.)

Scrivener is a powerful content-generation tool for writers. It is not a word processor in the normal sense. Instead, it is designed to let writers tackle larger projects by gathering multiple documents, notes, and research materials all in one place and rearranging them at will. At the end of the process, the finished document is compiled from selected elements for output to a variety of formats, including Word document, ebook, or direct to print.

The program puts everything you need for structuring, writing and editing long documents at your fingertips. On the left of the window, the binder allows you to navigate between the different parts of your manuscript, your notes, and research materials, with ease. It is much more convenient than having conventional open windows on the screen.

It also has a handy corkboard mode, where each chapter or scene is pinned to a virtual index card, which can then be labeled with a description, a title, etc. You can move the index cards around at will, and the text pinned to them moves around with them. In this way, you can quickly reorganize and restructure entire chapters or the whole book from a high-level outlining view; at any time, you can click on an index card and dive back into the scene's text. Scrivener makes it easy to switch between focusing on the details and stepping back to get a wider view of your composition.

Scrivener is intuitively organized around how the creative writing process actually works for most people—in a nonlinear, nonsequential manner, with more flexibility than the traditional word processor.

~ *Final Draft 8* (Final Draft Software. Mac/PC. www.writebrain.com/power_writer_main.htm. $299.)

Final Draft is the number-one selling word processor specifically designed for writing movie scripts, television episodics, and stage plays, and it has become an industry standard.

Film, radio, and television scripts have industry-standard layouts. Elements such as character names, dialogue, and action have specific margin and capitalization rules that differ from medium to medium. Although Final Draft is essentially a glorified word processor, anyone attempting to format a screenplay with Word will soon understand Final Draft's worth as a productivity tool.

One of the key features of Final Draft is its ability to split the interface into two panes horizontally or vertically. This means the script can be open in one pane and any of the other tools, such as Scene view, Index or Cards, can be open in the other. You can even opt to have the script open at different points in both panes at the same time.

Like the majority of its competitors, Final Draft uses a tab-and-enter method of text entry. Pressing the Tab key switches between elements, such as character name, action or dialogue, and once written, pressing *return* moves to the next element. The technique is simple, speedy and intuitive. Character names and locations also auto complete, so the only thing slowing down the process might be writers' block.

~ *Character Writer 3.1* (Typing Chimp Software. Mac/PC/Linux. www.characterpro.com/characterwriter/index.html. $69.99.)

Great stories require great characters, yet creating a vital, identifiable, sympathetic (even if evil) characters, is one of the hardest parts of developing a good tale.

Character Writer takes you through steps, asking you questions to help you develop a believable character. The program also makes suggestions for your characters in terms of behavior and goals. It even has a section for psychological disorders to help you define a fully embodied character. Beyond creating the basic character personality, it also helps you define relationships between characters.

Character Writer includes a built-in story generator and organizer. The story generator tab can create a countless permutation of story sequences. Once you have created your basic story structure, you can edit, develop, and organize until you think the story is perfect. Stuck for ideas? Character Writer offers generic story lines. It also plays well with other programs.

The Writing Mode feature keeps character profiles at your fingertips throughout the story-writing process, on whatever device you are working.

~ *MasterWriter 2.0* (MasterWriter. Mac/PC. www.masterwriter. com/creative_writer/index.html. $189.)

MasterWriter is more than a tool for writers: It is a searchable collection of phrases, rhymes, parts of speech and pop culture sayings. An interconnected system of dictionaries and databases help you find the best word or phrase for any story, script, novel, play, song or other writing. It is comprehensive creative writing software that allows writers to maintain their narrative flow through access to multiple resources in one application.

MasterWriter offers 33,000 phrases, sayings, and word combinations, as well as more than 100,000 rhymes and 36,000 rhyme phrases. In addition, this writing software has more than 12,000 icons and sayings from American and world culture, compiled in the Pop Culture feature.

One of the best features of this MasterWriter is Word Families, a reference dictionary and thesaurus in one. Simply type in a word and its various usages appear. More options are available by applying word filters, which let you extend or narrow your search for similar words. For example, click on Extended, and five pages of words and sayings appear.

Poets and picture book authors take note. You can search for rhymes to any word and broaden or narrow your searches. You can look for All Rhymes, Primary, Secondary, and Pop Culture reference rhymes. MasterWriter can even give you phrases that rhyme with a word or words. It has a feature called Sound-Alikes to get as close to a perfect rhyme as possible, with three options— Close, Wider, and X-Wide—to broaden your searches for near rhymes.

In addition, this software offers the only electronic version of the comprehensive Synonym Finder thesaurus. MasterWriter's built-in dictionary is the fourth edition of *The American Heritage Dictionary of the English Language.*

~ *Power Structure* and *Power Writer* (Script Perfection Enterprises. PC. www.write-brain.com/power_writer_main.htm. $199.95, $129.95)

Power Structure is novel and screenwriting software that contains templates, allows you to gather notes and materials into scenes and chapters, and helps develop a countless number of characters, scenes, and so on. Based on Power Structure's development tools, Power Writer focuses more heavily on the actual manuscript, allowing you to write anything from a short story all the way up to a full novel in one easy-to-use program. Its integrated Story Development and Outline Tools lets your writing proceed as one continuous act of creation from first idea to finished manuscript.

If you are working on a short story or nonfiction novel, Power Writer can help you craft a compelling work in no time. Its three main features are the outline view, composition frame, and story tools, which work together and allow you to document new ideas quickly. This makes editing and adjusting your story easy.

Outlines, notes, ideas, character arcs, and much more are always in sync with the actual text, regardless of how much you edit or rewrite. They are all right at your fingertips with a simple click of the mouse, or can just as easily be hidden so you can focus purely on your prose.

A characters section lets you flesh out everything you need to know about the characters in your story—physical attributes, psychologies, and their roles in the story. Another plus of the software in this section is the name bank. If you are having a hard time coming up with the right name for your character, this feature is sure to help.

Writers' Apps

If you use a tablet computer or smartphone, you are already familiar with the thousands of apps available for fun and productivity. Here is a sampling of what is available to help you with your writing tasks, including a brief description, devices for their use, and developer links.

~ *My Writing Spot* (iPhone/iPad/iPod Touch/Android. PT Software Solutions. http://www.mywritingnook.com. $4.99)

My Writing Spot is a simple, writing app that offers the same features as a typical work processor. It has autosave, word counts, password protection, document organization, and online websync.

~ *Writer's Studio* (miSoft. iPhone/iPad/iPod Touch. www.misoft.com. $3.99)

Audio and visual elements can be added to text in Writer's Studio. It is good for creating interactive materials.

~ *Story Tracker* (Andrew Nicolle. iPhone/iPad/iPod Touch. http://andrewnicolle.com/apps/storytracker. $6.99)

Story Tracker is an organization app that tracks stories that have been submitted, where they have been submitted, which publishers accepted or rejected them, income from the submissions, and more. The app also can also backup and export to a desktop database.

~ *ScriptWrite* (Filter Apps. iPhone/iPad. http://filterapps. wordpress.com. $3.99.)
A Mac-based word processing app, ScriptWrite focuses on the needs of screenwriters. It creates a seamless page, not separate pages or categories, to maximize the flow of writing.

~ *Screenplay* (Black Mana Studios. iPhone/iPad. www.blackmana.com/products/screenplay. $4.99.)
The word processing app Screenplay is integrated with Final Draft, one of the standard desktop screenwriting programs. It has some useful features, like a find/replace function, and the ability to import and export to Final Draft 8.

~ The Brainstormer (Tapnik. iPhone/iPad/iPod Touch. www.tapnik.com/projects. $1.99.)
To get over writer's block or simply brainstorm, the Brainstormer can help. The app uses three spinning wheels organized into themes, subjects, locations, and so on, that randomly generate ideas for stories.

~ Word Press. (Automatic. iPhone/iPad. http://ios.wordpress. org. Free.)
WordPress is a popular free blogging application, well-known to most web users. Its app is a universal program that operates much as its desktop version does. You can post entries, add, edit, and remove copy, images, tags, and categories. The app makes it easy to get writings online.

~ *Dropbox*. (Dropbox. Mac/iPhone/iPad. www.dropbox.com. Free.)

DropBox is a free cloud storage service (up to 2 GB, more for a fee) that works across desktops, the iPad, and iPhone. Users can share documents, photos, and videos across various devices, and they will sync as updated.

~ *FreeNote* (Flyable. Android. www.appbrain.com/app/ freenote-note-everything/com.suishouxie.freenote. Free.)

A notetaking app, FreeNote that combines manual handwriting and keyword typewriting. You can even draw illustrations using this app. Additional features include voice, photo and video support, calendar, alarm and a to-do list. This app works with stylus pens.

~ *Documents to Go* (Data Viz. iPad/iPhone/iPod Touch/ Android. www.dataviz.com/DTG_iphone.html?redirect=iphone. $9.99.)

Having Documents to Go is like having Microsoft Office on your smartphone. It creates and edits Word documents, with the usual functions: cut, copy, paste, editing, bulleted and numbered lists, pictures, tables, word count. Files can be password-protected. It also creates Excel and PowerPoint documents.

~ *Auto Call Recorder* (Appstar Solutions. Android. http:// appstarsolutions.blogspot.com. $6.99.)

For phone interviews, Android users can record calls automatically or selectively. Recorded calls can be played, saved to internal storage or an SD card, and shared.

Critique Groups "Get It"

By Judy Bradbury

Without a critique group, a writer often feels adrift. Is my character believable? Have I set up a plausible problem? Does the setting come alive? Do I get from plot point A to plot point B in a logical fashion? Although as the author I know what is going on, is anything unclear to the reader?

Critique groups offer authors a safe and welcome harbor where they can find advice, a fresh eye, and critical review. Critique groups also offer camaraderie, a shoulder to cry on as well as a shoulder to pat with warm congratulations, and several shoulders to bolster and sustain you through the muddled middles and insipid reviews. They can share publishing information and network with you. Best of all, critique groups composed of well-matched members *get* you and what you do with your precious writing hours. You do not have to explain the surge of satisfaction you feel when you score an amazing plot twist or develop a singularly affecting character or have a submission accepted.

Critique groups come in many sizes and shapes, and their schedules and formats vary. Some groups are large, with sub-groups that shift and flow depending on the work being reviewed. Many groups are small, with four to seven members, and some groups are actually two-person partnerships. Groups may meet every two weeks or once a month, but there are others that gather annually or biannually for a much-anticipated retreat.

At the Table

In alphabetical order, here is a list of the authors included in the article.

~ **Marsha Hayles** (www.marshahayles.com) has written a number of picture books for young children. Her debut novel, *Breathing Room* (Henry Holt), is an illustrated middle-grade story set in a sanitorium treating tuberculosis, and was released in June 2012.

~ **Anna Grossnickle Hines** (www.aghines.com) was once dubbed the "sorceress of the ordinary." She has penned move than 60 books for children including the popular *Daddy Makes the Best Spaghetti* (Sandpiper). Recent releases include *I Am a Backhoe* (Tricycle Press) and *Peaceful Pieces: Poems and Quilts About Peace* (Henry Holt). Her books of themed poems often are illustrated with handmade quilts she created specifically to accompany the verse.

~ **Joan Holub** (www.joanholub.com) is the author of 135 books for children, including *Zero the Hero* (Henry Holt), *Ballet Stars* (Random House), and the Goddess Girls tween series (co-authored with Suzanne Williams; Aladdin).

~ **Ruta Sepetys** (www.rutasepetys.com) is the author of *Between Shades of Gray* (Philomel), an international best-selling historical fiction novel about the Soviet imprisonment and deportation of Lithuanians in the 1940s. The book has won several awards, among them the 2012 Golden Kite Award for Fiction.

~ **Joyce Sidman** (www.joycesidman.com) is the author of the 2011 Newbery Honor book *Dark Emperor and Other Poems of the Night* (Houghton Mifflin) and the 2010 Caldecott Honor book *Red Sings From Treetops: A Year in Colors* (illustrated by Pamela Zagarenski; Houghton Mifflin). Her *Swirl by Swirl: Spirals in Nature* (Houghton Mifflin) garnered numerous awards as well.

~ **Lisa Wheeler** (www.lisawheelerbooks.com) is the author of more than 30 children's books. They include *Dino-Football* (Carolrhoda), *Spinster Goose: Twisted Rhymes for Naughty Children* (Atheneum), and the Ready-to-Read Fitch & Chip series (Simon& Schuster), as well as nonfiction titles such as *Mammoths on the Move* (Harcourt).

Some groups meet online while others find a library, accommodating restaurant, or someone's home in which to convene. Groups may concentrate on one genre—say young adult fiction or mysteries—while others review a mix of genres. Whatever the format, the goal is the same: meeting and working together with a shared objective of improving each member's work, shaping stories, poems, and nonfiction into the best they can be before they are sent out to be considered for publication.

Assembled here is a panel of published children's authors who belong to variously configured critique groups and who graciously agreed to offer insights into what they find works well, what does not, the joys and the drawbacks of being a member of a critique group, advice they would give to those considering joining or forming a group, and why they personally find a critique group helpful—even essential—to their professional lives. Their experiences may help you as you consider critiquing.

Let's Begin

~ Please briefly describe your critique group. How long have you been a member of the group?

Hayles: "I belong to a traditional critique group made up of four writers that meets on a monthly basis to discuss works in progress; an online critique group of six writers that responds in a timely fashion to a picture book manuscript at any stage of the process; and a one-on-one critique partnership that reviews only a completed draft of the manuscript. For the purposes of this roundtable, I will focus on my one-on-one critique partnership with Linda Sue Park. I'm not sure of the exact year we started working together, but I am thinking we've been together at least 13 or 14 years now. I do know we started after I'd sold my first picture book and before Linda Sue won the Newbery Award."

Hines: "Our writing group is quite different from the usual critique group in that we are geographically scattered and only meet twice a year. It has actually evolved into more of a retreat group than a critique group. We've been together since the mid-nineties—or the eighties, if you count the years we met at a writer's workshop in Port Townsend."

Holub: "Our group consists of four members. We write a mix of board books, picture books, easy readers, and middle-grade/YA novels, and we've been together for over ten years. "

Sepetys: "Our critique group consists of six people and we meet at the library twice a month. I have been part of our group for over seven years."

Sidman: "I consider a group an essential part of writing. I've been a member of a group since I first started writing for children in 1989. However, I've moved and changed groups several times. My present writers' group is composed of six women. It has grown and changed as members have left and joined. But the core of this group started about ten years ago. We are all seasoned writers, with published books under our belts and a serious commitment to children's literature."

Wheeler: "I have been a member of several groups (most defunct) since 1995. The group I will describe here is an online group of six published children's book authors that has been together for ten to twelve years. We come from four different states, and we focus on picture books."

~ *How did your critique group get started?*

Holub: "We started with three members, two published and one not. We met through our regional SCBWI (Society of Children's Book Writers and Illustrators) group, when we were all serving on the local board in one capacity or another."

Sepetys: "Our group met via the SCBWI regional Midsouth listserv. One of the members posted that they were looking for a group in the area and several of us responded."

Wheeler: "I knew some of the members from a previous group that had fallen apart. We also invited a few others we knew personally. Over the years, a couple of the writers left. But the six of us have stayed strong."

Hines: "We originally met at Centrum Writer's Workshop in Port Townsend, Washington, where Jane Yolen taught a children's writing class in which each of us took part. Jane alternated between a beginner's class and an advanced class. In the years she taught beginners, a number of us came as independent students, meeting for daily critique and sharing sessions on our own. Eventually some of us began gathering at other times during the year as well, sometimes meeting at my home in Pennsylvania from which we could make day trips to New York to meet with publishers. Four to six of us continue to meet twice a year at my current home in Gualala, California, which is ideally set up for retreats."

Hayles: "Linda Sue attended one of our local writer's meetings and happened to sit next to me. Throughout the meeting, she scribbled me questions, and I scribbled responses back; we had an instant rapport. We soon became part of a critique group with several members. Linda Sue processes information at lightning speed—faster than anyone else I know—and unfortunately, another member of the group was her mirror opposite and needed to go through things slowly and methodically. The chemistry just didn't work. But Linda Sue and I realized that we could work well one-on-one. And so began our partnership."

~ *Describe how your critique group works.*

Holub: "We meet once a month for two to three hours at a bookstore, someone's home, or anywhere with an available table and chairs. We bring copies of our work, about five to ten pages, which the author reads aloud. We then discuss as a group, with lots of back and forth between everyone."

Sepetys: "We email each other our work and read it in advance of the meeting. At the meeting, we discuss the work, ask questions, and make suggestions."

Sidman: "We each bring our work and take turns reading

aloud. Since we have become friends as well, we start with a period of catching up with our lives, then begin reading. Each author brings hard copies of her work for each member, which are handed out for us to scribble on as it is read aloud. Then we start the discussion, focusing first on the strengths of the piece, then on questions we have or parts that seemed off. I would say that we emphasize support and celebration over competitiveness. We always share marketing tips and help each other toward the goal of an excellent published piece."

Wheeler: "We are fairly loose. When a member has a piece that needs to be critiqued, we send it to the whole group in the

> "We emphasize support and celebration over competitiveness. We always share marketing tips and help each other toward the goal of an excellent published piece."

body of an email. The only rule is that we are not allowed to read anyone else's critique until we offer our own. One of the unwritten rules is that we are allowed to be hard on each other. Since we are all published, we have grown a thick skin, and it doesn't do any of us any good to sugarcoat a critique. We do not take turns, etc. The fact is, for most of what I write I may not need a critique. But when something isn't working or is very different from what I normally write, I am eager to get the opinions of the group members. I think we all operate this way in the group, and so, often it can be months between [email critique] submissions."

Hayles: "Linda Sue and I work one-on-one and critique any kind of manuscript (picture book, novel, short story, poem) our partner has to offer. In my other critique groups, we tend to share works in process, but Linda Sue and I exchange finished drafts."

Hines: "Since we meet [on retreat] for a week at a time, most of our logistics center around meals and daily schedules. We meet for breakfast, which we jointly prepare, then go to our rooms for writing. We meet again for lunch, and then return to writing until about 5 PM when we go out for a walk. Each of us plans and heads up the preparation of one dinner; any remaining dinners are filled in with leftovers or pizza. In the evening we meet to critique if anyone is ready and wanting feedback, or one of us might bring up a burning issue she or he wants to talk about. Some years we have met for critiques in the afternoon as well, but more and more that is seen as valuable writing time. At meal-times, during walks, and anytime two or more of us bump into one another, we are likely to discuss issues pertaining to writing, books, and the publishing business. Though we don't do a lot of critiquing, it is an intensely focused week—and a whole lot of fun."

~ *What do you find of most value in belonging to a critique group?*

Sidman: "For me, the group is a *third eye*—a place to try out a polished draft of a piece before I send it to my editor. My group catches errors, inconsistencies, and vagueness that I cannot always see. Beyond that, we are like a band of sisters—always there to encourage, commiserate, and celebrate. I would be lost without this group."

Sepetys: "I most value the honest, objective input from five very different human beings. If several of the members independently have the same comment or suggestion for my manuscript, I know I need to make the change."

Wheeler: "It is wonderful to have five professionals at my fingertips. Their advice is invaluable, and I take everything they suggest to heart."

Holub: "I need that honest feedback from critique partners I trust before I send a manuscript out to an editor. It also helps to have ongoing meetings scheduled so that I'm always working on something new to present to my *crit* group."

Hines: "I value the camaraderie and support. These people have become very dear friends, and they understand what I do!"

Hayles: "Linda Sue is an amazing writer and such an intelligent reader. She offers insight at every level of the manuscript. Her radar may flag problems with point of view, a grammatical glitch, plot structure, tone, dialogue, word choice, pacing. She pays attention to each scene and its place in the overall structure of the work, and she's not afraid to ask why any word, sentence, paragraph, or chapter is there. But instead of saying, 'Work at revising this,' she wisely encourages me to *play* at trying another possibility. I love that distinction and find it most helpful. But in the end, I think what I appreciate most about working with Linda Sue is her boundless enthusiasm for all things literary. This enthusiasm is at the heart of her support of me as a writer and really for all writers. Linda Sue truly wants everyone to shine."

~ What is the biggest challenge of being a member of a critique group?

Hines: "For our group that would be finding the dates when everyone can come. When I first started participating in group critiquing experiences, I think the biggest challenge was sorting out just what each critiquer's gifts and limitations were. Some people can write spell-binding novels, but they just don't seem to *get* a picture book for the very young. I had to learn to listen to it all and then apply what felt true to me and my story."

Sepetys: "Scheduling is a feat. We all have very different lives, so sometimes it can be hard to coordinate."

Sidman: "To be honest, it's scheduling. It's so hard to find a time we can all meet. We try for monthly meetings. Also, group chemistry can be important. Right now, my group has terrific chemistry—a great mix of liveliness, seriousness, and wisdom. But there have been times when we've had too few members, or members who weren't really committed, and the meetings just didn't work as well."

Holub: "When we started out, our meetings sometimes ran long, or someone might get more time during the meeting and someone else got shorted. We solved this easily by having a digital timer sitting in the middle of our table. If we have a two-hour meeting with four authors in attendance, each gets one half-hour. When the buzzer goes off, we quickly wind up our thoughts and move on to the next author."

Wheeler: "For me, the biggest challenge is when a critique comes in and I am in the middle of a busy traveling season. (I do school visits and tend to be very active between January and May.) I am always eager to read the new manuscript but have to be sure my head is in the right place when I critique it. I don't want to rush it and miss something."

Hayles: "We've both had instances where we wanted to push back at the comments the other has given. For example, Linda Sue suggested I consider cutting one of my favorite moments in *Breathing Room*, as well as rearranging some of the final chapters. Of course, I didn't want to do any of that and had a very intense argument in my head with her as I read through her comments. That is, until I played with her suggestions. Then I knew she was right. *Breathing Room*—and everything I write—is stronger because of her."

~ *What advice would you offer regarding critique groups?*

Hayles: "I know my good fortune at having this unique partnership with Linda Sue Park. We worked together before she won the Newbery Medal, and though her schedule has become busier because of her success, our critique process remains pretty much the same. We found what works well for us both and have stuck with it. I think it is important to find someone you can respect and trust as a reader and a writer—and as a friend, too."

Wheeler: "I find it valuable to streamline membership. For instance, if you write middle-grade novels, I think it would be beneficial to join a group of authors who write in that genre. My group is all picture book writers. This doesn't work for everyone, but I love belonging to a group of picture book writers because they get it. They know the beast and know when it isn't working. I once was in a group where the only *label* was that everyone wrote for children. So I might submit my 350-word picture book one week and have to critique a 30,000-word novel the next. This didn't work for me. I didn't feel comfortable critiquing that genre and kept trying to cut words and slim each sentence down to picture book length. It was maddening! But others who are in such a group have told me they love it because they learn about all the genres this way. So, I guess it is a personal thing. All I know is that once I joined a streamlined group, my picture book writing got stronger."

Holub: "I once visited a second-grade classroom of students who'd written stories that they were reading aloud to the class. They then raised hands to offer critiques. The teacher's critique rule was to first give two compliments to the author, and then to offer one suggestion for improvement. This was a valuable lesson that can be applied to our professional writing critique groups. Although it's important to suggest ways an author could improve a story, it's also important to say what you think is already working well in the story. Otherwise, the author may change the very thing you liked in her next revision. And in this business where there's so much potential for rejection, authors need honest encouragement from friends!"

Sepetys: "I'd say to look for a group who is committed, that you can grow and evolve with over many years. The longer you work with the group, the trust will deepen and it will feel more like a creative partnership than a critique. I would never have published a book without my critique group. I couldn't have done it without them!"

Sidman: "Find people you trust. Establish some guidelines, but don't turn it into a classroom. Experiment with format. If the

Resource Books

- ~ *No Red Pen: Writers, Writing Groups & Critique,* by Victoria A. Hudson (CreateSpace).
- ~ *Writing Alone and with Others,* by Pat Schneider (Oxford University Press).
- ~ *Writing Alone, Writing Together: A Guide for Writers and Writing Groups,* by Judy Reeves (New World Library).
- ~ *The Writing & Critique Group Survival Guide: How to Give and Receive Feedback, Self-Edit, and Make Revisions,* by Becky Levine (Writer's Digest Books).
- ~ *The Writing Group Book: Creating and Sustaining a Successful Writing Group,* edited by Lisa Rosenthal (Chicago Review Press).

group isn't working for you, discuss this with members and see if there might be a solution—a new meeting venue or new members, perhaps. Groups reflect the people in them. Choose your members carefully; these will be people that will be seeing your very soul on paper. You will be vulnerable, and trust is paramount."

Hines: "It is good when a group forms from a class or other shared experience because it gives the group a common base from which to start. If I were to start a group without that base, I think it would be important to build it in some way. General advice: Be kind and respectful. Recognize the gifts of each member in the group and don't be too thin-skinned. Not everyone will get what you do, but even if they don't, they may have points that you can learn from. Listen, evaluate, and use what works for you."

The verb *critique* means to review, analyze, assess, and discuss. As you seek out a writers' critique group, reflect on what type of group might work best for you and fit well in your schedule. Search for others who share your perspective on writing for children and whose interests, personalities, and commitment seem best-suited to yours. Then grab a pen and your planning calendar, and prepare for an invigorating, collaborative, and satisfying professional experience that's kept alive by caring, writerly friends who get it.

Markets

Style

Business

Research

Ideas

Contests

Indexes

Like Found Money

Make the Most of Your Research

By Michael Cooper

After you spend weeks or months, or perhaps years, researching and writing a story, article, or book, what do you do with that gigabyte of anecdotes, little-known facts, and interviews with fascinating people? You want to make the most of your hard work. Once you have used parts of your research in a first project, mine it for other writing projects, or use the research to market yourself.

My first experience of wringing multiple articles out of one batch of research notes happened in the early 1980s, a couple of years after I began freelancing in New York City. *Outdoor Life Magazine* sent me to Alaska for three weeks to travel the width and breath of the state for an article on outdoor things to do and see. When I wrapped up the article, I started shuffling through my suitcase full of brochures, local guidebooks, and notes, looking for other ideas to sell. They were like found money:

~ The *Wall Street Journal* bought a short article about sled-dog racing.

~ The *Washington Post* travel section published a feature on visiting Nome.

~ *ASTA Travel News*, an American Society of Travel Agents publication, used an article on Alaska cruise ship vacations. And the editor gave me several other assignments unrelated to Alaska.

~ *American Spirit,* the American Airlines in-flight magazine, ran a piece about a scenic train trip between Anchorage and Seward.

~ A marketing firm promoting Alaskan tourism for the state paid me to write an article for an advertising insert in *Travel & Leisure,* and to write a couple of features with my byline for a press kit distributed to newspapers. Those features ran in the *Boston Inquirer* and the *Los Angeles Times.*

I do not remember the exact figure, but that one trip to Alaska probably earned me $5,000 or so, which in the 1980s was good money.

Stretch & Promote

These days I mostly write nonfiction trade books for kids and young adults. But the idea is the same: Stretch the value of my research. The added benefit is that the articles help promote my books. Here are a couple of examples.

Houghton Mifflin published *Indian School* about a dozen years ago. It was about the Carlisle Indian Industrial School, the first of several federal boarding schools for Indians established in the late nineteenth century. At the time, the *Washington Post* regularly ran articles about interesting day trips in a section called Nearby Escapes. Knowing the editors wanted completed articles rather than queries, I submitted an article about visiting the Indian school in Carlisle, Pennsylvania, which is a two-hour drive from D.C. Visitors could stroll the shady campus, which is now the Army War College, and see the nineteenth-century brick buildings constructed by young Indians. Then they could visit the local historical society to see an exhibit about the school. Three months after I submitted the article, the *Post* published it and I received $500 payment and a good writing credit.

More recently, I used the research from *Up Front: Theodore Roosevelt* (Viking), to write a 750-word article for *Highlights for*

Children titled "Over, Under Or Through, But Never Around." It described how our twenty-sixth president, who was a fitness buff, enjoyed taking unsuspecting White House lunch guests—usually formally dressed ambassadors, generals, and cabinet members— on three- and four-hour hikes along the Potomac River, wading streams and climbing boulders. Roosevelt is consistently ranked among the top five most popular American presidents, so I am holding on to my research notes because I suspect he will be a good source of articles for years to come.

A Case Study

My experience with Alaska and Roosevelt has taught me that research on broad, topical, or perennially popular subjects yields more articles and more sales. My most recent book bears that out.

The first chapter of *Ten Famous American Fires* (Macmillan) is about the devastating fire in 1760 that destroyed a large part of Boston; the tenth and last chapter is about a California wildfire that burned one-fifth of suburban San Diego County. The fires are the dramatic focus. The backstory is about technology, urban life, and the development of public services.

While I was doing my research for the book, I kept a notepad beside me or an open Word document on my laptop so I could jot down article ideas and their sources. When I was away from my desk, such as in my dentist's waiting room browsing through a stack of magazines, I recorded ideas on my iPhone by voice memo. I used to tell myself I would not forget an idea if it is truly good. But I have learned better. By the time I finished the research for *Ten Famous American Fires,* I had written down lots of article ideas.

Six months before the book was published, I began sending out query letters. One article idea was the history of the fire drill, which dates from the efforts of nineteenth-century cotton mill owners to make their mills safer. I sent the query first to *American History*. If it was not accepted there, I would send it to another history magazine, probably *Smithsonian*. And I planned a 750-word feature for a kids' publication such as *Highlights* or *Cobblestone*, an American history magazine.

Another idea for the same market was about the first volunteer fire companies in Philadelphia and Boston. They were serious about fighting fires, but they were also high-class social clubs with members such as Benjamin Franklin, Paul Revere, and John Adams.

And who doesn't like a good horse story? Fire departments after the Civil War used horses to pull steam fire engines. These well-trained workhorses were also mascots for firemen and for the community. I thought this would be a good article for kids' magazines or for a horse magazine such as *Blaze*.

Finally, Fire Prevention Week itself was an opportunity to pitch fire-related articles on a topic such as why Fire Prevention Week always includes October 8, the day of the Great Chicago Fire of 1871. This short piece was good for my local newspapers. There is little money in publishing in local newspapers, but they reach several hundred thousand people so they are good vehicles for self-promotion.

Anniversaries are popular hooks to hang stories on. In my research, I look for anniversaries of important events, annual observances, and the birthdays of significant people. I keep the dates on a Google calendar. If I have an article idea related to a date, six to nine months ahead of time I send out queries.

Another way I have been able to make the most of my research is to review books. I spent several weeks researching and writing a book proposal on the Holocaust. It was turned down, but I later had the opportunity to use my knowledge of the subject and of the previous books written about it to review three kids' books for the *Washington Post*. There are fewer book review sections in newspapers these days, but newspapers still run some reviews and many magazines publish reviews.

Where to Turn

When I am brainstorming article ideas, I have a regular list of potential markets that I turn to first. But with my research on American fires I looked beyond the usual list and came up with lots of ideas. It just took a little brainstorming and a little research to find them.

I use a variety of sources to locate potential magazine markets. Looking for new markets for my fire-related articles, I browsed the different categories of magazines in *Best of the Magazine Markets for Writers 2013* (Writer's Institute Publications). The career category made me think about an article on what it takes to be a fire fighter. The travel category brought to mind an article on fire museums. The health and fitness category made me think about an article on how fire fighters keep in shape.

Until recently, I had not considered submitting to Canadian magazines, but if the angle is right, these publications can be open to U.S. writers and offer more possibilities for reusing your research—even some of your already written and published articles. Some of the most popular are *Chatelaine* (chatelaine.com), which covers fashion, food, home, travel, and money; *The Walrus* (walrusmagazine.com), a general interest magazine that is sort of like the *Saturday Review*; and *Zoomer, Canada's Boomer Lifestyle Magazine* (zoomermag.com). Magazinescanada.ca lists about 300 magazines with brief descriptions and website links.

One of the best ways I have found to research publications is to browse the titles listed on Amazon and the Barnes & Noble website (www.barnesandnoble.com). Publications are divided into the usual categories—automotive, health, travel, and so on—which can prompt ideas, just as the *Best of the Magazine Markets for Writers 2013* categories do, and may lead to new markets. Barnes & Noble lists about 1,000 English language publications. Some 38,000 publications are listed on Amazon, but many of those are in foreign languages. The Amazon listings are more detailed, plus they usually include photos of covers and of the features and columns inside the magazines. The readers' comments are interesting too.

Multimedia

Since this is an age of multimedia, for *Ten Famous American Fires* I created a Keynote (Apple's answer to PowerPoint) presentation to show to local libraries, school groups, and civic organizations. This is a good way to promote my work and myself. Plus, I usually charge for school visits and some organizations give honorariums.

Having done photo research for my book, I had identified plenty of interesting photos to use. Seven of the fires I covered occurred in the twentieth and twenty-first centuries, so the Keynote presentation also included film footage. I added footage of the 1906 San Francisco earthquake and fire from the Library of Congress. For the two most recent fires in my book, I found YouTube videos.

When I am doing research that is particularly interesting, either because of the subject or the methodology, I write about it on my blog. Finally, I put research information on my website. After my biography of John Paul Jones was published several years ago, I posted photos of Jones's mummified corpse. I received email comments such as "way cool" or "Great photo. Okay if I download a copy?" For *Ten Famous American Fires,* I put up dramatic photos of fires and of handsome fire horses. And I posted facts such as that in the U.S. a fire department answers an alarm every 30 seconds.

Once I got into the habit of thinking about how to use my research in multiple ways, I have always had more ideas than I could possibly follow up on. And that is a good thing.

Taking Notes

Foundations of Research

By Patricia Curtis Pfitsch

"**W**e call ourselves *writers*," says author Ann Bausum. "We don't call ourselves *researchers*. But if your job is to write nonfiction, you're only going to be able to do that well if you've done the best possible work you can do as a researcher. Find the system that works for you as a researcher—that's going to give you the power you need to be the best writer." One of the most invisible, and yet most important parts of that research system is taking notes.

There is no right way to take and organize research notes. "You just have to figure out what works for you and what you're comfortable with," says Gail Jarrow, author of *The Amazing Harry Kellar, Great American Magician* (Calkins Creek). Nevertheless, professional writers' systems do have some characteristics in common.

Link Facts to Sources

Good note-taking systems keep each piece of information firmly connected to the source it came from. As she reads her sources, Bausum, whose book *Freedom Riders: John Lewis and Jim Zwerg on the Front Lines of the Civil Rights Movement* (National Geographic Children's Books) was a Sibert Honor Book, she flags each fact she wants to include in her book with an N. When done reading, she types each flagged fact on a notecard with the bibliographic information for the source at the top. "It is quite a maddening and labor-intensive approach," Bausum admits, "but it makes the writing process go so much better for me that it's worth the extra time. When I'm writing, I can just write." She does not get distracted wondering, "Now who said that again?" or "Where did I get that fact?"

Jarrow takes notes on paper by hand and then files them in a three-ring binder. At the top of each page she writes the source and author's name. "Every time I write something down, I write in the [left hand margin] the page from which I'm taking that note. Later, if I have to go back and confirm it or find it because my editor wants to actually see the source, I know exactly where I found that fact." Even though most of her books do not have footnotes, when Jarrow is writing her first or second draft she includes bibliographic information in the text. "When I put in a fact, I always put a reference to where that fact is, the author's name, and page number." Later, she takes that information out of the text, but she still has that earlier draft if she needs it.

Chris Eboch's latest book for children is *The Eyes of Pharaoh* (Pig River Press). She also writes romantic suspense for adults under the name Kris Bock, and she writes nonfiction for all ages. She types notes into her computer, organizing them by subtopic. She records the bibliographic information for each source at the top of her document, adding the call number and library where she found the book. Then she begins making notes at the appropriate topic heading. "If I'm using books in my personal library, I just make a brief identifying note such as *royalty clothing description* and reference the page number, rather than writing out all the details." She copies and pastes information from websites, making sure to include the URL for the specific page, not just the site's home page. "By making sure I know exactly where I found a piece of information, I can easily find the original source."

Sometimes Christine Kohler, author of *Words Alive! Christian Writers' Skills and Prompts* (Amazon Digital Services), and *Music Performance: Vocals & Band* (Rosen), does not actually take notes at all. When her sources are newspaper and magazine articles or books, "I copy the pages, then reread and highlight the information," she explains. With book sources, she may read the entire book or use the index to locate specific information. "If I want something from [a certain] page, I put a sticky note on it and write on the sticky note a name or a fact that will help me organize that information into the right chapter or subtopic." After she is finished with the book, she photocopies all the pages with sticky notes and transfers the note from the book to her paper.

"When I open a book, I type all the bibliography information in the correct format into a document I title Works Cited," Kohler says. She does the same with a URL. She then types or cuts and pastes important notes into the document.

Nancy Coffelt, whose work is included in the latest Uncle John's Bathroom Readers for Kids series, keeps most of her research on the computer. She begins a project by doing a Google search on her topic. "Then I bookmark the sites I think I might use. That's my first file. I make sure I [note] my web addresses for any online sources." She takes notes on her computer from online sources, and when she is collecting information from books she types in what she needs as well. At the library, she makes notes in a notebook. "Then I translate my scrawls into a Word document and save that in the appropriate folder."

Use Note-taking to Organize Your Draft

Your note-taking system can help you organize your draft as well as your research information. Bausum often ends up with hundreds, even thousands, of notecards for one book project. "As I'm reading, and especially as I'm typing the notecards, I add key words. When I'm done, I can take over a huge physical, flat space and start tossing those notecards into piles based on keywords. Those keywords become the subsets of paragraphs and chapters of a book. By the time I'm ready to write I have an outline for

Technology for Notes

Many writers developed their research and note-taking systems 'back in the day' before computers came within reach for individual use. Today they can use new digital and online technologies to refine their process, saving time and increasing accuracy.

Writer Ann Bausum uses a bibliographic software program called Citation (citationonline.net/brochure.asp) to help her create note cards. "It has allowed me to streamline the typing. Basically I type into a template. I can flag the notecards with keywords and then type them out and physically handle them later." She does not have to retype the bibliographic information on each card; that is automated by the template. "The software program also builds a bibliography while you're using it. When you're all done and you've entered your nine million notecards, you can ask the program to generate your bibliography and it will do that. It may not come out perfectly formatted but it's close enough to make it so much easier to prepare the material that becomes the published bibliography." Bausum admits that while there are other programs that allow writers to keep their notecards virtually on the computer, she is not interested in taking that step. "I'm just twentieth century enough to really like the tactile sensation of handling the notecard."

To save time, author Gail Jarrow takes a simple digital camera with her when she does research at museums. She photographs relevant pages of documents so she can refer to them later. "They have the rules online and you just read them. A lot of museums say right off the bat that you can do it, though you can't use the flash."

When Chris Eboch wrote her first historical fiction novel she took notes on paper with a different heading for each sheet. "Now I do much the same thing," she says, "but I type my notes directly into the computer. I keep them in a single document, but I use Microsoft Word's Document Map function so I can easily jump to the appropriate section."

When Christine Kohler was doing the research for *Turkey in the News: Past, Present, Future* (Enslow), she contacted a professor from the University of Hawaii who had written a book about Turkish issues. "This professor, whom I've never met, introduced me to a Turkish journalist who put me in contact with people I needed to interview when I could

Technology for Notes

not get answers from news articles." Years ago this kind of research would have been done through the mail, but Kohler was able to use email to make all her contacts.

Kristi Holl visits Pinterest (pinterest.com) to find photos of places and things she needs to describe. She also uses Evernote—an application downloaded from the Internet (evernote.com). "Online research is a snap with Evernote. The free version works well for me. You can capture the URL automatically—a big help—and copy the whole web page into Evernote." She rarely copies things by hand word for word. "I either photocopy it at home or I read from the book using voice activation software and create quick documents that way."

For writers who rely on computers to store most of their research materials, Nancy Coffelt has an important piece of advice. "Either back up your files on an external hard drive or subscribe to online backup. You will have a computer meltdown at some point. Buying a new computer is a hassle. Losing information is a catastrophe."

Other Note-Taking Software
- ActionMethod: www.actionmethod.com
- Basecamp: basecamp.com
- Catch: catch.com
- Notational Velocity: notational.net. Mac only.
- Ominfocus: www.omnigroup.com. For Apple products.
- OneNote: part of Microsoft Office, and available for iPhone and Windows Phone
- Springpad: springpad.com
- Simplenote: simplenoteapp.com
- Trello: trello.com
- WorkFlowy: workflowy.com

the book organized in outline form, divided into chapters and so forth. It allows that writing process to be infused with a narrative power that would be hard to sustain if I didn't literally have the facts at my fingertips pre-filed and ready to go."

Kohler also organizes all her information into subtopics. "If I'm writing a long book, like the one on Turkey where I had to write about the beginning of people on Earth in that region through the twenty-first century, then I put each subtopic into a separate file folder. Even my books can be stacked on a table or my desk and bookcases, in different piles depending on the subtopic. I'll put the notes in order on my typing easel, and glance at the facts while I'm composing the article or book chapter on the computer.

Jarrow creates her outline before she starts taking notes. "I just do enough reading to see the broad picture, and then think about how I want to tell the story." She assigns each chapter of her outline a Roman numeral. Only then does she begin researching in depth. "I'm reading a fact and I'm thinking about where in the book it would go. So in addition to the source's page number, I also put in the margin the Roman numeral of the chapter where it would go." When she is ready to write chapter two, for example, "I will go back and look through my notes and my eye will go right to Roman numeral II and I'll reread things." She also has folders for each chapter where she keeps ideas, and copies of articles that pertain to that chapter's topic. "For me, it's the way to stay organized—the way to be visual about everything and to remind myself of information."

Photos & Audio Files

Be sure your system provides for photos, videos, and audio files. "When I write mysteries," says Kristi Holl, author of the Boarding School Mysteries (Zonderkidz), among other titles, "I always try to visit actual places: to take photos (to describe things more accurately); to talk to locals (who know the best anecdotes);

and to poke around, walk the streets, and hike the paths." On these trips Holl collects maps, brochures, and other visual research materials. "I use a three-ring binder for written notes and photocopies from books, plus pocket folders to hold brochures and postcards. I use colored tabs to organize the notes so I can find things quickly." Holl also goes to museums. Instead of spending time to read each poster or display, she takes photos if curators allow it. "When I put the digital photos on my desktop computer, the files are large enough to read each display."

When Holl is writing, she goes to the photos and other visuals. "I put myself back in the place I visited. I pretend to be the character and view the settings through her eyes. I also try to view the setting photos through the eyes of other characters, for conflict possibilities. For example, [I might note,] 'The cave below the cliff looks like a fabulous place to explore to a child; it looks like a good hiding place for a villain; and, to the mother it looks like a horrible accident waiting to happen.' All three ideas are useful to the plot."

Bausum sometimes uses photos and video files in a similar way. Her latest book, *Marching to the Mountaintop: How Poverty, Labor Fights and Civil Rights Set the Stage for Martin Luther King Jr.'s Final Hours* (National Geographic Children's Books), is about a labor strike in Memphis. "It's the sanitation strike that draws Dr. King to Memphis, and that's what he's [involved in] when he's killed," she says. "I looked at hundreds of photographs from this series of protests. Many of them are people carrying signs. I may never see a reference in a printed source about every single text that's on these signs, but I see photographs that show the content." She makes note cards for this kind of information. In her current work in progress, she has been using newsreel archives of protests in rural Mississippi. "One of the things you can capture off [the newsreels] are sounds. So, just the sounds of nature in the background are something I've made notes of because that should be introduced into the text."

Avoid Plagiarism

Your note-taking system can and should help you avoid plagiarism—the copying of another writer's words. "I always put the text from the source verbatim into my note card," says Bausum. "That's the way I'm most comfortable because then there's never ever any question in my mind what language was used, what terminology was used. I don't have to worry: 'Did I paraphrase what they said and now I'm paraphrasing it back to somebody else's language?' I really want the raw source right there—it totally takes plagiarism out of the equation."

Jarrow agrees. "The most important thing is to figure out a way not to plagiarize. It is such an easy thing to do inadvertently." Jarrow also often includes the exact words of her sources in her notes. "Sometimes it's faster to do that than to paraphrase. I don't want to stop and think about paraphrasing. So I use quotation marks around everything that I have copied word for word."

Eboch also uses quotation marks when she copies word-for-word, and she flags paraphrasing as well. "I'll make a note that it's my original interpretation. That's especially helpful if I'm working at a museum or with a reference book I can't take home. Otherwise, when I have my sources at my desk, my notes reference the page number of the original material so I can quickly check both the information and the phrasing."

"When I am writing a rough draft," says Holl, "and I use some quoted information, I color that part in red. It alerts me to go back when I'm done and be sure I summarize and change it enough so that I haven't used someone else's words."

Coffelt starts thinking about her own individual voice in her nonfiction from the very beginning, when she is still taking notes. "I don't copy and paste as I want to distance my voice from what I'm reading. It's important that I truly understand the material." To avoid plagiarism, she even checks her adjectives. "Because I can use up to a dozen sources for an article, it can be tricky, but since the thought of even inadvertent plagiarism is so awful to think about, I double-check my finished article against all my sources to make sure my words are truly all mine."

Kohler, too, finds that her own voice helps her avoid plagiarism. "When I have many, many sources, and I've researched deep enough and absorbed the material until I'm saturated with understanding, then I compose something fresh in my own voice, style and words," she explains.

You can capture sounds off old newsreels. "Just the sounds of nature in the background are something I've made notes of because that should be introduced into the text."

Whatever system you devise for taking notes and organizing your research, says Holl, "Be consistent. Do it from the very beginning of the project." Kohler advises, "Keep it simple, but detailed enough that in revisions with the editor you can expand upon or prove your case with multiple sources. Books go back to the library. Websites change, even disappear. That's why I copy everything."

Even with a system that works for you, recording and organizing research might not be your favorite part of the process. Bausum suggests when deciding on a topic, choose something you are passionate about. "Then you can love as much of this process as possible. If not write about what you know, write about what you want to know, and then the research will be a joy."

What's in a Name?

Researching & Choosing the Perfect Names for Characters

By Chris Eboch

Shakespeare wrote, "A rose by any other name would smell as sweet." With all due respect to the Bard, names are more important than that. Giving your characters the right names can influence how readers see them and even help you develop the characters' personalities. The wrong name can prevent readers from connecting with a character. Author and writing teacher Darcy Pattison provides an example: "Supposedly, in the first draft of *Gone with the Wind,* Scarlett O'Hara was named Pansy. That's not a name for the strong heroine we find in the final story."

To find a suitable character name, some authors simply consider people they know, whether friends or enemies. Jacqueline Horsfall says, "I use the names of my friends' kids or family members for positive, not negative, characters. Everyone thinks this is a hoot, especially the kids, and they look forward to seeing themselves in my published stories. [It's] a little bit of celebrity status for them, something to show their friends and boast about. In my YA novel *For the Love of Strangers* (Leap Books), I named the teacher after my grown niece, also a teacher. She was so thrilled that she showed the book to all the faculty members, who in turn bought copies for the school—an unintended perk, but happily so."

Jonathan Miller, author of mysteries such as *Rattlesnake Lawyer* (Cool Titles), draws on real life in another way. "I sometimes name villains or victims after old enemies. The victim in one novel was named after two childhood bullies. The first name was the first-grade bully. The last name was the ninth-grade bully." What better revenge than to kill off old enemies (in fiction, of course)?

For other authors, choosing names requires research. Books of baby names or sources of historically popular names help, especially when writing about foreign places or past times. Penny Raife Durant says, "When I was writing the novelization of my uncle's life from 1944 to 1956, I had names for all the American people involved. I had the names of my aunt's Italian family, but no others. I had to invent characters she would have come to know at Grottaglie Air Base and the town, and in Rome and aboard the *Andrea Doria*. The *Writer's Digest Character Naming Sourcebook* includes the meaning of the names, rather like a baby name book. I chose Agnese (ag NAY zay) for the woman who was a huge help to my aunt. The name means *pure*, and I love the Italian pronunciation."

Books and other sources of name lists can be a big help, but some people prefer a more hands-on approach. Freelance editor and proofreader Karen S. Elliott says, "I conducted research on a real person, my great-grandfather James Day. I had genealogical charts, completed by my mother's generation, but I wanted to experience more. I visited places where Welsh miner James settled in the Pennsylvania coal region. While there, I talked to historical society representatives, toured the coal mine where great-grandfather worked, and spent days in the mine's museum. I visited the county records and read microfiche, old newspapers, and historical publications. While reading the historical documents, I made note of interesting names of the times. I use these names for additional filler characters in my historical memoir and fiction."

Drawing on Meaning

For many writers, discovering the perfect name contributes to a character's development. "It's important for me to know up front the meaning of the name," Pattison says. "But, as I get into the story—third draft or so—it gets less important. In other words, it helps me to develop the character, but once the character is set in my mind, I don't worry so much about the name."

Scientist and writer Mike Space says, "When I get an idea for a novel, I outline the story and develop a character list. I like a character's name to reflect his or her personality. One way I will create a character's name is by doing computer searches on their personality traits. I find plugging the personality trait, plus *name meaning*, into a search engine works better than looking at any specific site. For example, the protagonist in my most recent story was so attractive she could make any man fall in love with her. I did a name search on *love* and among many name results found Hadraniel, which means *angel of love*. I shortened the name to Haddie and it worked perfectly."

"When my character has the perfect name, many other things fall into place as well."

Many authors have favorite resources for finding meaningful names. Vijaya Bodach, an author of many science books and an aspiring novelist, says, "When my character has the perfect name, many other things fall into place as well. As such, I always research the meanings of the names. I do not care whether my readers know the meaning, but it helps me stay focused. In my latest work in progress, *Damaged*, I had named the main character Pari, because she was like a fairy child. But something didn't sit right. After I finished the first draft, I looked through my name book and hit upon Rebecca. It means *bound, binding, servant of God*. It evoked the sense of being shackled and that is exactly how my character feels, so she is Rebecca now. As for her older sister, I hit upon the perfect name from the start: Joy. She is joyful."

While some authors do not care if readers understand a name's meaning, others intentionally create names that have positive or negative associations. Georgia Beaverson, who writes fantasy under the pen name Aiden Beaverson, says, "I love to make names reflect the nature of the character. It's a little nod to Charles Dickens, I guess. For instance, in my novel *The Hidden Arrow of Maether* (Delacorte), the girl protagonist is promised in marriage to an older man. I wanted his name to match my protagonist's repugnant feelings toward him, so I named him Tykk. The word is hard and abrupt and the sound makes the reader think of a blood-sucking insect. In another novel, the middle-school biology teacher is called Drippe, which absolutely suits his weak personality."

Creating Other Worlds

For authors writing science fiction or fantasy, naming is more complicated, but drawing on name lists and considering meaning can still provide inspiration. To create unusual worlds and bring them to life, many authors look to foreign cultures as sources. Beaverson says, "Because I write fantasy and magical realism or paranormal, I tend to choose Celtic or Scandinavian names."

Writer Vaughn Roycroft says, "One of the first things I did when I started my epic fantasy series in progress, A Legacy of Broken Oaths, was to come up with the names. The process of naming not just the characters but the nations, tribes, clans, cities, seas, and religious elements was elemental to world-building. Since the series is rooted in the epic culture clash between the Goths and the Roman Empire, I relied heavily on Gothic and Latin, making lists of words from the two languages I thought pertinent to the story. I particularly enjoyed naming my Roman antagonists, inventing their names from Latin root words. For example, Malvius is rooted in the Latin *malevelle*, meaning *of evil intent*. And Turgian is from the Latin *turgere*, meaning *to swell*, as in his head, with pride. In my experience, the essence of story emerges with world-building, and world-building emerges from the naming process."

Janice Hardy, author of the Healing Wars Trilogy (Balzer+Bray/HarperCollins), says, "I like to use whatever geographic area or culture I explored to create my world. I was inspired by Lake Victoria in Africa when I was world building for *The Shifter,* so I peppered the series with Afrikaans words as names. The main city, Geveg, means *struggle*, which I thought was perfect for a city struggling for independence. The villain in the second book is named Vyand, which means *enemy*. The names give clues about who a character is, and it's a lot of fun when a reader emails me and asks, 'Did you mean to name that character *betrayal*, because they totally did that.'"

This technique can work for some historical fiction. For my own Mayan historical adventure for kids, *The Well of Sacrifice,* I found an archaeology book that interpreted the name glyphs of ancient kings and queens into modern English. I borrowed names that suggested the characters' personalities. I chose Eveningstar for the heroine, while her flighty sister got the fragile name Feather Dawn. And how could a character named Great Skull Zero not be a villain?

Soft Names, Hard Names

While many authors focus on the meaning of names, the sound of a name is also important. Pattison says, "My BA is in speech pathology, my MA in audiology. One of the classes I enjoyed most was phonetics, which is the study of sounds. From that study comes an understanding of how sounds are made in the mouth, how they sound when spoken, etc."

"If you want a soothing, peace-loving character, use names with the soft consonants: Shayla, Mary, Rose, Will," Pattison recommends. "A whiny character? Use nasal sounds: Noreen, Angie, Nick. A villain? Use names with the sibilant sounds: Chaz, Seth, Zheng. A difficult teacher? Use hard sounds in his or her name: Mrs. Quark, Mr. Judd. Use names with a single syllable that also end with a stopping sound for characters that are jumpy, uncertain, or who are curt: Mart, Jan, Pym."

Pattison points out, "There are no rights and wrongs here; it's

More Tips on Naming

~ Try to vary the number of syllables in your main characters' names, avoid rhyming names, and make sure names do not start with the same letter. It is much easier to keep Eve, Leslie, and Jessica straight than Jenny, Jody, and Judy. This is especially true in fantasy and science fiction books using unusual names: Naming three characters El-ron, El-mon, and El-non will be confusing.

~ Consider using memorable names (Dylan, Hunter) rather than common ones (Dan, Bob). If a plain name best suits your main character, use unusual names for secondary characters.

~ In general, refer to characters consistently. If you vary between first name, last name, and nicknames, readers will struggle to keep track.

~ There may be times to break these rules, but do so only with good reason. For example, you can suggest character relationships by whether they call each other by a formal name, first name, or nickname.

just the way the name sounds—not what it means, not the denotations or connotations—pure sound. Pay attention to the different types of consonants and it might lead you to a great name. It's definitely not an exact science. It's more of a call for writers to be aware of the sound of things, especially something as important as a name."

Writers have many options for choosing perfect character names. And that's a good thing, because in truth, Rose by another name might not sound as sweet.

Inspiring Mind, Body, Soul

Research in Religion & Spirituality

By Mary Northrup

From ancient to modern times, for countless millions and for each individual, religion and spirituality have been of far-reaching importance personally, socially, and historically. They thus offer countless topics for writers. Whether you are researching for a book or an article, for an adult audience or for children, myriad resources will help you explore the many dimensions of religion and spirituality.

Writers and researchers can find print and electronic sources on religion in general; on particular faiths, religious denominations, or religious practices; and on theology. Spirituality comprises many streams, not just mainstream religions, including New Age, *alternative* religions such as Wicca, belief in a higher power not necessarily God, belief in many gods, astrology, mysticism, meditation, naturalism, and more.

A good place to start the search is at your local library. You will find books, magazines, and online databases that cover religion and spirituality, and the reference librarians can point out sources you may not know, helping with search terms, or introducing you to local resources. At the library, start by dipping into reference books, especially if you are unfamiliar with your subject. These encyclopedias, dictionaries, biographical sources, and even atlases provide you with an overview of your topic or pertinent facts to get you started.

The Bounty of Books

The library catalogue is your gateway to books. Search by keyword or subject to find what you need. If you are in the mood for browsing (and this is a good way to uncover some treasures), look for religious books in the 200s in a library that uses the Dewey Decimal Classification system, and BL through BX in a library that uses the Library of Congress Classification (LOC) system.

Most public and small college libraries use the Dewey system, while larger research university libraries use the LOC system. Which type of library is best for your research? Public libraries generally carry popular books, magazines, and databases suitable for the general adult public. Academic libraries tend to acquire scholarly sources, geared for the undergraduate or graduate student. The libraries at private religious colleges or universities could be your best source, since they will carry more religious books and other sources in their collections.

Your library may be part of a network of libraries, which enables you to search one book catalogue and find sources that you can order on interlibrary loan. Beyond that, most libraries allow, and even encourage, users to request books that do not appear in the catalogue, which they will try to find in other libraries throughout the country. You can also search WorldCat (www.worldcat.org), a database of books and the libraries that hold them. Some public libraries let you make a request through WorldCat via a connection to your library's website, and have those items sent on interlibrary loan. Check with a librarian to find out more.

Do not forget ebooks. Your library may have them available through the catalogue to view onscreen or to download to an ereader or tablet.

Like much in the field of religion and spirituality, books run the gamut from ancient texts to volumes on modern issues, from scholarly treatments to intensely personal memoirs. Your topic and the search terms you use in the catalogue should bring up what you need. Optimize your results by being as specific as possible. For example, if you are researching yoga and need to know about its history, search *yoga* and *history* to find books that specifically deal with this topic. To narrow down even more, add search terms: *yoga, history, transformation, ego, discipline, healing.*

Most libraries have copies of religious sacred texts on their shelves: the Bible, Qur'an, Book of Mormon, Upanishads, Tao Te Ching, and others. Many of these are now found on the web in their entireties. Some websites contain the full text of thousands of books no longer under copyright; these often include the sacred literature of religions. (See a list of websites on page 294, under *Texts online.*)

When searching for books, whether in the reference section, the circulating collection, or online, think of all related subjects that may apply to your topic. Art and architecture, literature, philosophy and ethics, archaeology, anthropology, and history can be closely aligned with religion and spirituality and are worth investigating, depending on your topic.

Magazines and Journals for All Tastes

Most libraries carry a collection of periodicals for browsing, and sometimes for checking out. These individual periodicals may be all-inclusive in their coverage of religion and spirituality or cover one faith or denomination. These, like books, run the gamut from scholarly to popular, with the popular titles most likely appearing in public libraries. Feature articles, news, commentary, and book reviews of books appear in these publications.

A look through *Magazines for Libraries, 20th edition* (ProQuest) under the categories of (1) Religion and Spirituality and (2) Well-Being reveals a wide diversity of periodicals that are considered standard for public and academic libraries. Catholic, Jewish, Muslim, Protestant Christian, Evangelical, Hindu, Buddhist, and Humanist publications all appear, as do periodicals that cover multiple reliions, or that address nature spirituality, shamanism, paganism, and other varieties of spirituality.

Connecting to More with Online Databases

Besides browsing through magazines or journals or faithfully reading them weekly or monthly, you may choose to search for articles through an online database. Your local public library probably subscribes to a number of these services, which you can access either in the library or at home using your library card number. If you are a student or employee at a college or university, the library at your institution also subscribes to databases, and may have some of the general ones as well as the more scholarly databases. In either case, look for the following.

- ATLA Religion Database (American Theological Library Association)
- Infotrac Religion and Philosophy
- JSTOR (Use Advanced Search to search through more than 70 scholarly religion journals.)
- ProQuest Religion
- Religion and Philosophy Collection (EBSCOhost)

In addition, religious and spiritual topics may be reported in magazines and journals that are not exclusively religious in nature, and therefore may not show up in religious databases. So you may also want to search the following general periodical databases, which carry millions of articles from popular and scholarly publications.

- Academic OneFile and General OneFile (Infotrac)
- Academic Search and MasterFILE (EBSCOhost)
- ProQuest Research Library

Plentiful Websites

Many writers prefer to start their research on the Internet. If you have done any searching at all concerning religion or spirituality, you know the wide diversity of sites available. Even more than books or periodicals, websites must be evaluated. If an author is identified, that is a plus. Many sites, however, aggregate pieces or provide information without bylines. So it is important to identify the publisher of the site and determine whether the information is trustworthy. For example, the BBC Religion website is sponsored by the British Broadcasting Corporation, a known and trusted media company. If in doubt about a source, look for a link to an About Us page on the website you are exploring. It may give you a clue as to the publisher, its mission, and purpose.

Directory sites:

These sites do not provide content, but instead are collections of links to other sites. They are good places to start your research.

~ Internet Public Library. http://www.ipl.org. Click on Resources by Subject, then Arts and Humanities, then Religion and Theology.

~ Virtual Religion Index. http://virtualreligion.net/vri/index.html. Click on one of the topics in the long list or search the site.

Content sites:

~ Adherents.com. www.adherents.com. Find more than 43,000 statistics in this treasure trove. They range from the common, such as lists of the major world religions by size, to the obscure, such as the religious affiliation of famous science fiction and fantasy writers.

~ BBC Religion. www.bbc.co.uk/religion. From podcasts to quizzes to a multifaith calendar that lists religious holy days and festivals, this site is filled with information. Check out the list of religions (www.bbc.co.uk/religion/religions) to become familiar with the beliefs, customs, history, structure, worship, and subdivisions of 20 religions.

~ Beliefnet. www.beliefnet.com. With the tagline "Inspiration, Spirituality, Faith," this site includes articles, news, prayers, and features to encourage believers and searchers on many spiritual paths. Wellness is included, with pieces on meditation, yoga, and personal growth.

~ Patheos. www.patheos.com. A source with articles, stories, blogs, and columns covering most of the major faiths, as well as atheist and pagan topics. With many ways to connect today—Facebook, Twitter, newsletters, and RSS feeds—this site aims to open dialogue and engage readers.

~ Pew Forum on Religion & Public Life. www.pewforum.org. Through surveys and research, the Pew Research Center's Forum on Religion & Public Life "seeks to promote a deeper understanding of the issues at the intersection of religion and public affairs." The site has statistics and demographic information as well as unbiased analyses of some of society's major hot button issues.

~ Religion Link. www.religionlink.com. A source of story ideas and sources for journalists, compiled by journalists. Each piece provides an overview of the topic and a long list of sources, both national and regional. It includes a Religion Stylebook, which covers usage, spelling, and pronunciation.

~ Religious Tolerance. www.religioustolerance.org. Explore more than 6,000 essays on world religions, nontheistic beliefs, spirituality and ethics, and the Hot Topics section, which covers controversial issues.

Texts online:

~ Christian Classics Ethereal Library. www.ccel.org. Read the full text of classic Christian writings in this easy-to-use site. Search by title, author, subject, or scripture passage, or browse by title, author, format, language, or subject.

~ Internet Sacred Text Archive. www.sacred-texts.com. Explore a large selection of online books covering religion, mythology, and folklore. The major religions' texts are included here, as well as Native American, gnosticism, prophecy, tarot, and many others.

~ Religion–Online. www.religion-online.org. Find more than 6,000 scholarly Christian full-text books, articles, and chapters on a variety of topics, including ethics, social issues, theology, culture,

Market Information & News

~ *Publishers Weekly* is a great source for staying up to date on what is going on in the publishing world. This magazine provides feature articles, which sometimes cover religion or spirituality, news, and book reviews which regularly include religion/spirituality for children and adults. Watch for the spring and fall religion issues, which focus on new books by publisher, and the quarterly religion update, which includes articles on trends, author profiles, and some reviews. You can also subscribe free to the *PW* eletter on religious publishing.

Annual market guides are good sources for searching for book or magazine publishers interested in writing on religion and spirituality. Try these:

From Writer's Institute Publications (www.writersbookstore.com):
~ *The Best of the Magazine Markets for Writers*. Look at the category index for Fiction: Inspirational/Spiritual, New Age/Metaphysical, and Religion/Belief Systems.
~ *Book Markets for Children's Writers*. Look at the category index for Religious (Fiction) and Religious (Nonfiction).
~ *Magazine Markets for Children's Writers*. Look at the category index for Religious (Fiction) and Religious (Nonfiction).

From Writer's Digest Books:
~ *Children's Writer's and Illustrator's Market*. In the subject index, see Religion under Book Publishers and under Magazines, for both fiction and nonfiction markets.
~ *Writer's Market*. See Astrology, Metaphysical and New Age, and Religious under Consumer Magazines, and Church Administration and Ministry under Trade Journals.

From Tyndale House Publishers:
~ *The Christian Writer's Market Guide*

and more.

~ Bartleby.com. www.bartleby.com. Some religious texts are included in this reference source, including the King James Bible, *Lives of the Saints,* Bagavad-Gita, and Koran chapters.

~ Project Gutenberg. www.gutenberg.org. This huge collection of online books includes some religious writings. Browse or search over 39,000 titles. For just a taste, search *spiritual* or *religious*.

Experts

Not all information comes to writers and researchers through a printed page or a screen. Sometimes people can be the best sources. Talk to a member of the clergy. Contact a local seminary or theological school if there is one in your area. Professors of theology or religious studies are good sources. You may also find experts in bookstore owners, in particular those who run religious or spirituality-based stores. Depending on the focus of your book or article, interviews with adherents of a particular religion or practitioners of a type of spirituality may also be invaluable.

Nostalgia: Getting It Right

By Susan Sundwall

The song "Remember" that is so poignantly offered in the 1998 movie *You've Got Mail* strikes at the heart of what it means to experience *nostalgia*. It is a deep pining for something long ago and far away, a sentiment echoed in the first two lines of Harry Nilson's song. Nostalgia is a universal emotion exploited in movies, books, essays, magazine articles, music, and poetry—making the market possibilites for nostalgic writing nearly endless. But because nostalgia is also a condition wrapped completely in memories and longing, writers of nostalgia should pause and exercise caution, about subject, style, quality, and audience.

Personal & Collective Memory

It is helpful to understand all the ways nostalgia manifests itself. Along with purely sweet memories, it often also contains a bittersweet component. Mental health experts like Christi Wright, a therapist in New York state, believe nostalgia is a positive force. "Nostalgia helps us cope with change and, from a mental health perspective, it assists us to begin the mental process of adaptation by mediating negative thought states."

Researchers at the University of Southampton in the U.K. have found nostalgia to be a potent mood booster. Since memories often star the important people in our lives, they may give us a comforting sense of belonging. According to research reported in *Psychology Today*, psychologist and Associate Professor Tim Wildschut found that people who write about a nostalgic event are more cheerful after the exercise, compared with people who write about an everyday experience. The research also showed that people who write about good memories report higher self-esteem and feel more positively about friendships and close relationships. ("Nostalgia Sweet Remembrance," by Marina Krakovsky. *Psychology Today.* www.psychologytoday.com/articles/200605/nostalgia-sweet-remembrance)

The nostalgia writer may seek to elicit both the pleasant and unpleasant components of a remembered emotion. This is especially true for those who write about situations that took place in war years or times of great social upheaval. Wright explains the connection between trauma and nostalgia: "Now I realize people do wax nostalgic when they are engaged in positive activities, but if you listen, the talk will invariably turn to loss, i.e., trauma. Not in a dour, sad way, but in a wistful way."

As an example she imagines someone commenting, "Whatever happened to that floor sweeper anyway? He sure was a nice fellow." Wright explains that in a shared nostalgic moment, we may "all know what happened to [the floor sweeper], but we don't want to or need to say it. Nostalgia is a coping mechanism and it reduces blood pressure and calms the brain by engaging the grief centers of the brain in a productive way. This is why it is so important to reminisce after the death of a loved one, or go to the place where your house once stood after it was swept up in a tornado. These acts help us cope."

The best nostalgia writing pulls the reader into a bygone era using personal memories and blending them with historical events and times. We tap into the collective memory and empathize with others who share similar sentimental yearnings and experiences. Even though memories blur and are perhaps idealized over time, those changes in "reality" do not necessarily work against writing a good nostalgic piece.

Ken Tate, Editor of *Looking Back* and *Good Old Days* magazines, says, "If you were sitting on your grandfather's knee listening to the story of his family's migration west during the Great Depression, he might well not have every stopping place or watering hole along the route right, but that would not invalidate his story and its importance to you. This is in no way giving license for a nostalgic article to take liberty with facts, but it should salve the history buff's ire if something doesn't exactly measure up to the test of history."

Balance Memory & Fact

Striking a balance between memory and fact can be delicate. We have memories because of daily events, some of great import, but maybe only to us. If you want to impress the feel of an era on your readers, flesh out your story with details of that time. If you cannot remember which war Uncle John fought in, find out. If you do not, everything you write after that will be skewed and confusing to your reader. Fighting in the European theater in World War II was very different than being in Korea in 1952, even if the experience of war also has universality.

You may be writing an article or story that is not nostalgic in its primary purpose, but touches on the nostalgic, sometimes unexpectedly. Publications that invite folklore are a prime example.

"*Farmers' Almanac* is synonymous with nostalgia, and while we try hard to keep [the magazine] current, we appreciate the extent to which people enjoy nostalgia," says Managing Editor Sandi Duncan. "Weather lore and other folklore are always topics that gain great attention, whether in the print edition or online. Sometimes to us, the weather lore seems old in that we knew about the rhyme or reason [behind it,] but when we share it again with our audiences, there is a great response."

Linda O'Connell is a multi-genre writer and award-winning poet who reminds writers that nostalgia informs too. She says, "Everyone has shared similar life experiences. Nostalgia transports us to our early comfort levels, when times seemed easier, before our lives were so harried. Readers of all ages know what perspiration feels like rolling off the forehead, but generations

Revelations

Award-winning writer Linda O'Connell shares her experiences writing for the Chicken Soup for the Soul series:

"I have written numerous articles for magazines and newspapers, but my greatest satisfaction comes from writing personal essays. My dad was functionally illiterate but he could tell a story that kept listeners spellbound. I believe that the personal essay is a creative form of authentic storytelling that can span the generations.

"To date, I have been published in 15 Chicken Soup for the Soul titles. All of my stories are based on my experiences. "A Working Mom's Retirement Plan," published in *Chicken Soup for the Working Mom's Soul*, is a blend of humor, inspiration and nostalgia. I detailed how, although I love being a preschool teacher, I aspired to be in the creative arts: journalism, photography, acting. After my kids were grown, I looked back on my life and realized that I had attained my aspirations . . . . Although I never earned a journalism degree, I honed my writing skills each night as I wrote in my childrens' journals . . . . I didn't become a professional photographer, but I spent a fortune on film, flash bulbs, albums and eventually large plastic tubs as an archive for family photos. Acting? Never on stage, but I certainly deserved an Academy Award for my performance on a school bus."

"My personal essays have a unique slant. In *Chicken Soup for the Soul Food and Love*, I assumed most writers would submit stories about chocolate and romance. I wrote about how I was tempted by the *bad boy*, a piece of apple walnut cake that I rediscovered in a deli. My story evolved into a true account of friendship between Rose, my late best friend, and me, and an apple walnut cake we baked together.

"'Listen to the Children,' published in *Chicken Soup Devotionals for Moms*, about an incident that happened between me and our three-year-old granddaughter, was a long shot. I assumed the editors wanted stories written by and for moms, but I submitted anyway. It was accepted because moms of all ages could relate to a story from a grandma's perspective. My advice to writers: Think out of the box; take a chance.

"My personal essays have appeared in numerous anthologies and also literary magazines. The closer I write to the heart, the better my chance of acceptance."

ago folks cooled under electric fans and prior to that, paper fans. Today's kids are electronically connected and live in climate-controlled houses. They don't know what telephone booths are and they text instead of using typewriters. When writing nostalgia, not only do I strive to entertain, but also to inform."

Personal & Family Research

Once you have a nostalgia topic selected, and an editor who agrees it is a good one, you need to combine your memories with real research that will give your writing meaning and weight.

> "Kids don't know what telephone booths are and they text instead of typing. When writing nostalgia, not only do I strive to entertain, but to inform."

A few years ago a regional newspaper published a story I had written about my father. As I wrote, I was determined to state accurately why it was that he left the family to work in Greenland right after the Korean War. Family lore contended it had something to do with airplanes, but I was not sure about much else. So I contacted one of my brothers who, along with one of my sisters, has kept our family stories alive. Tim was my first resource and steered me in the right direction. I was able to access public domain material from the U.S. Air Force and discovered that at that time civilians had been contracted to construct airstrips at Thule Airbase in Greenland. Dad had gone there to make enough money to move the family out of poverty in Minnesota and into, he hoped, the boom times in California. By the time I had thoroughly researched the period and the people, I had more information than I needed, but it felt good to have solid facts to weave with my memories. That research gave weight and veracity to my story.

"With the assumption that, when writing nostalgia, the story [originates] from the writer's personal cache of memories," says Tate, "the tools [then] become a little more generalized. First, start with family sources. Run the story by parents (if still living), siblings, and other, older members of the family. Do their recollections jibe with your own? Be sure to look through family photographs for some verification. Was the car your parents drove in 1958 indeed a 1960 Studebaker? Photos have a way of firming up memories and providing some independent verification of basic facts. The writer may need to be a sleuth after that."

O'Connell says, "Sometimes when I stir a dust-covered memory, I must approach family members. Believe me, their memories are as individual as each of their personalities, so I write as truthfully as possible from my own perspective. I also search the Internet with key words: *nostalgia* and the topic."

At *Farmers' Almanac,* Duncan agrees about research and primary sources, which only the writers themselves can provide for their personal nostalgia: "We count a lot on our freelancers and copy editors to research topics. Online [research] is okay, but meeting people and doing some family tree type of history is better."

Expanding out from your own family stories to online research can open many possibilities. I can attest to the vast amount of material availbable on Ancestry.com, for instance. My sister Elizabeth took up the gauntlet of family historian and used this site to access the manifest from the ship that brought our paternal grandparents to the U.S. from Sweden. She also contacted relatives in Northern Minnesota who were able to provide long-held family photos. The site can be used to access information about various eras, to enhance your story.

Stay focused and dismiss anything that will muddy your own story, whether it originates in memories or research. For instance, in the piece about my father, I did not think it necessary to mention that my Uncle Vern, his brother, had gone with him to Greenland. I could have gone off on a tangent about that aspect of the story, but my reader would not have cared.

"Use library and/or Internet sources to help verify information garnered from family sources and old photographs," says Tate, at *Looking Back* and *Good Old Days*. He continues, "If you write about your own memories, there is a much better chance of getting the story right, unless self-delusion gets in the way. Nostalgia, with its bittersweet memories, is inherently first person in its telling. As long as the story/information/sources are within the one generation of the writer's life, it will make the facts easier to verify."

Another multimedia source is the History Channel, whose website lists topics that include Eras and Decades, People, Events, World War II, and even holidays in all their vast array. Plumbing the depths of the topics on this site can enrich the nostalgic angle of your story, and memory sparkers abound. For even more scholarly possibilities, do not neglect the Library of Congress resources (loc.gov), including the sections American Memory, Veterans History, and Sound Recordings.

The town historian is a resource many writers overlook. Our local historian, former teacher Dominick C. Lizzi, spent 15 years gleaning records, searching out maps, photos, and obtaining access to the records of Valatie, New York, residents. His is an exhaustive piece of work and a rich resource . Lizzi has his counterpart in thousands of towns and cities across the country. Go and find the one you need.

What Editors Say

After your personal memory becomes an idea, you perform the necessary wider research, and you complete your article or story, comes the marketing of your nostalgia. Where are the markets? What do editors want to see more often?

"We get hundreds of submissions each month, so it is definitely a buyer's market," says Tate at *Looking Back* and *Good Old Days*. "We

Nostalgia Markets

~ *Blurt Magazine:* 140 Southwood Ave., Silver Spring, MD 20901. http://blurt-online.com. Editor, Scott Crawford.

~ *Capper's:* Ogden Publications, 1503 SW 42nd St., Topeka, KS 66609. www.ogdenpubs.com/writers/cappers. Editor, Hank Will.

~ *Catholic Forester:* 355 Shuman Boulevard, P.O. Box 3012, Naperville, IL 60566. www.catholicforester.org/servicecenter/catholicforestermagazine/WriterandArtistGuidelines.aspx Editor, Patricia Baron.

~ *Chicken Soup for the Soul:* P.O. Box 700, Cos Cob, CT 06807. www.chickensoup.com. Editor, D'ette Corona.

~ *Christian Science Monitor:* 210 Massachusetts Ave., Boston MA 02115. www.csmonitor.com/About/Contributor-guidelines#homeforum. Editor, John Yemma.

~ *Country Woman*: 5400 S. 60th St., Greendale, WI 53129. www.country-womanmagazine.com/contributor-guidelines. Editor, Lori Lau Grzybowski.

~ *Good Old Days* and *Looking Back:* 306 East Parr Road, Berne, IN 46711. www.goodolddaysmagazine.com, www.lookingbackmagazine.com. Editor, Ken Tate.

~ *Grand Magazine:* 4791 Baywood Point Dr S, St. Petersburg FL, 33711. www.grandmagazine.com. Editor, Christine Crosby.

~ *Grit*: 1503 S.W. 42nd St. Topeka, KS 66609. www.grit.com/guidelines.aspx Editor, Caleb Regan.

~ **Kiwi Publishing:** P.O. Box 3852, Woodbridge, CT 06525. www.thinthreads.com/submit.php. Editor, Stacy Battat.

~ *Lutheran Digest:* 6160 Carmen Ave., Inver Grove Heights, MN 55076. www.lutherandigest.com. Editor, Nick Skapyak.

get way too many Christmas-related stories each year (because of the nostalgic nature of the holiday), and fewer stories related to some of the other holidays. Any well-written article about memories of the writer's life are welcome. Humor and wit are a definite plus."

Farmers' Almanac has a list of favorites, says Duncan: "weather lore, where words originate, *remember-when* types of stories."

Do not be dismayed if in some publications you research you

Nostalgia Markets

- *Montana Magazine:* P.O. Box 5630,Helena, MT 59604. www.montana-magazine.com. Editor, Beverly Magley.
- **Not Your Mother's Book:** P.O. Box 607, Orangevale, CA 95662. http://publishingsyndicate.com/publishing_syndicate/submissions/nymb_submit_guidelines.html. Editors, Linda O'Connell and Diana Graveman.
- *Old Farmers' Almanac:* P.O. Box 1609, Lewiston, Maine 04240. www.almanac.com/content/writers-guidelines. Editor, Sandi Duncan.
- *Range Magazine:* 106 East Adams, Suite 201, Carson City, NV 89706. www.rangemagazine.com/guidelines/index.htm. Editor, Carolyn Joy Hadley.
- *Reminisce Magazine:* 5400 S. 60th St., Greendale, Wisconsin 53129. www.reminisce.com/submit-a-story. Editor, John Burlingham.
- *The Saturday Evening Post:* 1100 Waterway Blvd., Indianapolis, IN 46202. www.saturdayeveningpost.com/about/submission-guidelines. Editor, Jackie Leo.
- *Significant Living:* N7528 Aanstad Rd, P.O. Box 5000, Iola, WI 54945. www.significantliving.org/writers-guidelines.html. Editor, Diana Jones.
- **Telling Our Stories Press:** 185 AJK Blvd., #246 Lewisburg, PA 17837. http://tellingourstoriespress.com/pb/wp_ff7ee108/wp_ff7ee108.html. Editor, Co Co Harris.
- **Valley Living:** Media for Living, 1251 Virginia Ave., Harrisonburg, VA 22802. www.mediaforliving.org/about. Editor, Melodie Davis.
- *Yankee Magazine:* P.O. Box 520, Dublin, NH 03444. www.yankeemagazine.com/contact/contactus/guidelines. Editor, Debby Despres.

do not see *nostalgia* as a submissions topic. Search the magazine, newspaper, or book publisher's website and archives. You will not see nostalgia listed on the *Saturday Evening Post* site, but when you read the most popular articles listed you will find titles like "I Wish I Could Be Andy Taylor. He's Nicer," or "What the Operators Heard in 1907." Both of these topics simply drip nostalgia. The same could be said for the magazine's iconic covers.

O'Connell's favorite websites to help locate nostalgia markets are Funds for Writers (www.fundsforwriters.com); Christian Writers Submissions (www.christwriters.info); the Practicing Writer (groups.yahoo.com/group/practicing-writer); Ask Wendy, the Query Queen (http://askwendy.wordpress.com); and *Reminisce Magazine* (www.reminisce.com).

O'Connell is also the co-creator of *Not Your Mother's Book . . . On Family*, a collection of stories published by the Publishing Syndicate, which has about 40 titles in development. She is looking for submissions. "I am definitely seeking nostalgic, true, first-person stories that are fresh, edgy, quirky and/or humorous. We are not seeking sad, or sweet and sappy stories." For example, she says, "Tell on your sibling. What sort of antics occurred at your dinner table or at your grandparent's house?"

Elements of nostalgia abound in writing that is done for magazines, memoirs, anthologies, and ebooks. For all, the one task you must accomplish for a good nostalgic piece is to remember.

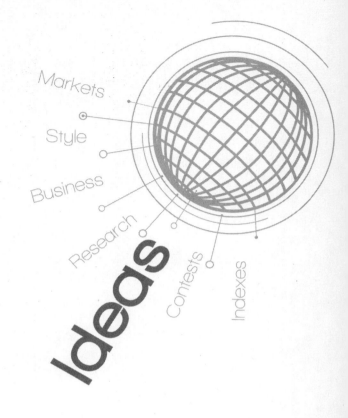

Markets

Style

Business

Research

Ideas

Contests

Indexes

Creativity

Where Does It Come From & How Do I Get Some?

By Christina Hamlett

"Oh, I could never write a book! I'm just not that creative." If you've heard people say that—or if you have ever said it yourself—you are are engaging in the same chicken-and-egg debate about creativity's origins and causality that has argued for centuries. If everyone is born with creativity, why doesn't everyone use it to best advantage? Conversely, if it is a skill that can only be learned, how do we account for individuals who become creative despite their lack of access to the right education, tools, and encouragement?

Nature versus Nurture

Pasteur's dictum that "chance favors the prepared mind" may have referred to scientific experimentation, but it also applies to the concept of mastering creative forces, at various levels of consciousness. Creative people combine the preparation of being able to observe anomalies—people, situations, events—that are not as they *should* be, and the masterful ability to take them to another level of understanding.

Dr. Joan C. King (www.cellular-wisdom.com), a former Dominican nun turned neuroscientist, spent three decades researching this issue as Professor and Department Chair at Tufts University School of Medicine. As one of the few voices talking about creativity from a scientific, cellular-level perspective, she says, "I believe that every individual cell in our bodies is *creative*, adding up to each of us having the inherent ability to be creative. In other words, we each have our own unique fingerprint of creativity."

Within that context, however, is the question of whether creativity is a constant trait, an occasional state of being, or something that is only defined by specific outcomes. Is a toddler banging on metal pots with a spoon, for instance, participating in a creative act, or do we not label it as such until the noise

Each of us has "our own unique fingerprint of creativity."

resembles a sound we interpret as music? By the same token, can we applaud something as a truly creative product if it's the result of imitation, trial-and-error, or deductive/inductive reasoning?

Internationally acclaimed artist and designer Pablo Solomon (www.pablosolomon.com) believes that the biggest question is whether children are really creative or just appear to be so. "If a child were pressured to *create* a specific new product or slogan or whatever, would that child be able to stay on task and yet be creative?" The perception that children are creative, he continues, derives from five simple facts: "(1) They don't have preconceived notions of how to do things; (2) they're not influenced by societal pressures; (3) they're not concerned about outcomes; (4) they don't have financial or time constraints; and (5) they're not trying to fit a sexually stereotypical mold. Can you teach creativity? I really don't think so, but I do think you can teach people to shed their fears of rejection, failure, and ridicule that often prevent them from allowing their minds the freedom to think what no one else appears to be thinking."

Nancy B. Irwin, a doctor of clinical psychology and hypnotherapy (www.drnancyirwin.com), advances the observation that "[c]reativity comes from both nature and nurture. Certainly there's a creativity gene (those who are more right-brained); this explains the nature. The nurturing of this innate talent can either be squelched by rigid, close-minded *practical*' caregivers—'Stop daydreaming! What are your chances of being a writer? Join the real world!'—or be encouraged by loving, open-minded, supportive caregivers. There's also a third piece: the individual's personal choice. There are some people who may inherently have less creative talent, yet are so passionate about it that they learn to use and enhance what creativity they do possess. Sometimes these people go further because they just work harder."

Right Brain versus Left Brain

"Creativity may be most readily accessible to those born with right-brain dominance," says Laura Oliver, author of *The Story Within: New Insights and Inspiration for Writers* (Penguin) (www.thestorywithin.com). "This is the tendency to seek patterns, recognize resemblances, and understand metaphor; in other words, those of us who see George Washington's likeness in a cloud but can't remember his name. Like blue eyes, right-brain dominance may be an inherited trait, but creativity begins by understanding everyone has the creative hardware; some of us just need help accessing it. Like any behavior, original expression grows stronger when expected, nurtured, and rewarded. And here's where the left brain comes in: The left brain—that logical hemisphere and source of computer-like, linear thinking—can't stand inconsistency. The left brain absolutely must make your inner and outer world match so you know you're sane! This means that when you tell yourself you're creative, your left brain will begin to look for evidence that you are. This, in turn, reinforces the right brain's efforts to make associations and put things together in a new way."

"Different temperaments get creative in different ways," says Jen Lilienstein, founder of Kidzmet (www.kidzmet.com), a resource for parents and teachers that identifies the "unique learning languages" of children. "Unleashing creativity depends on which Jungian cognitive processes an individual happens to prefer," says Lilienstein. "For example, in order for *intuitive* types to get creative, they need to get tantalized by possibilities. For *sensing* types to relish creating, they need to be given tangible objects to enhance/improve. For *feeling* types to get creative, they need to key into the human benefit of their creativity. For *thinking* types to create, they need to see the logical benefit of the creative direction."

In 2007, author Suzanne Kingsbury founded Wild Words, a resource organization for writers that is based on neuro-theologic research that has been done at Penn and Harvard. "Studies have found that ceasing activity in the part of the brain associated with negativity/resistance helps us be creative and access our imagination. Creativity is inherent. Children play, they make believe, they see fairies in the woods, turn bedrooms into enchanted forests and carpets into hot lava. We unlearn creativity as we mature. In order to recapture that which is *lost*, we need to learn to set aside the conditioned part of ourselves—the part that has traditionally been called left brain—so we can suspend the need for hard evidence and play imaginatively on the page."

Defining Creativity

The word *creativity* is so commonly tied to artistic pursuits that we often forget it exists in other fields of endeavor. "The creativity that writes a symphony isn't the same creativity that designs a new jet engine," says author Joseph A. Bailey, a veteran TV comedy writer (*The Muppets, Sesame Street,* and author of *Memoirs of a Muppets Writer*) who spent 20 years putting words in the mouths of frogs, pigs, and a loopy Swedish chef. "The composer hears original music in his head while the engineer is watching gears and belts go around. Those creative processes can also be found in numerical operations, languages, and the natural sciences." While Bailey believes that creativity is an inherited trait, he is just as positive that it can also be directed. "After you discover your particular gift of creativity, you still have to acquire the complementary craft. In other words, you can't write the next *War and Peace* if you can't compose a decent sentence."

"I used to think I was strictly a numbers person," says freelance writer and editor Eartha Watts-Hicks (www.earthatone.com). "I have a degree in business administration with a concentration in accounting. My introduction to writing came when my English professor explained the skill to me in formula form. Before that, I just couldn't get it! What I learned is that writing is passion, observation, expression, and imagination. If we're not passionate and imaginative, we can easily observe and record. The gift itself may be God given, but in the event we're not blessed with that talent, the technique can still be acquired through learning the skill, practice, critiques—and rewrites!"

How is it that you can be creative in some areas but a total dud in others? Janet Pfeiffer, President and CEO of Pfeiffer Power Seminars, attributes her 20-year creative evolution as an author and award-winning amateur nature photographer to the practice of associating with, and keenly observing, others who are creative in arenas with which she is not familiar. "I have zero ability to decorate my house, so I began watching HGTV and paying close attention to the way designers think. They take ordinary items and find ways to repurpose them. They constantly think outside the box, taking risks when mixing colors, textures, styles, etc. I listen to song lyrics and notice the unique ways lyricists take something ordinary like 'I love you' and express it as 'My heart beats only for you.' By subscribing to the process of these creative people, my writing style (and home decorating skills) have grown."

Exercising Your Creative Muse

You cannot expect to run a marathon successfully if your body is not in shape. Why should it be any different when you approach the hurdle representing your writing career? If you want a more powerful creative self, you need to put it on a strength-training regimen that you have the discipline to commit to on a consistent basis. For starters:

~ Study paintings and make up stories about the people depicted.
~ Rewrite the first line of whatever book you are reading—in 20 different ways.
~ Compose your next shopping list as a rhyming poem.
~ Make origami birds out of every rejection letter you have received.

You must dismiss any notions that creativity can only be learned when you are young. Murray Grossan, M.D., author of *Stressed? Anxiety? Your Cure Is in the Mirror* (CreateSpace), believes that practicing creativity is a vital secret to staying young and being healthy. "My book challenges seniors to design a perfect spa, imagine what a future hospital would be like, and think about how they'd build a house on the moon or a car for Mars." Grossan's exercises also incorporate memorization games with a creativity component. "Memorize shopping lists by gross distortions such as giant tomatoes pierced by celery stalks."

"Creativity isn't merely the ability to produce an item such as a painting or a book," says Edie Weinstein, author of *The Bliss Mistress Guide to Transforming the Ordinary into the Extraordinary* (Balboa Press). "We're each the canvas on which we daily recreate ourselves. Creativity can be honed with practice and encouragement, but deep down you need to thoroughly love what you do. Find joy in the creative process, not merely the finished product, by experimenting with what lights you up. Explore with all of your senses awake and aware. That is your artistry."

"Before I start to write," says Bailey, "I spend some time working on a crossword puzzle. It loosens up your thinking. Is the clue a noun or a verb? Is there a theme? Is it a pun? Is it a joke? And, all this time, you're working with words."

"One of the biggest mistakes many young aspiring designers and artists make," Solomon says, "is to focus so heavily on being creative that they never develop the technical skills, discipline, focus, and tenacity to turn their ideas into reality. My advice is to drop your preconceived ideas, consider anything that pops up and evaluate its possibility later. You have to believe creativity is out there and available to anyone who opens his or her mind. The Japanese have a great term for this called *mind of no mind*. That is to be totally aware, yet with no predetermined thoughts."

Can you firmly tune out the naysayers in your life, including that pesky one in your head? "I urge every writer to quiet their chattering cerebral cortex," says King, "and look within to discover, and bring out, their creativity."

Watts-Hicks recommends reading books on the craft of writing to uncover a formula that works for you. "Take notes constantly. Record everything that impresses you in your travels and all the reasons why—the abrasive texture of bricks, the stench of a fish market remaining in your clothing, a metal playground slide and the resultant burns on your thighs after taking your child on a play-date. Anything can spark a story's beginning! Set a regular writing schedule and stick to it, even if you're not producing the number of pages you believe a *real* writer should. Give yourself permission to write terribly, too; your goal isn't to be perfect but to improve."

Kingsbury emphasizes that play is essential to the creation of great art. "If you aren't having fun, stop! Lose time by doing something physical; great writing forgets time and starts in the body. Go stack wood, garden, paint a room. Have your early efforts at expressing yourself been 'creatively abused' by others? Confront those demons! Write it out, how you felt about it, and your defense. Read this defense every day; in time this will take deeper root than the demon's voice." She also recommends joining a noncritical writing group. "Once you know your strengths, any weakness in your craft will fall away."

Like Kingsbury, Oliver is a proponent of engaging in repetitive motor movements that put the left, logical, brain into neutral and allow the evocative right brain free reign. "Ironing, driving, taking a shower, polishing silver, folding laundry, running or walking—anything you do by rote, on autopilot, gives rise to creative thought. When you write, do so with abandon. Follow the energy, take every side road. Your inner artist may have found a better route, or even a more gratifying destination. Get specific: Not 'how am I going to resolve my plot,' but 'what should my character do when the phone rings?' Write down every wild, nonsensical idea that comes to you. Imagine that you're catching fireflies on a dark night and their collective light will be the only one by which you find your way home."

If your last vestige of procrastination is that you are just waiting for your muse to get in the right mood, consider these words from the incomparable Pearl S. Buck: "I don't wait for moods. You accomplish nothing if you do that. Your mind must know it has got to get down to work."

You heard the lady. Go start creating!

Identifying Strong Topics

Where Research & Idea Development Meet

By Carmen Goldthwaite

Whether lying in a hammock contemplating nature, taking the dog for a stroll, donning white gloves in a hushed library to handle special archival papers, or taking a trip: Ideas sprout in many places. They may have lain dormant in memories. They may have circled in thoughts and questions. At some point, they snag your attention.

When that happens, the passive research of a stroll, a library visit, a trip, begin to fuel more active pursuits and expressions. You begin to ask questions, research answers, and generate more questions. In that process, ideas can be tested to see how they might work in a story, article, or book.

"Watching a movie, some random image will strike lightning and begin this evolutionary process," says young adult novelist Rosemary Clement-Moore, whose recent title is *Brimstone* (Ember/Random House). "The sprout comes up, nurturing more and more ideas." She describes her passive research process in this way: "I feel like my brain is pulling it all in—everything I read, see on TV or in a movie goes past my head, goes into the brain, and sits there in primordial ooze until it crawls out. I don't know when it will crawl out."

Visual Research & Ideas

Time travel and mystery author J. Suzanne Frank grabs visuals from travel, as ideas and research begin to expand. A writer, teacher, and Director of The Writer's Path at SMU, Frank says of her time travel mysteries: "I try to visit the places I write about because the spirit of an ancient location is so evocative. It also creates palettes of visuals that are going to be repeated, color schemes or motifs that are woven into the story and have that meaning, the symbolic meaning to that culture in that book." Frank's books include *Shadows on the Aegean* and *Sunrise on the Mediterranean* (Grand Central Publishing), and mysteries in the fashion industry, which are written under the pseudonym Chloe Green. Her newest book is *Laws of Migration* (Tyrus Books).

Mystery writer and winner of the Agatha Award for writing for children and young adults, Daniel J. Hale acknowledges a similar ideation and research process, but centered on a camera. "Typically, what I do is start with an idea." Then he grabs his digital or video camera and heads out to explore a city or neighborhood, "capturing the light. I'm a big fan of light," he says. "I start seeing something—a trend, cars, a house, etc., and it will shape what I end up doing."

Hale's photo-imaging sparked one early morning while taking his dog for a walk. In his area of Dallas, lots of construction was taking place. "Because I liked the light, I started noticing all the turrets" and that became a feature he explored for a Dallas-set mystery. The turrets did not make it into the book, but other such investigations did, including a walk alongside a small lake. "At the end of the lake is a spillway, and over it, a wooden footbridge," says Hale, who then admits to liking chase scenes. "I had crossed this bridge. Giant concrete teddy bears were at the end. I thought I'd jog across, [which] made this drumming sound. I went back, and [video recorded myself] running with the drumming sound in the background—and that led to the very end of the book." The yet-untitled book explores Dallas, its "haves and have-not's, in a way that would not be off-putting [to] either camp." The whole concept for the book originated when Hale "started taking pictures, video, or stills."

Compare Hale's visual process of research—stretching out an idea to see what works and what does not—to Clement-Moore's. She turns to the arts, particularly poetry and ballet. "I'm always looking for some image that shows there's a story there" in poems, and "I watch everything about ballet," which inspired Clement-Moore's YA novel *The Splendor Falls* (Delacorte). "I wanted to play with the idea of deceptive fragility with a character, a ballerina," she says.

Tell Everyone You Know

Both Hale and Clement-Moore subscribe to the wisdom to "tell everyone you know" as they develop and research writing ideas.

Hale enjoys a host of friends across the U. S. and Europe. As his ideas unfold, he talks to them and they become part of his research. "People will tell you things that [make you say,] 'Oh, I'd never thought of before.'" For his novel *White Out*—co-written with his nephew Matthew LaBrot (Top Publications)—Hale says a conversation with a friend in France allowed him to clarify a key detail. He learned that the French do not get take-out hot chocolate from a café. "My character should know [that]," Hale says. Learning that cultural detail came about by talking about a potential story with his friend.

Frank says much the same. When writing her fashion mysteries, including *Fashion Victim* (Kensington), she says she asked people "their stories all the time and because I wasn't writing nonfiction it was a great jumping-off point" for her to learn more about the fashion industry, which serves as the world for her characters. "I was learning the intricacies of how the business worked." At the same time, Frank also did research into crime, to learn "how to kill people," all to make story and character fit together. Frank believes in "full immersion" in the worlds she writes about.

In Clement-Moore's novel *Highway to Hell* (Delacorte), she wanted her characters to investigate the *Chupacabra*, or *goat sucker*, the Mexican legend akin to Big Foot. "I grew up in the ranching culture in South Texas and heard about the Chupacabra and started investigating." Her family and students fed her information and stories because they knew of her curiosity for the folklore surrounding the legend and its potential role in the novel she was writing. "It led me to a whole field of people who look for Big Foot and Loch Ness monsters and the like."

Asking questions that direct her to people who reveal facts and stories has sent Clement-Moore on many quests. The process helps her form her character's world. Her folktale pursuit resulted in "investigating the current ranching industry on a big scale." She went home to South Texas and from people there she "learned about the dying breed of the Mexican cowboy, one culture so formative in Texas." The pursuit next led Clement-Moore to study the geology of oil wells.

Asking questions, listening to people's stories, then asking more questions, she says, "You learn more than you'd ever put in your books. [You] have to weave it in, [as] the character's backstory." Knowing so much more than she would ever use in one book, Clement-Moore is careful not to write an *info dump* but, "I really enjoy dropping those tidbits in so the readers can go look [them] up." She also describes her research as "like an iceberg" that holds her story up, echoing Ernest Hemingway, who wrote:

> If a writer of prose knows enough about what he is writing he may omit things that he knows and the reader, if the writer is writing truly enough, will have a feeling of those things as strongly as though the writer had stated them. The dignity of movement of an iceberg is due to only one-eighth of it being above water. (*Death in the Afternoon*)

Research-First Approach

Nonfiction author Jim Crutchfield is a more traditional researcher. He loves the library and books in general. When he has an idea but does not have much information, he hits the hall of books and papers. "I love to go to a research library." For nonfiction, he says, "You have to be as impeccable as you can in the research. The research drives the project."

Whether or not an idea proves viable for an article or book, Crutchfield feels the research that supports it will never be in vain. "Invariably when I research I find two to three ideas and make a note to come back and follow [them]." Often his reading fuels his excitement about ideas, many of which end up in his writing as anecdotes, as articles, or to propel other full-length books.

Frank also enjoys the book-adventure aspect. "Research always leads my story. I like books," she says. "I will start off with a kernel of an idea, but as I research somebody's theory, it presents such interesting possibilities." One such discovery of a possibility found its way into the pages of her second time-travel novel, *Shadows on the Aegean*. She read about the fall of the Minoan Empire and the fall of Atlantis, and crafted her story around the idea that the fall of Minoa was the basis of the legend of Atlantis. Mindful that she is writing novels, Frank describes herself as a "researcher blending fact and fiction in a way that rings true in a fiction world."

While it is hard to replace curiosity, passion, and excitement as ingredients for writing strong stories, authors agree that without research ideas would leave them with a blank page or blinking cursor. Nonfiction author and novelist Johnny D. Boggs agrees "Research comes first. It's where you find what really grabs you." He recommends, "Write about your passion, [for] fiction or nonfiction, and start digging into it. Go back to the contemporary accounts, the period newspaper, the archive collections at major libraries or historical societies." Fortunately, many of these are now available online.

With his research-first approach, Boggs is like the other authors interviewed here: "I'll often be reading something and just come across something that I'd like to really learn more about. And then start digging from there." Today, as much as writers are naturally book lovers and relish a good research library, it is impossible not to acknowledge the ease that the Internet has brought into the research and idea development process. But as a former journalist, Boggs touts the practice of "shoe leather journalism," and relies on interviews too for research.

Fellow journalist Ken Wells, who works for Bloomberg News and writes nonfiction books and novels on the side, often starts his pursuit of an idea with a question. After reporting from the drowned Louisiana parish of St. Bernard, an area he knew well from college and early reporting days, he formulated this question: Why have people lived since 1752 in an area that has experienced 30 to 40 major storms over recent centuries?

Wells took a "deep dive" into books, interviews, and the Internet to find the answer. Shoe leather journalism led him to a "real, local historian down there whose family had been among the founders of New Orleans. He kept meticulous records." Wells interviewed and read about the Arcadians who settled the area, as well as shrimpers and their families. Wells also had a shrimper take him to precise places, so he could recreate the scenes he wanted to bring alive in his nonfiction *The Good Pirates of the Forgotten Bayous* (Yale University Press), and later the novel, *Crawfish Mountain* (Random House).

Wells emerged with stories, and an answer to his question also posed as a question by his novel's protagonist: "How can we leave? I have to live on or near my boat. Every day I look around and judge the wind, the moon, the tide, to judge where the shrimp are running."

Surprising answers often await interviewers and researchers like Wells and Boggs. Questions, curiosity, a germ of an idea, fed and nourished by investigation, fire the engine of stories and sometimes change the researcher, the writer, in the process.

"I Wish I Had a Book About..."

Teacher & Librarian Needs

By Judy Bradbury

The interests of children and young adults mirror our culture, changing as the world we live in changes. What once held the attention of a six year-old might seem passé today. Teens historically chase trends, and what was hot yesterday is not today. Advances in technology, breakthroughs in science, and national and international politics affect our world, eventually influencing what kids seek to explore in books or other reading material. Our world is a continually changing landscape and to snare the interest of today's readers, authors must be aware of societal trends, and in what prompts a child to reach for a particular book before bed or on a rainy Saturday—despite the competition of other media and technology.

In education, the Common Core Standards (CCS) have changed the landscape of U.S. classrooms as schools endeavor to better the system from preschool through high school, and ready future generations for post-secondary education or careers. Adopted by just about every state in the union, the CCS have altered the way teachers organize and deliver instruction to a certain degree, but mainly they have identified key features that ought to be present in best practices in instruction. Along with the adoption of common standards comes a fresh look at the types of books that ought to be available on classroom and library shelves—both their quantitative and qualitative aspects and the complexity of text at various stages of literacy development. The CCS are a big deal in education, and they have altered the way teachers and school media specialists look at literacy.

For this article, public and school librarians, teachers, students, and independent bookstore owners from locations across the country were invited to offer their insight on topics they feel are underserved in currently published books for children and young adults. The responses received appear below, listed according to subject or general category. For more ideas about what topics might fill a gap, mine your local professionals. Ask the children's librarians in your public library, the teachers and school media specialists in your children's elementary, middle, or high schools, and independent bookstore owners for topics sought after by the children they service.

General

~ Nonfiction: "We need more literary informational texts!"

~ Transitional books to take children from picture books to chapter books: "Similar to Junie B. Jones books.")

~ Protagonists with homosexual parents.

~ More Latino literature.

~ Bilingual books in English and Spanish, English and other languages, and stories from immigrant cultures.

~ Illegal aliens: the current political debate.

~ "I would like to see a well-written book or two on school lockdown drills aimed at primary students. Several years ago my school board began mandating regular lockdown drills for elementary as well as secondary schools in our district, and I suspect that this is common in many schools in the US. I've looked for books to use with the younger students on this topic, and haven't found one. There are a number of books on fire drills and the *whys* and *hows* of fire drills, but I have not found a picture book on lockdown drills. Maybe it's too hard to put such a topic together for primary students (grades 1-3), but if there was a read-aloud type book on this topic, I'd buy it."

~ Role models: What is a role model? What makes a good role model? What makes a bad one? What makes a timeless one?

~ Stories in which the main character is physically or mentally handicapped.

Animals: Fiction & Nonfiction

~ Stories about dogs.

~ Dog series for advanced readers.

~ Hedgehogs and shrews.

~ Horse stories: "Young girls still love them."

~ Two-toed and three-toed ground sloths.

~ True accounts or realistic fiction about rescued animals, wildlife rescue, and rehabilitation of birds, mammals, and other species.

~ Wild water buffalo.

~ Reemergence of endangered species.

Family-Related Fiction

~ Stories about grandparents suffering from chronic illnesses who have become too ill to travel to visit their grandchildren.

~ Getting ready to visit a loved one in a nursing home.

~ Foreclosure leads to loss of a place to live for a family and its pets; fiction or nonfiction about feelings associated with the trauma, embarrassment, and recovery from loss of one's home.

~ Books for kids whose parents—especially moms—are serving overseas in the armed forces

History

~ The American Revolution, for primary-grade students.

~ Craft books related to history topics: American history, Eurasian history, world cultures.

~ World religions.

~ Wars: history of, reasons for, avoidance of.

Science

~ Survival skills for natural disasters.

~ Excellent, well-written books with a focus on basic concepts in science.

~ Crafts related to common science topics.

~ Science experiment books that offer clear, easy-to-follow directions for safely carrying out the experiments.

~ Nonfiction books for middle-grade readers that offer a balanced discussion of global warming from both sides of the issue of whether it exists at all, is a problem for Earth, and how to address global warming.

~ "Rocks! We need lots more interesting rock books for kids under 10 years of age."

~ "I've spent years looking for interesting and appropriate books on earth science."

~ Astronomy.

~ Geology for students below fifth grade.

~ A book that explains how rainbows form for middle-grade readers, grades three to five.

~ Gardening.

Sports Fiction & Nonfiction

~ Sports books geared toward girls that are *not* about cheerleading or gymnastics.

~ Books in which girls play softball, basketball, soccer, track and field, and swim competitively.

~ Hunting.

~ Fishing.

~ Soccer.

~ Wrestling.

Other

~ Astrology.

~ UFOs.

~ Alien encounters.

~ Crop circles.

~ Sign language.

~ Crime.

Young Adult

~ Cutting, self-mutilation.

~ Tattoos.

~ Ghost stories.

~ Horror stories.

~ Urban fiction.

~ The psychology of gangs.

~ Romance for middle school readers ("This is always tough to find!")

~ "Biographies written for adolescents and young adults that are relevant, enjoyable to read and real to the person's life, but also inspiring. Am I asking too much? I find biographies are either written for the elementary school reader or they're scholarly, academic tomes."

Teachers and school librarians inhabit the world of children. They have a knack for intuiting what kids of a certain age hunger for when they reach for a book. They also know what is lacking in the marketplace to supplement their curriculum and scaffold learning (the tailored support given students to help them meet goals) in the content areas. Working day by day, side by side with children of various ages, reading abilities, and interests, these professionals are naturally aware of what topics are underrepresented in today's trade book offerings—what topics they wish would be covered for a child of a certain age.

Public librarians in large urban areas or county lending systems handle and read reviews of hundreds of books on a monthly basis. Online sources as well as advance reading copies (ARCs) enable them to choose the best books for their shelves. Like teachers,

Professional Resources

- **American Library Association:** www.ala.org
- *Book List:* www.booklistonline.com
- **Bowker:** www.bowker.com/en-US
- *Bulletin of the Center for Children's Books:* bccb.lis.illinois.edu
- **Children's Book Council:** www.cbcbooks.org
- *Horn Book:* www.hbook.com
- **International Reading Association:** www.reading.org
- *Kirkus Reviews:* www.kirkusreviews.com
- *Publishers Weekly:* www.publishersweekly.com
- *School Library Journal:* www.schoollibraryjournal.com

librarians strive to meet the needs of their readers and strike a balance between patrons' interests and their abilities. Librarians and teachers ultimately hope to instill a love of books and nurture lifelong reading habits. Better readers make better students and better students are more successful in school and often in life. Teachers and librarians make careful decisions about what books they will purchase for their classroom or library shelves as well as those they will store virtually in e-readers because money in schools and public library systems is achingly tight.

Teaching professionals, librarians, and bookstore employees are valuable resources. They can help authors better understand the market and why some books are eagerly snatched up by children and teens while others are left behind to collect dust. Teaching and library media professionals and bookstore employees alike can aid authors in zeroing in on gaps in the marketplace that need filling. Ultimately, the common goal for all of us is to put a book in a child's hands that will make its way to his or her heart. And that begins with having available for the child the right book at the right time. If you write that special book on an underrepresented topic, the book that makes a difference in a child's life could be yours.

Develop & Use Story Maps

By Christina Hamlett

If you woke up tomorrow morning and decided to go to Spain for the first time, you probably would not get in your car and simply start driving. While it is one thing to embrace spontaneity if you already live next door in Portugal and have friends to meet you when you arrive, journeys of greater distance require that at least a portion of your prep time includes studying a map.

The same can be said of writing. How often, for instance, do you know where you want your heroes and villains to end up by the final chapter but are not sure how, exactly, to get them there? Without an outline or chart to guide the process, you are not just putting your characters at risk of wandering around aimlessly, and slogging the pace, but also causing your readers to abandon them out of confusion and frustration.

A story map is a visual layout of all the moving and stationary parts that comprise your plot. In addition to settings, timeframes and major events, it is a depiction of your characters' interrelationships and their respective dreams, fears, goals, and obstacles. Like a regular road map, it is a tool that also lends itself to improvisation, inviting you to linger in some spots longer than others and to utilize shortcuts if you happen to notice an alternative route that will get you to your destination more quickly.

The Matrix

The most simple story map is a matrix, a basic grid that shows you at a glance *who wants what.* You can create this online in Word by clicking on Insert/Table and defining the number of columns and rows you want, or using a piece of graph paper and a ruler. For example, for five characters, create 36 squares (6 across and 6 down).

You will write your character names across the top, and down the left-hand side list of all the major elements that are at stake in the story. These could be generic themes such as reward, revenge, and escape or they could be objects, events, or quests: marriage, treasure, job promotion, destroying monsters, new car, saving the homestead, stardom, and so on.

The next step is to go down the column under each character's name and make a check mark for each quest that applies. If applicable, use color coding for primary and secondary goals. You may discover, for instance, that multiple players are after the treasure and will be in competition. In contrast, the matrix may reveal that Julie's only goal is to get a gold ring on her left hand but her boyfriend Zach is obsessed with destroying monsters. If these two are the love interest in your plot, these conflicting primary motivations represent a red flag. Your story will need to develop common ground that will bring them together.

When completed, your matrix will look something like this:

	Victor	Patti	Zach	Roger	Julie
Treasure	x	x		x	
Marriage				x	x
Homestead		x			
Monsters			x		
Stardom	x				

At a glance you have an overview of your characters' motivations, potential threats to their quests, and opportunities for collaboration or compromise. This matrix is also useful if you are writing murder mysteries and need to chart your suspects' whereabouts, or if your plot transpires over several decades and you want to track who was doing what during incremental time periods.

The Storyboard

The storyboard mapping technique uses a comic strip layout and simple drawings to depict settings, characters, and major plot points for development. The best part is that you do not need any artistic talent to make it work for you.

At its most elemental level, the first option is to fill your story panels with the same kind of silly stick figures, houses, cars, animals and trees you probably drew as a child. You need only as much or as little detail as will help jog your memory when you actually start writing your scenes. The panels can also contain short snippets of dialogue or keywords relevant to the actions that are transpiring.

If your characters' physical activities go beyond your drawing ability—bicycling, canoeing, parachuting—your second option is to use a search engine and look for "images for stick figure pictures." This will yield a number of websites. You can also go to stock photo websites such as Bigstock (www.bigistock.com), Shutterstock (www.shutterstock.com), or Stockphoto (www.istock-photo.com) if you prefer placeholder images of rooms, buildings, landscapes, famous landmarks, wildlife, and inanimate objects that are realistic versus abstract. Venturing beyond all of the royalty-free turf is permissible as well, provided that the pictures incorporated in your storyboard are for your eyes only and are not used for any commercial purposes.

Another story mapping approach is to create your own cartoon strip. To get started, a free website called Pixton (www.pixton.com) allows you to set up multiple panels, insert indoor and outdoor backdrops, select and pose a variety of characters, change color schemes and facial expressions, enlarge or shrink or reposition frame elements, and create dialogue bubbles.

If you thrive on feedback, Pixton has an interactive component that lets you share your serialized storyboard with a community of fellow cartoonists. This is practical if you want to experiment with different scene placements or alternative endings. And who knows? You might even start a preliminary buzz of curiosity about your book, an essential ingredient in keeping you motivated.

The Circles of Life

Circles are frequently used to create story outlines. These arise from the connectivity design of business flow charts representing structural hierarchy, assigned roles, and interfaces. With some slight modification, one of the most common models lends itself easily to the mapping concept.

This one is a character arc map that calls for five concentric circles of different sizes that share the same center, like a target. Use a large piece of paper to draw the following:

Starting at the center and moving outward, label each circle in the following order: individual, partner, family, community, world. Draw a line from the smallest circle out to the side and create a list of what your hero is most obsessed with on a strictly personal level (i.e., looks, money, popularity, etc.). Draw a line out from the next circle and identify what your hero most wants from a partnership, whether it is marriage, friendship, business relationship, etc. Repeat this pattern for the remaining three circles. What this gives you is a map of how your hero may or— may not—evolve from an egocentric mentality into a selfless role that ultimately wants what is best for humanity, even if it carries high risk for himself.

This story map can also be used to illustrate where your different characters are in their developmental stages. Instead of, or in addition to, drawing lines and making lists, this version places character names into each circle. The hero, for instance, may be the center of his own universe while his father's core focus is on protecting the family's interests at any cost. Meanwhile, the hero's girlfriend occupies the outermost circle of spirituality and would rather fight for a social cause than draw any personal attention to herself.

Note that the farther apart your characters are on this circle chart, the harder and more implausible it will be to bring them together.

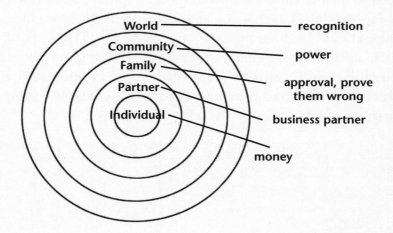

By the Numbers

As commonplace as *three-act structure* is in a working writer's vocabulary, thinking in terms of thirds is not something that comes naturally to most people when they are plotting a story. As a result, their beginnings may take too long to get off the ground, their middles meander off-course, and their endings have a slapdash feel to them. The solution to this is a four-act structure that allows you to parse out the action from start to finish based on some easy math.

Whether you use four columns labeled Act 1, Act 2, Act 3 and

Act 4 or list these down the left side of a page like an outline, you simply divide the estimated number of pages in your project by the number 4. Whatever number you come up with is your allotment of pages for each of the four acts. This does not just work for novels and short stories; it works for stage and screen projects as well because these adhere to the rule that 1 page = 1 minute.

If, for example, you are writing a 100-page novella, you have 25 pages to spend on each act. To use this approach as a story map, make a short list in a column identifying which characters need to be introduced and what has to happen within that particular time block before you can move on to the next column. These should be no more than a few sentences. This form of linear documentation lets you see if you're trying to compress too much "stuff" into one act at the expense of other sections in which very little transpires by comparison. See the following example.

	Act I	Act II	Act III	Act IV
Wally	Ignored at school by Brandy, whom he really likes.			
Brandy	Obsessed with *Twilight*; thinks vampires are cool.			
Ernie	Wally's friend. Teases Wally and says to become a vampire himself.			
Andrea	Wally's friend, student assistant in the drama department. Agrees to transform Wally into a faux vampire, for a price			

The Maze

Everyone is familiar with puzzle mazes in which Mr. Mouse has to navigate his way through a labyrinth in order to reach The Cheese located in the opposite corner. Along this one-way-in and one-way-out route are corridors that lead to dead ends or sometimes encounters with traps, cats, and poison.

The maze format of story mapping gives you an aerial view of your plot in progress and is easy to create at the PuzzleMaker section of the Discovery Education website (puzzlemaker.discovery-education.com/AdvMazeSetupForm.asp). Five different maze shapes are available here and involve varying levels of complexity.

The sample below is a 20 x 20 Escape model with each square being 8 pixels and utilizing random paths. The S represents the starting point for your main character and the E is the ending point of his or her efforts—the final escape, acquisition of treasure, true love, and so on.

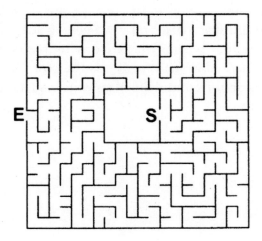

Once you have your maze designed, you can either magnify the image on your screen or take it to your neighborhood printers and have it enlarged to poster size.

If you are working off your screen, use the Insert tab in Word to place clip art images throughout the corridors between your character's starting point and the exit. It can be a single icon such as a mousetrap, fire, or hazard sign that represents every obstacle in your plot or you can individualize each of the threats or setbacks your character encounters. If your maze story map is on a larger, table-top scale, your obstacle markers can be board game pieces, wrapped candy, or color Post-It Notes. Each time your character encounters an obstacle in either of these platforms, it can either be permanently removed from the maze or transferred to a different spot closer to the exit point.

Whichever style of story map you use for your project, the goal is the same: to display plainly the interrelatedness of your characters and events, as well as encourage the exploration of alternative outcomes. Too often, a writer's strong fixation on how everything is *supposed* to work out at the end creates tunnel vision that obscures the ability to develop character motivations fully, escalate the conflict, and sustain momentum.

By adapting these models to fit your chosen genre and using them as a prewriting activity, you will become adept at recognizing whether it is your players that are driving the plot forward (fueling their personal growth) or if it is the plot that is driving your characters' actions and delivering your readers to exciting new destinations.

Add-ons

Help Sell Your Story with Sidebars, Addenda, & More

By Sue Bradford Edwards

Make your work appealing: Most writers realize that this is the best way to sell their work. Yet very few writers take advantage of the appeal that sidebars and other supplemental materials have for editors. "Most writers rarely think about supplemental things," says Jim Wrinn, Editor of *Trains*.

Nick Skapyak, Editor of *The Lutheran Digest,* agrees. "I don't see too many add-ons, actually," he says. "I wish I did!"

From special-interest magazines like *Trains* to religious publications like *The Lutheran Digest* to general-interest glossies or small newsletters, the add-ons that you can include with submissions are as varied as the markets that use them. Some markets prefer visual materials such as timelines, charts, graphs, or other graphics that are used to summarize or elaborate on information found in the main body of the article. Other publications focus on sidebars that are text-rich additions containing resources, definitions, or a craft or activity. Electronic publications offer yet another range of possibilities such as downloadable supplements, apps, or video clips.

To know what supplemental information would be best to include in your query or submission, first study the publication and the audience it serves.

Understand Your Audience

When including add-ons with an article, the key is to provide relevant material that relates to or expands on the main story.

Rachael Heyboer, Editor of *Christian Home and School,* can always tell when a writer has not read or researched the publication and is submitting based solely on the magazine's name. "We aren't home schoolers. We send our magazine to parents of our member schools. The goal is to include articles that deal with home life with a Christian school experience."

This means preparing material relevant to parents whose children attend Christian schools. "First you need a quality article that fits with the theme and the overall goal of our publication," says Heyboer. "An article about behavior management for your kids could include a sidebar on extra reading, further information, websites, or further bullet points. If you reference a book, I want a sidebar about why you referenced it and more on the book."

Patrice Pages, Editor of *ChemMatters*, faces a slightly different challenge. "As far as I know, *ChemMatters* is the only publication that seeks to demystify a specific scientific field (in this case, chemistry) for high school students," says Pages, who explains that he knows of no such magazine for biology or physics students. "*ChemMatters* explains to students why chemistry is important and why they need to learn it in the classroom, and how it affects their everyday lives." One issue on art and chemistry featured articles on the chemistry behind stained glass and pottery. Because the articles are written for students, and not teachers, scientific concepts need to be explained in lay terms.

While most writers grasp that they are writing for a classroom publication, they do not always understand what this means in terms of content. The teachers already have textbooks at their disposal. Textbook writing is not what they need.

The few sidebars Pages receives often miss the mark. "We don't want experiments. Teachers use textbooks with lots of activities, so we don't want to replicate what is already out there." In *ChemMatters*, sidebars explain terminology when an explanation in the body of the article would simply slow down the flow of the story.

Beer-and-Pizza Effect

In addition to streamlining an article, add-ons are a way to pull the reader into a topic. "We'd love to see more short sidebars, timelines, quirky things that are another entry point for readers. Just about anything that gives the reader a quick fun read. Something that can take them down another avenue. Things that are fun, clever, logical offshoots. The ones that I really look for are the logical progression of where the reader would take [the subject] themselves," says *Trains*'s Wrinn.

Wrinn calls this progression the *beer-and-pizza effect.* If his railway enthusiast readers were talking about a particular rail subject over beer and pizza, what additional topics would come up? Where would the conversation go next? What questions might they ask?

The August 2012 issue of *Trains* illustrates. It features two stories on the one hundred and fiftieth anniversary of the Union Pacific Railroad. One story was strictly a business history. The other was a creation mythology about how the Union Pacific came to be. The author of the latter article included an offbeat sidebar. "It was made up of humorous newspaper headlines," says Wrinn, "on how long it would take to build the transcontinental railway today." Wrinn's readers responded. "The sidebar has brought as much feedback as main story."

Presenting information in a visual fashion, such as the timeline mentioned by Wrinn, also pulls readers into articles. Heyboer suggests "a chart or graph that covers information from the article but pulls it together visually."

Online content is another way to pull readers into a topic in a print publication, explains Sheila Seifert, *Thriving Family* Editorial Director of Parenting. "*Thriving Family* sees few-to-no web/digital suggestoins that complement articles. Authors should include an idea for charts, downloadable PDFs, a corresponding article, a map, a craft or recipe, a game, DVD suggestion, audio suggestion, Facebook post, Tweet, Pinterest idea, quiz, or other items. If a writer suggests an add-on and the *Thriving Family* editors like it, the author

Be Creative

When you consider what might make a good add-on, begin by studying the publication. "Look at *Trains*," says Editor Jim Wrinn. "See what sidebars and offshoots we do today. We have an audience who has an expectation of what *Trains* is going to look and feel like; they know what the DNA is." A reader would immediately spot an ill-conceived sidebar in a favorite publication. But first, so will the editor, who will turn it down in a submission.

Use your article itself as a base for sidebar ideas. "Most articles have some type of call to action. A humor article might want the reader to laugh. An informative article might want the reader to become aware of an issue. A how-to article might want the reader to produce an amazing craft. If the writer explores the article's call to action, then the writer can decide how to offer additional add-ons," says Sheila Seifert, Editorial Director of *Thriving Family*. " In a humor article, perhaps the add-on would be a related cartoon or a sidebar that offers a humorous take about one small point in the piece. In an informative article, try a video clip suggestion that offers insight from another perspective, a sidebar that details a real family's experience or that digs deeper into one aspect of the topic, or a downloadable page that offers connection points of what the reader can do next. In a how-to article, it might be the pattern that's needed or a video that shows how to do a difficult step."

Get in the reader's head and brainstorm the possibilities. "Try to put yourself behind the reader's glasses. If you were reading the piece, where would your mind wander? Consider the centerpiece of your story and branch off from there," says Nick Skapyak, Editor of *The Lutheran Digest*. "Come up with 3-4 ideas and see which one has enough information to merit writing another 150-250 words."

Follow these steps and you will find yourself not only selling articles but also a host of accompanying supplements.

could receive an additional assignment creating the add-on. I am surprised that more writers don't offer possible web/digital ideas with their article submissions." Supplemental material can add to your income, as well as your article.

Keeping Things Tight

Not only do sidebars and other supplemental material enable writers to expand on a story, they also help writers keep their prose lean. Says Wrinn,"The tendency for most writers is to write long and try to put everything in the mainbar."

Essential facts that break the flow of a story are perfect candidates for sidebar material. "Scientific facts can slow the flow of the story if it takes several paragraphs to explain them. Put them in a sidebar," says Pages. "When we have a concept that needs further explanation, I wish writers understood how to summarize it in the main body and put the details in a sidebar."

Supplemental material also allows writers to present information on a tangentially related topic that can benefit readers of the main article. "I recently had a mainbar about a railroad in West Virginia. It has to find a unique way to get its trains through a narrow valley with a rushing river," says Wrinn. He immediately saw the value of a piece on how the railroad solved a unique problem. But the article itself created a problem for readers: It left them with very little knowledge about day-to-day operations within the railroad itself. Wrinn suggested that the author add material about what the railroad does on a daily basis, and that became a sidebar.

Interviews also make for strong sidebars. "Interviews are also something we like to have," says Pages. The interview can tell how the person uses chemistry to solve a particular problem, but this leaves interested students with no idea how to pursue a similar career unless the author addresses this in a sidebar.

The Lutheran Digest's Skapyak also likes to see sidebars that add human interest details to a factual piece and vice versa. "I'd like to see add-ons that add interest value to a piece. For example, if a story is a personal experience piece about how an apple pie bridged a gap between two families or two people, an add-on featuring facts about apple pie—when it was *invented*, strange ways people eat it, etc.— would be of interest. Ideally, in this case, the recipe for the apple pie mentioned in the story would be a perfect fit!"

"When I do see add-ons, I am drawn to those that tie up loose ends," says Skapyak. "Using the [apple pie] example, the article is a personal experience. Tying it up with some interesting facts would catch my attention. [Alternatively,] if the piece were largely informational, say about fireworks, a short, possibly personal experience or historical anecdote wherein fireworks were central to the plot would also tie up loose ends for me."

Most important, make sure the information is relevant. "An add-on that is merely busywork or more words will be rejected. When authors are thinking about add-ons, they need to consider how the items will save the readers time or money, or how the add-on will clarify something that has been discussed," says Seifert. "In this age of enhanced publications, *Thriving Family* looks at each article for its ability to be enhanced. The more writers work with us in this area, the more we may want to work with them."

Include sidebars and charts, or suggestions for add-ons, with your main submission. They will catch the attention of busy editors who often have to create this additional content themselves. It is just another way to make your work appealing and thus make a sale.

Exercises to Inspire Imagination

By Christina Hamlett

My former mother-in-law was an avid collector of cookbooks. The best ones, she always said, were those that were written with such passion and clarity "you can practically smell the flavors right off the page." Engaging a reader in that level of sensory connection is more than just an artful blend of wordsmithing and sumptuous color photographs. It is the author's intimate knowledge of the culinary arts, the hands-on expertise, that gives the recipes the authenticity a non-cook might find hard to articulate. Cooking is a skill set that actively engages all five senses: the texture of ingredients, the tantalizing aromas, the sound of the sizzle, the ability to distinguish sweet, sour, salty, and bitter flavors, and the sight of an appealing meal.

In contrast, what we have been taught since grade school about the craft of writing largely focuses on the stimuli we receive through our eyes and ears. Yes, we are writing about what we know as a product of our observations and experiences, but how much more imagination could we unleash if we put the rest of our senses to the task?

The Psychology of Smell

Memory and smell have long been intertwined, with imprinting that starts at birth. The brain's ability to associate smells with particular emotions, events, and people is why the faintest whiff of perfume, cookie dough, or burnt rubber can immediately transport us to the past and trigger sharp memories of a lost love, Christmas at Grandma's, or a car accident we were lucky to walk away from. In my own experience, for instance, I cannot smell cows without remembering every detail of the rainy afternoon our Girl Scout troop went on a field trip to a dairy farm. Yep, those wet Holsteins are still running around in my head, despite the passage of 50 years.

Scents can also affect our mood without having any connection to the past. As an example, my imagination always conjures a late 1800s manor house library whenever I encounter someone smoking a Cavendish blend of vanilla pipe tobacco or wearing sandalwood aftershave. Certain aromas of incense invite moonlit images of gypsy caravans, while new-car smell, fresh cut lumber, and hedgerows of star jasmine promote an inexplicable sense of optimism.

Tactile Techniques

Feeling a day of playing hooky coming on? The art of a convincing call-in to report to your boss that you are under the weather when you're really perfectly fine is all in the staging. It is more than just about having props within reach that make you repeatedly sneeze; it is about working up a breathless, heated sweat, plunging your hands in ice water for 45 seconds before you call, and donning your most unattractive, ratty bathrobe and zipping it up to the neck. In a nutshell, whatever you make your body *feel* will manifest in the way you describe your symptoms to a listener.

If you tend to be analytical in your approach to writing, try focusing instead on how things feel in order to broaden your creativity. Consider, for instance, that our largest sensory organ— skin—contains more than four million receptors for detecting textures, temperatures, and sensations like tingling, vibrations, and pressure. The rapid speed with which the brain interprets whether an external stimulus is safe or harmful means that you

Olfactory Exercises

~ *What does your neighborhood smell like?* Whether it is a big city, suburbia, or the countryside, take a half-hour walk and breathe deeply, making note of the various aromas emanating from gardens, garbage, industrial sites, bodies of water, restaurants, and the open windows of neighbors' kitchens. Write a series of flash fiction stories in which each scent you have recorded is associated with a character or event.

~ *Follow that nose.* With the exception of fresh seafood, coffee blends, and certain fruits, you probably do not pay much attention to supermarket smells. For this exercise, have a trusted friend come with you as you walk through the aisles of a grocery store either with your eyes closed or blind-folded. Each time a distinctive aroma hits your nostrils, use a mini-recorder to describe how the scent makes you feel. For the second part of this exercise, open your eyes and visit the aisles that sell packaged and canned goods as well as cleaning supplies. Assess whether the label designs and colors influence your expectations of what a product smells like (i.e., do you assume a detergent in a yellow box will smell like lemons?). Create a series of advertising slogans in which scent is the hook.

~ *Non-Scents.* Many realities around you defy olfactory association (unless, perhaps, you have synesthesia). Colors, for instance. Emotions. Household appliances. Yet that is exactly what this exercise is all about. For each of the following, describe its attributes in terms of a smell: (1) grey, (2) warm towels, (3) clouds, (4) melancholy, (5) jewelry, (6) tax returns, (7) superstition, (8) red, (9) mist, (10) microwave.

are likely to give little thought to your sense of touch unless you are comparing fabrics, testing durability, feeling your way through a dark room, engaging in intimacy, or reading Braille.

A Matter of Taste

There is a reason they call some food *comfort food*. Whether it is a favorite sandwich, pasta, a pot pie, meatloaf, or even a bowl of oatmeal, comfort foods are those that evoke sentimental

Tactile Exercises

~ Borrow a page from Halloween haunted houses for this first one. Have a friend set out 10 bowls containing elements such as cooked pasta, crumpled potato chips or cereal, buttermilk, mud, mashed potatoes, grapes, seaweed, a wiglet, wet sponge pieces, a cold lumpy soup, wet socks, cottage cheese, candy corn, mashed bananas, gummy worms, and rubber bugs. Put on a blindfold and allow yourself to be guided to put your hand into each bowl. Rather than trying to guess what it really contains, give your imagination free rein to envision something horrifying (i.e., a bowl full of squishy eyeballs). Write a flash fiction story based on the most lingering of these tactile sensations.

~ Put on a silk blouse, or shirt and soft pants. Sit in your most comfy spot, and compose a short romantic scene on your laptop or in a notebook. Next, put on something that is scratchy and too tight, sit in a straight-backed wooden chair and rewrite the scene. Experiment some more by writing the scene in a room that is too cold, followed by one that is too hot and stuffy. Write barefoot, first by wiggling your toes into a deep plush rug, then by putting your feet in a box lid full of gravel.

thoughts, are easy to fix, relieve physical ailments (chicken soup), or lower the emotional stress of a broken heart, a bad hair day, or feelings of guilt from spending too much money. Interestingly, studies have shown that what triggers the craving for a comfort food differs between the sexes: Men are drawn to it because they are feeling positive and women because they are feeling negative.

Our perceptions of what something will taste like are as much a product of the diversity of flavors we were exposed to during childhood as it is to the power of suggestion by the person doing the selling or serving. If, for instance, your older brother told you that brussels sprouts tasted like greasy, grimy gopher guts, your taste buds would be primed to spit out the first bite before it even reached your lips. Conversely, if a sommelier commends your wine selection and says you have chosen an excellent year, isn't

Taste Exercises

~ Make a list of your favorite comfort foods. In short story format, relate your earliest memory of each one, including who prepared it, the occasion and setting, what kind of plate it was served on, what you drank with it, and what the weather was like. With practice you can train your brain to recall a deeper level of detail that can subsequently enrich your writing.

~ Barring any allergies or food restrictions, commit to trying one new food each week. Ethnic cuisine is good for this exercise because you will not only be exposed to ingredients and herbs with which you're unfamiliar but different cooking methods as well. Make a conscious effort to study textures and thoroughly taste every flavor. Write flash fiction in which your main character eats this meal for the first time.

~ For each of the following tastes, assign a musical instrument that best captures its personality: (1) baked potato, (2) carrots, (3) gelatin, (4) steak, (5) bran muffin, (6) popcorn, (7) fudge, (8) champagne, (9) tofu, (10) marmalade.

the *vino* going to taste that much better than if he said, "Uh, yeah, sure, it's okay I guess."

The refinement of our sense of taste is also influenced by the environment in which we eat, and not just how fast we consume the food. The higher and more persistent or frenzied the noise level, the more we lose the ability to gauge the saltiness and sweetness of food. Play calming music at roughly the same level as a normal conversation and the food will not only be more flavorful, but you will also be able to think more clearly and creatively.

Do You Hear What I Hear?

Your ears serve two important purposes, the more obvious one being their ability to let you hear and distinguish sounds. The second is to assist you in keeping your balance. Hearing is believed to be the last of our senses to go—a useful tidbit to remember if you are in the presence of someone unconscious.

Auditory Exercises

~ If your television has this function, blacken the screen and listen to a show with which you are not familiar. (An alternative is to tape a piece of cardboard over the screen or simply sit with your back toward the TV.) Write down your impressions of how the characters look, what the setting is, and any other pertinent guesses based on a strictly auditory experience. For a television show or movie, make note of how the inclusion of music and sound effects influences the mood, especially in a horror film.

~ Put in a pair of earplugs at a noisy community park. (Be mindful of personal safety, of course.) Write a flash fiction piece about a character who can no longer hear birds singing, children laughing, dogs barking, or people playing sports.

~ Write a letter describing a concert experience to a fictitious recipient who has never heard music.

~ Listen to a style of music that differs from your regular fare. Play it multiple times, each time singling out and focusing on just one instrument or singer.

Hospitals have no shortage of stories in which patients that awakened from a coma could recall everything their visitors said, including secret confessions and fractious debates about how to divvy up the estate.

For people with hearing impairments stemming from congenital defects or as the result of an accident or disease, studies have shown that the brain can compensate for the loss by rewiring and directing normally hearing-related tasks to the other senses, thus enhancing them. These include such skills as a keener sense of peripheral vision and depth perception, a higher sensitivity to movement, and a more strongly defined sense of smell.

Seeing Is (Sometimes) Believing
Vision is generally considered the most complex of our senses

because of the volume of data our brain receives through our eyes, and because of the processes that enable us to distinguish colors and shapes, judge distances, navigate in different levels of light, and recognize familiar sights. The majority of information we have about the world tends to come to us through our peepers. The eyes, however, can play tricks on us: mirages, optical illusions, even mistaken identities, and brain-teaser optical illusions. (See www.illusions.org, www.eyetricks.com/illusions.htm, and www.123opticalillusions.com.)

The Innocence Project (www.innocenceproject.org) argues that in about 75 percent of overturned criminal convictions, the culprit is mistaken eyewitnesss identifications. Nor should we forget that in 1961 the Museum of Modern Art in New York City proudly put on display a work by Henri Matisse called *La Bateau*. The painting was enjoyed by all for 47 days—the time it took for someone to finally realize it was hanging upside down.

Last But Not Least

No discussion of a writer's ability to explore new facets of creativity would be complete without mention of the sixth sense: extrasensory perception.

Whether you call it instinct, gut feelings, hunches, intuition, or flirtations with spirituality, this sixth sense is an invaluable tool for those occasions when you find yourself stalled in a mental cul de sac. By turning off distractions, meditating, and jotting down whatever free-form phrases or images float into your head, you can take the first steps to tune into an ESP frequency. Combine this with a diligent practice of listening to those initial impressions you get about people, surroundings, and events. You may be surprised by what your subconscious is really trying to tell you, and leading you to write.

The Language of Ideas

Idea Generators & Exercises

By Susan Tierney

Words and phrases are the tools of a author's trade, the brushes and paint of the writing canvas. Every word we use is conceptual—that is the nature of language—and the richness of a language is often found in its idiomatic expressions. Common or unusual, words and phrases embody ideas. As the examples below illustrate, they can also be a source of new ideas. Read through the origins of the expressions included, and use the idea suggestions or exercises to generate your own new, colorful ideas on your writing canvas.

According to Hoyle

Origin: The British Sir Edmond Hoyle wrote the authoritative rule book for the popular card game *whist* in 1742, and several other books on the rules and strategies behind cards, chess, and backgammon. *According to Hoyle* came to mean following the rules, obeying authority, and behaving correctly.

Ideas:

~ A history of card games, or games across various cultures or ages; a history of other games, such as chess, and their significance socially.

~ A scene, with dialogue, in which *poker face* takes on thematic meaning for a story.

~ Modern electronic games have been named for Hoyle,

including Hoyle Casino and Hoyle Card Games. Write reviews of modern versions of card and other games of strategy.

Ace up your sleeve

Origin: This expression means having a hidden advantage, like a playing card in your possession that fellow players do not suspect —one hidden up your sleeve. The sixteenth-century Scottish poet William Dunbar wrote of "ane false caird in to his sleif" (a false card into his sleeve). The ace originally refered to the single dot or pip on dice, and later to the single pip on a card. A similar expression is *ace in the hole.*

Ideas:

~ What is the mechanism for slipping a card up your sleeve without others knowing? Investigate magic tricks and sleight of hand.

~ Explore the history of con games like three-card monte, which dates to at least the fifteenth century. Or write an article exposing modern con games that take advantage of consumers, such as those recently making the news after hurricane Sandy.

~ Use a con, or con artist, as the core of a scene for a story, or the inspiration behind an entire story arc.

Achilles heel

Origin: From Homer's epic poem about the war between Troy and the Greeks, this phrase refers to the Greek hero Achilles's only physical weakness. According to myth, Achilles's mother dipped him in the river Styx as an infant because its waters would make him invincible, but the place she held the baby—at the heel of his foot—was not fully immersed, and therefore the only place on his body not protected. In the Trojan War, the great Greek warrior was killed by a poison arrow to his heel. The phrase *achilles heel* came to mean a place of weakness in an otherwise strong person that can lead to their downfall.

Ideas:

~ Outline a story arc for a YA novel about the teenage Achilles beginning to come to grip with his invincibility and his vulnerability. Does teenage hubris or angst dominate? Who are the friends who come to age with him, foreshadowing the war to come and his fate?

~ In medicine and science, research the Achilles heel, or other such anatomical vulnerabilities. Discover how they impact various stages of life, from childhood to old age.

~ The physical skills of the classical warriors were mythologized. Look at the modern sports and athletic skills of javelin throwing, discus, shot put, and the marathon, and come up with angles for three articles on them. Focus on (1) the athletes; (2) the mathematics and physics behind such sports; or (3) the sociocultural aspect of such sports in ancient and modern times.

Acid test

Origin: Nitric acid (*aquafortis*) was once used to test gold by alchemists. It has the quality of being able to dissolve most metals, but gold is resistant to it. An *acid test* reveals definitively if something is real or fake.

Ideas:

~ The science behind CSI (crime scene investigations) has been strong in the popular consciousness for more than a decade now, thanks to television procedurals, and the popularity does not seem to be diminishing. Come up with specifics for five forensics-based articles or stories that would fascinate the general interest reader. They could involve forensics in any of these categories: accounting, anthropology, archaeology, entomology, psychology, or technology.

~ Create a solution to a mystery story using *aquafortis* as the mechanism of discovery. How would using that solution be echoed by an *acid test* of one of the characters, main or secondary, who has a secret? Or use alchemy as a theme in a short story, historical or contemporary. The alchemy may be literal or metaphoric.

~ Nitric acid is sometimes used to stain wood. Explore traditional artisanal techniques in woodworking or other crafts. Or look into the chemistry behind *aquafortis* and the original principles of alchemy—which contributed to the development of chemistry as a science—and construct an article for young readers. Research how *aquafortis* was used in various trades, including jewelry making, mosaics, and metalwork.

Across the board

Origin: Used in horse racing, *across the board* refers to the notice board at a track that indicates odds for the order in which horses will finish in a race. A bet is across the board when equal money is placed on a horse to win, place, and show. The expression has come to mean all-embracing.

Ideas:

~ Construct a travel piece based on racetracks in your region, nationally, or internationally.

~ Explore the history of horse racing. What different styles are there? What cultural dimensions has it had? Economic?

~ Set a story in a particular era of racing, with horses at the center of your plot.

~ Learn more about the health needs of horses and come up with three different articles on the subject for different audiences, from children to adults. Or look into how horses have been involved in human health issues.

~ Write about the mathematical principles behind different kinds of gambling.

Add insult to injury

Origin: Originating in classical fables, *add insult to injury* is a phrase that was spoken by a fly to a bald man who hit himself on the head to swat the insect. According to *The American Heritage*

Dictionary of Idioms, "The fly then jeered, 'You want to avenge an insect's sting with death; what will you do to yourself, who have added insult to injury?'" The expression may have been coined by the Roman fabulist Phaedrus, and it first appeared in English in 1748 in *The Foundling,* a play by Edward Moore. The meaning is to make a bad thing worse.

Ideas:

~ Recall a situation or action in your own life that made a bad thing worse. Write a personal experience piece. Or, create a scene for a story based on your recollection. Try to expand it into a full plot line.

~ Find an ancient fable that appeals to you and retell it in a modern way. Include a tag line or moral.

~ Brainstorm the possibilities for articles on flies for a variety of markets: health/sanitation, keeping your home free of insects, science article for young people, the role of different kinds of flies in ecosystems, and so on.

Agony column

Origin: Newspapers once carried columns in which people advertised about missing relatives or friends—the agony of loss. *Agony column* has also at times referred to advice columns.

Ideas:

~ Use an agony column as a plot device in a mystery or other genre of fiction.

~ Make an agony columnist your protagonist. What could be the character's own central pain?

~ Investigate the history of newspapers and uncover other kinds of columns and reporting common in the past, but no longer popular. Construct an article for readers interested in writing, journalism, social changes, or nostalgia.

~ In "Sherlock Holmes, The Adventure of the Red Circle," Sir Arthur Conan Doyle referred to agony columns. Use the following description to start a modern story of your own:

He took down the great book in which, day by day, he filed the agony columns of the various London journals. 'Dear me!' said he, turning over the pages, 'What a chorus of groans, cries, and bleatings! What a rag-bag of singular happenings! But surely the most valuable hunting ground that ever was given to a student of the unusual!'"

Albatross around one's neck

Origin: A symbol and image famously from Samuel Taylor Coleridge's *The Rime of the Ancient Mariner*, an *albatross around the neck* is something no one wants: a burden or sense of guilt that cannot seem to be removed.

Ideas:

~ Center a story on a character's albatross—a mistake with unforeseen consequences that the character cannot shake. Create an image comparable to the burden and stigma of the albatross, with more immediate meaning for a contemporary audience.

~ Where do albatrosses live? What unique qualities do they have? Explore their nature and existence.

~ Coleridge had an enormous influence, with his close friend William Wordsworth, on the direction of English poetry through the publication of their joint volume of poetry, *Lyrical Ballads*. Research Coleridge and consider him (or someone like him) as a character at the core of a novel; explore Coleridge's friendship with Wordsworth and his sister Dorothy.

~ How are the challenges in the lives of mariners today similar to those in Coleridge's time, 200 years ago?

At loggerheads

Origin: "Ah you whoreson logger-head, you were borne to doe me shame," wrote Shakespeare in *Love's Labours Lost* (Act IV, Scene iii, v. 1544). *At loggerheads* means to be fighting head-to-head over something, often fruitlessly. A *logger* was a dialectical term for a block of wood, usually one that was tied to a horse's leg to keep it from escaping. Loggerhead is synonymous with *blockhead*.

Ideas:

~ Write a scene where two characters are literally at logger-heads—their legs chained to blocks, and arguing vociferously. How did they get into that situation? What are they arguing about? What kind of colorful names (like *blockhead*) might they use against each other?

~ *Loggerheads* has been given as a name to a snapping turtle, also called the *alligator snapper*. Investigate this particular animal, and devise an article for children about it. Or research interesting common names for other animals, and how they came to be.

~ A loggerhead is also an antique iron shipbuilding tool, used for melting pitch. Come up with ideas for articles on unusual antique tools. Or what kinds of stories can you imagine that would incorporate an antique tool as part of the plot line?

~ Loggerheads is the name of several towns around the world, including two in England, one in Wales, and a small island in Florida. Choose one as a setting that highlights why two fictional characters are engaged in what seems a futile conflict, and devise a resolution.

Back to square one

Origin: The origin of *back to square one* is debated, usually among three possibilities. Strangely, the expression only appears in print for the first time in 1952. The theories are: (1) From at least the 1600s, *scotch* meant a line drawn on the ground, thus the game of *hopscotch*, with its jumping over lines; *back to square one* meant to return to the first line in the game. (2) The phrase derived from a twentieth-century game, Snakes and Ladders, in which players who rolled the wrong number on their dice were sent sliding down a ladder back to an earlier square on the game board. This is responsible for the first print reference. (3) In a now generally disputed theory, the reference was to diagrams consisting of a numbered grid that were used to explain play on the soccer pitch, especially in BBC match commentaries starting in 1927.

Ideas:

~ Use a child's game, such as hopscotch or Snakes and Ladders, as the central image of a short story. Reflect the progress of the game in the actions, conflicts, setbacks, and so on, of your characters. Why does your protagonist have to go back to square one, and what happens next?

~ Famed sociobiologist and author of *The Naked Ape,* Desmond Morris also wrote a noted book called *The Soccer Tribe.* In it, he discussed the rituals and tribe-like behavior of *soccer* (football) fans, players, and commentators internationally and their place in culture. Develop an article on the rituals of soccer or another sport in the U.S. or worldwide. Or look at how the rituals of a sport have changed in recent years. Are baseball's rituals the same in 2012 as they were in 1927 or 1961, for example? What new rituals, such as bringing children onto the pitch pregame, may have developed in soccer/football, and what does it mean culturally?

Banana republic

Origin: Short story writer O. Henry used this expression in 1904 in his *Cabbages and Kings.* The author, whose real name was William Sydney Porter, had visited Honduras a few years before, and he coined *banana republic* to refer to a small, corrupt, usually Central American nation that relied on a single product, such as bananas, to survive economically.

Ideas:

~ From O. Henry to Graham Greene to Woody Allen, banana republics have been used as settings for stories that are humorous, cynical, and/or tragic. Ironically, O. Henry—Porter—was probably guilty of embezzlement at a bank, was indicted, and fled to Honduras to avoid trial. Explore the possibilities of irony in a story, creating your own banana republic as a fictional world. It may be as large as a nation or small as a village.

~ Research one or more modern Central American nations and come up with article ideas on their current industries, agriculture, and culture. Target young people's magazines.

~ Find out about other writers who have been in trouble with the law. Did they use their experiences, as O. Henry did, in their writing? Tell their stories. Possibilities include Thomas Malory, Christopher Marlowe, Fyodor Dostoyevsky, William Burroughs, Norman Mailer, Ken Kesey.

Baptism by fire

Origin: While obviously referring to the biblical concept of baptism, and John the Baptist's statement that "the one to come," Jesus, would baptize with the Holy Spirit and with fire (*Matthew* 3:11), this figure of speech also often refers to the experience of entering the battlefield. It uses the image of fire, therefore, in two ways, referring to flames and to guns. In general usage, *baptism by fire* means being thrown into a difficult situation that is initiating, purifying, or a means of learning.

Ideas:

~ Conceptualize a story about bullying in which one of the characters' perspectives is that a particular experience is a baptism by fire—necessary and toughening—and the consequences of that experience on someone's life.

~ Think of a situation in which you felt like you were baptized by fire, whether in your faith life, your business life, or in your family or daily life. Write a personal essay about the experience.

~ For a work of historical fiction, select a war or wartime period and imagine a central scene in which the protagonist undergoes a baptism by fire. Give this classic, but somewhat common theme (*War and Peace, Red Badge of Courage*) new dimensions.

~ Some politicians undergo baptisms by fire—George W. Bush after 9/11 and Hurricane Katrina and perhaps Barack Obama with the financial collapse. Think of a politician (or judge, corporate leader, or other public figure) who has either risen to the challenge, or collapsed under fire, and write an analysis or history, or use the real event as the germ of a fictional story.

Beat about the bush

Origin: This phrase dates to the Middle Ages, and refers to the practice of using sticks to hit around bushes, and flush out birds or other prey, for hunters to net or shoot. The concept is that the person who is *beating about the bush* is not getting directly to the purpose of the hunt and capturing the animal personally.

Ideas:

~ Write a scene in which a villain is resisting telling the protagonist (who does not yet know the antagonist is a miscreant) a piece of information, beating about the bush. If he did tell, it would remove an important obstacle from the protagonist's path, and expose the villainy.

~ Go to your library or online sites and look at the hunting scenes in illuminated medieval manuscripts. Take one and create character sketches for the people depicted, and begin to compose a story about the scene. Try, for example, *The Book of Hours of the Duke of Berry* (www.metmuseum.org/Collections/ search-the-collections/70010729).

~ If you have an interest in hunting, fishing, or other outdoor activities, research new products or techniques in that hobby or sport. Come up with five ideas for product reviews or technique comparisons. Identify potential markets for each, and tailor the ideas to each market.

Beyond the pale:

Origin: The Pale (originally from the Latin word *palus*, a fence stake, or part of a stockade) was an area surrounding Dublin that was controlled by England as early as the Norman Conquest. *Beyond the pale*, according to the English, was unsafe, unfortified territory where their laws did not hold because of Irish control. The phrase came to mean people, or actions, outside of acceptable society, behavior, or law.

Ideas:

~ Outline a Celtic fantasy in which characters within and beyond the pale interact. Create a backstory for a protagonist. Or, translate the same concept to a Western, or to a hard science fiction story.

~ The practice of creating a pale existed in other cultures and times. Catherine the Great of Russia ostracized Jews to the borders of the country, in an eighteenth-century pale. Look into this history, or other times when peoples were made to live in prescribed regions. What was the cultural and sociological impact?

~ Are there segments of society today, in our country or in any other, that are still viewed as beyond the pale? Explore the possibilities for an article or story.

~ Related to the original usage, the Irish were considered uncivilized and barbaric, unacceptable. That meaning remains today in *beyond the pale*. Create two characters, one who might be seen as uncivilized in overt ways and who is looked down on by a second character, who is outwardly civilized but morally barbaric. Engage them in dialogue.

~ What archaeological topics can you generate from the concept of the Latin *palus*—wooden or other stockades? For example, in 2012, Civil War stockade walls surrounding a prisoner of war camp were discovered in Georgia's Magnolia Springs State Park. (chronicle.augusta.com/ news/metro/2012-10-11/civil-war-stockade-walls-found-camp-lawton).

Carte blanche

Origin: A *carte blanche* is literally a white (French *blanche*), or blank paper signifying the right of someone to do whatever they please in some regard. Its derivation is from card games. The phrase referred to a hand with no face cards, but special value. Another theory, however, says *carte blanche* comes from a military battle term: An unconditional surrender was represented by a white paper containing only the defeated leader's signature, as an indication that the vanquisher dictated all terms.

Ideas:

~ Outline a thriller in which a *carte blanche* starts the action rolling, perhaps in a James Bond-like style.

~ For a middle-grade novel, begin with a character learning the concept of *carte blanche*, demanding one in some way from an adult, and discovering that having such freedom has consequences.

~ Select four real life personalities, contemporary or historical, who intrigue you. Write an act of a play in which the four play cards around a table. One of them is dealt a *carte blanche*, a hand that can lead to winning the game—but will it?

~ If *carte blanche* means the ability to do whatever you choose in a given circumstance, write a persuasive essay about some situation, whether personal, social, or political, in which you believe someone acted on a virtual *carte blanche*. Discuss how that freedom was either fraught with dangers or handled wisely. Or write a profile of an individual who you believe used power well, or not.

Cry uncle

Origin: Cry uncle, as most every child knows, means "I give up!" Why cry for your uncle? The originally American phrase may date to a joke printed in the children's pages of 1890s newspapers, about a man trying unsuccessfully to teach a parrot to say *uncle*.

Ideas:

~ Write your own humorous story for children or teens about someone trying to teach a parrot to speak. Explore the themes of frustration and surrender, with your main character learning something in the end.

~ Find fresh angles for writing a how-to on training a parrot, a dog, or another animal. Investigate theories in animal training, interviewing animal trainers on the varieties of techniques possible.

~ Go to your local library or historical archives and peruse newspapers from the 1890s, or as far back as you care to go. See what ideas jump from the pages. Develop ideas for nonfiction or fiction projects.

Go off half-cocked

Origin: In some early firearms, the hammer (or cock), could be put in a halfway position to let the user prepare to fire. But the gun could either go off unintentionally, or when meant to fire, fail. The expression *go off half-cocked* came to mean to do something without complete preparation or success. The connotation is also that there is incompetence, a risk of danger, and possibly anger involved.

Ideas:

~ Use a weapon of any kind that misfires or hits an unexpected target as the turning point in a story. Before the event, what was life like for your characters? After the event? How might the *thing*, the weapon, serve as an image or metaphor throughout your story?

~ Set a story during the American Revolution, centering it on a teenager coming of age. Since *half-cocked* can also suggest someone who does not know what they are doing, follow your young character through a series of events where he or she is learning self-control amid the chaos of war.

~ Research the science behind the mechanisms of weapons, and generate how-things-work articles. Look for unusual weapons and how they work, or how they led to other inventions useful to society.

~ Markets for antique and other guns are many, in general and in publishing. Look for magazines interested in information on them, and brainstorm three articles.

Hail Mary pass

Origin: A *Hail Mary pass* originated as an expression in football at Catholic universities in the 1920s or 1930s. It referred to a long forward pass made with little time left in the game, and in desperation. The phrase became more generally known in 1975 when Roger Staubach, a quarterback with the Dallas Cowboys and a Catholic, used a variation of the expression after playing a game against the Minnesota Vikings. The phrase has come to be used in contexts outside football for a sudden action, or last-ditch effort, taken to save what appears to be a losing situation.

Ideas:

~ *Hail Mary pass* is often used in business and political commentary today. Think of historical or contemporary situations in which last-minute actions changed the end result of a conflict or potential loss. Write an opinion piece or analysis.

~ Consider how the concept of a Hail Mary pass can work into a piece of fiction. Using football as theme, construct a story in which your protagonist symbolically throws a winning pass—takes an extreme action that may or may not save the day. How does the action affect your protagonist psychologically?

~ Prayers like the Hail Mary are a form of dialogue and poetry. Explore the role and forms of prayer in your culture, or in other cultures. Alternatively, investigate meditation and philosophical or intellectual counterparts to prayer. Develop potential articles on the subject; or compose prayers for devotional publications; or develop a fictional character whose prayer life is central to his or her personality and actions.

Knock on wood

Origin: The superstition of knocking on wood to avoid having bad luck probably originated in ancient beliefs about nature. In ancient Greece, nature deities like wood nymphs were believed to live in trees. In Celtic religions in Britain, trees were sacred and had spiritual power. *Knocking on wood* would represent a petition, or prayer. The Christian practice of touching the cross, the symbol of Christ's crucifixion, and asking for a blessing may also be part of the meaning of *knock on wood*.

Ideas:

~ Search out folk stories from your own family traditions, or through reading and research, and choose one or two to retell, first in a historical way and then in a modern version.

~ Superstitions may reveal aspects of a society. Look for new, contemporary superstitions to write about. One possibility is the Argentinan octopus that supposedly predicted the winner of soccer's last World Cup. Different cultures, professions, and events hold onto traditions not based on logic. Consider sailors and fisherman, marriage and pregnancy, and stage actors. Investigate the superstitions of a group and why they continue.

~ Use a superstitious nature as the driving force of a fictional character. That nature could be the major flaw that keeps your character from reaching a goal, or a villain's motivation, and it must be overcome to resolve the story. The story could be historical or contemporary, real life or fantasy.

La-di-da

Origin: La-di-da may have derived from the words *lard, laird,* and *lardy* (meaning *lord*) in the eighteenth century as a purposeful and foppish mispronunciation to denote affected speech and behavior. It also became an oath.

~ Write a page of dialogue for historical fiction, contrasting classes or cultures and reflected the differences in their dialogue. Set your scene in eighteenth-century Britain, America, or anywhere else in the past.

~ Expand on the theme implicit in the dialogue you wrote: Begin to conceive a story in which class or cultural differences inform the conflict and growth of characters.

~ Explore the use of oaths or curses in contemporary times. Consider changes in the media acceptance of oaths, and the use of rough language by children, teens, and adults.

On a wing and a prayer

Origin: Originating as a line of dialogue in a 1942 American movie made about World War II, *Flying Tigers,* this phrase referred an attacked, damaged plane and a pilot trying to make it home. The next year, a song was written based on the phrase, "Coming in on a Wing and a Prayer." It suggests two meanings of *wing*, one the plane's wing and the other connected to prayer, an angel's wing.

Ideas:

~ Movies about war and its aftermath have often been reflective of their times. Write reviews of some of these that analyze them in retrospect. Then begin writing reviews of current films. Find periodical or online markets, including blogs, in need of reviews. Among the war movie possibilities from different decades are *Sergeant York, Twelve O'Clock High, The Best Years of Our Lives, The Bridge on the River Kwai, Patton, MASH, The Deer Hunter, Born on the Fourth of July, Full Metal Jacket, Saving Private Ryan, Jarhead,* and *The Hurt Locker.*

~ Over the centuries, ballads and songs echo the times in which they are popular. Make notes about the *voice*—not the singer, but the message and sound—behind a particular song or type of music and how they speak to the audience and the times. Turn your thoughts into an essay or review. Or, interview sources knowledgeable about music for an informational article.

~ Use a lyrical, musical writing style to begin a verse novel. The subject might be war, a family's struggles, or a character's internal battles and attempts to survive *on a wing and a prayer.*

Pie in the sky

Origin: Originating in an American labor union song from 1906, *pie in the sky* refers to believing fruitlessly that a reward will come, despite current turmoil. The expression is attributed to labor activist Joe Hill, who used it in a parody of a Salvation Army hymn, "In the Sweet Bye-and-Bye." Hill wrote, "You will eat, bye and bye,/ In the glorious land above the sky!/Work and pray, live on hay,/ You'll get pie in the sky when you die" ("The Preacher and the Slave"). The phrase and the parody criticize those who promise heaven or a later reward, rather than feeding the poor or providing jobs today.

Ideas:

~ Sketch out a character like the real life Joe Hill. Place him or her in a setting such as 1906, or another period of financial unrest and unemployment in the U.S. What kind of figure might this character be in the current economic times? Alternatively, find angles for articles, either for young people or adults, on Hill or other historical figures from this period.

~ What labor issues are of concern in the U.S. today, regionally or nationally? In the Western world as a whole, or in Third World countries? Find markets for informational articles, or political or social commentary related to these issues. An example might be the recent employee protests against Walmart.

~ Writers have at times taken stands on the cause of the labor movement, workers, or the social issues of the working class. Read the work of one or more of authors such as George Bernard Shaw, Upton Sinclair, John Steinbeck, and George Orwell. Or, read writers of an opposite perspective, like Ayn Rand. Find story ideas or inspiration in their writings, but modernize them.

Small potatoes

Origin: The expression *small potatoes* means something of little significance, or trivial. It dates to at least 1836. It may be related to the British usage *small beer,* which referred originally to inexpensive beer with low alcohol content; since the 1700s *small beer* has been idiomatic for something weak.

Ideas:

~ The potatoes we eat today can all be traced back to one variety from Chile, dating to 500 BC. Develop article ideas based on potatoes in the categories of food history; cooking techniques and recipes; cultural history; nutrition (almost all a potato's is just under the skin); or other uses of the tuber, such as children's activities—making prints, experiments, games.

~ Investigate the food culture of Chile, or other Latin American cultures. How has it spread to the rest of the world, and what impact does it have on modern gastronomy?

~ The potato famine that ended in the deaths of a million people and emigration of another million in nineteenth-century Ireland rose from the confluence of the potato blight; social conditions; and political decisions that failed to react to the crisis effectively. Consider how the Great Famine might be the setting for fiction or a jumping off-point for nonfiction about famine generally. Or, use it as inspiration for historical fiction, or a fantasy novel setting and plot. How has *an Gorta Mór*—the Great Hunger—become folkloric?

Soft soap

Origin: Soft soap does not derive from soap and its lathering or softening capabilities, but from *soft solder*, a process of combining tin and lead. Over time the phrase became *soft sawder*, and finally *soft soap*. Its meaning is to flatter and convince.

Ideas:

~ How-to articles can almost always find markets. For do-it-yourselfers or people who are not naturally handy, write an article on how to do simple soldering for household fixes. What other such tasks would work for a how-to article, for print or online DIY markets?

~ Find publishing markets for audiences of skilled workers, such welders, plumbers, those who work in electronics, or jewelry makers, or sculptors.

~ For young readers, outline an article on the chemistry behind soldering, and its uses. You might discuss the metals used, the alloys created, the processes possible, flux, and the tools used now or in the past. Consider the possibility of a craft article.

~ Develop a soft-soaping secondary character who manipulates a protagonist by flattery or powers of persuasion. Write a scene in which the soft-soaping behavior becomes a turning point for your main character. For possible inspiration, look to Charles Dickens's Uriah Heep in *David Copperfield*.

Markets

Style

Business

Research

Ideas

Indexes

Contests

Grants Boost Writing Careers

By Michael Cooper

Need a few thousand extra dollars, or a month in a villa in northern Italy, or a door-opening boost to your writing career? Apply for a grant. While some writers have won multiple grants, others do not bother with them. But there are many reasons to add grant applications to your to-do list. Grants and fellowships can not only pay some of the bills, they have additional benefits far exceeding their dollar value.

Just ask Paul Bergstraesser, a writer who teaches at the University of Wyoming. In 2012, he won a $25,000 National Endowment for the Arts (NEA) literary fellowship. "A confidence boost from a NEA fellowship is probably the single greatest outcome," says Bergstraesser, "and it feels like doors into the writing community will be opened more easily in the coming years. I've already been contacted by an agent about my work because of the fellowship, a connection that probably wouldn't have happened as quickly without the award. Finally, I see the award as a boost to my teaching career."

Grants Large & Small

The NEA Fellowships, Fulbrights, and other big-name grants are competitive, but not as much as one might think. "We received 1,179 eligible applications for fiscal year 2012," says Brenna Berger, a division specialist in the NEA's Literature office.

"We regularly receive around 1,100 eligible applications each year and that number is steady for both prose and poetry years." As many as 40 writing fellowships can be awarded annually. So that is almost a 1 in 28 chance of winning a career-enhancing NEA fellowship.

Surprisingly, some of the lesser-known grants have only a handful of applicants. Every other year the Kentucky Arts Council (KAC) awards the Al Smith Fellowships in fiction and in nonfiction. In 2012, I applied for the fiction fellowship. I did not win. But after the winners were announced, I learned how few people had applied. KAC Executive Director Lori Meadows told me that in 2012 only 12 people applied for the three $6,000 fiction fellowships and 11 applied for the three $6,000 nonfiction fellowships.

Grants from national organizations, of course, receive a lot more applications, but they are not necessarily swamped. The Society for Children's Writers and Illustrators (SCBWI), a Los Angeles-based organization with 22,000 members worldwide, awards numerous grants, including annual work-in-progress grants in four categories: nonfiction, contemporary novel, multi-cultural writing, and general work. Applicants have to belong to SCBWI, which is open to anyone for a $70 a year membership fee. The winner in each work-in-progress category receives a $2,000 grant and the runner-up receives $500. "Last year we received about 500 applications in the four categories," explains Chelsea Mooser, SCBWI Director of Outreach. "Most applications are in the general and contemporary categories."

Why Writers Do Not Apply

Back in July 2012 I sent emails to several hundred members of two professional writing organizations asking about their experiences applying for grants. About 40 people responded. Here are some of the responses.

Jacqueline Jules, a writer in northern Virginia, replied succinctly,

"I have never applied for a writing grant. I never thought it was worth my time. It's hard to win contests."

Kurt Hampe, a writer in Louisville, Kentucky, explained, "I've toyed with the notion a couple times, but I haven't for a couple reasons. One, I didn't desperately need the grant, so I didn't want to deal with the learning curve (did I just admit that?). And two, I haven't relied on my fiction to cover the bills, so I felt like I was better off focusing on the writing than on the grant writing."

Many writers who replied to my query *had* won grants. "I've applied, and have received grants twice from the Ohio Arts Council," wrote Stephanie Tolan, "and then because I'd won an OAC grant I was eligible to apply for a summer residency at the Fine Arts Work Center (FAWC) in Provincetown, where I was given an apartment, a small stipend, and three months to do nothing but write (and hang out at the beach when I wanted). I also was given the opportunity to take three classes (for free) at the FAWC—one of which was [on] books as art, which was a fabulous class and great fun!"

Brenda Seabrooke, a writer now living in Florida and a 1994 NEA fellow, responded, "I applied to the West Virginia Writers Commission (or something like that), and was rejected using the same material that got the Endowment grant. I also applied to Emerson College [and won] what was then called the Sophie de Liedel Award for two weeks at Kasteel Wel, a castle in southeast Holland that the college owns. It was exciting."

Poet and writer Ellen Birkett Morris has received six grants. The most recent was a KAC 2012 Al Smith Fellowship in fiction. Grants are "a stepping stone in terms of further recognition of my work," Morris believes. "An arts council grant followed by a well-received book might open the door to NEA grants or other awards. It was also tremendously encouraging at a pivotal time in the development of my writing."

One Writer's Fulbright

A Fulbright fellowship "proved to be one of the most transformative periods in my life—not just for myself but for my writing as well," Franz Knupfer believes. After completing his MFA at Johns Hopkins, Knupfer applied to the Fulbright Program, which is sponsored by the U.S. Department of State's Bureau of Education and Cultural Affairs. He later wrote about his Fulbright experience for Poets & Writers magazine.

In his article Knupfer, who is deaf, explained that he wanted to go to Katmandu to work at a school for the deaf and write short stories about the experience. A Fulbright advisor at Hopkins told him that "having a creative project wouldn't make my proposal less competitive but rather more unique."

Because Western Europe is the most popular destination for Fulbright fellows, Knupfer picked Nepal, in part because he thought there would be less competition. He was right. In the 2009-2010 year there were only 48 Fulbright applications for five available grants to Nepal.

"Many writers," Knupfer's article explained, "aren't aware that it [the Fulbright Program] is a potential source of funding for artists. While it's true that 58 percent of Fulbright grants are given for academic projects and only 6 percent fund projects in the arts, this is partially due to the fact that few artists apply."

Fulbright fellows are varied, Knupfer says. "They are students, researchers, and teachers . . . . They are also visual and performing artists, journalists, and professionals." And nearly a third of the applicants aren't affiliated with a university or other U. S. institution. There are only a couple of hard-and-fast rules Knupfer says. Be an American citizen and have a BA.

Knupfer, who now lives in Colorado, summed up his Fulbright experience. "My values were tested and transformed, my worldview widened. I began to see much of my work while an MFA student as solipsistic—I'd written about what I knew, which happened to be myself. In Nepal, I began to write about something larger."

Knupfer's article is "Fulbright grants: an untapped resource for writers" in the September/October 2010 Poets & Writers magazine.

Specialized Grants

There are many kinds of grants for writers. Some are for writers at certain stages of their careers. The New York Public Library gives an annual Young Lions Fiction Award of $10,000 to writers who are U.S. citizens under age 35. The SCBWI offers a $2,000 grant for mid-list writers who haven't sold a book in two years. The Guggenheim writing fellowships are awarded "on the basis of achievement and exceptional promise."

Many grants are limited to specific genders or genres. Kore Press in Tucson, Arizona, offers an annual $1,000 grant for a "female-identified poet." Graywolf Press in Minneapolis annually gives a $12,000 grant to unpublished creative nonfiction writers.

Other grants are intended for writers in specific places. The PEN American Center in New York gives $1,000 fellowships to emerging poets, fiction writers, and nonfiction writers who are from underrepresented communities such as inner-city Los Angeles. Every state has an arts council and most award grants and fellowships to their state's artists.

Some grants send writers to interesting places. The National Science Foundation's Antarctic Artists and Writers Program provides round-trip economy airfare and accommodations to that frozen continent for writers who need to do firsthand research there. For a somewhat plusher destination the Rockefeller Foundation fellowships give writers 30-day residencies at its Bellagio Center, a villa overlooking Lake Como in northern Italy.

A number of grants are for specific uses such as research and travel or for giving readings and workshops. The Amy Lowell Travelling Scholarship, amounting to $52,000, is awarded annually to enable one or two U.S. poets to travel and study abroad. Poets & Writers magazine gives grants ranging from $50 to $1500 for readings and workshops in New York and California and in eight large cities outside those states.

How Difficult Are the Applications?

"The SCBWI grant application was very straightforward and involved the same work that we do to create a nonfiction proposal and query for a publisher," explained Chicago writer Laurie Lawlor, who has received two SCBWI work-in-progress grants. "The most recent grant covered research expenses for a biography of Jack London. All the work that I did in creating the proposal I feel is beneficial to the actual pitching of the project. In other words, there was no wasting of effort in the SCBWI grant application."

My own KAC 2012 Al Smith fellowship application was quite easy. Using the online application, I prepared a brief biography. And I submitted two short writing samples, several pages from one of my published books and the first eight pages of the novel I was working on. But later I began to suspect it was too easy. Email exchanges with two of the winners made me realize that I probably did not put enough effort into my application, which might be typical of first-time or occasional grant applicants.

Here is how Morris prepared her successful Al Smith application: "I spent several week putting together my thoughts on my journey as an artist, classes I took, mastery I achieved, classes I taught, and writing goals. I worked to make sure that they got a sense of my development as an artist and could see that I had reached a level of mastery that merited the fellowship."

KAC's Meadows explains about common mistakes applicants make: They often "do not read the guidelines before starting the application, or before calling the arts council to ask for assistance."

Breener, at the NEA, also said applicants not following the guidelines is a recurring problem. "In order to ensure a level playing field for all applicants, we do adhere to the guidelines. While the process can be daunting, it is doable. We are always happy to help applicants as they prepare their applications and spend quite a bit of time walking them through the process."

At SCBWI the problem is a bit different. "The most common problem would probably just be sending a manuscript that hasn't

Resources

~ The Foundation Center is probably the most important source of information about foundations in the U.S. and perhaps in the world. It's headquartered in New York City and has field offices in Cleveland, Washington, D.C., Atlanta, and San Francisco. Each location has a library that's open to the public and full of information about grants and how to apply for them. The Foundation Center also has some 450 "cooperating collections" at universities, public libraries, and other institutions around the country. Or let your fingers do the walking by subscribing to the Foundation Directory Online for $29.95 a month. You'll find more information at www.foundationcenter.org.

~ The New York Foundation for the Arts maintains a free online database called NYFA Source that is, according to its website, "the most extensive national directory of awards, publications, and services for artists." It can be accessed at www.nyfa.org.

~ Pen American Center offers a one year subscription to its online database of some 1500 domestic and foreign grants, prizes, fellowships, and residencies. The annual fee is $10 for PEN members and $12 for non-members. Go to www.pen.org.

~ Poets & Writers magazine offers subscribers an online index of some 450 grants, prizes, and fellowships searchable by genre. P&W also has other helpful programs such as a calendar of application deadlines, lists of recent winners, and a blog about contests. Subscriptions to P&W are $19.95 a year. The magazine's online address is www.pw.org.

been revised at all yet," Mooser said. "Although the grant is for a work in progress, the winners are typically applicants who have already gotten feedback from their critique group or colleagues at an SCBWI event and have done some revisions on the piece they are submitting."

What advice do grant winners have for writers applying for grants? Lawlor's advice is "know what you're planning, do your research about previous grants given, and present an honest and thoughtful proposal."

"When one thinks a manuscript is ready" to submit with a grant application, don't rush to get it in the mail, Seabrooke cautions, "wait awhile and look at it again."

The process of applying for grants, many writers agree, is similar to submitting manuscripts to magazines, agents, and publishers. There will certainly be rejections, but be persistent and one day you will find yourself reading a letter that begins, "Congratulations."

Contests & Awards

For Adult & Children's Writers

Abilene Writers Guild Annual Contest

P.O. Box 2562, Abilene, TX 79604
www.abilenewritersguild.org

This annual competition is open to all writers and awards prizes in ten categories, including children's stories, novels, poetry, flash fiction, memoir/nostalgia, and general interest articles. Guidelines vary for each category. Visit the website to download the annual contest guidelines. Entry fee, $5 for short pieces; $10 for novel entries. *Deadline:* Submissions are accepted from October 1 to November 30. *Award:* First place in each category, $100; $65, second place; $35, third place.

Jane Addams Children's Book Award

Marianne I. Baker, Chair MSC 6909, 7210B Memorial Hall, James Madison University, 800 S. Main Street, Harrisonburg, VA 22807
www.janeaddamspeace.org

Honoring authors and illustrators of children's literature who reach standards of excellence while promoting the themes of peace, social justice, equality of the sexes, and a unified world, this award competition is held annually. Books of fiction, nonfiction, or poetry targeting children ages 2 through 12 that were published in the year preceding the contest are eligible. *Deadline:* December 31. *Award:* Honorary certificate and a cash award.

Alligator Juniper's National Writing Contest

Prescott College, 220 Grove Avenue, Prescott, AZ 86301

www.prescott.edu/experience/publications/alligatorjuniper

Alligator Juniper is published annually by Prescott College, and features the winners in national contests. This contest accepts original, unpublished entries in the categories of fiction, creative nonfiction, and poetry. Fiction and nonfiction entries should not exceed 30 pages. Poetry, limit 5 poems per entry. Entry fee, $15. *Deadline:* October 1. Contest opens August 15. *Award:* First prize in each category, $1,000 and publication in *Alligator Juniper*.

American Book Awards

Before Columbus Foundation, The Raymond House, 655–13th
    Street, Suite 302, Oakland, CA 94612

www.beforecolumbusfoundation.com/submission.html

These awards are sponsored by the Before Columbus Foundation, a nonprofit educational and service group that promotes multicultural literature and widens the audience for cultural and ethnic diversity in American writing. The awards are given for excellence and an outstanding contribution to American literature. Two copies of a book may be submitted by anyone—author, publisher, agent—for consideration in the next year. All genres are eligibile, including adult books, children's books, anthologies, and multimedia. No fees or forms are requested. *Deadline:* December 31. *Award:* Given in a ceremony at the University of California, Berkeley.

Sherwood Anderson Fiction Award

Mid-American Review, Dept. of English, Box W, Bowling Green
    State University, Bowling Green, OH 43403

www.bgsu.edu/studentlife/organizations/midamericanreview

Sponsored by *Mid-American Review,* the literary journal of Bowling Green State University, this competition is open to all writers and accepts short story entries of high literary merit. Entries may be in any genre of fiction, but must be original, unpublished material. Entry fee, $10. *Deadline:* November 15. *Award:* First place, $1,000 and publication in *Mid-American Review.* Four finalists are also considered for publication.

Arizona Authors Association Literary Contest

Contest Coordinator, 6145 W. Echo Lane, Glendale, AZ 85302
www.azauthors.com

This annual contest sponsored by the Arizona Authors Association and Five Star Publications and is open to all writers in English. It accepts unpublished and published works in categories including short stories, poetry, essays, articles, true stories, and novels. In 2011, two special categories included short stories from Arizona residents, set in the state or with Arizonans as characters; and an essay with an Arizona theme, setting, or narrator. Each category is divided into three groups: elementary school; junior high and high school; and college and adults. Entry fee, $15-$30. *Deadline:* January 1 and July 1. *Award:* Category winners, First prize, $100; second prize, $50; third prize, $25 and publication in *Arizona Literary Magazine.*

Atlantic Writing Competition

Writers' Federation of Nova Scotia, 1113 Marginal Road, Halifax
NS B3H 4P7 Canada
www.writers.ns.ca

Open to writers living in Atlantic Canada, this annual competition accepts entries of adult novels, YA novels, short stories, poetry, writing for children, plays, and magazine articles or essays. Previously unpublished material only. Entry fees: novel categories, $35; all other categories, $25. WFNS members receive a $5 discount on entry fees. Published authors may not enter the competition in the genre that they have been published. Limit one entry per category. *Deadline:* November 9. *Award:* First-through third-place winners in each category receive awards ranging from $200 to $50.

Autumn House Poetry, Fiction, and Nonfiction Contests
P.O. Box 60100, Pittsburgh, PA 15211
www.autumnhouse.org

Autumn House Press sponsors this annual contest that accepts collections of fiction, poetry, and for the first time, nonfiction. All fiction genres are welcome. Poetry collections, 50 to 80 pages. Fiction, 200–300 pages. Nonfiction, 200-300 pages on any subject; forms include personal essays, memoir, travel, historical narratives, nature or science writing. Entry fee, $30. *Deadline:* June 30. *Award:* Winning entry is published by Autumn House Press, and awarded $2,500 and a $1,500 travel grant. All entries are considered for publication.

AWP Award Series
Association of Writers & Writing Programs, Carty House, Mail Stop 1E3, George Mason University, Fairfax, VA 22030-4444
www.awpwriter.org/contests/series.htm

The nonprofit Association of Writers & Writing Programs holds this annual award series for fiction, creative nonfiction, and poetry. The competition is open to all writers; guidelines are available at the website. *Deadline:* Entries must be postmarked between January 1 and February 28. *Award:* Poetry and short fiction winners, $5,500 and publication; novel and nonfiction winners, $2,500 and publication.

Marilyn Baillie Picture Book Award
Canadian Children's Book Centre (CCBC), 40 Orchard View
   Blvd., Suite 101, Toronto ON M4R 1B9 Canada
www.bookcentre.ca

Fiction, nonfiction, or poetry in picture book form, for readers ages three to eight, is eligible for this award. It is given to "outstanding" books "in which the author and illustrator achieve artistic and literary unity." Titles published in the year preceding the contest are eligible for entry. Winners are chosen by a jury appointed by the CCBC. *Deadline:* December. *Award:* $20,000 and a certificate.

Doris Bakwin Award for Writing

Carolina Wren Press, 120 Morris Street, Durham, NC 27701
carolinawrenpress.org/submissions/contests

This biennial contest, held in odd-numbered years, seeks collections of shorts stories, novels, and memoirs written by women. It encourages submissions from new and established writers and accepts unpublished material only. Guidelines are posted on the website in late summer. Entry fee, $20. *Deadline:* March 15. *Award:* $1,000, and publication by Carolina Wren Press, which also runs the Carolina Wren Press Poetry Series, a contest held in even-numbered years.

Baltimore Review Competition

P.O. Box 529, Fork, MD 21051
www.baltimorereview.org

The newly relaunched online *Baltimore Review* is continuing to hold an annual competition for original, unpublished poetry, fiction, or creative nonfiction. Entry fee, $10. Submit via the website. *Deadline:* August 1 to November 30. *Award:* First place, $300 and publication in *Baltimore Review*; second place, $200; third place, $100.

Bartleby Snopes Annual Writing Contest

www.bartlebysnopes.com

In 2013, the online literary journal *Bartleby Snopes* is sponsoring its fifth writing contest. The contests focus on dialogue, the most recent requiring a short story, to 2,000 words, composed entirely of dialogue. Stories must be original and unpublished; work posted on blogs, boards, websites is considered published and therefore ineligible. Entry fee, $10; multiple entries are allowed. Submit via the website submissions manager. Do not include your personal information on manuscript pages. *Deadline:* September 15. *Award:* Winner, $250+; four honorable mentions will receive $10 each. All pieces are published in the January issue of *Bartleby Snopes*.

Pura Belpré Medal

American Library Association, 50 East Huron, Chicago, IL 60611
www.ala.org/alsc/awardsgrants/bookmedia/belpremedal

This annual award is named in honor of Pura Belpré, the first Latina librarian at the New York Public Library. Medals are presented to a Latino/Latina writer and to an illustrator in recognition of literature that best portrays and celebrates the Latino cultural experience for young readers. Authors and illustrators must be residents or citizens of U.S. or Puerto Rico; submissions must be published in the U.S. or Puerto Rico in the contest year. Fiction and nonfiction published in Spanish, English, or bilingual format are eligible. *Deadline:* December 31. *Award:* Winners are presented with medals at a June celebration.

Geoffrey Bilson Award for Historical Fiction for Young People

Canadian Children's Book Centre (CCBC), 40 Orchard View
  Blvd., Suite 217, Toronto ON M4R 1B9 Canada
www.bookcentre.ca/award

Books of historical fiction for young people by Canadian authors are celebrated by this annual contest. Books published in the year preceding the contest are eligible for entry. Winners are chosen by a jury appointed by the CCBC. Picture books, short story collections by more than one author, and plots involving time travel are not eligible. *Deadline:* December. *Award:* $5,000 and a certificate.

The *Boston Globe-Horn Book* Awards
The Horn Book, 56 Roland Street, Suite 200, Boston, MA 02129
www.hbook.com

These prestigious awards celebrate excellence in literature for children and young adults. A committee of three judges evaluates books submitted by U.S. publishers and selects a winner and up to two Honor Books in the categories of picture book, fiction and poetry, and nonfiction. No entry fee. *Deadline:* May 15. *Award:* Winners receive $500 and an engraved silver bowl. Honor recipients receive an engraved plate.

Boulevard Short Fiction Contest for Emerging Writers
6614 Clayton Road, PMB 325, Richmond Heights, MO 63117
www.boulevardmagazine.org/partners.html

Writers who have not yet published a book of fiction, creative nonfiction, or poetry with a nationally distributed press are eligible to compete in this annual contest. Entries must be original, unpublished work, to 8,000 words. Entry fee, $15. *Deadline:* December 31. *Award:* $1,500 and publication in *Boulevard*.

Briar Cliff Review Writing Competition
3303 Rebecca Street, Sioux City, IA 51104-2100
www.briarcliff.edu/bcreview

This annual contest accepts unpublished entries of fiction, creative nonfiction, and poetry. Fiction and creative nonfiction should not exceed 6,000 words. Poetry entries may include up to three poems. Entry fee, $20. *Deadline:* November 1. *Award:* First prize in each category is $1,000 and publication in *Briar Cliff Review*.

Marilyn Brown Novel Award

Jen Wahlquist, English Literature Dept., Mail Stop 153, Utah
   Valley University, 800 West University Pkwy., Orem, UT 84058
www.uvu.edu/english/marilyn_brown_novel/index.html

Under the stewardship of Utah Valley University's English
Depart-ment, this award is given annually for the best unpublished literary mainstream novel focusing on realistic cultural
experiences of the Utah Region, or Latter-day Saints experiences.
No science fiction or fantasy; mainstream literature only.
Minimum of 200 pages; no maximum. No entry fee. Limit one
entry per competition. *Deadline:* October 1. *Award:* $1,000.

Randolph Caldecott Medal

American Library Association (ALA), 50 E. Huron, Chicago, IL
   60611
www.ala.org

Named in honor of the English illustrator, Randolph Caldecott,
this award is presented to the artist of the most distinguished
American picture book for children published in the preceding
year. It is open to all U.S. citizens. Honor books are also recognized. *Deadline:* December 31. *Award:* The winner is announced at
the ALA Midwinter Meeting and is presented with the Caldecott
Medal at an awards banquet.

California Book Awards

595 Market Street, San Francisco, CA 94105
www.commonwealthclub.org/bookawards

This contest was established to find the best California writers
and spotlight the high-quality literature produced in the state.
The competition awards California authors with gold and silver
medals in recognition of outstanding literary works. Awards are
presented in the categories of fiction, nonfiction, poetry, first
work of fiction, Californiana, YA literature, juvenile literature,

and notable contribution to publishing. Submit six copies of entry. No entry fee. *Deadline:* December 17. *Award:* Consists of 6 to 8 gold medals and up to 6 silver medals.

Canadian Library Association's Book of the Year for Children
10 Abilene Dr., Toronto, ON M9A 2M8 Canada
www.cla.ca

Recognizing Canadian works of children's literature for ages 12 and under, this award is presented annually to works of creative writing (fiction, poetry, narrative, nonfiction, and retellings) by Canadian citizens. All titles submitted for this award must be published in the year preceding the contest. *Deadline:* December 31. *Award:* Winner receives a leather-bound copy of their book.

Canadian Writer's Journal Short Fiction Contest
Box 1178, New Liskeard ON P0J 1P0 Canada
www.cwj.ca/04-00fiction.htm

This contest, sponsored by *Canadian Writer's Journal*, accepts unpublished work by Canadians in any genre, to 2,500 words. Awards are presented in March and September. Each entry must be accompanied by a brief author biography. Entry fee, $10. *Deadline:* April 30. *Award:* First place, $150; second and third place, $100 and $50, respectively. Winning entries are published in *Canadian Writer's Journal*.

CAPA Competition
Connecticut Authors and Publishers Association, c/o Daniel Uitti,
   223 Buckingham Street, Oakville, CT 06779
aboutcapa.com/writing_contest.htm

This annual contest accepts entries of short stories (to 2,000 words), children's stories (to 2,000 words), personal essays (to 1,500 words), and poetry (to 30 lines). The competition is open to all writers and accepts multiple entries, provided each entry is accompanied by an official entry form. Submit four copies of entry. Entry fee, $10 per story/personal essay or up to three poems. *Deadline:* December 24. *Award:* First place, $100; second place, $50. Winning entries are published in CAPA's newsletter.

Children's Writer Contests
93 Long Ridge Road, West Redding, CT 06896
www.thechildrenswriter.com

Every year *Children's Writer* newsletter sponsors two contests, each with a specific theme and requirements. Upcoming themes vary, as do the age ranges of the intended audience of children—from preschool to high school. Recent contests have included poetry and middle-grade mysteries. No entry fee for subscribers; $15 entry fee includes an eight-month subscription. Multiple entries are accepted. *Deadline:* February and October. *Award:* Cash prizes vary, with first place as much as $500. Winning entries are published in *Children's Writer*.

Christopher Awards
5 Hanover Square, 11th Floor, New York, NY 10004
www.christophers.org

These annual awards are sponsored by the Christophers, a Catholic organization with a ministry of communications. The awards recognize artistic work in publishing, film and television that creates a positive change in society and promotes self-worth. Profiles of courage, stories of determination, and chronicles of constructive action and empowerment are accepted. All entries must be published in the year preceding the contest. *Deadline:* November. *Award:* Winners are presented with bronze medallions at a ceremony in New York City.

Crossquarter Short Science Fiction Contest
P.O. Box 23749, Santa Fe, NM 87502

www.crossquarter.com/contest.html

Short story entries of science fiction, fantasy, and urban fantasy are accepted in this annual competition. The contest is sponsored by Crossquarter Publishing and looks for entries that portray the best of the human spirit. Entries should not exceed 7,500 words. Submissions must be electronic. Entry fee, $15. *Deadline:* March 15. *Award:* First place, $250; second- to fourth-place, from $125 to $50; fifth- through fifteenth-place, honorable mention. All winners will receive publication by Crossquarter Publishing.

Sheldon Currie Fiction Prize
The Antigonish Review, P.O. Box 5000, Street Francis Xavier
   University, Antigonish NS B2G 2W5 Canada
antigonishreview.com

The Sheldon Currie Fiction Prize is held each year. It is open to well-written, unpublished short stories on any subject matter. Entries should not exceed 20 pages. Entry fee, $30 from the U.S. and $25 from Canada; $40 from outside North America. *Deadline:* July 31. *Award:* First place, $600; second place, $400; third place, $200. The three winning entries are published in the *Antigonish Review.*

Delacorte Press Contest for a First Young Adult Novel
1745 Broadway, 9th Floor, New York, NY 10019
www.randomhouse.com/kids/writingcontests

This annual contest encourages young adult contemporary fiction. It is open to writers living in the U.S. and Canada who have not yet published a YA novel. Manuscripts should be between 100 and 224 typed pages. Limit two entries per competition. All entries must feature a contemporary setting and plot suitable for readers ages 12 to 18. *Deadline:* Submissions must be postmarked between October 1 and December 31. *Award:* Book contract with Random House, advance on royalties of $7,500, and $1,500 cash.

The Amanda Davis Highwire Fiction Award

849 Valencia Street, San Francisco, CA 94110

www.mcsweeneys.net/pages/the-amanda-davis-highwire-
fiction-award

The San Francisco-based publisher McSweeney's has presented this memorial award biannually since 2004. It was created in honor of book and short story author Amanda Davis, who died in a plane crash. The award is given to a woman writer younger than 32 "who both embodies Amanda's personal strengths—warmth, generosity, a passion for community—and who needs some time to finish a book in progress." Submit a work-in-progress, 5,000–40,000 words, and a brief explanation of financial status via Submittable (www.submittable.com), to amanda-davis.submittable.com. A mailed hard copy submission is also acceptable. See online guidelines for more details. Fee, $20. *Deadline:* December 15. *Award:* $2,500.

Jack Dyer Fiction Prize

Dept. of English, Faner Hall 2380, Mail Code 4503, Southern
Illinois University–Carbondale, 1000 Faner Dr., Carbondale,
IL 62901

craborchardreview.siuc.edu/dyer.html

Open to U.S. residents, this annual competition is sponsored by *Crab Orchard Review,* the literary journal of Southern Illinois University–Carbondale. It is open to submissions of unpublished fiction, to 6,000 words. Entry fee, $20 per entry. Limit 3 entries per competition. *Deadline:* Postmarked between March 1 and May 4. *Award:* Publication in the winter/spring *Crab Orchard Review* and a payment of $2,000.

Margaret A. Edwards Award

50 East Huron Street, Chicago, IL 60611

www.ala.org/yalso/edwards

This award was established by the American Library Association's Young Adult Services Association and honors a living author for a body of work and special contribution to YA literature. The winner's writing will have been popular over a period of time and is generally recognized as helping teens to become better aware of who they are and their role in society. Nominations are accepted from librarians and teens. *Deadline:* November 1. *Award:* $2,000, and a citation presented during the annual ALA conference.

Arthur Ellis Awards

4C-240 Westwood Road, Guelph, ON N1H 7W9 Canada
www.crimewriterscanada.com/awards

The Arthur Ellis Awards were established to honor excellence in Canadian mystery and crime writing. The contest is open to writers living in Canada or Canadian writers living elsewhere in the world. It accepts published entries in several categories, including best short story, best nonfiction, best first novel, best juvenile novel, best novel, best crime writing in French, as well as the best unpublished crime novel. Processing fee, $35 for books, $15 for short stories. *Deadline:* December 15. *Award:* Winners receive a wooden statue at the annual awards dinner.

William Faulkner–William Wisdom Creative Writing Competition

624 Pirate's Alley, New Orleans, LA 70116-3254
www.wordsandmusic.org/competition.html

This annual competition was set up to preserve the storytelling heritage of New Orleans and the Deep South by Pirate's Alley Faulkner Society. Unpublished entries are accepted in seven categories: novel, novella, novel-in-progress, short story, essay, poetry, and short story by a high school student. Entry fees range from $10 to $75, depending on category. Visit the website for complete guidelines. *Deadline:* Entries must be received between January 1 and May 15. *Award:* Publication in the Faulkner Society's annual literary journal, *The Double Dealer.* Ranges from $750 to $7,500.

Shubert Fendrich Memorial Playwriting Contest

P.O. Box 4267, Englewood, CO 80155-4267

www.pioneerdrama.com

This competition encourages the development of quality theatrical material for educational and community theaters. It is open to playwrights who have not been published by Pioneer Drama Service. Manuscripts must have a running time between 20 and 90 minutes. *Deadline:* Ongoing. *Award:* Publishing contract and advance against royalties of $1,000.

Fineline Competition for Prose Poems, Short Shorts

Mid-American Review, Dept. of English, Bowling Green State
    University, Bowling Green, OH 43403

www.bgsu.edu/studentlife/organizations/midamericanreview

The literary journal of Bowling Green State University, *Mid-American Review,* sponsors this competition for literary quality prose poems and short, short stories. Entries must be original and unpublished material. Length, no longer than 500 words. Submit a set of three prose poems or stories. Verse will be automatically disqualified. Entry fee, $10. *Deadline:* June 1. *Award:* First place, $1,000 and publication in *Mid-American Review.*

H. E. Francis Award

Dept. of English, Morton Hall, Room 222, University of Alabama,
    Huntsville, AL 35899

www.uah.edu/hefranciscontest

This annual award is sponsored by the Ruth Hindman Foundation and the University of Alabama–Huntsville English Department. It accepts original, unpublished short stories that are judged by a nationally known panel of editors. Manuscripts must not exceed 5,000 words. Entry fee, $15. *Deadline:* December 31. *Award:* $1,000.

Don Freeman Memorial Grant-in-Aid
8271 Beverly Boulevard, Los Angeles, CA 90048
www.scbwi.org/Pages.aspx/Don-Freeman-Grant

Members of the Society of Children's Book Writers and Illustrators who intend to make picture books their primary contribution to children's literature are eligible for this grant, which is underwritten by Amazon.com. The grant is presented annually to help artists further their understanding, training, and work in the picture book genre. *Deadline:* Entries must be postmarked between February 15 and March 15. *Award:* Winner, $2,000; runner-up, $500.

John Gardner Memorial Prize for Fiction
Harpur Palate, English Dept., Binghamton University, Box 6000, Binghamton, NY 13902-6000
harpurpalate.binghamton.edu

This contest was established to honor John Gardner's dedication to the creative writing program at Binghamton University. It is open to all writers and accepts previously unpublished short story entries. Entries should not exceed 8,000 words. Entry fee, $15 (includes a one-year subscription to *Harpur Palate*). *Deadline:* February 1 to April 15. *Award:* $500 and publication in the summer issue of *Harpur Palate.*

Glimmer Train Contests
4763 SW Maplewood, P.O. Box 80430, Portland, OR 97209
www.glimmertrain.com/writguid1.html

Glimmer Train sponsors a contests each month of the year, including Family Matters, Fiction Open, Short Story Award for New Writers, and Very Short Fiction. Lengths vary. Electronic submissions are preferred. *Deadlines:* Vary. *Award:* First place award ranges from $1,500 to $2,500 and includes publication in *Glimmer Train*, and 20 copies of the issue with the winning story.

The Golden Kite Awards
8271 Beverly Blvd., Los Angeles, CA 90048-4515
www.scbwi.org

Presented annually by the Society of Children's Book Writers & Illustrators, the Golden Kites recognize excellence in children's fiction, nonfiction, picture book text, and picture book illustration. SCBWI members whose work has been published in the year preceding the contest are eligible. *Deadline:* June 15 to December 3. *Award:* $2,500 and an expense-paid trip to the award ceremony at the Golden Kite luncheon during SCBWI's summer conference in August. Four honor book recipients also receive recognition.

The Guild Literary Complex Prose Awards
Guild Complex, P.O. Box 478880, Chicago, IL 60647-9998
guildcomplex.org

An annual contest for short fiction and nonfiction, open to Illinois residents over 21, is sponsored by Chicago's Guild Literary Complex. Submit one piece of original fiction or nonfiction, to 1,000 words. Entry fee, $5. Mail entries, or email to contest@guildcomplex.org, with "Prose Awards" in the subject line, and either a PDF or Word document attached. Do not include your name or other identifying information on the manuscript itself. *Deadline:* September. *Award:* $250 for the winner in each category. Winners read their fiction or nonfiction at an October event at the Chopin Theater in Wicker Park.

Gulf Coast Writer's Association Let's Write Contest
P.O. Box 10294, Gulfport, MS 39505
www.gcwriters.org

The Gulf Coast Writer's Association has held this literary contest for 25 years. It is open to all writers of fiction, nonfiction, and poetry. It accepts entries in all genres except erotica, horror, or stories with graphic violence, or exhibiting any religious, racial, or moral prejudice. Submissions must be original, unpublished work. Fiction and nonfiction, to 2,500 words; poetry, 3 poems, to 50 lines. Entry fee, $8. Mail entry with a cover letter including your information, the entry's category, and word count. Or, email via the website page. *Deadline:* January 15 to April 15. *Award:* First place, $100; second place, $60; third place; $25, and publication in the association's *Magnolia Quarterly*.

John Guyon Literary Nonfiction Prize
Dept. of English, Faner Hall 2380, Mail Code 4503, Southern Illinois University–Carbondale, 1000 Faner Dr., Carbondale, IL 62901
craborchardreview.siuc.edu

Sponsored by *Crab Orchard Review*, the literary journal of Southern Illinois University–Carbondale, this competition awards excellence in original, previously unpublished literary nonfiction. The contest is open to U.S. residents. Entries should not exceed 6,500 words. Entry fee, $20 per entry (maximum 3 entries). *Deadline:* Postmarked between March and May. *Award:* $2,000 and publication in the winter/spring *Crab Orchard Review*.

Lorian Hemingway Short Story Competition
P.O. Box 993, Key West, FL 33041
www.shortstorycompetition.com

Writers of short fiction whose work has not been published in a nationally distributed publication with a circulation of 5,000 or more are eligible to enter this competition, which receives submissions from around the world. It accepts original, unpublished short stories of up to 3,500 words. There are no restrictions on theme. Entry fee, $15 for entries postmarked by May 1; $20 for those postmarked by May 15. Online submissions accepted, with the same deadlines. *Deadline:* May 15. *Award:* First place, $2,500 and publication in *Cutthroat: A Journal of the Arts*; second and third place, $500.

Highlights for Children Fiction Contest
803 Church Street, Honesdale, PA 18431
www.highlights.com/highlights-fiction-contest

This annual contest sponsored by *Highlights for Children* is open to both published and unpublished writers over the age of 16. Not to exceed 500 words. Clearly mark Fiction Contest on the manuscript. No entry fee. *Deadline:* Submissions must be post-marked between January 1 and January 31. *Award:* Three prizes of $1,000 (or tuition for the Highlights Foundation Writers Workshop) and publication in *Highlights for Children*.

Monica Hughes Award for Science Fiction and Fantasy
Canadian Children's Book Centre (CCBC), 40 Orchard View
  Boulevard, Suite 217, Toronto ON M4R 1B9 Canada
www.bookcentre.ca

To be awarded first in 2012 by the Canadian Children's Book Centre, this award honors excellence in children's and young teen science fiction and fantasy. Books must be originally pub-lished between January 1 and December 31 of the previous year. Entries must be written by a Canadian. Acceptable subgenres or subjects include time travel, alternate or re-imagined histories, dystopian, utopian, aliens, steampunk, space operas, urban fan-tasies, the paranormal, domestic magic, faeries, talking animals, among others. Submit four copies of each title with a submis-sions form found on the website. *Deadline:* December 9. *Award:* $5,000 and a certificate.

The *Hunger Mountain* Creative Nonfiction Prize

CNF Prize, *Hunger Mountain*, Vermont College of Fine Arts, 36
  College Street, Montpelier, VT 05602
www.hungermtn.org/hunger-mountain-creative-nonfiction-prize

The literary journal *Hunger Mountain* holds this annual contest
for writers of creative nonfiction. Enter an original, unpublished
article, to 10,000 words. Entries may be submitted by mail, or
electronically via the online submissions manager. Do not
include your name or address on the entry itself. For hard copy
submissions, include an index card with the title, your name,
address, phone number, and email address. Submit multiple
entries separately. The contest is judged by the journal's editors
and guest judges. Fee, $20. *Deadline:* September 10. *Award:* First
place, $1,000, and publication in *Hunger Mountain;* two honor-
able mentions, $100 each.

Barbara Karlin Grant

Society of Children's Book Writers & Illustrators, Barbara Karlin
  Grant Sommitee, c/o Q. L. Pearce, 884 Atlanta Court,
  Claremont, CA 91711
www.scbwi.org

The Barbara Karlin grant was set up by SCBWI to recognize and
encourage aspiring picture book writers. It is presented to a full or
associate SCBWI member who has not yet published a picture
book. Works of fiction, nonfiction, retellings of fairy tales, folktales, or legends are eligible for consideration. Manuscripts
should not exceed eight pages. No entry fee. New applications
and procedures are posted on the website each year. *Deadline:*
Submissions must be postmarked no earlier than February 15 and
received no later than March 15. *Award:* $2,000; runner-up, $500.

Iowa Short Fiction Award

Iowa Writers' Workshop, 507 North Clinton Street, 102 Dey
  House, Iowa City, IA 52242-1000
www.uiowapress.org/authors/iowa-short-fiction.htm

This annual competition of the Iowa Writers' Workshop at the
University of Iowa calls for collections of short stories. It is open
to writers living in the U.S. and abroad who have not previously
published a volume of prose fiction. Manuscripts should be at
least 150 double-spaced pages. No entry fee. *Deadline:* Entries
should be postmarked between August 1 and September 30.
Award: Award-winning manuscripts are published by the
University of Iowa Press.

Coretta Scott King Book Awards

50 East Huron Street, Chicago, IL 60611-2795
www.ala.org

Honoring Martin Luther King Jr. and his wife, Coretta Scott
King, for their courage and determination, this award promotes
the artistic expression of the African American experience
through literature and graphic arts. Sponsored by the American
Library Association, the awards are given to African American
authors and illustrators for inspirational and educational contributions to children's and YA literature. Submit via online submissions form. *Deadline:* December 1. *Award:* A plaque and $1,000,
will be presented at the Coretta Scott King Award Breakfast at the
annual ALA conference.

E. M. Koeppel Short Fiction Award

P.O. Box 140310, Gainesville, FL 32614
www.writecorner.com

Unpublished fiction in any genre is the focus of this annual
competition open to all writers. Submissions should not exceed
3,000 words. Entry fee, $15; $10 for each additional entry.

Deadline: October 1 through April 30. *Award:* $1,100; editors' choice awards, $100 each.

David J. Langum Sr. Prizes in American Historical Fiction and American Legal History or Biography
The Langum Charitable Trust, 2809 Berkeley Drive, Birmingham, AL 35242
www.langumtrust.org

The Langum Charitable Trust is a nonprofit that encourages high-quality historical writing addressed to the general public rather than to academics. The prize for American historical fiction is awarded annually to the book published in the preceding year that best demonstrates excellence in both fiction and history. The competition is open to works by any publisher, but not to self-published or subsidized books. The Langum Trust's prize for works of legal history or biography is awarded to an original book published in the preceding year by a university press; the winner is most accessible to the general public, and "rooted in sound scholarship." *Deadline:* December 1. *Award:* $1,000.

Literary Juice Flash Fiction Contest
www.literaryjuice.com

The new online literary journal *Literary Juice*, publishing bimonthly since January 2011, is running a flash fiction contest. The journal specializes in risky, witty, highly creative, even "bizarre" work. Contest entries, to 700 words, must be original and unpublished, and may be in any fiction genre except novel excerpts. Entry fee, $5. Submit via the online submissions manager only. Multiple submissions allowed. Simultaneous submissions allowed; notify *Literary Juice* if your submission is accepted elsewhere before the contest concludes. *Deadline:* February 15. *Award:* $200 and publication in *Literary Juice*. A runner-up will receive $50 and publication.

Magazine Merit Award

Society of Children's Books Writers & Illustrators, 8271 Beverly
   Boulevard, Los Angeles, CA 90048
www.scbwi.org/Pages.aspx/Magazine-Merit-Award

The Society of Children's Book Writers & Illustrators sponsors
this annual award in recognition of outstanding original magazine
work written for young people. It accepts published entries in the
categories of fiction, nonfiction, illustration, and poetry. SCBWI
members only. No entry fee. Submit four copies of each entry,
with proof of publication date. *Deadline:* December 15. *Award:*
Winners in each category receive a plaque.

Memoirs Ink Writing Contest

10866 Washington Boulevard, Suite 518, Culver City, CA 90232
www.memoirsink.com/contests

Held twice each year, this contest accepts original personal
essays, memoirs, or stories based on autobiographical experiences.
Entries must be previously unpublished and written in the first
person. The contest is open to all writers, but accepts submissions
in English only. Entries may be up to 1,500 words for the
February contest; and to 3,000 words for the August contest.
Entry fee, $17; $2 discount for previous entrants. Multiple submissions are accepted. *Deadline:* February 15 and August 1. *Award:*
First place, $1,000; second place, $500; third place, $250.

Micro Award

Alan Presley, PSC 817, Box 23, FPO, AE 09622-0023
www.microaward.org

The Micro Award recognizes fiction under 1,000 words, otherwise known as flash fiction or nanofiction. Submissions must be
prose fiction published either in print or electronically in the
year preceding the award. Self-published fiction is eligible.
Authors may submit one story; editors may submit two stories

from their publications. *Deadline:* October 1 to December 31
Award: $500.

Milkweed Prize for Children's Literature

Milkweed Editions, 1011 Washington Avenue South, Suite 300,
   Minneapolis, MN 55415
www.milkweed.org

Fiction for readers ages 8 to 13 is the focus of this annual
competition sponsored by Milkweed Editions. The prize was
established to encourage authors to write for children. Submissions
with high literary merit that embody humane values and contribute to cultural understanding. No entry fee. *Deadline:* Ongoing.
Award: $10,000 cash prize and publication by Milkweed Editions.

Minotaur Books/MWA Competition

175 Fifth Avenue, New York, NY 10010
www.mysterywriters.org/?q=Contests-Writers

Open to writers over 18 who have not published a novel, this
competition is sponsored by Minotaur Books in conjunction with
the Mystery Writers of America. It accepts original, book-length
manuscripts in which murder or another serious crime is central to
the plot. Submit questions to mbmwafirstcrimenovelcompetition@
stmartins.com. *Deadline:* Online entry form must be completed by
December 17. *Award:* Publishing contract from St. Martin's Press/
Minotaur Books and $10,000 cash advance against royalties.

The Howard Frank Mosher Short Fiction Prize

HFMSFP, *Hunger Mountain,* Vermont College of Fine Arts, 36
   College Street, Montpelier, VT 05602
www.hungermtn.org/short-fiction-prize

The literary journal *Hunger Mountain* holds this annual contest
for writers of short fiction. Enter an original, unpublished short
story, to 10,000 words. Entries may be submitted by mail, or via

the online submissions manager. Do not include your name or address on the entry itself. For hard copy submissions, include an index card with the title, your name, address, phone number, and email address. Submit multiple entries separately. The contest is judged by the journal's editors and guest judges. *Deadline:* June 30. *Award:* First-place, $1,000, and publication in *Hunger Mountain;* two honorable mentions, $100 each, and consideration for publication.

Mythopoeic Society Fantasy Awards
306 Edmon Low Library, Oklahoma State University, Stillwater, OK 74078
www.mythsoc.org/awards

Honoring outstanding fantasy books for young readers that are written in the tradition of J. R. R. Tolkien and C. S. Lewis, this award is presented to picture books through YA novels, adult fantasy, and scholarly books. Entries are nominated by members of the Mythopoeic Society. Books and collections by a single author are eligible for two years after publication. *Deadline:* February 28. *Award:* A statuette.

National Book Awards
National Book Foundation, 90 Broad Street., Suite 604, New York, NY 10004
www.nationalbook.org

The National Book Award recognizes outstanding literature for young people and adults. Awards are given for fiction, nonfiction, poetry, and YA literture. Full-length books, collections of stories, and collections of essays or poems are eligible. All entries must be published in the U.S. during the year preceding the contest. This competition is open to U.S. citizens only; books published or scheduled to be published in the previous year only. Entry fee, $125. Entries must be submitted by publishers. *Deadline:* Entry forms must be postmarked by June 15; books, bound galleys, or bound manuscripts due by August 1. *Award:* Category winners, $10,000; Four finalists, $1,000.

National Children's Theatre Medal

280 Miracle Mile, Coral Gables, FL 33134

www.actorsplayhouse.org

Held yearly, this competition is sponsored by the Actors Playhouse at the Miracle Theatre. It welcomes submission of unpublished musicals that are appropriate for children ages 5 to 12. Submissions should feature a cast with no more than 8 adults, who may play multiple roles. Works that received limited production exposure, workshops, or staged readings are encouraged, as are musicals with simple settings that appeal to both children and adults. Running time, 45 to 60 minutes. Entry fee, $10. Include sheet music and the submission form found at the website. *Deadline:* Entries must be postmarked by April 1. *Award:* $500 and a full production of the play at the National Children's Theatre Festival in May.

The John Newbery Medal

American Library Association, 50 East Huron Street, Chicago, IL 60611

www.ala.org/alsc/awardsgrants/bookmedia

This prestigious medal is presented by the Association for Library Service to Children to honor the year's most distinguished contribution to American literature for children up to the age of 14. Titles eligible for consideration must have been written by a U.S. author and published in the year preceding the contest. Books are judged on literary quality and overall presentation for children. Nominations are accepted from ALSC members only. *Deadline:* December 31. *Award:* The Newbery Medal is presented to the winning author at the ALA midwinter banquet.

New Millennium Writings Award
P.O. Box 2463, Room M2, Knoxville, TN 37901
www.newmillenniumwritings.com/awards.php

This annual contest is sponsored by *New Millennium Writings,* a literary journal. It accepts entries in the categories of short-short fiction, fiction, nonfiction, and poetry. It accepts previously unpublished material, and material that has been published online or in a print publication with a circulation under 5,000. Short-short fiction, to 1,000 words. Fiction and nonfiction, to 6,000 words. Poetry, to three poems, five pages total. Entry fee, $17 per submission. Submit online or via mail. *Deadline:* June 17. *Award:* $1,000.

New Voices Award
Lee & Low Books, 95 Madison Avenue, New York, NY 10016
www.leeandlow.com/p/new_voices_award.mhtml

Encouraging writers of color who have not published a children's picture book, this annual award is sponsored by Lee & Low Books. It welcomes original material that addresses the needs of children of color, ages 5 to 12. Works of fiction, nonfiction, and poetry are accepted, but folklore and stories about animals are not. Entries should not exceed 1,500 words and must be accompanied by a cover letter with the author's contact information and relevant cultural/ethnic information. Limit two submissions per entrant. No entry fee. *Deadline:* Submissions will be accepted between May 1 and September 30. *Award:* $1,000 and publishing contract with Lee & Low Books; Honor Award winner, $500.

Ohio State University Prize in Short Fiction
Ohio State University Press, 180 Pressey Hall, 1070 Carmack
   Road, Columbus, OH 43210-1002
www.ohiostatepress.org

This annual award recognizes and awards excellence in a collection of short stories or novellas, or a combination, published or unpublished. Manuscripts must be between 150 and 300 typed pages; individual stories or novellas in the collection may not exceed 125 pages. Entry fee: $20. *Deadline:* Submissions must be postmarked in January. *Award:* Winning author receives publication, with a $1,500 advance against royalties.

On-the-Verge Emerging Voices Award

Society of Children's Book Writers and Illustrators, 8271 Beverly
  Boulevard., Los Angeles, CA 90048
www.scbwi.org

In 2012, SCBWI created this award "to foster the emergence of diverse voices in children's books" and honor writers and illustrators from traditionally under-represented cultures in children's literature. The award will be given annually to two writers or illustrators. Manuscripts must be original, unpublished, unagented, not under contract, and written in English; authors must be over 18. Entries and applications should be emailed to voices@scbwi.org. Include an autiobiography, to 250 words; a description of why the work represents an under-represented culture, to 250 words; a synopsis, to 250 words; and a PDF of the complete manuscript. *Deadline:* November 15. *Award:* All-expenses paid trip to the SCBWI winter conference, a year's membership to SCBWI, an SCBWI mentor for a year.

Orbis Pictus Award for Outstanding Nonfiction
  for Children

National Council of Teachers of English, Orbis Pictus Committee
  Chair, 1111 West Kenyon Road, Urbana, IL 61801-1096
www.ncte.org/awards/orbispictus

This award for excellence in children's nonfiction recognizes books used in kindergarten to eighth-grade classrooms characterized by outstanding accuracy, organization, design, and style. Eligible titles must be published in the year preceding the contest. Nominations may come from National Council of Teachers of

English (NCTE) members, or the education community. Text-books, historical fiction, folklore, and poetry are not eligible. To nominate a book, write to the committee chair with the author's name, title of book, publisher, copyright date, and a brief explanation of why you liked the book. *Deadline:* December 31. *Award:* A plaque at the NCTE Convention.

Pacific Northwest Writers Association Literary Contest

PMB 2717, 1420 NW Gilman Boulevard, Suite 2, Issaquah, WA 98027

www.pnwa.org

Sponsored by the Pacific Northwest Writers Association, this annual contest accepts unpublished entries in 12 categories that include: young adult novel, screen writing, mainstream, adult short topics, poetry, children's picture book/chapter book, historical, and romance. Each entrant receives two critiques of their work. Entry fee, $35 for members; $50 for nonmembers. Limit one entry per category. *Deadline:* February 15. *Award:* First place, $700 and the Zola Award; second place, $300.

The Katherine Paterson Prize for Young Adult and Children's Writing

KPP, *Hunger Mountain,* Vermont College of Fine Arts, 36 College Street, Montpelier, VT 05602

www.hungermtn.org/katherine-paterson-prize-for-young-adult-and-childrens-writing

The literary journal *Hunger Mountain* holds this annual contest for writers of picture books, and middle-grade and young adult literature. Enter an original, unpublished short story, to 10,000 words; it may be a picture book, short story, or novel excerpt. Entries may be submitted by mail, or electronically via the submissions manager. Do not include your name or address on the entry itself. For hard copy submissions, include an index card with the title, your name, address, phone number, and email address. Submit multiple entries separately. The contest is judged by the journal's editors and guest judges. *Deadline:* June 30. *Award:* First-place, $1,000, and publication in *Hunger Mountain;* two honorable mentions, $100 each, and consideration for publication.

PEN Center USA Literary Awards
269 South Beverly Dr., #1163, Beverly Hills, CA 90212
penusa.org/awards

Writers living west of the Mississippi River are honored for their literary achievements through this annual awards program. Entries that have been published in the year preceding the contest are accepted for nomination in the categories of including children's literature, graphic literature, fiction, creative nonfiction, journalism, drama, teleplay, research nonfiction, poetry, translation, and screenplay. Entry fee, $35 per entry. *Deadline:* Book category submissions, December 31; non-book category submissions, January 31. *Award:* Category winners, $1,000 and a free PEN membership.

PEN/Phyllis Naylor Working Writer Fellowship
588 Broadway, Suite 303, New York, NY 10012
www.pen.org/page.php/prmID/281

This fellowship provides support for promising authors in the field of children's or YA fiction. Eligible authors must have published at least two novels. Books must be published by a U.S. publisher. Likely candidates are those whose books have been well-reviewed but have not achieved high sales volume. Nominations are accepted from editors and fellow writers and should include a detailed letter of support; a list of the nominated author's published work and reviews; and a description of the nominee's financial resources. Three copies of the outline of a work in progress and 50 to 75 pages of the text must also be submitted. *Deadline:* Letters of nomination must be postmarked between October 15 and February 1. *Award:* $5,000 fellowship.

Phoebe Winter Fiction Contest

Phoebe 2C5, George Mason University, 4400 University Dr.,
    Fairfax, VA 22030
www.phoebejournal.com

This annual contest is sponsored by *Phoebe,* the literary journal of George Mason University. It accepts unpublished short fiction. Entries, to 7,500 words. Entry fee, $12 per submission. *Deadline:* December 15. *Award:* $1,000 and publication in *Phoebe.*

Pikes Peak Writers Fiction Contest

Pikes Peak Writers, P.O. Box 64273, Colorado Springs, CO 80962
www.ppwc.net

Open to writers who have not yet published book-length fiction or short stories, this contest accepts entries in the categories of children's books, YA, romance, mainstream, historical fiction, mystery/suspense, and science fiction/fantasy. Entry fee, $30. Critiques are available for $20. For book submissions, include a synopsis (to 1,250 words) and sample pages of the manuscript (beginning with chapter one or the prologue, to 4,000 words); short stories to 5,000 words. Describe the target market. Submissions must be sent electronically. *Deadline:* September 15 to November 15. *Award:* The Paul Gillete Award, First place, $100 or a refund of the Pikes Peak Conference fee; second place, $50; third place, $30.

Edgar Allan Poe Awards

Mystery Writers of America, 1140 Broadway, Suite 1507, New
    York, NY 10001
www.mysterywriters.org/?q=AwardsPrograms

The Mystery Writers of America sponsors these annual awards, which are considered among the most prestigious for writers. They are presented for work published in the year preceding the contest in several categories that include best fact crime, best YA mystery, best juvenile mystery, best first novel by an American author, and best play. Books must be submitted by publisher. No entry fee. *Deadline:* Varies. *Award:* An Edgar Award is presented to each winner at a banquet; cash award.

Prairie Fire Press Contests
423-100 Arthur Street, Winnipeg MB R3B 1H3 Canada
www.prairiefire.ca/contests.html

Two annual competitions honor works of creative nonfiction and short fiction. Creative fiction entries should not exceed 5,000 words and must be unpublished. Short fiction, to 10,000 words. Entry fee, $32. *Deadline:* November 30. *Award:* First prize, $1,250; second prize, $500; third prize, $250. Winning entries are published in *Prairie Fire* magazine.

**Michael L. Printz Award for Excellence in Young
 Adult Literature**
50 East Huron Street, Chicago, IL 60611
www.ala.org/yalsa/printz

This award, from the Young Adult Library Services Association and *Booklist*, recognizes excellence in YA literature. Anthologies and works of fiction, nonfiction, and poetry that target ages 12 to 18 and were published in the preceding year are eligible. ALA committee members may nominate titles. Entries are judged on overall literary merit, taking into consideration theme, voice, setting, style, and design. Controversial topics are not discouraged. *Deadline:* December 1. *Award:* An award seal, presented at the ALA midwinter conference.

Prism international Literary Nonfiction Contest

Creative Writing Program, University of British Columbia,
Buchanan E462, 1866 Main Mall, Vancouver BC V6T 1Z1
Canada
prismmagazine.ca/contests

This annual contest honors excellence in literary nonfiction. Entries of creative nonfiction may be on any subject, and should not exceed 6,000 words. Entry fee, $35 for Canadian; $40 for U.S.; $5 for each additional story (includes a one-year subscription to *Prism international*). *Deadline:* November 30. *Award:* Grand prize, $1,500 and publication in *Prism international*.

Prism international Short Fiction Contest

Creative Writing Program, University of British Columbia,
Buchanan E462, 1866 Main Mall, Vancouver BC V6T 1Z1
Canada
prismmagazine.ca/contests

This competition is open to all writers, with the exception of those currently enrolled in the creative arts program at the University of British Columbia. It looks for original, unpublished short stories up to 6,000 words. Entry fee, $35 for Canadian; $40 for U.S.; $5 for each additional story (includes a one-year subscription to *Prism international*). *Deadline:* January 25. *Award:* Grand prize, $2,000 and publication in *Prism international*. Three runner-up prizes of $300 and $200 are also awarded.

Roanoke Review Fiction Contest

221 College Lane, Salem, VA 24153
roanokereview.wordpress.com/

This annual contest is sponsored by the literary journal of Roanoke College and looks to encourage the writing of short fiction. It is open to all writers. Entries should not exceed 5,000 words. Entry fee, $15. All entrants receive a copy of the journal.

Enter online or via maill. *Deadline:* November. *Award:* First place, $1,000; second place, $500. Winning entries are published in the *Roanoke Review*.

San Antonio Writers Guild Writing Contest
P.O. Box 100717, San Antonio, TX 78201
www.sawritersguild.org

This competition accepts entries in the categories of novel, short story, flash fiction, essay/memoir, and poetry. It accepts previously unpublished submissions only. Word limits vary. Visit the website for complete information. Entry fee, $10 for members; $20 for nonmembers. *Deadline:* First Thursday in October. *Award:* First place, $150; second place, $75; third place $50.

The A. David Schwartz Fiction Prize
Cream City Review, Dept. of English, University of Wisconsin-
   Milwaukee, P.O. Box 413, Milwaukee, WI 53201
www.creamcityreview.org/submit/#contests

Sponsored by the literary journal of the University of Wisconsin, *Cream City Review,* and Karry W. Schwartz Bookshops, this prize is offered annually. The competition accepts previously unpublished works of fiction. Entries should not exceed 30 pages. Entry fee, $15. *Deadline:* December 31. *Award:* $1,000 and publication in *Cream City Review*.

Seven Hills Literary Contest
P.O. Box 3428, Tallahassee, FL 32315
www.tallahasseewriters.net

Sponsored by the Tallahassee Writers' Association, this annual contest offers prizes in the categories of best short story, creative nonfiction, flash fiction, and children's chapter books/stories (for children 4–8). The competition is open to all writers and accepts unpublished, original entries only. Entries should not exceed 2,500 words (500 words for flash fiction). Entry fee, $12 for members; $17 for nonmembers. *Deadline:* August 31. *Award:* First place, $100; second place, $75; third place, $50. Winners are published in *Seven Hills* literary journal.

Mary Shelley Award for Imaginative Fiction
Rosebud Magazine, N3310 Asje Road, Cambridge, WI 53523
www.rsbd.net/NEW

Established to promote speculative and imaginative fiction in a literary context, this contest accepts original, unpublished works of fantasy, fiction, horror, and mystery, as well as entries that stretch beyond the boundaries of these genres. Entries should be between 1,000 and 3,500 words. Entry fee, $10. *Deadline:* October. *Award:* First place winner receives $1,000 and publication in *Rosebud.* Four runners-up receive $100 and publication.

The Ruth Stone Poetry Prize
RSPP, *Hunger Mountain,* Vermont College of Fine Arts, 36 College Street, Montpelier, VT 05602
www.hungermtn.org/ruth-stone-poetry-prize

The literary journal *Hunger Mountain* holds this annual poetry contest. Submit three original, unpublished poems. Entries may be submitted by mail, or electronically via the submission manager. Do not include your name or address on the entry. For hard copy, include an index card with the title, your name, address, phone number, and email address. Submit multiple entries separately. The contest is judged by the journal's editors and guest judges. Fee, $20. *Deadline:* December 10. *Award:* First-place, $1,000, and publication in *Hunger Mountain* online; two honorable mentions, $100 each, and publication in *Hunger Mountain* online.

Kay Snow Writing Contest
2108 Buck Street, West Linn, OR 97068
www.willamettewriters.com

This annual competition, sponsored by the Willamette Writers, encourages writers to reach their personal goals. It accepts original, unpublished entries in the categories of adult fiction, adult nonfiction, juvenile short story or article, poetry, screenwriting, and student writing. Entry fee, $10 for members; $15 for non-members. Word lengths vary for each category. Visit the website for complete guidelines. *Deadline:* April 23. *Award:* Ranges from $10 to $300 in each catagory. The Liam Callen award, $500, is presented to the best overall entry.

Society of Midland Authors Awards
P.O. Box 10419, Chicago, IL 60610
www.midlandauthors.com/contest_about.html

Authors and poets who reside in, were born in, or have strong ties to any of the 12 Midwestern states are eligible to enter this annual contest. Awards are presented for adult fiction and non-fiction, biography, poetry, and children's fiction and nonfiction. Entries must have been published in the year preceding the contest. No entry fee. *Deadline:* February 15. *Award:* Cash award and a recognition plaque.

So to Speak **Contests**
George Mason University, MSN 2C5, 4400 University Dr., Fairfax, VA 22030
sotospeakjournal.org/contests/

So to Speak, a feminist literary journal, sponsors this contest for fiction, nonfiction, and poetry. Entries may also be personal essays, memoirs, and profiles. Fiction and nonfiction, to 4,500 words. Poetry, to five poems per submission, not to exceed 4,500 words. Entry fee, $15. *Deadline:* Nonfiction and poetry deadline, October 15. Fiction deadline, March 15. *Award:* First prize in each category is $500 and publication in *So to Speak.*

John Spray Mystery Award

Canadian Children's Book Centre (CCBC), 40 Orchard View
   Boulevard, Suite 217, Toronto ON M4R 1B9 Canada
www.bookcentre.ca

This award, established in 2011 by the Canadian Children's
Book Centre, honors outstanding mysteries for readers 8 to 16.
Entries may be thrillers, crime novels, or whodunits, and must be
written by a Canadian. Titles published in the year preceding the
contest are eligible for entry. No fantasy, science fiction, or graphic novels. *Deadline:* December 9. *Award:* $5,000 and a certificate.

SouthWest Writers Annual Contest

3721 Morris NE, Albuquerque, NM 87110
www.southwestwriters.com/contestAnnual.php

This annual contest is sponsored by SouthWest Writers and honors distinguished unpublished work in a variety of categories
including novel, short story, short nonfiction, personal essay,
book-length nonfiction, children's book, screenplay, and poetry.
Entry fees, word lengths, and other requirements vary for each
category; check website for specific information. Manuscript critiques are available for an additional fee. *Deadline:* May 1. *Award:*
First-place winners in each category receive $200; second-place,
$150; third-place, $100. First-place winners compete for a $1,500
Storyteller Award.

Stanley Drama Award

Wagner College, One Campus Road, Staten Island, NY 10301
www.wagner.edu/stanley_drama

The Stanley Drama Award was set up to encourage and reward
aspiring playwrights. The competition is open to original, full-
length plays or musicals, or a series of two or three related one-
act plays that have not been professionally produced or published as trade books. Musical entries must be accompanied by

an audiocassette or CD. Entry fee, $30. *Deadline:* October 31. *Award:* $2,000.

Sydney Taylor Manuscript Competition

Aileen Grossberg, 204 Park Street, Montclair, NJ 07042-2903
www.jewishlibraries.org/ajlweb/awards/st_ms.htm

This annual competition is open to original fiction containing Jewish content targeting children ages 8 to 11. Entries should deepen a child's understanding of Judaism. Manuscripts should be between 64 and 200 pages. Short stories, plays, and poetry are not eligible. No entry fee. Limit one entry per competition. *Deadline:* December 15. *Award:* $1,000.

Utah Original Writing Competition

617 East South Temple, Salt Lake City, UT 84102
arts.utah.gov/funding/competitions/writing.html

Since 1958, this annual competition has honored Utah's finest writers in several categories, including YA book, novel, personal essay, short story, poetry, and general nonfiction. The competition accepts unpublished entries from Utah residents only. Writers entering in the categories of novel, general nonfiction, book-length collection of poems, and juvenile book may not have a book published or accepted for publication in the category. Word lengths vary for each category. Check the website for complete information. No entry fee. *Deadline:* Entries are accepted beginning April 4 and must be postmarked by June 29. *Award:* To $1,000.

Laura Ingalls Wilder Medal

American Library Association, 50 East Huron Street, Chicago, IL 60611
www.ala.org

Every other year this award is presented to honor an author or illustrator whose body of work has contributed substantially to children's literature. It is open to books that were published in the U.S. during the year preceding the contest. Nominations are made by Association for Library Services to Children members. The winner is chosen by a team of children's librarians. *Deadline:* December 31. *Award:* A bronze medal is presented to the winner.

Tennessee Williams Fiction Contest
938 Lafayette Street, Suite 514, New Orleans, LA 70113
www.tennesseewilliams.net/index.php?topic=contests

This competition is open to writers who have not yet published a book of fiction. It accepts entries up to 7,000 words by hard copy or through the website. Entries are subject to blind judging. Author's name should not appear on manuscript itself. Include a cover letter with story title, name, and full contact information. Entry fee, $25. *Deadline:* Submissions are accepted between June 1 and November 15. *Award:* $1,500, airfare and accommodations at the Tennessee Williams Literary Festival, a reading at the festival, and publication in *Louisiana Literature*.

Tennessee Williams One-Act Play Competition
938 Lafayette St., Suite 514, New Orleans, LA 70113
www.tennesseewilliams.net/index.php?topic=contests

This annual contest recognizes and rewards excellence in one-act plays from writers around the world. The winning script should require minimal technical support and a small cast of characters. Multiple entries are accepted. Entry fee, $25 per entry. Plays should run no longer than one hour and must not have been previously produced or published. *Deadline:* November 1. *Award:* $1,500 and a full production of the play at the Tennessee Williams New Orleans Festival.

Paul A. Witty Short Story Award
Steven L. Layne, Chairing, Poetry and Prose Awards Subcommittee,

Judson University, 1151 North State Street, Elgin, IL 60123-1404
www.reading.org

The International Reading Association presents this annual award to a short story that was published in a magazine for children during the year of the contest. Submissions should be of the highest literary merit. No entry fee. *Deadline:* May 1 to November 15. *Award:* $1,000.

Work-in-Progress Grants
8271 Beverly Boulevard, Los Angeles, CA 90048
www.scbwi.org/Pages.aspx/WIP-Grant(1)

Each year, the Society of Children's Book Writers & Illustrators offers several grants to children's writers to complete projects that are not currently under contract. Grants are available to full and associate members of SCBWI in the categories of general work-in-progress; contemporary novel for young people; nonfiction research; and previously unpublished author. All applications should include a 750-word synopsis and a writing sample of no more than 2,500 words. *Deadline:* Submissions must be postmarked no earlier than February 15 and received no later than March 15. *Award:* Seven winners receive $2,000; seven runners-up receive $500.

***WOW! Women on Writing* Flash Fiction Contests**
www.wow-womenonwriting.com/contest.php

This ezine presents quarterly flash fiction contests to inspire creativity and communication and provide recognition to its winners. All styles of writing are welcome. Entries should be from 250 to 750 words. Accepts entries through the website only. Entry fee, $10, entry with critique, $20. *Deadline:* February 28; May 31; August 31; and November 30. *Award:* First place, $350; second place, $250; third place, $150; seven runners up; 10 honorable mentions. Winners also receive publication on the *WOW!* website.

The Write Now New Plays Competition and Workshop
900 S. Mitchell Dr., Tempe, AZ 85281
www.writenow.co/competition

Write Now is an organization that advocates for plays for children, and for new and established playwrights. Its biennial competition and workshop aims to strengthen the national drama community, and is a collaboration of the Indiana Repertory Theatre and Arizona's Childsplay at the Sybil B. Harrington Campus for Imagination and Wonder. The competition's history originates in the former Waldo M. and Grace C. Bonderman Youth Theatre Playwriting Competition. Submissions are accepted from playwrights 18 and over, one per competition. Four or more scripts become finalists and move on to the workshop for rehearsal and revision at Childsplay in Tempe, Arizona. Plays must be unpublished, although previous production in an educational or other nonprofessional setting is allowed. The audience may be any targeted group between kindergarten and high school. Musicals are not eligible for the 2013 competition. Submit electronically with the online entry form. *Deadline:* July 31. *Award:* The top four winners receive $1,000 and a staged reading of their plays.

Writers at Work Fiction Writing Competition
P.O. Box 540370, North Salt Lake, UT 84054-0370
www.writersatwork.org

Writers at Work, a nonprofit literary arts organization, sponsors this annual contest that recognizes emerging writers of fiction. Writers not yet published in the category of their entry are eligible to submit original work. Manuscripts must not exceed 7,500 words. Only online submissions are accepted. Entry fee, $20. *Deadline:* January 1 to March 1. *Award:* First prize, $1,000 and publication in *Quarterly West;* two honorable mentions in each category awarded $250.

Writer's Digest Annual Writing Competition

8469 Blue Ash Road, Suite 100, Cincinnati, OH 45236
www.writersdigest.com/competitions

This annual competition calls for entries in 10 different categories including children's/YA fiction, short stories, screenplays, magazine article, and plays. It accepts previously unpublished work only. Multiple entries are accepted. Word counts vary. Entry fee, $15 for the first poem and $10 for each additional poem; all other entries, $25 for the first manuscript and $15 for each additional manuscript submitted in the same online session. *Deadline:* See website. *Award:* Prizes vary by category.

Writers-Editors Network Annual International Writing Competition

P.O. Box A, North Stratford, NH 03590
www.writers-editors.com

Open to all writers, this contest honors authors of fiction, nonfiction, children's literature, and poetry. Entries of children's literature must be previously unpublished or self-published only. Poetry may be traditional or verse. Specific category guidelines are available at the website. Entry fees vary for each category. *Deadline:* March 15. *Award:* First- through third-place awards are $100, $75, and $50.

Writing for Children Competition

Writers' Union of Canada, 90 Richmond Street East, Suite 200, Toronto ON M5C 1P1 Canada
www.writersunion.ca

Canadian writers who have not yet published a book are eligible to enter this competition from the Writers' Union of Canada. It was established to encourage new Canadian talent in the field of children's literature. Entries should not exceed 1,500 words. Entry fee, $15. Multiple entries are accepted. *Deadline:* April 24. *Award:* $1,500.

Zoetrope: All-Story Short Fiction Contest
916 Kearny Street, San Francisco, CA 94133
www.all-story.com/contests.cgi

Sponsored by *Zoetrope: All-Story*, a magazine founded by Francis Ford Coppola, this annual contest seeks to encourage talented writers and to introduce those writers to leading literary agencies. Unpublished literary fiction of all genres are accepted. Submissions should be 5,000 words or less. Entries from outside the U.S. are welcome. Entry fee, $15 per story. *Deadline:* Entries are accepted between July 1 and October 1 . *Award:* First prize, $1,000; second prize, $500; third prize, $250. The three prize winners and seven honorable mentions are considered for representation by several prominent literary agencies.

Conferences

For Adult & Children's Writers

American Society of Journalists and Authors
  Annual Writers Conference
1501 Broadway, Suite 302, New York, NY 10036
www.asja.org/wc

Held each spring since 1971, this conference offers concurrent morning and afternoon panels, which are ranked to help beginning to advanced writers choose appropriately. More than 100 editors, authors, agents, and publicists take part in this weekend event, which allows time for keynote speeches and networking. *Date:* April 25–27. *Location:* New York, New York. *Cost:* $375 for members (early registration, $335); $385 for nonmembers (early registration, $345). One-day rates are also available.

Ann Arbor Book Festival Writer's Conference
1118 Granger Avenue, Ann Arbor, MI 4810
www.aabookfestival.org

Coinciding with the Ann Arbor Book Festival, this annual conference is a full Saturday event. Attendees can sign up for three small-group sessions focused on writing skills and one large-group session on publishing, all of which are led by a noted group of authors and instructors. *Date:* June. *Location:* Ann Arbor, Michigan. *Cost:* $100.

Annual Writers Conference at Penn

University of Pennsylvania, College of General Studies, 3440
   Market Street, #100, Philadelphia, PA 19104

www.pennwriters.org

Sponsored by Pennwriters, a multi-genre writer's organization,
this annual event joins writers of all levels and genres with
agents, editors, and fellow authors for three days of workshops,
critiques, pitch sessions, and networking. The option of a one-
day conference is available. *Date:* May. *Location:* Pittsburgh airport Marriott. *Cost:* $275 for three-day conference, including meals;
$194 for one day.

Antioch Writers' Workshop

c/o Antioch University Midwest 900 Dayton Street, Yellow
   Springs, OH 45387

www.antiochwritersworkshop.com

This weeklong conference features morning lectures and afternoon intensives, with evenings reserved for readings, panel discussions, and workshops. Programs focus on fiction, nonfiction,
screenwriting, playwriting, poetry, and the business of publishing. *Date:* July 16–23. *Location:* Yellow Springs, Ohio. *Cost:* $610
($550 for past registrants and local residents), plus $125 non-
refundable registration fee. *A la carte* tuition, $250–$325.
Manuscript critique, $75.

Appalachian Heritage Writers Symposium

Southwest Virginia Community College

P.O. Box SVCC, Richlands, VA 24641

appheritagewritersym.wordpress.com

Fiction, memoir, poetry, and children's writing workshops,
ands panel discussions, are offered during this two-day symposium.
Date: June. *Location:* Richlands, Virginia. *Cost:* $50; includes con-
tinental breakfast and awards luncheon. College credit, optional.

Arizona State University Writers Conference

P.O. Box 875002, Tempe, AZ 85287

www.asu.edu/pipercwcenter/conference

Intimate master classes, panel discussions on publishing and the writing life, readings, and conversations with faculty are the main components of this four-day conference. Its emphasis is on developing fiction, nonfiction, and poetry in a true community of writers. *Date:* February. *Location:* Tempe, Arizona. *Cost:* $325. Master class tuition (registration required), $125. Discounts are available.

Aspen Summer Words

110 E. Hallam, Suite 116, Aspen, CO 81611

www.aspenwritersfoundation.org

Aspen Summer Words is a six-day festival and retreat for writers in all their guises, from novelists and poets to filmmakers, songwriters, and comedians. The writing retreat includes workshops in fiction, memoir, poetry, young writers, and digital storytelling. Online applications are accepted through April 15. *Date:* June. *Location:* Aspen, Colorado. *Cost:* Application processing fee, $25. Five-day juried workshop, $665; $415, beginning fiction; two-day readers retreat, $233; other fees vary. Some scholarships are available.

Bay to Ocean Writer's Conference

P.O. Box 1773, Easton, MD 21601

www.baytoocean.com

The Eastern Shore Writers' Association sponsors this one-day conference of workshops, speeches, and panels on topics pertaining to the craft of writing and the business of publishing. Presenters include authors, editors, publishers, journalists, freelance writers, and literary agents. Manuscript reviews are offered. *Date:* February. *Location:* Chesapeake College, Wye Mills, Maryland. *Cost:* Contact for cost information.

Erma Bombeck Writers' Workshop

University of Dayton, 300 College Park, Dayton, OH 45469
www.humorwriters.org

"The workshop for humor writing, human interest writing, networking, and getting published," this event is held every other year. The next conference is scheduled for 2012. Past sessions covered such topics as writing a humor column for a national news-paper and creating humorous children's books. The faculty is made up of experienced and entertaining writers and publishing professionals. *Date:* April. *Location:* Dayton, Ohio. *Cost:* $375.

Canadian Authors Association CanWrite! Conference

74 Mississaga Street East, Suite 104, Orillia ON L3V 1V5 Canada
www.canwriteconference.com

Attendees will learn computer tips for making their writing life easier, and how to create PowerPoint presentations to enhance book launches. Other workshops will explore the world of ebooks and explain electronic rights for writers. Fiction, nonfiction, poetry, public speaking, and writing for young adults are some of the other sessions planned. *Date:* May. *Location:* Location of the next conference is yet to be confirmed. *Cost:* Full conference, $350 for members and $390 for nonmembers. One-day rates, $140 for members and $175 for nonmembers.

Cape Cod Writers' Conference

Cape Cod Writers' Center
P.O. Box 408, Osterville, MA 02655
www.capecodwriterscenter.org

Over the course of five days, attendees take part in morning and afternoon courses and master classes on the craft of writing romance, mystery, poetry, screenwriting, journalism, memoir, and children's fiction, among others. Panels, faculty readings, and speeches are also scheduled during this annual conference. *Date:* August. *Location:* Hyannis, Massachusetts. *Cost:* $185 per course; $150 for mentoring; $150 for manuscript evaluation. Registration fee, $35 (waived for members). Shorter courses are offered at lower rates.

Carolinas Writers Conference
South Piedmont Community College
P.O. Box 126, Polkton, NC 28135
ansoncountywritersclub.org

About 250 to 400 people attend this annual event, which focuses on the craft of writing and the promotion of reading. The program covers children's and YA writing; fiction, including the genres of romance, science fiction, fantasy, horror, and mystery; screenwriting; poetry; marketing; and publishing. *Date:* April. *Location:* Wadesboro, North Carolina. *Cost:* $30.

Cat Writers' Association Writers Conference
22841 Orchid Creek Lane, Lake Forest, CA 92630
www.catwriters.org

The business and technical aspects of a career that centers on writing about cats are explored at this three-day annual conference, which also offers panels and lecture sessions on various fiction genres, nonfiction, and writing for children and young adults. Private 15-minute appointments with editors/agents are available. *Date:* November. *Location:* Visit the website for location. *Cost:* $150 for members; $200 for nonmembers (early registration, $100 for members and $125 for nonmembers).

Chautauqua Institution Conferences
P.O. Box 28, Chautauqua, NY 14722
writers.ciweb.org

The Writers' Center at Chautauqua Institution sponsors weekly workshops during the summer months. Topics include business and technical writing, playwriting, autobiography/memoir, journalism, poetry, romance, mystery, and humor writing, among others. A four-day Writer's Festival is held as well, which features workshops, panel discussions, readings, and lectures. *Date:* Summer workshops, June, July, and August. Writers' Festival, June. *Location:* Chautauqua, New York. *Cost:* Summer workshops, $110 a week. Writers' Festival, $400 (10 percent discount for returnees.)

Colgate Writers' Conference
13 Oak Drive, Hamilton, NY 13346-1398
cwc.colgate.edu/home.aspx

Veteran and novice writers alike are welcome at this annual weeklong conference. Mornings are devoted to craft talks and workshops, while afternoons are set aside for individual consultations with instructors. Panel discussions, readings, and informal conversations round out the program. *Date:* June. *Location:* Hamilton, New York. *Cost:* $995 for residential attendees; $745 for day students; $1,245 for novel and memoir tutorial students. Discounts and fellowships are available.

DFW Writers' Conference
dfwwritersconference.org

Sponsored by the DFW (Dallas-Fort Worth) Writers' Workshop, this annual two-day conference offers writers at different levels of experience the opportunity to network with fellow writers and meet agents, published authors, and editors. Registration gives participants access to more than 40 classes on the art and business of writing, and includes agent appointments on a first-come, first-served basis. *Date:* May. *Location:* Hurst, Texas. *Cost:* $295.

East Texas Christian Writers Conference
East Texas Baptist University
One Tiger, Marshall, TX 75670
www.etbu.edu/news/cwc/workshops.htm

In addition to one-hour writing workshops scheduled for Saturday, this conference also holds pre-conference workshops on Friday afternoon. Workshops offer intense, personal, and practical application for those willing to get directly involved in the writing process. The conference gives aspiring writers the opportunity to have contact, conversation, and exchange of ideas with each other. *Date:* October. *Location:* Marshall, Texas. *Cost:* Individual, $90; student, $60. Fee covers the Friday evening banquet and attendance at five to six writing workshops on Saturday. Preconference workshops, additional $35–$45.

Green Mountain Writer's Conference
47 Hazel Street, Rutland, VT 05701
www.vermontwriters.com

At this annual weeklong conference, developing writers attend workshops run by professional authors who teach the craft of writing fiction, creative nonfiction, poetry, journalistic pieces, nature articles, essays, memoir, and biography. Working sessions and writing assignments are scheduled around readings and panel discussions. *Date:* August. *Location:* Tinmouth, Vermont. *Cost:* $525 (early registration, $500); includes snacks, lunches and readings.

Highlights Foundation Workshops
814 Court Street, Honesdale, PA 18431
www.highlightsfoundation.org

Long known for its annual summer conference for children's authors at New York's Chautauqua Institution, a dozen years ago the Highlights Foundation started moving toward smaller, specialized workshops, held year-round. It now offers nearly 40 workshops yearly. Each includes 10 to 30 participants and several faculty members, including editors, agents, publishers, academics, and art directors. The workshops take place at The Barn at Boyds Mills, a conference center and 21 cabins built on the original Poconos property of the founders of *Highlights for Children*. They generally take place either from Thursday to Sunday or Friday to Monday. In 2013, workshop topics include: children's books about agriculture that go beyond the barnyard; writing for boys; discovering stories in math; middle-grade novels; author opportunities after publication; the heart of the novel; the poetry novel; fantasy novels; poetry for all ages; a concentrated course in nonfiction; returning to an unfinished manuscript; young adult novels; fairy tales; historical fiction, and more. Applications available online. Tuition includes the workshop, lodging, food, and an airport shuttle, if required. See the website for details. *Dates:* Vary; check the online calendar. *Location:* Honesdale, Pennsylvania. *Cost:* Tuition varies. Payment plans are available. Scholarships are available.

Idaho Writers' League Annual Writers Conference
IWL Conference, 519 14th Avenue, Caldwell, ID 83605
www.idahowritersleague.com

This two-day conference offers morning and afternoon workshops, luncheons, and a banquet. The theme for this year's conference is Writing Up A Storm. Check website for list of workshop topics and presenters. *Date:* September. *Location:* Boise, Idaho. *Cost:* $155 for members ($135, early registration); $175 for nonmembers (early registration, $155).

Iowa Summer Writing Festival
C215 Seashore Hall, University of Iowa, Iowa City, IA 52242
www.continuetolearn.uiowa.edu/iswfest

Weeklong and weekend workshops are held over the course of six weeks and four weekends at this well-known annual event for serious writers. Some workshops are devoted to critiquing manuscripts that participants bring with them, others to generating new work through exercises and assignments. Writing for children and young adults, screenwriting, playwriting, poetry, travel writing, and nature writing are some of the many workshops offered. *Date:* June and July. *Location:* Iowa City, Iowa. *Cost:* $560 to $585 per week; includes special events, dinner on the Sunday evening of registration, and the Friday banquet. Weekend only, $280; includes Saturday breakfast.

Jackson Hole Writers Conference
P.O. Box 1974, Jackson, WY 83001
www.jacksonholewritersconference.com

In addition to workshops led by novelists, creative nonfiction writers, poets, agents, editors, and publishers, this conference offers three manuscript critiques. The 2010 conference offered classes on fiction, creative nonfiction, poetry, YA fiction, memoir, and magazine writing. This four-day event is held annually. *Date:* June. *Location:* Jackson Hole, Wyoming. *Cost:* $390; includes all conference events, the welcome cocktail party, and the barbecue. Manuscript critique, $30, or $110 for longer manuscripts.

James River Writers Conference
320 Hull Street, #136, Richmond, VA 23224
www.jamesriverwriters.org

In addition to workshops, panel discussions, and speeches, this conference offers the opportunity for one-on-one meetings with literary agents or editors and first-page critique sessions. Last year's two-day conference featured workshops on pitching articles, stories, and books; using Facebook to maximize exposure; and one-on-one meetings with agents. *Date:* October. *Location:*

Richmond, Virginia. *Cost:* $240; one-day only, $170. Preconference workshop, $40.

Jewish Authors Conference: Writing for Adult Readers

520 8th Avenue, 4th Floor, New York, NY 10018
jewishbookcouncil.org

The Jewish Book Council holds an annual day-long conference attented by authors, editors, agents, and publicists. The overall focus is publishing books on Jewish themes, Jewish publishing, and networking with others in the field. *Date:* December. *Location:* New York , New York. *Cost:* $139 ($119, early registration).

Jewish Children's Book Writers & Illustrators Conference

520 8th Avenue, 4th Floor, New York, NY 10018
jewishbookcouncil.org

Sponsored by the Jewish Book Council, which promotes public awareness of books that "reflect the rich variety of the Jewish experience," this day-long conference is held annually. It offers presentations from authors, literary agents, publishers, and editors designed to help new as well as published authors advance their careers. *Date:* November. *Location:* New York City, New York. *Cost:* $122.

Kentucky Women Writers Conference

232 East Maxwell Street, Lexington, KY 40506
www.uky.edu/WWK

This two-day conference, held annually since its inception in 1979, attracts women at all stages of their writing careers. Workshops are limited to 12 members each. Pre-registration is required, and enrollment is done on a first-come, first-served basis. Fiction, nonfiction, poetry, and writing for young adults are among the workshops offered. *Date:* September. *Location:* Lexington, Kentucky. *Cost:* $195 for two days; $30 for students.

Kenyon Review Writers Workshop
Kenyon College, Gambier, OH 43022
www.kenyonreview.org/workshops/writers

Generating and revising new writing are the focus of the *Kenyon Review* workshops in poetry, fiction, and literary nonfiction. The retreat is scheduled around morning workshops, private time for writing in the afternoon, and public readings in the evening by instructors, visiting writers, and participants. Applications are accepted January 1 to May 1. *Date:* June 15–22. *Location:* Kenyon College, *Cost:* $1,195; $200 discount for returning participants.

Manhattanville Summer Writers' Week
2900 Purchase Street, Purchase, NY 10577
www.mville.edu/graduate/academics/arts-a-sciences/mfa-in-creative-writing/summer-writers-week.html

Three-hour workshops are held each morning of this five-day conference. Participants choose from workshops offered in the categories of fiction, poetry, nonfiction, children's/YA, and alternative media Afternoons are devoted to special workshops, readings, sessions with editors and agents, and individual manuscript consultations. A major presenter is scheduled each year. *Date:* June. *Location:* Purchase, New York. *Cost:* $725; two graduate credits available for an additional fee.

Mendocino Coast Writers Conference
College of the Redwoods
P.O. Box 2087, Fort Bragg, CA 95437
www.mcwc.org

This three-day conference, which is limited to 100 participants, features all-day genre intensives. Those who wish to attend one of these novel, short fiction, memoir, or poetry intensives are required to pre-submit a sample of their work, which will be critiqued in the small group sessions. Those attending only the afternoon lectures and discussions are not required to send work in advance; however, those who wish to take advantage of a 30-minute consultation with an author, editor, or agent must pre-submit 10 pages of a manuscript. *Date:* July. *Location:* Mendocino Campus of College of the Redwoods, California. *Cost:* $575; early registration, $525. $60 fee for private consultation with conference faculty.

Northern Colorado Writers Conference
108 East Monroe Drive, Fort Collins, CO 80525
northerncoloradowriters.com

Writers of all genres and levels attend this annual two-day conference for inspiration and information. Sponsored by Northern Colorado Writers, the event offers over 20 workshops on a variety of topics for both fiction and nonfiction. Last year's program included an editor's panel, editor pitch sessions, and read and critique sessions with authors and editors. *Date:* March. *Location:* Fort Collins, Colorado. *Cost:* Visit the website for cost information.

North Wildwood Beach Writers' Conference
City of North Wildwood Financial Officer, City Hall, 901 Atlantic Avenue, North Wildwood, NJ 08260
www.nwbwc.com

Speakers, workshops, manuscript evaluations, contests, and a book bazaar are the components of this day-and-a-half event. Workshops cover writing for children and young adults; fiction writing, including romance; nonfiction writing, including journalism and memoir; screenwriting; and poetry. Other workshops cover marketing and the business of publishing. *Date:* June. *Location:* North Wildwood, New Jersey. *Cost:* See website for information.

Oklahoma Writers' Federation Writers Conference

Barbara Shepard, OWFI, P.O. Box 54302, Oklahoma City, OK
　73154

www.owfi.org

This annual three-day conference has been held for more than 45 years. Workshops generally cover writing and marketing fiction (including science fiction and thrillers) and nonfiction for children, young adults, and adults. The theme for the 2011 conference is "Story Weavers." *Date:* May. *Location:* Norman, Oklahoma. *Cost:* $175 (includes 2 days of seminars, two banquets); early registration, $150. Single-day seminars, $70 each. Extra workshops, $15–$25.

Outdoor Writers Association of America Annual Conference

615 Oak Street, Suite 201, Missoula, MT 59801

owaa.org

First held in 1927, this gathering attracts writers who specialize in informing the public about outdoor recreational activities and the responsible use of natural resources. Workshops and seminars focus on craft improvement as well as on issues of specific interest to those who write about the outdoors. Topics include the business and technical sides of writing, marketing, and publishing, photography, technology, and nature journalism. The three-day conference also devotes sessions to national and local news related to outdoor activities and conservation. *Date:* September. *Location:* Varies yearly; most recently, Fairbanks, Alaska. *Cost:* Visit the website for cost information.

Pet Writing Conference

The Pet Socialite, Inc., 362 Broome Street, #20, New York, NY
　10013

www.petwritingconference.com

Authors and journalists interested in writing about animals gather at this one-day event each year to attend seminars and workshops about the business side of pet writing, as well as for networking opportunities with veterinarians and representatives of animal organizations. One-on-one sessions with agents and book and magazine editors are also available. The timing of the conference coincides with the Westminster Kennel Club Dog Show, held nearby. *Date:* February. *Location:* New York, New York. *Cost:* Visit the website for registration information.

Pikes Peak Writers Conference

P.O. Box 64273, Colorado Springs, CO 809662
www.pikespeakwriters.com

This annual conference offers more than 30 workshops that focus on fiction writing for children and teens as well as for adults. In addition, agents and editors are available to attendees seeking to pitch their work. Manuscript evaluations and critique sessions round out the three-day program. *Date:* April. *Location:* Colorado Springs, Colorado. *Cost:* Visit the website for cost information.

St. David's Christian Writers' Conference

87 Pines Road East, Hadley, PA 16130
www.stdavidswriters.com

Three days of workshops led by nationally known authors and editors are the centerpiece of this Christian writing conference, which also offers one-on-one tutorials and professional critiques for additional fees. Keynote addresses and literary readings, evening meditations, and after-hours social events are other features of the conference. The theme for this year's conference is Loaves and Fishes. *Date:* June 18–22. *Location:* Grove City, Pennsylvania. *Cost:* Rates vary depending on whether participants are commuting or staying on campus. Visit website for this year's tuition costs.

San Francisco Writers Conference

1029 Jones Street, San Francisco, CA 94109

www.sfwriters.org

San Francisco Writers sponsors this President's Day Weekend conference, which features more than 50 workshops, panels, social events, and one-on-one networking with presenters. In addition, editors from major publishing houses participate in Ask-A-Pro sessions. Speed Dating for Agents is an optional add-on event. *Date:* February. *Location:* San Francisco, California. *Cost:* $695 (early registration, $625). Additional $50 to participate in Speed Dating for Agents.

Sewanee Writers' Conference

University of the South, 119 Gailor Hall, Stamler Center, 735
   University Avenue, Sewanee, TN 37383-1000

sewaneewriters.org

With a focus on fiction, playwriting, and poetry, the Sewanee Writers' Conference offers workshops that meet for five two-hour sessions on alternating days. Over the course of the 12-day program, participants attend daily readings, lectures on craft, panel discussions, and Q&A sessions with distinguished faculty members. *Date:* July/August. *Location:* Sewanee, Tennessee. *Cost:* Visit the website for cost information.

Society of Children's Book Writers & Illustrators Annual International Conferences

Society of Children's Books Writers & Illustrators, 8271 Beverly
   Boulevard, Los Angeles, CA 90048

www.scbwi.org

The annual summer conference, held for 42 years, was joined 14 years ago by a winter conference. Both offer workshops, master classes, manuscript and portfolio consultations, panel discussions, and a variety of keynote speeches over the course of their three-day programs. The faculty consists of more than 50 authors, illustrators, editors, and agents. *Date:* January and August. *Location:* Winter conference, New York, New York. Summer conference, Los Angeles, California. *Cost:* Visit the website for cost information.

SCBWI Big Sky Fall Conference
www.scbwi.org/Regional-Chapters.aspx?R=4&sec=Conf

The Montana chapter of SCBWI hosts this weekend gathering for attendees to "learn, write, and share" with fellow children's authors and illustrators. Opportunities for both critiques and intensives followed by roundtable discussions are offered. The conference features writing and illustrating workshops led by authors, editors, and agents centering around story, craft, and character. *Date:* September. *Location:* The 320 Ranch, near Yellowstone National Park. *Cost:* Visit the website for cost information.

SCBWI Carolinas Fall Conference
P.O. Box 1216, Conover, NC 28613
www.scbwicarolinas.org

The fall conference of the Carolinas SCBWI has been held for 20 years. Sessions and workshops covered writing for the middle-grade reader, picture book creation, and making an impression on the first page. Manuscript critiques are available for an additional fee. *Date:* September. *Location:* North Carolina. *Cost:* Visit website for registration information.

SCBWI Florida Regional Conference
scbwiflorida.com

The Barnyard is the theme for this year's three-day midwinter conference for SCBWI members. Scheduled throughout the weekend are workshops, first-page critiques, and writing and illustrating intensives. Time is also reserved for informal critique groups and keynote speeches on a variety of topics related to children's writing. For information, the current Regional Advisor, Linda Rodriguez Bernfeld, can be reached at lrbjsb@bellsouth.net. *Date:* January 18–20. *Location:* Miami, Florida. *Cost:* $175.

SCBWI Kansas Fall Conference
P.O. Box 3987, Olathe, KS 66063
www.kansas-scbwi.org

Writers at all stages of their careers gather at this two-day conference to attend workshops led by editors, agents, authors, illustrators, and other prominent professionals from the world of children's and young adult publishing. Panel discussions, keynote speeches, and manuscript critiques round out the event. *Date:* October. *Location:* Overland Park, Kansas. *Cost:* Costs vary depending on days attending, and sessions or critiques desired.

SCBWI MD/DE/WV Conferences
mddewvscbwi.org, aseraserburns.wordpress.com

This regional branch of the Society of Children's Book Writers and Illustrators holds spring, summer, and winter conferences or workshops. It offer swriters and illustrators of books for children and young adults a hands-on, craft-centered literary weekend in fiction and nonfiction. Individually focused break-out sessions are also available. *Date:* July. *Location:* Damascus, Maryland. *Cost:* Visit website for registration information.

SCBWI Michigan Spring & Fall Conferences
www.kidsbooklink.org

The workshops at this weekend conference are led by award-winning authors and illustrators, literary agents, and art directors and editors from major publishing houses. Although the conference is open to members and nonmembers, only SCBWI members are eligible to enter the lottery for a paid manuscript or portfolio critique. The current Regional Advisor is Leslie Helakosi and may be reached for information at lelhel@hotmail.com. *Date:* May, October. *Location:* Visit website for location information. *Cost:* Varies.

SCBWI Mid-Hudson Valley Conference
scbwi-easternny.org

The Mid-Hudson Valley SCBWI holds two conferences a year, in June and November. The spring conference is a single day, and the Falling Leaves Master Class takes place over a weekend. Breakout sessions, hands-on workshops, panel discussions round out the day, and manuscript critiques are available. *Date:* November. *Location:* Silver Bay, New York. *Cost:* Members, $225; nonmembers, $275.

SCBWI Midsouth Fall Conference
P.O. Box 396, Cordova, TN 38088
www.scbwi-midsouth.org

Editors and art directors from prominent publishing houses and bestselling authors are among the presenters at this weekend conference. Attendees may enter a fiction manuscript contest or illustrator contest. An art director/editor session on picture books, a talk about book packagers, and critiques for query letters were three new offerings at the 2010 conference. Individual paid manuscript and portfolio critiques are available. *Date:* September. *Location:* Nashville, Tennessee. *Cost:* Visit the website for cost information.

SCBWI Nevada Tahoe Writers' Retreat
P.O. Box 19084, Reno, NV 89511
www.nevadascbwi.org

The Nevada chapter of the Society of Children's Book Writers and Illustrators offers this hands-on, intensive weekend of group and one-on-one critiques with guest authors and literary agents, as well as workshops. *Date:* October or November. *Location:* Lake Tahoe, Nevada. *Cost:* $425 for members; $475 for nonmembers.

SCBWI New England Annual Conference
www.nescbwi.org

The 2012 conference embraces the theme is "Word by Word." Paid editor critiques, peer critiques, a query session with agents, keynote speeches, book signings, and book sales are scheduled around the workshops and writing intensives presented at this weekend conference. *Date:* May. *Location:* Springfield, MA. *Cost:* Visit the website for cost information.

SCBWI New Mexico Handsprings Conference
P.O. Box 1084, Socorro, NM 87801
www.scbwi-nm.org

The New Mexico SCBWI holds an annual retreat with presentations by successful authors and literary agents, in addtion to critiques, illustrator portfolio displays, mini book launches, and workshops. *Date:* November. *Location:* Hummingbird Music Camp, Jemez River, Albuquerque, New Mexico. *Cost:* Visit the website for cost information.

SCBWI Oregon Spring Conference
P.O. Box 336, Noti, OR 97461
www.scbwior.com

This annual conference brings together an esteemed team of professional authors, illustrators, editors, art directors, and agents. Features of the two-day event include first page sessions, intensives for illustrators, keynote presentations, master craft workshops, and individual manuscript and portfolio consultations. Continuing education credits are available. *Date:* May. *Location:* Portland, Oregon. *Cost:* Visit website for registration information.

SCBWI Rocky Mountain Conference
www.rmcscbwi.org

The Rocky Mountain chapter of SCBWI holds a fall conference each year. In addition to workshops presented by editors from some of the best-known New York City-based publishing houses, this conference offers manuscript critiques with editors, agents, and published authors; one-on-one portfolio reviews; and first-page critiques. A weekend conference, it attracts writers and illustrators from Colorado and Wyoming. *Dates:* September. *Location:* Lakewood, CO. *Cost:* Visit website for registration information.

SCBWI San Francisco North/East Bay Fall Conference
www.scbwinorthca.org

This one-day conference for children's writers and illustrators at all stages of their careers offers a program full of inspiration, craft development and mastery, marketing tips, and more. One of the two all-day sessions focuses on picture books. *Date:* October. *Location:* Oakland, California. *Cost:* Visit the website for cost information.

SCBWI Southern Breeze Fall Conference
P.O. Box 26282, Birmingham, AL 35260
www.southern-breeze.net

Four sessions comprised of approximately 30 workshops are offered at this two-day event where attendees can tailor the day to fit their specific interests. The faculty includes authors, illustrators, agents, art directors, editors, and other publishing professionals. Both private and group critiques are also available. *Date:* October. *Location:* Birmingham, Alabama. *Cost:* Visit website for registration information.

SCBWI Spring Spirit Conference

P.O. Box 487, Placerville, CA 95667

www.scbwi.org/Regional-Chapters.aspx?R=5

The California North/Central regional chapter of SCBWI hosts this one-day conference, which offers a diversity of workshop options for attending writers and illustrators. The event closes with a question- and-answer panel. Written manuscript and art sample critiques are available for an additional fee. Date: April 6. Location: Citrus Heights, California. Cost: Members, $135; non-members, $155.

SCBWI Texas: Austin Regional Conference

201 University Oaks Boulevard, Suite 1285 #170, Round Rock, TX 78665 www.austinscbwi.com

Kick it Up a Notch is the name of this year's regional confer-ence for people who write, illustrate, or share the passions for children's literature. Hour-long general assembly sessions are held throughout the course of this three-day gathering. In addition to small-group intensives, consultations with literary agents, editors, and accomplished authors and illustrators are available for an additional fee. Personal social media evaluations and portfolio reviews are also offered. *Date:* February. *Location:* Austin, Texas. *Cost:* See website for various registration prices.

SCBWI Texas: Houston Annual Conference

2013 Registration, c/o Mary E. Riser, 19 Spotted Fawn Court, The Woodlands, TX 77381-3895 www.scbwi-houston.org

This conference offers a full-day of networking with other writers and learning about the world of publishing through talks by impressive guest presenters. Author/editor critiques are available for an additional fee. *Date:* April 13. *Location:* Katy, Texas. *Cost:* $135, members; $160, nonmembers. Early registration, $120, members; $145, nonmembers.

SCBWI Tri-Region Workshops, Writer's Days, Retreats
www.scbwisocal.org/days/index.html

SCBWI Los Angeles, SCBWI San Bernardino/Riverside, and SCBWI Cen Cal hold a variety of events, including Writer's Days, retreats, each year. Spotlight presentations by authors and illustrators, an editors' panel, and speeches by representatives from major publishing houses are featured activities. Check the calendar on the website for dates, topics, and locations. *Dates:* Vary. *Location:* Vary. *Cost:* Visit website for registration information.

South Carolina Writers Workshop Conference
P.O. Box 7104, Columbia, SC 29202
www.myscww.org

This weekend conference begins on Friday morning with optional intensive workshops. Saturday and Sunday are filled with sessions on various career topics. In previous years, conferences have featured interactive *slush fest* sessions with agents and editors. One-on-one pitch sessions and critique appointments with conference faculty members are available for an additional fee. *Date:* October. *Location:* Myrtle Beach, South Carolina. *Cost:* Visit website for this year's registration information.

Southern California Writers' Conference
1010 University Avenue, #54, San Diego, CA 92103
www.writersconference.com

Interactive workshops, panels, special events, and one-on-one consultations are scheduled during this three-day conference. Planned workshops cover fiction, nonfiction, "read and critique," and business and marketing. Screenwriters, authors representing a variety of genres, agents, and editors are among the faculty members. *Date:* February. *Location:* San Diego, California. *Cost:* $425. Early registration discounts. Additional fees for critique sessions and one-on-one consultations.

Space Coast Writers' Guild Annual Conference
P.O. Box 262, Melbourne, FL 32902-0262
www.scwg.org

The goal of this two-day conference is to provide inspiration, entertainment, and encouragement for writers of all genres. The Guild brings together area authors with publishers, agents, and editors from around the country, and occasionally from around the world. A self-publishing workshop is among the presentations and workshops scheduled for this year's event. Others cover plays, YA novels, first chapters, breaking into publishing, memoirs, settings, and more. *Date:* January 26–27. *Location:* Cocoa Beach, Florida. *Cost:* $200, members; $240, nonmembers. Half-day and single-day rates are available.

Tin House Summer Writers Workshop
P.O. Box 10500, Portland, OR 97296
www.tinhouse.com/writers-workshop/

Held on the campus of Reed College, this weeklong program consists of morning workshops limited to 12 participants. Craft seminars and career panels are scheduled in the afternoons, with author readings held in the evenings. Workshops are led by the editors of *Tin House* and Tin House Books. For an additional fee, mentorships are available to participants who have completed a collection of stories or poems, a memoir, or a novel. *Date:* July. Applications are accepted beginning January 1 through March 15. *Location:* Portland, Oregon. *Cost:* Visit the website for cost information. Scholarships are available.

Wesleyan Writers Conference
294 High Street, Room 207, Middletown, CT 06459
www.wesleyan.edu/writing/conference

This conference, held for 57 years, welcomes all writers, from beginners to veterans. The five-day program consists of seminars, readings, panels, lectures, and optional manuscript consultations. Each seminar typically includes a lecture, a discussion, and optional writing exercises. Seminar topics include novel, short story, fiction techniques, narrative in fiction and nonfiction, poetry, literary journalism, short and long-form nonfiction, memoir, and multimedia and online work. Private manuscript consultations are available with faculty members or teaching fellows. Attendees also have the opportunity to meet with editors and agents who are looking for new writers. *Date:* June 13–16; one-day program available June 15. *Location:* Middletown, Connecticut. *Cost:* Day students, tuition, $975; with meals, $1,250. Boarding rate, $1,425. One-day, $225. Scholarships and fellowships are available.

Western Writers of America Convention
www.westernwriters.org

Workshops, panels, discussions with editors and authors, and book signings are all part of this five-day convention. Workshops focus on writing fiction and nonfiction—including writing for children and young adults—and all are geared toward preserving the rich history of the American West. The business side of publishing is also examined, as is marketing. *Date:* June 24–29. *Location:* Las Vegas, Nevada. *Cost:* Visit the website for updates.

Willamette Writers Conference
9045 SW Barbur Boulevard, Suite 5A, Portland, OR 97219-4027
www.willamettewriters.com

Participants have almost 100 workshops to choose from at this weekend conference. Topics include historical fiction, self-help books, children's books, screenplays, mysteries, romance, and science fiction, among many others. Literary agents, Hollywood agents and producers, and editors are among the workshop leaders. Only those attending the conference for the full three days may submit up to two manuscripts for advanced critiques for an additional fee. *Date:* August 2–4. *Location:* Portland, Oregon. *Cost:* Visit the website for cost information.

Winnipeg International Writers Festival
624-100 Arthur Street, Winnipeg MB R3B 1H3 Canada
www.thinairwinnipeg.ca

Workshops, lectures, interviews, keynote speeches, and readings fill the days of this weeklong festival, which has been held annually since 1997. More than 50 representatives from the publishing world offer presentations on playwriting, poetry, children's and young adult writing, journalism, mystery, horror, and other topics. Programs target children as well as adults, and are presented in both English and French. *Date:* September. *Location:* Winnipeg, Manitoba. *Cost:* Visit the website for updates.

Write on the Sound Writers' Conference
700 Main Street, Edmonds, WA 98020
www.ci.edmonds.wa.us/artscommission/wots.stm

Sponsored by the City of Edmonds Art Commission, this conference is a highly anticipated regional event that fills up early. With more than 30 workshops to choose from, it draws noted authors and other publishing professionals as faculty. The program begins on Friday afternoon with pre-conference workshops, and continues with two full days of workshops and other events on Saturday and Sunday. Manuscript critique appointments are available for an additional fee. *Date:* October. *Location:* Edmonds, Washington. *Cost:* Visit the website for cost information. The conference brochure will be available in July.

Writers in Paradise
4200 54th Avenue South, Street Petersburg, FL 33711
www.writersinparadise.com

This eight-day program from Eckerd College offers workshops on short story, novel, nonfiction, and YA writing. Lectures, panels, roundtable discussions, readings, and book signings fill out the rest of the schedule at this annual convention. Individual manuscript consultations are offered for an additional fee. *Date:* January 19–27. *Location:* St. Petersburg, Florida. *Cost:* $700; optional manuscript consultation, $200. Scholarships available.

The Write Stuff
Greater Lehigh Valley Writers Group
3650 Nazareth Pike, PMB #136, Bethlehem, PA 18020-1115
www.glvwg.org

This weekend conference has been held annually since 1993. In addition to writers' workshops, it offers sessions on the business of writing, panel discussions, manuscript critiques, opportunities to meet with agents and editors, and a book fair. *Date:* March 16–17. *Location:* Allentown, Pennsylvania. *Cost:* Visit the website for cost information.

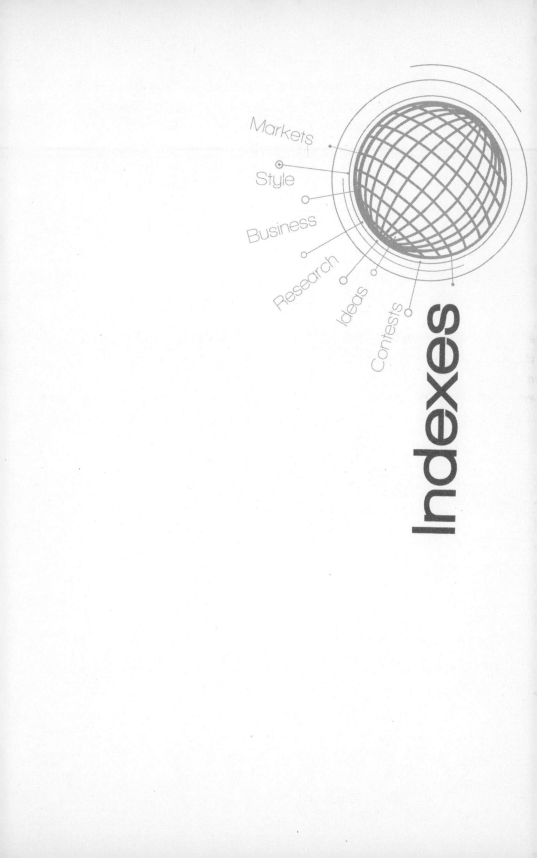

Markets

Style

Business

Research

Ideas

Contests

Indexes

W